ETHICS *for* PROFESSIONALS
in a
MULTICULTURAL WORLD

David E. Cooper
Northern Michigan University

PEARSON
Prentice
Hall

Upper Saddle River,
New Jersey 07458

Library of Congress Cataloging-in-Publication Data

Cooper, David E. (David Earl), (date)
    Ethics for professionals in a multicultural world / David E. Cooper.
    p. cm.
    Includes bibliographical references and index.
    ISBN 0-13-183093-7
    1. Professional ethics. I. Title.

  BJ1725.C62 2004
  174—dc21

2003045986

VP, Editorial Director: Charlyce Jones Owen
Senior Acquisitions Editor: Ross Miller
Editorial Assistant: Carla Worner
Marketing Manager: Claire Bitting
Marketing Assistant: Kim Daum
Production Editor: Jean Lapidus
Copy Editor: Stephen C. Hopkins
Manufacturing Buyer: Christina Helder
Cover Design: Bruce Kenselaar
Illustrator (Interior): Steven Mannion/Mirella Signoretto
Composition: Interactive Composition Corporation
Printer/Binder: Courier Companies, Inc.

Pearson Prentice Hall™ is a trademark of Pearson Education, Inc.
Pearson® is a registered trademark of Pearson plc
Prentice Hall® is a registered trademark of Pearson Education, Inc.

Pearson Education LTD.
Pearson Education Singapore, Pte. Ltd
Pearson Education, Canada, Ltd
Pearson Education-Japan
Pearson Education Australia PTY, Limited
Pearson Education North Asia Ltd
Pearson Educación de Mexico, S.A. de C.V.
Pearson Education Malaysia, Pte. Ltd
Editora Prentice-Hall Do Brasil, LTDA., Rio de Janeiro
Pearson Education, Upper Saddle River, N.J. 07458

10 9 8 7 6 5 4 3 2

ISBN 0-13-183093-7

Contents

Preface

This book is designed to serve those who find themselves in an intermediate position between the professional ethicist and the student studying for a career in a profession. It is an unfortunate fact of modern academic life that the books with the best ethical theories are couched in an academic jargon that makes them almost inaccessible to the average member of society. This is not necessarily an oversight, because the moral philosophers at the leading edge of our discipline are writing for people with Ph.D.'s in moral philosophy. But, a moral theory that cannot function in the lives of ordinary citizens is a moral theory that is not quite doing its job on the practical level. Thus, this text tries to make the concepts and moral theories of philosophers such as Kant, Mill, Rawls, Habermas, and their postmodern and feminist critics, accessible to those who are not professional philosophers.

The book has an interdisciplinary flavor, since I rely on my research in social science, child development, and clinical psychology to support some of my points. Over all, it is a philosophy teacher's response to the phenomenon of the "banality of evil" and other forms of administrative evil that occur when citizens with good motives make "professional" decisions that are ill conceived from the moral point of view. Wayward professionals are often bewildered about how they could have fallen so far off the moral track. When asked to speculate on this kind of issue, students sometimes claim that there is no moral track. Others say they are confused by the plurality of ethical and moral beliefs that now occupy the public sphere. Some adopt a postmodern skepticism about the possibility that there could ever be a justifiable universal consensus about moral fundamentals. Others seek comfort by focusing narrowly on a select code of ethics without worrying about whether or not the code is compatible with a broader philosophical vision for a just society. I believe these options contribute to moral drift and banal choices in situations of cross-cultural conflict, where a more sophisticated moral outlook is needed.

Contemporary life requires professionals as well as ordinary citizens to solve conflicts that cross religious, cultural, and technological boundaries within their own society as well as at the global level. Globalization is a complex phenomenon that is a source of hope for some and terror for others (Pensky, 2001, pp. vii–viii). On the one hand, it promises an increased growth of cross-cultural interrelationships that will help people transcend xenophobic ethnocentrism; on the other hand, it offers the threat of global markets devastating the political infrastructure of nation-states, leading to social and ecological crises and increased disparities in wealth. On the one hand, it promises that media contacts will cross hostile boundaries and shine a light on oppressive practices; on the other hand, it threatens to homogenize cultures and eradicate the source of unique individual cultural identities. On the one hand, it promises a growth in global political democratization that will move mankind away from totalitarianisms; on the other hand, it threatens the end of democracy because the rise of market-driven expert bureaucracies will dispense with direct citizen participation. All of this is very confusing. What these developments mean for codes of ethics and the practice of professionals is not yet clear.

Twenty-first–century citizens will need to develop a moral point of view that can adequately respond to these pressures. Given that professionals have a proven ability to master the esoteric knowledge of their field, the increasing need to develop sophisticated cross-cultural ways of relating will require them to take a leadership role in adjusting to the increased complexity of modern life. Because they will have to apply their intellectual skills to moral problems at both global and local levels, they are going to have to figure out how to locate professional codes of ethics in the broader milieu of an increasingly multicultural world. If they can master this task, their example will help the rest of us see how to approach conflicts from a point of view that has cross-cultural moral integrity. The main argument in this book is that there is a philosophically justified (i.e., rational) moral point of view that can serve to regulate (a) the evolution of codes of ethics for professions and (b) the adaptations that twenty-first–century citizens will have to make to their worldview in order to accommodate the growing complexity in our postmetaphysical, multicultural, and transnational world.

Over the years, I have used all the standard approaches to teaching ethics. Many of them simply increase the confusion students feel in the face of a smorgasbord of moral options. In particular, it is a mistake to present students with a bewildering array of alternative philosophical theories and/or cases that imply morality is about irresolvable moral dilemmas. Students need to be shown that pluralism does not have to remain a cause for bewilderment. A rational adjustment to pluralism can lead to what Habermas calls transcendence from within, leading to the moral point of view favored by most philosophers. I argue that "the moral point of view" is an ongoing developing perspective that is not only rationally justifiable, but is also a necessary practical accommodation to the forces evolving in the twenty-first century. Adopting this point of view with its practical implications for professional practice can diminish the possibility that we will drift into practices that promote what Hannah Arndt referred to as the "banality of evil."

Since Habermas is one of the leading moral philosophers of the age, I have worked his insights into every chapter of the book. I also feature Habermas's discourse ethics as one of the best contemporary responses to the postmodern angst over false universalization. The book discusses the friendly dispute between Rawls and Habermas, and argues that a proper interpretation of Rawls's veil of ignorance supports the virtue of rational moral empathy and democratic procedural rationality, both of which guide Habermas's discourse ethics at the application level.

Since this material is difficult to comprehend, students need to be eased into the complexity, rather than be bombarded with it all at once. To facilitate the transition, the text starts by introducing some fundamental distinctions that will be needed for later complex analysis. Accordingly, Chapter One is the longest chapter because it moves slowly from concrete to abstract issues, and introduces vocabulary and concepts that will be needed throughout the book to understand how the moral point of view ought to guide practical decisions. Some of the discussion about the relationship between rules, principles, and theory may seem too elementary, but I choose to err on the side of simplicity in the initial chapters.

A secondary goal of the book is to introduce a vocabulary that can help people think philosophically, so there is technical vocabulary in each chapter. However, the first time a technical term is used, it is cited in **bold italics,** and accompanied by its definition, also in *italics*. Because students have complained that they sometimes forget the meaning of a word and then are confused when they see it later in the book, I have added an alphabetical listing of key terms with their definitions in a glossary. Readers can quickly check the meaning of a term when they encounter it later in the book.

To make the book seem less intimidating, I have integrated illustrative anecdotes throughout the chapters. For example, in Chapter Three I use my graduate school encounter with a logical positivist logic teacher to show how moral muddle can lead even a man with a Ph.D. into adopting a naïve metaethical theory like emotivism. Since these anecdotes represent an informal philosophical interpretation of personal experience, they are flagged by a **For Instance** each time one of them is inserted. This kind of informality will not suit the tastes of all readers, but together with occasional illustrations, they help clarify abstract analytic points by giving readers a concrete image of the concepts being discussed.

Since students in pluralistic cultures do not necessarily share a background foundation of common life experiences, it is important to create a body of shared events that can serve to facilitate discussion. I use descriptions of a number of famous social psychology experiments and investigative reports to illustrate abstract and theoretical points, for example, the Zimbardo Prison Experiment, the Milgram Yale Authority Experiment, the Amnesty International study of Greek torturers, Lifton's study of Nazi doctors, etc. These illustrations are discussed with enough detail that together they begin to serve as a body of shared events to facilitate later discussion and comparisons.

I assume that before dealing with deep controversy people need to develop a body of philosophical concepts that can help them work through controversial issues. So my aim is to introduce key concepts early, but in a way that avoids the risk of causing premature personal discomfort that might be distracting. To accomplish this I use the case of the autistic genius Temple Grandin to illustrate how difficult it can be for a child who lacks normal procedural understanding to learn the meaning of a simple moral command such as "Be gentle with the cat." I also use other illustrations in a similar manner; for instance, the famous case of Phineas Gage is used to show how rational moral understanding depends on the normal human ability to integrate abstract knowledge with emotional commitment. These kinds of real life examples are fascinating in their own right, but they also help illustrate both the virtues and deficits to be found in any moral community. Throughout the text, there is a continuous emphasis on clarifying the virtues that are needed to function as a responsible moral agent who adopts the recommended point of view.

Since the final goal is to help people apply theory to real-life situations, the second chapter introduces a standard decision procedure from applied ethics, which recommends approaching cases by developing a "background" analysis, an analysis of "ideal theory," and an "implementation" strategy. This structure is used throughout the text to create a common framework for discussions. Since the entire book uses the model, the early chapters are devoted to backgrounding, the middle chapters to ideal theory, and the last chapter to theory of implementation. Thus, Chapters One through Three explore the background context of contemporary applied ethics by discussing the structure of moral inquiry, a normative definition of professional practice, and some common moral failures committed by professionals. These chapters call our attention to the need for a more sophisticated approach to ethics. Chapters Four and Five explore background empirical research on moral development, gender differences, and the way voice alters one's moral point of view. Next, ideal theories of rationality are explored in Chapters Six and Seven, and consequentialist and nonconsequentialist ideal theories are discussed in Chapters Eight and Nine. Finally, Chapter Ten discusses theory of implementation by illustrating how the ideal theories can be applied to actual cases. Because the book uses more empirical research than is standard in philosophical texts, the reader who wants a more traditional philosophical emphasis should read the book in the following order: Chapters One and Two to lay the conceptual groundwork for moral theory, Chapters Six and Seven to explore philosophical reasoning, Chapters Eight and Nine for the traditional Western theories of morality (including Habermas's discourse ethics), and Chapter Ten for illustrations on how to apply theory to practice.

This book is animated by my own beliefs about moral agency and professional life. The guiding assumption is that everyone can benefit from learning to use a theoretical perspective to judge practical value conflicts, especially in those contexts where our professional stations require us to intervene in the lives of "vulnerable" others in medicine, law, engineering, social work, teaching, parenting, and so forth. My faith in theory is based in part on personal experience. My own grasp of theory as well as my attempts to apply it to concrete cases continue to shape my behavior and add to the feeling of awe I have for the moral world. A theoretical orientation to values, of course, will not eliminate immorality from life, guarantee that we will always make the right decisions, or replace the importance of personal moral experience. But it can help diminish our human propensity to be ethically careless when we confront ethical dilemmas in our rapidly evolving pluralistic culture.

As every instructor knows, personal education accelerates once one begins to teach. I will end this lengthy preface by acknowledging my debt to all my students. Trying to teach them has taught me much more than I ever learned as a student, and, equally important, each semester their infectious enthusiasm adds to the quality of my life. I would also like to thank Northern Michigan University for the institutional support for the project, and Erin Schwiderson and Michelle Fish for the long hours and very competent help with editing and typing. I dedicate the text to the people who taught me about love and commitment, especially my children Katherine, Brian, Eliisa, Bill, and Nathan. My wife Mary deserves a special thank you for her patience and support.

⁓ Note To Students

There are certain reasoning strategies and conceptual tools that are not always explicitly taught but that are vital for success in the culture of higher education. Studies show that even though good students use the strategies, they cannot necessarily pass them on to other students because they are not always explicitly aware of their own skills (Ellis, 1994). This makes learning seem mysterious to those who have not learned the strategies, but there is no mystery here. Strategies can be mastered, and once acquired they increase general competence. If you will make use of them, I can guarantee your journey into the culture of academic philosophy not only will be interesting but also will broaden the repertoire of skills that you have for solving problems in general.

There are many ways to get to the same place. If you have a system that works for you, continue to use it. What I am going to suggest is that you broaden your skills by adding some new strategies. Experience will teach you which tools are most useful for different contexts. One of the best learning strategies is *active reading*. Too often students say, "I read this chapter six times and it still makes no sense." The problem is often passive reading. They start with the first word and read to the last word and do very little in the middle. If you are doing something wrong, doing it six times will not make it better. Remember, reading academic material is not like reading a story. It requires thought and reflection. I have been reading philosophy for 40 years. I still read new material at a rate of about 15 pages an hour. You have to give yourself time to reflect while you read.

Enter into a dialogue with the text. Ask questions about every paragraph. "What is this paragraph supposed to tell me?" "If I was going to be asked a question about this paragraph, what question would I be asked?" "Do I know the answer?" At the top of each page, write out questions that the page should answer. At the end of each section, write out a question that the information in the section could answer. And always keep a "global" perspective. "What are the questions that this discipline tries to answer?" "How does this particular bit of material contribute to that overall task?"

There are several steps to active reading. First, don't keep reading when you get confused. Stop. Then try to explicitly identify *where* you got confused. Second, try to *formulate a question* directed at your confusion; that is, a question that, when answered, will clear up your confusion or at least lead the way toward an investigation that will clear it up. Third, try to *specify some plans* for getting rid of the confusion. Take an active role in trying to generate a number of solutions to your questions. Fourth, try to *evaluate which possible solution is the best* and pay attention to how you came to your conclusion. Finally, *internalize the whole process* so that the steps used to clear up your confusion become part of your memory system. Write the steps down or visualize them in a familiar context.

This is the ideal time to think of questions that you can ask in class. Asking questions is crucial in becoming an active philosophy student. If students don't ask questions, the instructor is not getting feedback and may have a false idea about the students' understanding of the material. An academic blunder is apparent when the first test shows both the instructor and students that they have not been communicating.

One strategy for remembering new material is to make "maps" or schematic charts. Create charts that show how concepts are related. Keep the concepts from different theories on different maps so that you will not confuse the theories with one another. Then draw a master map that brings the smaller maps together so that you can compare theories. For example, you might draw a map for each moral theory, and then a larger one that highlights conceptual similarities and differences between the theories.

It is very hard to remember abstract terms because they are not usually tied to specific visual events. Maps can help us begin to visualize them in context. Why bother? Well, because visual memory seems to be almost inexhaustible. If you can attach abstract concepts to a visual image, you are far less likely to forget the terms. For example, "justice" is a very abstract concept often defined as "getting one's due" or "having one's rights respected." Students often have trouble remembering the definition (along with the hundred or so other abstract concepts they must remember). But when they visualize the definition, they report that it is much easier to remember. It does not matter how they visualize it, so long as they use their own memory system. Some students find it useful to *visualize* different rooms in their house, and then keep each philosophical theory in a different room. The individual terms of each theory can be attached to different objects in the room. For example you could remember "utility" by placing utilitarianism in the kitchen and associating "utility" with useful cooking utensils.

The strategies listed above are useful in any academic discipline. There are also strategies that have to be mastered in individual disciplines. Since each discipline focuses on questions and problems that are special to it, each has developed its own methods for trying to solve its particular problems. You increase your own ability to cope with the world when you master the problem-solving strategies of several different disciplines. Be sure to ask teachers or other experts for some guidance about what kind of skills are most useful for coming to terms with their discipline.

The author wishes to thank the following reviewers for their helpful suggestions: David Clarke, Southern Illinois University, and Christina M. Bellon, California State University Sacramento.

∽ References

ELLIS, DAVID B. (1994). *On becoming a master student.* Rapid City, SD: College Survival.
PENSKY, MAX. (2001). Editor's introduction. In Max Pensky (Trans. and Ed.), *Jurgen Habermas and the postnational constellation.* Cambridge, MA: The MIT Press.

David Cooper

PART I
PLURALISM, PROFESSIONAL ETHICS, AND MORAL MUDDLE

Chapter One

Communication, Social Pluralism, & Universal Morality

∼ A Foundation for Discussing Philosophical Ethics

This book is an introduction to applied philosophical ethics. I assume the average reader may never read the professional literature that shapes the worldview of philosophers who work in applied ethics, so my goal is to introduce new readers to some of the major insights from that literature. The book clarifies a particular version of the **Moral Point of View** (MPofV) that has been adopted by many professional ethicists. I argue that this point of view can provide a common universal moral foundation for the many codes of ethics that guide professional practices in settings where professionals must interact with clients who have diverse moral, religious, and cultural traditions. I believe that this foundation will also be useful to anyone who lives in a multicultural society. Furthermore, the MPofV can be interpreted so as to accommodate most of the concerns of the postmodern critics of universal moral theories. (These terms will be clarified later.)

It is not easy to present a theoretical point of view in a way that makes sense to people who are outside of the theoretical tradition. So the first problem is to figure out how to effectively communicate the reasons for the development of the MPofV to people who have not been trained as philosophers. To assist the reader, I will begin with some noncontroversial ideas that can serve as background reference points to support communication about this version of the MPofV. In this regard, the text begins with fairly informal discussions but becomes increasingly technical as it progresses. I will not define the actual boundaries of the MPofV until page 33, when these preliminary discussions will have set the stage for understanding why this way of interpreting moral experience had to evolve.

The Background Shapes the Foreground

> **For Study:**   Why are philosophers so concerned about the background conditions that influence how we interpret philosophical concepts?

Contemporary philosophers are keenly aware of the truth behind this slogan: **The background shapes the foreground.** Taken literally, it means that whether or not we can all "see" the same figure or event will depend on whether or not we share a background that can make the figure or event stand out in the same way for each of us. Preexisting background conditions affect how we interpret all the events we experience. Background influences can be both external (environmental, cultural, institutional factors, etc.) and internal (beliefs, desires, emotional predispositions, unique personal experiences, etc.). In short, we have to begin with the assumption that all our perceptions and thoughts about morality are heavily influenced by our own prior history. Why is this an important insight?

Our background predisposes us to see or understand certain things clearly and to look past or ignore other things that we might have noticed if we possessed a different background. Since our interpretations of moral experience are shaped by prior history, we have to wonder if the way various people think about morality can be valid. Because they study theories of knowledge, contemporary philosophers generally agree that all people (including philosophers) will naturally "project" different interpretations of reality onto the same events in the world. *Projection* is a *psychological capacity (often used as a defense) that allows a person to assume that an external reality embodies the same feelings, qualities, traits, beliefs, etc. that are found inside the person.* This natural tendency creates a special problem, because when differences in background cause people to project different interpretations, it complicates all attempts to reach agreement with strangers. The teacher who is sensitive to this diversity realizes that students who do not initially share all of the teacher's background experiences will not initially interpret events in the same way as the teacher. Even so, the extent of the differences can be startling.

For Instance:

I like to show my students a film called "The Death of Socrates" from the old CBS-TV series *You Are There*. The film reenacts the events surrounding the execution in Athens, Greece, of the famous philosopher Socrates in 304 B.C. The gimmick used in the film is to have modern CBS reporters, in this case Walter Cronkite, role-play news commentators who have traveled back in history. They interview actors who play the key historical figures who would have witnessed Socrates' execution. I have shown the film hundreds of times, and it continues to teach me the importance of paying attention to the initial background information available to an audience. Often students share enough of my background to agree that it is inspirational the way Socrates uses his philosophical beliefs to make sense of his execution. But just as often, I am startled by comments such as "What is a 'Socrates,' anyway?" or "Well, that was dumb. Why didn't he escape?" The reaction that startled me most occurred when I showed the film to student inmates behind the walls of a maximum-security prison. This was my first experience teaching at the prison, and I had not paid enough attention to the prisoners' background. Thus, I was not at all prepared for how they would see the figures in the "foreground" of the film.

The opening interview is with Aristophanes, a famous Greek poet and writer of comedies. The interviewer asks Aristophanes if he thinks Socrates "might yet be saved?" He replies, "I hope that he will, I think that he will not. But, valuing what is most precious to me, *my greatest concern at the moment is to protect myself*" [emphasis added]. While students at the university never openly react to Aristophanes' self-centered comment, a number of students at the prison spontaneously exclaimed: "Right on!" "All right!" "That dude knows where it's at." Later, some of these same students expressed contempt for Socrates. They thought he was a "chump" for calmly accepting his execution. They were seeing the film from a background that was radically different from my own. It had never occurred to me that anyone would see Aristophanes, rather than Socrates, as the hero of the film. I was in for an interesting semester.

Just as prisoners have special backgrounds that shape how they see events, so do philosophers. Thus, to understand the perspective found in mainstream philosophy, we will need to focus continually on the background conditions that have shaped the intellectual boundaries of mainstream philosophy. In fact, one could say that contemporary philosophers are almost obsessively concerned about this phenomenon. While each of them would like to think that their own way of interpreting the world accurately represents external reality, as philosophers they must acknowledge that there may be other ways of interpreting the world that work just as well for those "other people" who have different backgrounds. To avoid the possibility of false projections, then, many philosophers now just assume that they never see the world exactly as it really exists; they accept the idea that what they are seeing may only be one of several workable interpretations of the world. Some skeptics even go so far as to assert that there are no universal values and that there can never be any moral principles that ought to apply everywhere to everyone. But, does this mean every possible interpretation of the world is equally adequate? If so, how should we interpret concepts like "right and wrong," "true and false," and "liberation versus oppression"?

In spite of the obvious differences between people, we should not be too hasty in making generalizations about what people can and cannot share in common. In many ways we are different, but in many ways we are also the same. It is also possible for people to improve by becoming more aware and more critical of their own propensity to project. Thus, on a personal level many have already discovered that some background perspectives from which they have judged issues in science and morality have been inadequate. Thus, it is not only possible to improve but it is even possible that there might be a perspective that is better than all the rest. The problem is this: How would we ever know that a particular perspective is not just another projection from another ordinary background? We will discuss this vexing question throughout the book, but for now we can begin by considering an interesting observation from a renowned developmental psychologist.

The philosopher Abe Edel remarked at a social and political philosophy conference in the mid-1970s that he had once asked the developmental psychologist Erick Erickson if he knew how to design an environment that could make everyone happy. Erickson said, "No, I don't know how to do that, people are too diverse." When looked at from this angle, a universal background seems impossible; diversity seems to be the only reality. However, after a brief pause, Erickson added that he thought he could design an environment that would make all babies happy. From a developmental perspective, this makes complete sense. The older we get, the more diverse we become as we develop new interpretations of biological needs, are exposed to different culturally based understandings, and participate in our own development by choosing experiences unique to our own situation. But at the core, there may be some basis in human experience for an underlying foundation that can support cross-cultural, universal understandings about moral issues. Since Erickson seems more confident when associating a universal strategy for happiness with babies, perhaps we should also begin in the same place. We have all been babies (really) and have seen babies, so we can use this overlapping common experience as a place to begin. Let's take a brief look at research that shows how babies can be developmentally the same even while displaying surface differences. This will help develop some preliminary background concepts that will make it easier to talk about the possibility of universal moral values.

Surprisingly, as we shall see, this research is actually quite relevant for helping us understand some of the moral disagreements that occur later in life.

Communication Requires Shared Procedural Knowledge

> **For Study:** Why does all communication depend on shared-background procedural knowledge?

The careful study of how babies extend their understanding from early experiences to later ones teaches us that body-based understanding is crucial to the later development of symbolic capacities. Psychologists who study infant development call a baby's prelinguistic ability to crawl, grab objects, or respond to facial expressions *procedural knowledge.* Roughly, this refers to "... knowledge which requires certain capabilities [to] which [we] have no conscious access" (Dornes, 1996, p. 44). We display this kind of knowledge whenever *bodily procedures allow us to do things automatically without reflection or conscious awareness.* This is the same phenomenon studied by psychologists who do research on procedural memory. "When we find ourselves in specific situations where this information might be useful, there just seems to be a 'memory' there that we can rely on" (Cooper, Burns, Leith, and Pelton-Cooper, 1998, p. 22).

What we call *declarative knowledge* refers to all those skills and beliefs that can be *expressed consciously in symbolic form using words and signs.* Thus, declarative knowledge is more abstract than procedural knowledge. As Dornes (p. 45) says, "Declarative knowledge is symbolic and can be remembered" (and talked about), whereas "procedural knowledge is nonsymbolic and is 'acted' on" (but provides the necessary background for the possibility of declarative talk). There are two forms of procedural knowledge. The primary form is either present from birth or is learned so early it is prelinguistic. For instance, "being able to walk is based on knowledge which is gained in the process of learning to walk, but this knowledge has in comparison to changing gears or learning to drive never been declarative/explicit" (p. 45). To make it declarative would require us to go back and consciously investigate the bodily mechanisms that govern walking. After such research, we would be able to talk about how the procedural mechanisms work, putting us in a better position to teach adult accident victims who have lost their procedural understanding of walking. The secondary form of procedural knowledge involves that information that was originally learned consciously on a declarative level through teaching but then became procedural when it became habitual through "automatisation," such as our ability to ride a bicycle without reflection (Dornes, p. 45ff).

Insofar as babies around the world have to share certain fundamental bodily experiences to thrive, we should expect some common, biologically based procedural knowledge to exist in all people. If we focus our adult attention on this common prelinguistic knowledge, it may help us understand why there is a foundation for shared human understanding contained in all languages. No matter where they are from, everywhere people use their language to talk about the same kinds of physical and social activities. For instance, no matter where on earth babies are raised, they have to learn on a procedural level to walk and respond to the feel of gravity. They have experiences of up and down, back and forth, day (light) and night (dark), dry and wet, etc. Every baby experiences nurture and hunger, support and falling, protection and exposure, social acceptance and rejection, social boundaries or limits, and a social space within which they must live. Thus, around the world, to turn this procedural understanding into declarative knowledge, all languages address the issues that come with these and other common bodily experiences. People can understand what the basic terms in these languages mean because they already share a procedural understanding of how the body functions in physical and social space. To see how understanding the concept of procedural knowledge can help us understand some of the basic differences in moral understanding that show up at the declarative level, let's consider an unusual case where lack of common procedural understanding interfered with someone's ability to respond to the simple moral instruction: "Be gentle with the cat."

The Example of Temple Grandin

For Study: How does the Temple Grandin case illustrate that people need common background procedural understanding before they can use abstract moral concepts to communicate with each other?

Temple Grandin is a high-functioning autistic woman who has earned a Ph.D. in animal science, is a professor at Colorado State University, has published hundreds of articles and several books, and is a highly successful businesswoman who designs facilities for handling livestock. Since it is very difficult for the autistic to function in standard social settings, her accomplishments are quite extraordinary. *Autism* is *primarily a genetic disability*, and it is usually quite apparent by the age of three, when autistic children begin to show *a fierce degree of sensitivity to stimulation*. Because they experience ordinary sensations with excruciating intensity, the autistic *can't stand many typical human interactions even though they may desire them*. Thus, although Ms. Grandin reports that she longed to be hugged when she was a child, she was also terrified of such contact (cited in Sacks, 1995, p. 263). Her heightened sensations made a simple hug feel overwhelming. Because autistic children can't stand this kind of stimulation, they often avoid or resist physical contact with those who love them. As a result, they do not experience the normal prerequisite bodily interactions that teach children how to procedurally understand and deal with subtle human emotions.

This means that as adults they *lack the procedural information needed to understand complex emotional interactions,* such as romance, humor, deception, intrigue, and sympathy. Their approach to emotional life is so simple and direct that normal adults find their behavior to be quite disconcerting.

In a film on the development of the social brain, researcher S. B. Cohen (1995) used a device called "Charlie and the four sweets" to illustrate the difference between normal children and autistic children. Charlie is a simple line drawing of a face, and the only clue to what Charlie desires is to be found in his gaze. When Charlie is surrounded by four candy bars, normal three-year-old children can tell by his gaze which of the candies Charlie wants. If you change the picture so he is looking at a different candy, they will notice the change. But autistic children find this task to be very difficult. When asked, "Which candy does Charlie desire?" they give random answers. These children are often quite intelligent in other ways, but it becomes clear that they do not use Charlie's gaze as a clue to get their answer. The film points out that, in a sense, autistic children suffer from a kind of "mind blindness." They seem oblivious to the idea that another person may have internal mental states that can be interpreted by looking at the person's facial expressions. Because they lack the procedural understanding that should help them interpret normal signs of human interest and emotions, they are easily deceived and often perplexed in social situations that require procedural emotional understanding. The rich storytelling that gives meaning to social emotions and motives never becomes a part of autistic children's social experience. However, "'high-functioning' autistic

Figure 1.1 Most children can identify the emotions of others simply by "reading faces," but this ability is missing in autistic children. (Cohen, 1995)

individuals . . . with Asperger's syndrome can tell us of their experiences, their inner feelings and states, whereas [for] those with classical autism . . . there is no window, and we can only infer" (Sacks, 1995, p. 246–47).

Because Grandin has Asperger's syndrome, she is able to give us some fascinating glimpses into her world. This opportunity is especially educational because it shows how hard it is to share abstract insights when there is a deficit in the ability to share the bodily experiences needed to create the prerequisite procedural understanding. Grandin (1995, pp. 132–33) says that she identifies with two of the characters in the *Star Trek* science fiction shows—the Vulcan, Mr. Spock, and the android, Mr. Data. These fictional characters are pure intellect, and like her, they have to try to understand human emotions from the outside.

> As a child, I was like an animal that had no instincts to guide me; I just had to learn by trial and error. I was always observing, trying to work out the best way to behave, but I never fit in. I had to think about every social interaction. When other students swooned over the Beatles, I called their reaction an ISP—interesting sociological phenomenon. I was a scientist trying to figure out the ways of the natives. I wanted to participate, but I did not know how (Grandin, 1995, p. 132).

> Much of the time, I feel like an anthropologist on Mars. (Cited in Sacks, p. 259)

Notice how she uses "anthropologist on Mars" as a verbal device to help us understand what it means to be autistic. Anthropologists study people in other cultures with whom they often have very little shared surface experience. Thus, they try to interpret what is happening on the inside of the culture by observing from the outside. Anthropologists can, however, normally depend on some shared procedural knowledge with the people they study. But would we have shared procedural knowledge with a Martian? Without shared procedural knowledge of autism it is as hard for normal people to understand Grandin's inner world from the outside as it is for her to understand the inner emotional world of normal people. Can anything be done to help us communicate across such differences so that we can reach mutual understanding? For her part, Grandin has made remarkable progress. One technique she uses is to store observational data of standard human emotional interactions in her memory, as in a mental videotape library (Grandin, 1995, p. 137). Then, when she confronts an emotionally confusing situation, even though she cannot share the feelings involved, she can run an appropriate tape from her memory and imitate the behavior of the people on her mental tape.

Grandin says this approach helped to a degree, but her major breakthrough in understanding the emotional world of others came from making adaptations to a "squeeze machine" that allowed her to sooth her agitated nervous system. That is, since she had never responded in a normal manner to the experience of being hugged, Grandin had trouble understanding the concepts and emotions that develop because of this soothing bodily experience.

However, she eventually discovered a unique way to get in touch with this kind of experience. She was led to her discovery by way of her genius for understanding animals. Grandin points out that she has a lot in common with cows (Grandin, pp. 142–56). Like her, they are easily excited by sudden or intense stimuli, and thus they are rarely calm in stressful environments. Because Grandin was raised on a farm, she was familiar with the "squeeze machine" designed to hold cattle steady while their horns are removed or when they are branded. When the inverted V-shaped contraption closes around its body and gently squeezes, a cow becomes relaxed and calm. Since she had an empathic physiological understanding of a cow's excitable way of life, Grandin felt on an intuitive procedural level that a similar kind of squeeze machine could also help her experience calm relaxation.

Using her understanding of mechanical principles, Grandin designed an upright V-shaped squeeze machine with padded boards that could put gentle pressure along the length of her own body while she lay in it. Hydraulic gauges allowed her to control the amount of pressure. After some experimentation, she discovered how to give herself gentle squeezes that could calm her nervous system. An hour of squeezes would give her several hours of relief, which allowed her to go to college. She was even more pleased to find that her new bodily experiences in the machine provided the physiological foundation needed for understanding forms of empathy and some of the abstract ethical concepts that had eluded her in the past. The meanings of many ethical terms only become fully available to us after we have experienced the bodily sensations that serve as the experiential foundation for the abstract terms. With no experience of gentle hugging, how was Grandin supposed to interpret the moral command "Be gentle with the cat?" She says,

> To have feelings of gentleness, one must experience gentle bodily comfort. . . . It was difficult for me to understand the idea of kindness until I had been soothed myself. . . . After I experienced the soothing feeling of being held [by her squeeze machine], I was able to transfer that good feeling to the cat. As I became gentler, the cat began to stay with me, and this helped me understand the ideas of reciprocity and gentleness. (Grandin, pp. 142–56)

When we talk to another person using abstract words like "reciprocity" and "gentleness," we automatically assume that they have the same procedural understanding based on the same early bodily experiences as we do. But Temple Grandin did not have access to this normal life world. Until she experienced gentle touching, she could not understand the instruction to be gentle with the cat while petting it, and until she could be gentle, she could not learn about reciprocity from the cat (i.e., if you will pet me gently, I won't run away, I will reciprocate by staying here with you). Her new experiences with her mechanical companion opened new doors of understanding for her.

> From the time I started using my squeeze machine, . . . It was clear that the plea-
> surable feelings were those associated with love for other people. I built a ma-
> chine that would apply the soothing, comforting contact that I craved as well as
> the physical affection I couldn't tolerate when I was young. I would have been as
> hard and as unfeeling as a rock if I had not built my squeeze machine and fol-
> lowed through with its use. The relaxing feeling of being held washes negative
> thoughts away. I believe that the brain needs to receive comforting sensory input.
> Gentle touching teaches kindness. (Grandin, pp. 82–83)

It may seem strange to think that someone would have to learn the biological basis for gentle love from a machine rather than from a mother, but the
message in this case is not strange. To develop shared universal understanding,
we need some shared universal experiences. And those who are radically different from the norm cannot automatically be expected to learn and understand even universal values in the ways that are standard for the average
person. As we shall see, to blindly assume that everyone learns as we do is to
confuse the fact of a universal value's existence with the separate task of finding appropriate means for dealing with such values in different contexts. When
we judge only on the basis of our own experience, we will be inclined to reject
or misinterpret solutions to common problems that are developed by people
who are different. This is, of course, what happened to Grandin. When word
of her machine got out, psychiatrists viewed it as a form of regression. They
told her mother that using the machine would impede any chance Temple had
for normal emotional development. Her mother was distressed by this advice
and wanted her daughter to stop using the machine. Under this pressure,
Grandin also began to wonder if she should continue. But luckily, she was a
very independent young woman. She persevered in its use and even improved
on its design. She reports that although she still finds it difficult to understand
people who are motivated primarily by complex emotion, her empathy for the
human situation continues to develop.

> Motivated by love, my mother worked with me and kept me out of institutions.
> Yet sometimes she feels that I don't love her. She is a person for whom emotional
> relationships are more important than intellect and logic. It pains her that I
> kicked like a wild animal when I was a baby and that I had to use the squeeze ma-
> chine to get the feeling of love and kindness. The irony is that if I had given up
> the machine [as the psychiatrists wanted], I would have been a cold, hard rock.
> Without the machine, I would have had no kind feelings toward her. I had to feel
> physical comfort in order to feel love. (Grandin, pp. 90–91)

The importance of shared procedural background for shared human understanding cannot be overestimated. We will return to this notion throughout
the book—to ask questions about the background experiences that are necessary for high moral functioning. At this point, it is mainly important to

remember that diversity in human experience appears to be as normal as similarity. If we are going to be sensitive to other people, we cannot automatically assume that they share our background procedural understanding or that our perspective on how we ought to apply shared values will serve equally well as a standard for them. At the very least, we should try to understand what experiences others have had before judging or formulating policies that affect them. If we fail to do this, we will probably misrepresent their interpretations of events, and consequently we may fail to understand any unique accommodations that need to be made to satisfy both their particular and universal needs.

Self-Critical Dialogue Helps To Balance Perspectives

> **For Study:** Philosophy has adopted the norms behind critical self-reflective dialogue. How is this supposed to help philosophers in ethics with their concerns about the standard person problem?

When making judgments about what *ought* to be, we must proceed with caution. While there are many similarities among the belief systems people hold, there are differences as well. Too often, policymakers have assumed that just because everybody is the same on an abstract level (e.g., all men are created equal), they are also very similar in terms of what they need on a concrete level in their current local situation. For instance, all children are the same in that they need love and affection. But it is not possible to meet Grandin's universal need for affection by treating her like other children. She needs a much more refined intervention. In a similar way, all children need education and ought to be taught to read. But a school board should not assume that children can all learn to read in the same way. Children with reading disabilities need a different kind of intervention, even though the educational goal is the same for all. Thus, to construct a sound universal philosophy, we have to correlate abstract moral values with concrete local differences. When we forget to take differences between people into account, we are especially vulnerable to a type of error in judgment we'll call the *standard person problem.* This refers to those occasions when some group *assumes without reflection that its beliefs can accurately serve as a standard for judging everyone else's experience as well, just because historically the group's particular beliefs have always worked well for it.*

Because contemporary philosophers are so aware of the standard person problem, they realize they must take steps to diminish the likelihood that their own background presuppositions will create unintended, pernicious forms of bias during investigations. Thus, the discipline has adopted the norms behind *critical, self-reflective dialogue* to protect itself from itself. This means philosophers feel an obligation *to engage in critical dialogue with those who have opposing points of view, so that their own background assumptions will be evaluated at the same time that they are being used to analyze and judge all the other background assumptions that are used to attribute meaning to human experience.* Although it seems paradoxical to use one's background to evaluate one's own background, this task appears unavoidable if we want to diminish the level of bias. As a means to this critical goal, philosophers know that honest dialogue with those who hold opposing points of view is essential. Thus, most philosophers have chosen to make other values (such as self-preservation, power, tradition, wealth, and prestige) subservient to the task of trying to reach greater understanding through self-critical, rational dialogue about underlying foundational assumptions.

Since Grandin's story illustrates that it is possible for people to be different even on a procedural level, why shouldn't we simply give up on the idea that people can share universal understanding about things like morality? Perhaps all there is in the world is difference, and the idea that there ought to be universal moral norms is absurd. I think the complexity of human life guarantees that there are, and probably always will be, groups of people whose background context will lead them to disagree about moral values. But just because we cannot begin with a preestablished universal consensus does not mean we cannot begin. The point is to avoid committing the standard person problem whenever possible. So we must initiate a dialogue about the possibility of universally valid moral values that does not start from a moral point of view already based on hopelessly controversial assumptions. Are there any fairly noncontroversial assertions about humanity that we can use as a starting point to initiate cross-cultural discussions?

Humans Are Story-Telling Animals

> **For Study:**   How do humans get meaning in their life? What social and natural constraints place limits on the variety of ways language can be used to give meaning to our moral experiences?

As beings who *make-meaning,* the essence of human social existence is captured in our conscious attempt to tell stories that will attribute public meaning to our common experiences according to the symbolically expressed belief system of our community. The easiest way to understand the idea that conscious creatures create meaning is to think about the way a family passes on its heritage from generation to generation by telling stories about relatives. When a community's story gets very abstract and complicated, it becomes the system of beliefs that sustains the entire community. The use of language to convey meaning in this way is a universal phenomenon; people do this in all language communities in their constant ongoing quest to interpret their world. In fact, MacIntyre (1981) asserts that to be human is to be "essentially a story-telling animal" (p. 201). Every normal child is born into a language community that passes interpretive stories on from generation to generation. Thus, everyone experiences themselves in ways that are meaningful according to the stories they learned in their language community.

The more complex the system of symbols used, the more sophisticated and convoluted the interpretation of the world that gets told to each generation. However, the stories (or belief systems) that are passed from generation to generation are more than just stories to the members of a language community. Most people believe that the content that storytellers pass on about the world is true in some fundamental sense. Others believe that because the content of belief systems appears to be so different from culture to culture, it is far-fetched to think that there could be a common universal truth behind all of them. At first glance, the only fact that seems to be universal is that everyone needs to belong to some cultural story to survive as a human being.

Because different life experiences can lead to different interpretations of the world, some contemporary philosophers believe that it no longer makes good sense for philosophers to adopt the traditional strategy of trying to judge the truth of stories. They argue that what is important is to have access to an interpretation of the world, whether or not it is true in some cosmic sense. They say modern people would be better off if they would lighten up and become more playful with their interpretations—that is, we should all remember interpretations are only stories, so don't take them so seriously that you become indignant when someone questions your story's veracity. Given the possibility for such playfulness, some philosophers wonder: "Are the stories all culturally arbitrary, or are there some transcendent universal norms of religion, science, or

Figure 1.2 People pass down their stories—and their cultural values— from generation to generation, using a symbolic form of expression. (All illustrations courtesy of Brandon Reintjes, Marquette, MI, 1998)

morality behind at least some of the interpretations various language communities give to human experience?" How much leeway do we have to play with the content of cultural beliefs when we use them to give meaning to our experiences? I will argue that we can't make playful fictional claims at will and still be taken seriously by those who hear us. There are both natural and logical constraints that structure the type of stories that can be used by a civilization.

In the first place, the symbols used to communicate are not privately owned—they evolve in a community to serve communication between its members. Thus, the story that gets told will be constrained by the public history of the language community that sponsors the story. For most of human history, when members of language communities told their stories, they could generally rely on a background consensus among community members about the nature of human existence. *Life-world* is the term Habermas (1996) uses to denote *the historical heritage of a language community that makes the world seem "always already familiar."* It is composed of a "sprawling, deeply set, and unshakable rock of background assumptions, loyalties, and skills. . . . [What is interesting about this kind of] background knowledge is its peculiar prepredicative and precategorical character, . . . [it is a kind of forgotten] foundation of meaning inhabiting everyday practice and experience" (p. 22). In other words, since the language of a life-world is learned on a procedural level, we know it and its meanings in a tacit manner before we begin to develop declarative understanding about language itself. So the basics of language use are given to us before we become choosers who can begin to "play" with stories. We are not free to simply learn a language at will, we have to take it and its social content as it is given to us.

Second, language and its content are not taught to us as though it is all a matter of play. We are supposed to be serious about the community's interpretation of reality. So we are not free to simply playfully modify it at will unless we first announce that we are going to create some fiction as a matter of play. The willingness of tribal members to avoid creating confusion by honestly communicating according to the rules of their tribe's language is part of the glue that holds a community together.

Third, an important element of human well-being is intimately connected with the way stories are shared by members of a family, tribe, community, etc. As long as people share a life-world, they will live under a protective umbrella of background assumptions about the nature of the world that will initially provide each of them with a sense of "place" that is tied to their common belief about the meaning of their shared life. This consensus about background beliefs serves as a foundation for all future discussions between members of the community. It provides a sense of solidarity that allows people to engage in discourse without having to dispute every assumption that makes discourse possible. People will not want to "play" with their community's story for fear of disrupting its ability to provide a sense of place or well-being that can prevent the kind of alienation often found in pluralistic settings.

Figure 1.3 In a tribal society, sharing the same life-world is like being under a protective umbrella of shared values.

Fourth, other things being equal, there would be no motivation to tell a story that would deviate wildly from the standards of a person's language community. Each individual's attempt to tell the story of their own life will be judged to be believable only if it makes sense to other members of their life-world. An individual's story will be judged to be nonsense when the language community finds it incoherent—like the stories told by schizophrenics.

Finally, language is not created out of arbitrary mental fictions, there is an empirical foundation supporting language use. In the first place, people use language to communicate with others about what their bodies experience in the world. Insofar as all our more abstract conceptions depend on our ability to carry meaning upward from the bodily based and prelinguistic experiences of infancy and childhood, the stories we share will also be partly constrained by what our bodies are capable of experiencing in common and what we have or have not already experienced. In other words, because we all live bodily on the same planet, it is not an accident that shared language is also constrained by what the body can physically experience. (This point is compatible with the belief that how we experience our world is partly a social construction.)

But, what about making cross-cultural comparisons? Is it possible for cultures to share the same basic stories? It would be very useful if different language communities shared some background universal norms that were in fact respected in the stories found in all cultures. These norms could serve as a foundation upon which to build cross-cultural communication. One way to explore this possibility is to look for similarities between the common metaphors that people use to communicate ideas to new members of their life-world, for example, as when metaphors are used to teach children to understand the more abstract levels of tribal belief.

Metaphors Facilitate Communication

> **For Study:**   What experiences do all humans share that can help them construct metaphors to facilitate moral communication across cultures?

Metaphors are *language constructions that can be used to carry meaning from one context to another in order to clarify the second context.* For instance, the following metaphorical usage represents a perspective found in ancient Greece: "Women are sheep; they need to be tended and cared for." This sentence invites us to transfer meaning from the category of sheep to the category of women. But metaphors require interpretation. They can be revealing or misleading depending on how meaning is transferred. For example, are we supposed to think that women have wool or that women need a shepherd? A plausible interpretation by people who have experience with sheep would focus on the fact that sheep cannot take care of themselves; they need a shepherd to look after them. With a good shepherd, the sheep will be safe and content. The implication is that women are likewise vulnerable and need a father or husband for protection and care. Now notice how a different meaning is conveyed to the category of women if we switch metaphors and say, "Women are slaves." Slaves are people who should be free to govern themselves but are owned by a master who uses them for his own purposes. Thus, the metaphor implies that women ought to be free but are instead oppressed. Even if a master is a kind shepherd, the woman who ought to be free will still resent being the slave of the kind shepherd.

According to Lakoff and Johnson (1980), most of the important concepts used to give meaning to human experience can be traced back to the human imagination's capacity to create these kinds of *metaphorical extensions* to *carry meaning from one level or domain of experience to another.* This imaginative capacity makes it possible for us to take understanding we gained from previous bodily experiences and, using metaphors, extend that concrete understanding to increasingly abstract intellectual levels of experience. Our ability to do this is procedural, since we do it so automatically and begin at such an early age that we are often unaware that we know how to do it.

The bodily experiences that serve as a beginning foundation in all meaning systems include basic things like learning to accommodate gravity; that is, all humans experience verticality (up and down). This common experience leads to embodied images of verticality that make sense to anyone on a prelinguistic procedural level. We can extend this procedural knowledge of verticality to more abstract levels by creating metaphors that extend the body's awareness in order to capture abstract ideas of quantity, for example, "More is up and less is down." If our bodies did not experience the world according to vertical schemas, we would not be able to convey meaning with the following metaphorical usages: "*Prices keep going up; The number of books published each year keeps rising; His gross earnings fell; Turn down the heat.* [These] and many other examples, suggest that we understand MORE (increase) as being oriented UP (involving the verticality schema)" (Johnson, 1987, p. xv). In short, the way the body functions is structured. We can use metaphors to project that structure and create more abstract domains of understanding. But, our ability to use these metaphors to extend meaning to more abstract levels is not arbitrary because we have to rely on a background of shared experience. We cannot just project meaning at will, we have to use "input" that makes physical sense across domains of human experience. In other words, it doesn't work to say "Turn up the temperature, I want to cool down." The metaphorical usage is contrary to the experience of verticality that structures the way we create meaning. Human interactions with gravity make "up and down" part of the background that shapes how people tell their stories.

Once a particular metaphorical usage becomes common in a language community, it takes on independent status as a common concept and loses its metaphorical function. So, what does or does not count as a metaphor can be controversial. However, Lakoff and Johnson (1980) argue that our socially significant perceptions (if not all perceptions) are substantially determined by background metaphorical systems that originated in our prelinguistic bodily experiences.

These considerations imply that to accurately portray what is going on in philosophical stories, we must put the body back into our accounts of mind and human reason. Traditionally, the body had been ignored by the developing human sciences because of the fear that the body was tainted by irrational emotions and impulses, which seemed contrary to abstract rationality's goal of logically transcending the sensuous world. But this traditional Platonic picture, which infects the human sciences, must be adjusted to take into account what we now know about human development. How our nervous system interacts with the world sets limits on what the rational intellect can do and how far removed from the physical our stories can become without beginning to sound like nonsense.

The implication of this theory is that because metaphorical extensions of bodily experience underlie our abstract philosophical theories, then to fully understand many of the metaphors in another's philosophical story, we have to share at least some of the same bodily experiences. Remember, Grandin could not understand the concept of gentleness until she relied on a kind of metaphorical extension from her squeeze machine to her interactions with her cat. It was as if she said, "Ahhh! If my hands are a squeeze machine, then I should give the cat little squeezes like I get from my machine. That would be gentleness." If the body's experiences are part of the background information that determines which basic metaphors are available when imagination tries to extend old meanings to help us interpret new experiences, then there should be a physical basis for universal understanding. That is, because we all live on the same planet, it is not an accident that different language communities use light as a metaphor for understanding ("I can see what you mean") and darkness as a metaphor for the inability to understand ("I don't understand you, I'm in the dark").

In morality, the background concrete metaphors we use to construct our symbolic systems determine what kind of meanings make sense to us when we begin to evaluate the adequacy of human relations in the wider world. If there are socially significant bodily experiences that represent a universal procedural knowledge shared by members of all groups, perhaps this common experiential basis will lead to some overlapping metaphorical moral concepts that can serve as a universal foundation for guiding professional relationships around the world. A nice thought, but is it realistic? To explore this issue, we need to turn to some of the common philosophical concepts used in discussions of morality, and speculate on whether or not they originate in human experiences that seem to be universal. In order to stay in touch with the most common of human experiences, I'll begin with a reconstruction of a simplistic but clear idea of early moral life.

∾ "The Good Old Days" of Tribal Ethics

> **For Study:** Why do people have to be socialized? Why does the bag of virtues approach work well in tribal societies?

I think it is harder today to know what we ought to do than it was many years ago—not because universal moral ideals have become obsolete or because people have lost their moral virtues, but because the conditions under which virtuous people must apply ideals have become immeasurably more complex. To clarify this point, we will sketch out the simple picture of the good old days that mirrors the fairly romantic way some contemporary social critics conceive of the past. This picture will be accurate to the extent that it draws our attention to some of the features of life that formerly created moral solidarity in small communities. However, this picture should not seduce people into thinking it represents a social reality to which we can return (or which ever existed in pure form). Although we cannot solve the so-called decline in morality by recreating the past, we may be able to make some positive progress in understanding modern morality if we reconstruct some common tribal concepts to make them trustworthy guides in a world that has become much more difficult to navigate.

Historically, all tribes use similar socialization techniques to create new members. *Socialization* refers to the *process of training a person to become a fit member of a social group* and is basically the same phenomenon that anthropologists refer to as *enculturation*—the *"process of being educated into a way of life"* (Moody-Adams, 1997, p. 21). Once we have developed the procedural understandings that allow us to habitually obey the norms of our social setting, we have been successfully socialized into our life-world. Socialization is, of course, a necessary prerequisite for the existence of the human species itself. Children will never become adults without a social group that is willing to socialize them, and without adults there won't be a next generation. Thus, as Aristotle pointed out over 2,000 years ago, human beings are social animals designed by nature for living in a society after being socialized.

Unless something goes terribly wrong, as in exceptional cases of abuse, all children are socialized by the adult members of their tribe in such a way that they will share the cultural values of the older generation. The psychological term for this process is *introjection,* which means *to unconsciously internalize values that originated externally.* Introjection happens to us; it is not a matter of choice. Thus, those who introject values into us choose many of our deepest feelings about religion, family, love, sex, food, tastes, and general lifestyle preferences. Because childhood socialization is a clear case of control by the external environment into which we are born, it is more appropriate to hold the tribe responsible for introjected values than to hold individuals responsible, especially regarding those values that function at the procedural level. As a general rule, a tribe has the responsibility to see that its children are properly socialized so that their introjected values will make sense from a moral point of view that is acceptable to the tribe.

As mentioned above, most people living in homogenous societies share a common life-world made up of an "unshakable rock of background assumptions, loyalties, and skills" (Habermas, 1996). As a simple way to refer to such communities, I will call this a "tribal" form of existence. The shared background makes the world seem "always already familiar" (p. 22) to each member of the tribe. Because everyone in a homogeneous tribe has roughly the same social values introjected into them, the values feel like objective absolutes that are part of the fabric of nature. When there is no comparative basis from which to criticize the sources of introjection that gave members their traditional values, then basic moral beliefs can function like a system of taboos. In a *taboo* system *fundamental moral beliefs are treated as so sacred that ordinary citizens are prohibited from evaluating or judging them.* Since moral taboos are to be followed without question, the main virtue a moral agent needs is blind loyalty to the rules of the tribe. Under these conditions, a tribe will not develop self-critical social philosophy.

When compared with pluralistic cultures, socializing the next generation in a tribal society would seem relatively simple. Imagine how straightforward issues would be if we had only one set of major social norms to transmit to each tribal member. In many ways the process would be similar to teaching children to memorize the Boy or Girl Scout Code (a scout is trustworthy, brave, clean, loyal, reverent, courteous, kind, thrifty, helpful, etc.). Young scouts are not encouraged to pay attention to the intrinsic differences between these values; they merely learn to recite them. Kohlberg and Turiel (1971) refer to this style of moral socialization as the *"bag of virtues"* (p. 412) approach to moral education, because authority figures allow the next generation in the tribe to *assume that the values are of the same logical type so that it is appropriate to lump them together in an "absolute bag" to be obeyed without question.*

Tribal values can fulfill their community function even if they are *arbitrary,* meaning that *there are no independent reasons that can explain and justify the values,* because no one is challenging them or asking for deep justifications. That is, even arbitrary tribal values can create group solidarity, stable expectations, and a sense that everyone shares a natural heritage. As long as each tribal member adopts the values without question, this method works well; in fact, in a developmental sense it is necessary to treat family values as taboos when children are too young to discuss the purpose of social values. Tribal values clearly passed on in this way promote continuity between generations, especially when people of all ages assist in the socialization process. Because this kind of intimate early socialization provides each member with a clear, stable sense of social identity, people will be far less likely to suffer from the anxiety about the meaning of life that afflicts so many modern adolescents. Their basic need for a sense of place is satisfied by the historical social integrity of their tribe's life-world.

Levels of Abstraction and Justification

> **For Study:** Why do we need to pay attention to the different levels of abstraction when we formulate a justification for our actions?

Even in tribal settings there are types of value conflicts that occur which involve people, animals, the environment, spiritual beings, and so forth. In this text, we will discuss only value conflicts that occur between two or more people. Narrowing the focus will simplify our task, but it will not make the task simple. In the first place, to make sense of a value conflict on even a tribal level, we need to understand the background context within which the conflict occurs. (Remember, the background shapes the foreground.) Because any action must be historically or socially situated before its full meaning can be understood, we will have to explore various background contexts throughout the text. In the first place, one of the most important contexts in any moral conflict is the institutional setting that defines the roles of the people involved. Since we are interested in all contexts that are covered by obligatory rules, we will define an **institution** in a very broad way to mean *any rule-governed relationship*. Any time we occupy a station in a marriage, family, job, friendship, school, or church, etc., we are governed by the rules of an institution. Institutional rules tell us in an immediate, concrete way what we ought to believe in a local situation and how we ought to behave. So the first step in justifying a claim about what ought to be requires us to point to the rule that governs the situation, for example: "You ought to buckle up!" "Why?" "It's the law."

While there might be room for some individual initiative in carrying out one's tribal role, the important obligations of tribal life would be prescribed by clear institutional rights and duties of station that applied to all the men and women of the tribe. For example, the labels "husband" and "wife" make sense because they are based on concrete social expectations tied to introjected procedural understandings that are the same for all members of the life-world. When there is no way to make comparisons with other tribes, then standardized duties of station dominate the way men and women court, marry, and parent, leaving little room for individual lifestyle choice in these matters.

Duties of station include *all the special duties (and rights) that apply to people who move into an institutional setting to take responsibility for the specific social roles defined in the settings' code*. For example, because of their special role, doctors have rights and duties that do not apply to ordinary people, such as the right to practice medicine and also the duty to medically assist victims of accidents. The logical structure of these duties of station is inherently **intersubjective**. This means that *the way these settings function is determined by the shared expectations of everyone in the setting*. In all **social settings**, then, *functional members develop shared intersubjective procedural expectations about how a person who performs social actions in the setting ought to behave*. When someone deviates he or she will be quickly brought back in line with outright condemnation or gossip or other modes of social control. The more codified and legalistic systems of obligations get expressed in **codes of ethics,** which are the *published rules and principles that regulate the behavior of office holders within particular institutional settings*. These codes are written in varying degrees of complexity, and include everything from the Boy and Girl Scout codes to the ethical codes of professional associations.

Even with clear ethical codes specifying the extent of the duties of station, there would, of course, still be value conflicts in tribal settings. But, the conflicts would be resolved in a fairly straightforward, traditional manner. Members of the tribe would justify the resolution by appealing to the priorities established by the rules of traditional tribal hierarchies. At the moment, for the sake of clarity, I am making use of a device called *ceteris paribus* to stay focused on the pure case and ignore possible exceptions to the rule. *Ceteris paribus* is Latin for *"other things being equal."* So, other things being equal, we can assume that in an isolated tribe there would be few serious value conflicts that challenge the status quo of the fundamental tribal rules. We will return to this issue later when we consider complaints that might arise from tribal minorities.

To get a feel for how the justification of an action begins at the level of ethical rules, let's consider a simple conflict between a desire to act on a personal preference and a set of rules that should be familiar to most of us. Because I want to show how metaphors can be used to facilitate the socialization process, I will choose as my example the reconstruction of an event that gave me the opportunity to socialize my children into the tribal practice of driving. While approaching a stop light with my children in the car, I suddenly stopped my car and said: "Nuts!" My young, inexperienced daughter asked: "What's wrong? Why did the car stop?" Without an explanation of context, my action appeared to be no more than a meaningless physical event to her. As a parent and tribal member, it is my duty of station to socialize her into the mysteries of driving. The simplest explanation would be to clarify the context for my action by bringing her attention to the rule that governed my decision. I told her: "I stopped the car on purpose. The reason I said "nuts" is because I didn't want to stop now. But the light turned red, so I had to stop."

This explanation was supposed to reveal that although I wanted to continue, I chose to obey a rule of the road that says cars have to stop at red lights no matter the personal preferences of the driver. My daughter didn't understand the rules of the road, so she surprised me by saying: "If you didn't want to stop, then why did you?" She was wondering why I did not act on my personal preference and keep going. In reality, I said something to the effect that the law is the law; but, as a good tribal member, I should have contributed to the socialization process by helping my daughter understand that there are duties of station that apply to drivers on public streets. But how could I have explained that to a young child? Since my daughter has procedural understanding that family members have to obey the commands given by the adults in the family, I could use her knowledge of our family context to create some metaphorical extensions that would help her understand the rights and duties that apply to drivers.

To socialize my daughter, I will help her transfer her procedural commitment to intersubjective family rules to the more abstract commitment needed to respect the rules of the road. Thus, I will tell my daughter: "You know how we have rules in the family that we all have to obey so everyone will be protected, like no hitting or spitting? Well the family of drivers has rules too, and they have to be followed. Just as you have to follow our family's rules and not hit your brother without a very good excuse, well, it would also be wrong for me to violate the rules of the family of drivers without a very good excuse. Traffic laws demand that I override my own preferences in certain situations. So, I have to obey the rule, which says: 'You can go only if the light is green. You must stop when it turns red.'"

This explanation should satisfy those who have been socialized to feel a commitment to the intersubjective rules of family life—but my even younger son was in the backseat. Suppose he is still so self-centered that he resents all rules (or is a budding philosopher who craves deeper explanations). He may challenge the very nature of tribal social practices by asking: "But, why do we have to have rules anyway?" From his perspective, traffic lights seem to be arbitrary restraints on his personal preferences, and he may not see why they are good for the family of drivers. And of course, because there are some stoplights that seem to be rather arbitrary, he may have a point. To help him see that the rules might make rational sense as part of an important intersubjective practice, I will need to explain that there is yet another more abstract background level that can justify the rules. *Moral principles* are used to *prescribe intersubjective reasons for acting. They both explain and justify rules and actions to other members of the community*. In short, principles serve as good reasons for creating rules between people. They tell us why a tribe ought to create rules of the road in the first place. Although such principles often function like background procedural norms influencing choices, we can make them declarative by openly discussing them.

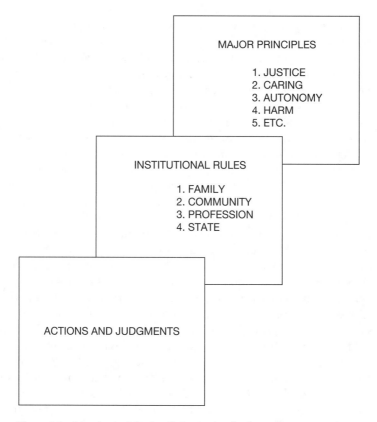

MAJOR PRINCIPLES

1. JUSTICE
2. CARING
3. AUTONOMY
4. HARM
5. ETC.

INSTITUTIONAL RULES

1. FAMILY
2. COMMUNITY
3. PROFESSION
4. STATE

ACTIONS AND JUDGMENTS

Figure 1.4 Moral principles justify institutional rules.

To socialize new members to have an emotional commitment to principles, we will have to use metaphorical extensions that can help to transfer already learned lower-level commitments to the higher levels of abstraction required by principles. In short, I would make use of my son's procedural commitment to the family to try and explain why we need higher levels of commitment. I could say: "You know how it makes you mad for your sister to take your toys without asking?" "Ya!" "Well you know how we made a rule that says she has to ask before she can play with your toys. Do you think that is a good rule?" "Yes." "Well if she has to ask you, then it is only fair that you also have to ask her, right? That way each of you is protected as a family member. See how useful rules can be? They help us apply principles like *'Be fair'* that we all need for protection."

I would also bring up the issue of the rights of station possessed by family members. Just like everyone in the family has a right to use the family's bathroom and shower, everyone in the family of drivers has a right to share the tribe's highway (the principle of justice). Think about what might happen if there were no rules and everyone tried to take their turn whenever they wanted to. Eventually someone would crash into someone else. So, while people are taking their fair turn, we need some way to coordinate their timing to avoid harm (the principle of harm prevention). Just as we have rules in the house to govern when to take turns and tools like locks on the bathroom door to protect someone's privacy, we need rules and tools to properly apply the principles of justice and harm prevention that govern the tribe's use of the road. So, the traffic light is a tool that makes sure everyone is treated fairly and it also prevents harm. "Isn't that a good idea?" Hopefully, my son will agree.

By situating my response to the stop light in this abstract, intersubjective context, I have demonstrated that following the rules is justified by moral principles. All tribes have these kinds of background moral principles. They are used to rationally justify commitment to rules when someone questions them. For children in ordinary tribal circumstances, fundamental principles are treated like taboos that are moral facts. Since we cannot challenge a fact, most children would stop asking questions at this point. How soon members of a tribe stop asking "why" questions will, of course, depend on their historical background and how much space is provided for internal criticism of rules.

Moody-Adams (1997) points out that in real tribal societies there is always some conceptual "space" for internal tribal criticism of rules and principles whenever (1) there is some group that suffers from institutional rules and (2) it is reasonable to "presume that most of those who generally reap some of the benefits of the institutional practice [created by the principles and rules] would not have chosen to be members of groups that suffer most of the burdens" (p. 85). In addition, opportunities for critical reflection could also arise during moments of **liminality,** a condition that *exists temporarily when a tribal member enters a rite of passage that allows him or her to take on a new tribal role* (Turner, 1974, pp. 13–14, cited in Moody-Adams, p. 69). During such moments internal comparison and criticism become possible as one reflects on her changing status. Perhaps a critic won't agree with the principles used, or will disagree about the way the principles have been implemented, or will just want to see where they will get to if they keep asking "why?" For whatever reason, if people keep asking, they will eventually have to go behind principles to explore the interpretive stories that create the kind of background context that is used to justify the level of moral principles.

When we challenge fundamental principles, we are asking for a justification that is so abstract it can only be answered by grounding the principles in some all-encompassing theoretical framework. Thus, at this level of abstraction, justifications may refer to a foundational taboo system the tribe uses to give ultimate meaning in their life-world. When we reach this point in a justification of actions, rules, and, then, principles, we are referring to the abstract taboo system, or in modern terms, the abstract **theory,** that contains the basic ***ideals*** we expect to find in *the perfect state of affairs that tribal members think should exist when things are what they ought to be.* This is their vision of how life ought to be "other things being equal."

Given social homogeneity and universal biological needs, members of traditional language communities could rely on a massive background of metaphysical consensus about the nature of their existence. Thus, for our purposes, we will define a ***metaphysical society*** as a life-world that *relies on a common system of beliefs about the ultimate nature of reality and the place of citizens in that reality.* With a system of shared metaphysical beliefs functioning as a background, all activities could be explained and justified by showing how they fit into the tribe's shared metaphysical system. In the romantic conception of the "good old days," conventional people would not challenge the legitimacy of the moral hierarchy that ascends through local laws, to background principles, to the community's abstract ideals. Since social rules are essential to humanity's social existence, in a well-structured metaphysical society they would be sacred. As Adam Smith (1982) says "rules of morality are the commands and laws of the Deity" (163).

When morality is based in this way on a sacred metaphysical foundation, the virtue of moral integrity can be assumed to be an essential part of the good life. Thus, Adam Smith assumed that everyone's reason for being moral was his or her own self-interest, because self-interest was intimately tied to moral integrity. For much of human history, beliefs about ***the good*** (*happiness*) and ***the right*** (*duty*) were simply two sides of the same coin (especially when rewards and punishments accompanying moral behavior were thought to carry over into an eternal afterlife). As we shall see, however, this compatibility is much more tenuous in postmetaphysical pluralistic societies. Violating duty is sometimes rewarded and doing duty does not always lead to personal happiness. For instance, when moral motives like loyalty and honor lead to intersubjective social commitments that require one to die for his or her country, the chance for personal happiness ends. It is clear that doing what is right is not logically

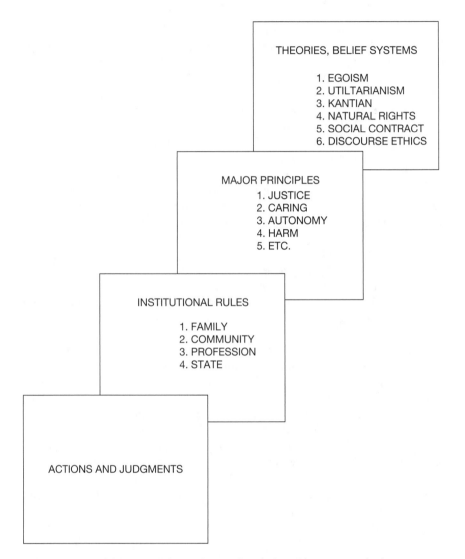

Figure 1.5   Moral theories justify moral principles which justify institutional rules.

or causally tied to getting what one desires on a personal level. (We will explore these complex value relationships in more detail in Chapter Four).

∿ Today's World of Social Pluralism

For Study: Why are introjected arbitrary values less likely to create legitimation problems in tribal ethics? Why does social pluralism complicate moral choice? Why are arbitrary values more likely to create legitimation problems in pluralistic cultures? In what way does pluralism contribute to moral growth?

When groups (or tribes) with different lifestyles, metaphysical beliefs, and moral points of view are living in the same political space, we have the conditions for *social pluralism.* Under these circumstances, even if we have been thoroughly socialized in tribe A, we will still be in a position to compare ourselves with those socialized in tribe B. As mentioned above, in tribal societies "internal" criticism would probably not arise unless some subgroup was disadvantaged or there was a condition of "liminality." In pluralistic cultures, however, there is also the possibility for a new kind of "external" criticism. When external comparisons between groups become possible, people may even begin to question the legitimacy of their own tribal and family socialization process.

In the contemporary world, philosophers can no longer rely on a shared metaphysics to ground moral norms. Modern societies are now composed of a variety of subgroups that have different ways of understanding themselves according to different background metaphysical assumptions. Thus, we have entered into a *"post" metaphysical age* (Habermas, 1998), where *consensus on background moral principles has to be reached without relying on the assumption that everyone conceives of the ultimate nature of the world in the same way.* Pluralism has, thus, created a general skepticism that surrounds all metaphysical and universal moral claims.

Furthermore, individuals often belong to several different and incompatible institutions at the same time. Gloria Anzaldua (1987) refers to this condition as life in the *"borderlands," the space between cultures.* She says that in the modern world everyone is not raised in a uniform, even if oppressive, community capable of providing everyone with the same stable intersubjective heritage. Although she received a good traditional Catholic upbringing in a small village for the first seven years of her life, she discovered that she had to develop an increasingly broader self-conception in order to survive and thrive in the more complicated pluralistic world that confronted her in her later years.

> Woman does not feel safe when her own culture, and white culture, are critical of her; when the males of all races hunt her as prey.
>
> Alienated from her mother culture, "alien" in the dominant culture, the woman of color does not feel safe within the inner life of her Self. Petrified, she can't respond, her face caught between *los intersticios,* the spaces between the different worlds she inhabits. (p. 20)

Although Anzaldua is referring specifically to women, a similar condition is experienced by men who are not members of the mainstream privileged group that has the power to set social agendas. Under such conditions of value pluralism, we are confronted with fundamental value choices that can cause a paralyzing sense of confusion and vulnerability, or "muddle" (symbolized by the question mark in the center of Figure 1.6). In a pluralistic culture, what does it mean to be a man or woman, a solid citizen, a loyal employee, a moral person, a husband or wife, a mother or father? Which version of a social role

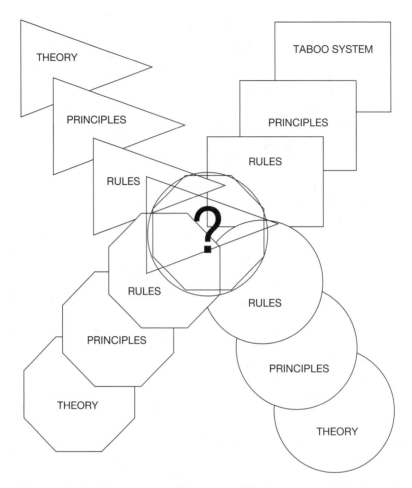

Figure 1.6 Pluralism creates confusion or muddle about personal identity and ethical and moral values.

is right from a universal moral point of view? Which version is better from a personal point of view? Which is better from the point of view of various institutional codes of ethics? These kinds of fundamental value questions are becoming more common every day around the world. A tribe would have to remain very isolated or extremely totalitarian to avoid the confusion such questions can cause.

In closed tribal settings lack of comparisons allows the primary benefits of tribal life (sense of self, social solidarity, security, moral confidence, etc.) to be maintained even when some duties of station can be seen to be arbitrary from an external, nontribal point of view. For most of us, however, the simple "good old days" of tribal certainty and security are gone forever. External value comparisons have given individuals the possibility of evaluating the most dominant values in their tribe's life-world. When comparisons suggest that some of the values that require us to make sacrifices for a traditional lifestyle could be arbitrary, then the possibility that there are less arbitrary alternatives that are not so burdensome often leads to confusion, even with regard to something as basic as our identity or our gender. When burdensome duties of station are arbitrary, then members who bear the greatest burdens may begin to experience a *legitimation crisis*—wherein *a significant number of the tribe's members begin to challenge the legitimacy of the tribe's basic institutions.* Tribal members may withhold their automatic compliance to traditional social roles. This, of course, will cause considerable anger among the older members who have already conformed to those roles. Inevitably, it will become more difficult to maintain the strong sense of place, solidarity, and security that was available when there was little choice.

For these reasons, when people ask for justifications of the various duties found at different levels, we ought to have something reasonable to say. In other words, if I want my children's loyalty forever, I should only impose values that I can justify to them. If I say, "There isn't a reason for the rule; I am just bigger than you. Do it because I say so!" then there will come a day when they will walk away, and rightfully so. This is especially true in the modern world, now that so many of us live without the stability provided by ancient, protected traditions.

We have lost the metaphysical support for Smith's (1982, p. 163) feeling of "reverence" for moral rules of conduct. Since morality had to become secular in order to make room for freedom of worship, there is no longer general agreement that morality will pay off in terms of personal happiness or in eternal salvation. As a result, the concept of *the good life (happiness)* has become differentiated from the concept of **what is morally right** (*duty*), resulting in personal motivation becoming detached from moral commitment (Habermas 1998, p. 34). That is, "being moral" and "living a happy life" are no longer assumed to be automatically compatible endeavors. Smith's faith in the sacred value of rules of conduct begins to look irrational to anyone who associates happiness with self-centered personal gain, unless of course, moral conduct only means concern for rules that benefit one's own preferences—especially in business settings where transactions are often between strangers. Under these conditions, for many people, universal morality and talk of the sacred now seem rather quaint, if not absurd. To the radical individualist, then, integrity between strangers begins to look like a game for the fool who doesn't understand "the way it is."

For whole societies the "sacred substance" (Habermas, 1996, p. 443) that represented a metaphysical umbrella of shared religious and moral meaning has been shredded by science and pluralism. So many people are ready to doubt any worldview, that finding a life with any lasting meaning has become increasingly difficult. In the words of Max Weber, the plurality of worldviews has led to a general "disenchantment of the world" (cited by Rehg, 1996,

Figure 1.7 In contemporary Western society, the life-world's protective umbrella of shared values has been shredded by pluralism.

p. xvii), so that people find it more and more difficult to assume without question that their lives can have shared social and cosmic meaning. Under these conditions, more and more people in industrialized societies are listening to a voice that says, "The world is so confusing; I don't know what to believe. I can't trust my umbrella. I wish I could find a wise professional to advise me."

Because these developments challenge the very nature of a stable social status quo and the principles used to justify it, people who wish to defend the foundations of their life-world from assaults by those from another life-world will have to move to an even higher level of abstraction. Taboo systems will have to evolve into flexible, universal moral theories that have some deep universal appeal. When people are forced to defend their ethical choices to people from a different heritage, they begin to construct those moral theories that are of special interest to philosophers. These *moral theories try to organize abstract concepts into rational frameworks that can provide the broad background intersubjective value contexts people will need to formulate universal justifications under conditions of pluralism.* If these theories are to be taken seriously by everyone, they will have to be compatible with a moral point of view (MPofV) that is impartially based, so that it can help us avoid the standard person problem.

∼ A Special Vocabulary Defines the Moral Point of View

> **For Study:** Why do philosophy and ethics have to be normative disciplines? Why do universal moral claims need to be supported by cross-cultural public reasons? Why can't personal or group feelings serve as a justification for universal moral claims? Why must the moral point of view emphasize impartiality?

Academic philosophers use a special vocabulary and style of thought to argue for the possibility of an impartial MPofV that can help philosophers evaluate the fundamental issues of moral experience. To portray the viewpoint of contemporary philosophy, we will begin with some preliminary definitions from that special vocabulary. In the first place, we can define *academic philosophy* as *a discipline that engages in self-critical, public dialogue about the adequacy of the belief systems that communities use to give meaning to their experiences.* The goal is to discover if there is some perspective, or way of giving meaning to the world, that is more adequate than all the others. To put it another way, philosophers know there are many different perspectives or interpretations of moral experience and they want to know if all of them are equally adequate. In general, philosophers assume that everyone *ought* to adopt the most valid positions; but they are not claiming that people always will. This assumption about what ought to be means philosophy is a *normative discipline.* That is, the discipline *not only describes the norms that serve as the foundation for various belief systems, but it also makes prescriptive judgments about the validity of the norms and belief systems.* To carry out its normative task, philosophy will have to go beyond descriptive disciplines like the sciences, because again, the goal is not just to give a scientific description of the various belief systems in the world, but also to judge the adequacy of those systems so that our prescriptions will be right rather than wrong.

The word "ethics" is often used in a casual manner to be synonymous with morality, as when it is used to refer to the general moral duties in a group's code of ethics. However, "ethics" can also be used in a more technical way to refer to the academic discipline that studies the adequacy of the moral values of different groups. In this text there will be times when the term is used both ways, but for now we will define *ethics* as *a dialogical academic discipline that tries to understand in a rational, self-critical manner* (as opposed to understanding in ways that are esthetic, religious, economic, patriotic, etc.) *how we ought to resolve various kinds of value conflicts.* As a subdiscipline in philosophy, the discipline of ethics is normative to the core since the goal of this academic study is to discover which moral systems are the most valid. (Again, this is the opposite of science, which would try to describe moral systems and how people do in fact treat each other.) If we lived in a different world where there was universal agreement about the principles and rules that prescribe what people ought to do, there would be no need for an academic discipline like ethics.

Moral values can be defined as all those *commitments we hold that make us think of some things as right and other things as wrong or some things as morally good and others as morally bad*. Thus, from a descriptive anthropological perspective, it is clear that every community has a broad *community morality,* that is, *a system of shared intersubjective norms that give all members of a specific community mutually understood expectations of how they ought to treat one another*. These community moral prescriptions are easier to understand when they are embodied in less abstract lower-level **ethical codes.** *Codes of ethics* are *written for specific groups within a society and involve the fairly concrete rules and principles needed to govern institutions and their officeholders*. In other words, this first level includes the concrete ethical guidelines that create duties of station for specific social groups like the family, the military, fraternal organizations, professional associations, etc. The rights and duties that come with the first-level "codes of ethics" and the second-level "community moralities" are usually taught to members of tribes during the socialization process. These values are, therefore, fairly clear and **concrete** (either you are a dentist or you are not, either you are a member of the Nadu tribe or you are not). When rights and duties are attributed to a **universal morality,** however, they transcend both first-level codes of ethics and second-level community morality. It is this third level of morality that provides a background context for judging the adequacy of the first two levels. It *prescribes rights and duties for everyone, no matter what their station or what community they inhabit*. For instance, a theory such as the one expressed in the U.S. Declaration of Independence asserts that people have universal human rights no matter whom they may be. Consider: "We hold these truths to be self-evident, that all men are created equal, that they are endowed by their Creator with certain inalienable rights, that among these are life, liberty, and the pursuit of happiness." This is an amazing claim that is in conflict with most of the power structures that have been allowed in community moralities throughout the history of mankind. Proving that everyone has rights or that everyone ought to do something is not an easy task. Thus, in the academic study of ethics we will have to make sense of this level by creating an abstract *moral theory* that *can justify the claim that there are moral values that can have universal validity*. This kind of theory by its very nature is going to be controversial and difficult to understand. Since this level is supposed to have priority over both professional codes of ethics and community moralities, we will need to explore how to keep these three different levels compatible.

Before we can convince people about the legitimacy of universal moral claims, we all have to reach a consensus about an appropriate moral point of view from which to judge the validity of the reasons used to support broad universal claims. In ethics there is a general consensus that *the moral point of view* from which to judge and make claims has to be *a standpoint that is impartial* (Habermas, 1993, p. 48). It is important to note, however, that even though a consensus has emerged in the history of philosophy regarding the logical need for impartiality, it has turned out to be very difficult to properly characterize the nature of moral impartiality. At a minimum, philosophers are now aware that they must be constantly on guard against letting unintended, harmful, or pernicious biases slip into their justifications of moral and ethical claims.

The most popular current consensus in ethics maintains that **for a moral point of view to be impartial,** it must (1) meet publicly acknowledged rational standards, (2) satisfy conditions of universality—that is, in principle be compatible with what all honest people could agree to after deliberation, (3) be self-critical rather than ideological, and (4) promote generalized empathy and respect among all people. (An additional condition will be added in Chapter Six.) The meaning and reasons for these conditions will be clarified later. (I used to claim these were requirements of the "Western" moral point of view. Two philosophers from Asia objected that the same concerns are found in non-Western cosmopolitan philosophies, so I have dropped the qualification "Western.") Because people also disagree about the best way to avoid pernicious forms of bias, we will also need to evaluate the adequacy of various application strategies for morality. We will return to these normative issues again and again as the text unfolds. At this point, however, it is more important to explore the most abstract level of justification found in academic ethics. We can approach this level by consulting six popular theories.

Six Possible Principles of Universal Morality

> **For Study:**   Why do most theories formulate foundational normative principles? Why are moral theories ultimately practical in their implications?

When resolving value conflicts, every moral theory assumes that it is more important to pay attention to some background features than others. Moral theories draw our attention to these important background features by formulating *foundational principles* that *indicate which values ought to be given top priority in all our moral decisions.* These principles are the most basic because all the other principles created at lower levels are interpreted by reference to how they fit with a theory's foundational principle. Even though these foundational normative prescriptions refer to ideal states of affairs, they are still inherently **practical** since the *abstract, morally binding statements ought to lead* *to local actions that will make concrete changes in the real world.* Thus, foundational principles are not just a matter of theory; they must help us develop practical guidelines about how to act locally.

There are at least six different moral theories compatible with the MPofV that are in competition with each other for our moral allegiance. The moral prescriptions found in their foundational principles are supposed to help establish a basic set of priorities that can help resolve cross-cultural conflicts. In later chapters we will look at the arguments for these different universal theories, but for now, we will only look at the form each of these six principles must take before they can function as impartial, foundational moral principles to regulate lower-level secondary principles of the kind we find in codes of ethics. Although a reader might like an immediate explanation of the meaning of each of these principles, I am not going to pursue that discussion here. The differences between these six principles are important and not easy to explain. It will be useful, therefore, to develop more background information before we delve into the complex nature of each theory. If you can't wait, then skip to Chapters Eight and Nine for a deeper explanation of each theory.

1. **Ethical Egoism:**   "Everyone ought to act to promote his or her own best interest."
2. **Utilitarianism:**   "Everyone ought to act to promote the greatest amount of happiness for everyone."
3. **Natural Rights Theory:**   "Everyone ought to act in accordance with everyone's inalienable, indefeasible natural rights."
4. **Social Contract Theory:**   "Everyone ought to act in accordance with the principles that *would* be chosen *if* free and equal rational people were to enter a social contract to establish a moral community."
5. **Kantian Duty Ethics:**   "Everyone ought to always treat people as ends unto themselves and never use them as a means only."
6. **Discourse Ethics:**   "Just those action norms are valid to which all possibly affected persons could agree as participants in rational discourses" (Habermas, 1996, p. 107).

Virtue Ethics, Another Possibility

> **For Study:** Why is it impossible to give one foundational principle for virtue ethics? What is practical wisdom?

The six principles listed above do not exhaust possible approaches to moral inquiry. For example, we might wonder, why a principle representing traditional virtues like honesty, courage, prudence, justice, charity, and so forth, is not listed. A ***virtue*** is a *human strength or skill that helps us live like we ought to.* MacIntyre (1981) points out that we can call a capacity or skill a virtue only when a social context requires us to develop that particular skill. The ***cardinal virtues*** are those that represent *the highest ideals or forms of conduct in a particular life-world.* For example, with their background emphasis upon leading a rational life, the classical Greeks chose as their cardinal virtues: wisdom, justice, courage, and temperance—all of which contribute to remaining rational. Since virtues make us stronger moral agents, if nothing else, surely socialization procedures should enhance such virtues rather than destroy them. ***Virtue ethics*** emphasizes attaining these strengths, but it does not focus on a single foundational principle. It simply tells us to develop *those traits of character (virtues) that help moral agents function well in situations calling for moral judgment.* This approach can be illustrated with a simple summary of Aristotle's theory of virtue ethics.

Aristotle focused on clarifying the concept of virtue itself. He argued that it was virtuous to choose the proper amount of emotion and/or action called for in a particular situation and that extremes of emotions and/or actions were vices. Thus, it is virtuous to strive for the ***golden mean,*** which refers to *the appropriate amount.* For instance, how much champagne should a person drink at a wedding? Too much is the vice of drunkenness, too little the vice of rudeness—it prevents one from toasting the bride and groom. Each participant should drink a virtuous amount, but the amount will be different for each, depending on his or her role in the wedding. It takes practical wisdom to know how to figure out how much is appropriate (the mean amount) in every occasion. In all communities there are people who possess the necessary ***practical wisdom.*** These people *have the capacity to judge wisely in a variety of practical situations; that is, they are virtuous.* How do they do it? Two thousand years ago Aristotle argued that people with practical wisdom have the capacity to follow the "right rule" whatever the situation (Ross, Trans., 1941, pp. 957–59, 1022–29). In this context, the "right rule" is not a law or code; it is synonymous with the morally right thing to do. Aristotle is arguing that people with practical wisdom have the virtues needed to balance all relevant variables in any circumstance to avoid acting in ways that are so extreme that they amount to vice. This is sometimes called "case wisdom" in the professions.

There is no reason to disagree with Aristotle. Of course, we should strive to be virtuous and avoid vices. But, exactly how are those of us who lack practical wisdom supposed to calculate the proportionate amount of emotion and/or action on all occasions? Advocates of each of the six theories listed in the previous section would say: "Wise people always ought to use our principle when they search for the 'right rule' in every situation." But Aristotle would not agree that it is feasible to give a foundational principle that ought to be used all the time. He believed the "right rule" was relative for different occasions, thus the term only means the practical capacity to appropriately judge in the various contexts. So, rather than follow the dictates of a major principle,

Aristotle advises beginners in ethics to focus on imitating the behavior of obviously virtuous people. In this way, beginners would themselves develop the habits of virtuous action. Wisdom in practical affairs must be learned on the job, so to speak, since it is not easy to summarize in a single principle the virtues needed for wise practice in all local situations.

The premise of this book is that we need to adopt a combination of the principles approach and the virtues approach to ethics. Certain virtues are essential for philosophical ethical deliberation about how to follow principles. That is, to properly use any of the six foundational moral principles mentioned previously, a person must first master certain common human virtues. Several chapters have been devoted to discussing how moral virtues develop and how they help professionals implement major philosophical principles at the more concrete levels where codes of ethics apply. Why is it so important for ordinary citizens to develop the virtues that support practical wisdom? Because in complex pluralistic environments, everyone is going to have to be prepared to engage in complex deliberation about how universal principles ought to be applied to local contexts.

∽ Metaethics and the Difference Between Justification and Application

> **For Study:**   Why does metaethics naturally emerge in pluralistic cultures? What is the difference between traditional courses in philosophical ethics and applied ethics? Why is the discourse of justification different from the discourse of application (use *ceteris paribus* and *prima facie* in your answer)?

Obviously, as the existence of the six foundational moral principles and virtue ethics clearly demonstrate, people who are serious about morality can still disagree with one another about which theory ought to guide their choice of principles. When debates begin about which moral theory is the most adequate background guide, we are forced to turn to the most abstract level of philosophical ethics in order to consider questions about the nature of ethical language and the structure of ethical theories themselves. *Metaethics* is a study that *attempts to answer questions about the nature of a moral point of view, the nature of moral theories, the meaning of moral terms, and the types of reasons that can serve as justifications in morality.* Since this level of study leads to theories about theories, it is about as abstract as ethical studies can get. Metaethics is not an end in itself; it developed to help us clarify what we are doing when we use normative moral theories. Since metaethics focuses on the logical or analytical study of moral terms, it does not necessarily lead to moral prescriptions about what we ought to do. Thus, it should not be confused with normative ethics, which does try to make moral prescriptions. Eventually, however, the goal is to discover criteria that can be of practical use when we try to figure out why some moral theories are normatively better than others. Thus, while much of this text will focus on metaethical considerations, the goal is to help prescribe a normative background for moral deliberation.

Value conflicts can arise on any of the conceptual levels (represented in Figure 1.8), since a disagreement can involve different desires, judgments, intentions, rules, principles, or theories. A different type of justification is correspondingly appropriate in each case, depending on the level of the conflict. For instance, a conflict over the appropriateness of rules in a particular institution might be settled by reference to shared principles—for example, if parents disagree about whether to set a child's bed time at 9 P.M. or 10 P.M., they may be able to resolve the disagreement over the rules if they agree on a principle of autonomy that says children should be free to choose between the alternatives themselves. If we can agree that the rule is an appropriate application of background principles, then the rule is justified. But a conflict over principles cannot be settled by appealing to lower-level rules. Instead, we would have to go to the next level of abstraction to find a common theory that can resolve our dispute over principles. Thus, to avoid confusion when trying to resolve value conflicts, it is important to have some metaethical clarity about the logical nature of the tasks being performed at different levels.

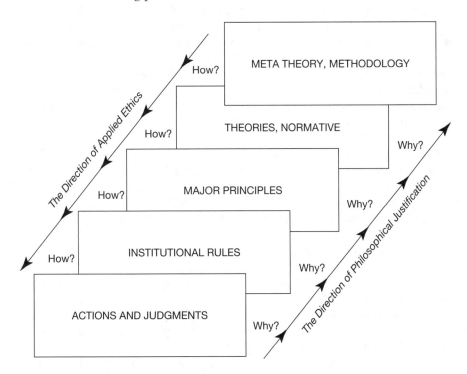

Figure 1.8 Applied ethics changes the direction of reflection.

One aim of academic philosophy is to study all the theories that have been developed to try to answer the "why" questions that arise under conditions of pluralism when people ask for a justification of moral claims at various levels. Most traditional courses in *philosophical ethics have focused on evaluating the various arguments that are used to justify background ideals expressed in universal principles* such as those mentioned earlier. These traditional courses do not devote much time to considering how the justified ideals ought to be applied to concrete cases, thus many people consider these courses to be too abstract to be of any practical use.

On the other hand, courses in *applied ethics* have been consciously designed to reverse the normal philosophical progression toward creating increasingly abstract and all-encompassing background theoretical ideals. These courses *investigate how theoretically justified abstract ideals expressed in foundational principles can be applied at lower and lower concrete levels to help resolve the kinds of value conflicts that arise in local contexts.*

Contemporary applied ethics courses acknowledge that to avoid confusion, two different logical tasks need to be addressed when constructing a moral system. The first task involves *justification discourse,* which is the *intersubjective attempt to find a theoretical justification of the universal ideals prescribed in foundational principles* (sometimes called *ideal theory*). This is the primary subject matter studied in traditional courses in philosophical ethics. This task has to be supplemented with the second task of *application discourse,* which tries to *figure out how to intelligently apply background ideals to diverse concrete situations.* This endeavor is sometimes called the *theory of implementation.* True practical wisdom in Aristotle's sense requires an understanding of both levels, since the resolution of concrete conflicts always presupposes some commitment to background foundational ideals (even if these commitments are not always explicitly acknowledged).

In his study of application discourse, Gunther (1993) argues that justification discourse and application discourse have different functions in morality. *Justification discourse* strives for abstract impartiality. Its goal is *to justify background universal ideals that apply to all groups; thus it has to restrict the complexity of discussions by ignoring local contingencies.* For instance, one could say, "I know inequalities exist in the world, but, *ceteris paribus (other things being equal),* I think everyone ought to have an equal right to life, liberty, and the pursuit of happiness." At this level of theoretical consideration we have to assume "other things are equal" in order to impartially determine which background universal, foundational principles should establish an ideal status quo from the MPofV.

As Wilkins (1970) points out, the "other things being equal" qualification places a moral claim in an agreed-upon neutral moral context so it can be treated as a noncontroversial assertion (p. 161). By holding contexts steady in this way, philosophers can agree on general *prima facie* rights and duties that can serve as background foundations or ideals against which we can compare real local situations. For instance, "Other things being equal, all people have a right to life," or "Other things being equal, you should always tell the truth". "A *prima facie* obligation is *an obligation for which there is a strong but not always conclusive reason for doing whatever the obligation requires*" (Wilkins, 1994, p. 92) (emphasis added).

The *prima facie* norms justified at the *ceteris paribus* level represent the ideal moral status quo from which we are supposed to begin deliberations at more concrete levels. For instance, my daughter knows the moral rule, "You ought not to hit your brother." This gives her a *prima facie* obligation not to hit, other things being equal. It places the **burden of proof** on her *to come up with good reasons that can demonstrate that the* ceteris paribus *qualification does not hold in a particular situation.* If my daughter can meet the burden of proof, then it might be justifiable to hit her brother ("Dad, I know other things being equal I should not hit Brian, but there was a special circumstance. I had to wake him up, the house was on fire"). The same logic holds for other moral values. Whatever the initial *ceteris paribus* consensus about theoretical *prima facie* universal norms, when people begin to apply the norms to concrete cases, other things are *seldom* equal. Thus at the applied level the goal changes. We shift focus so as to intentionally pay attention to all the features that are unique to the local context. Because we don't want to ignore relevant information, we say, "Now, *all things considered,* what is the best way to apply the universal norms in this context?"

For instance, if a murderer asks you where his next victim is hiding, then other things are not equal. "All things considered," in this case you should choose saving a life over telling the truth, so you ought to lie about the victim's hiding place. "All things considered" invites us to look at local contingencies that complicate the application of moral rules and principles. At first glance, it might appear that there are times when universal principles do not apply. But, notice that an exception to the general moral principle about telling the truth is allowed only because a stronger moral consideration overrides the *prima facie* duty to tell the truth. "Override" is a term that has special significance in application situations. It is the opposite of "violating" a principle or rule because it requires prior moral deliberation leading to a moral justification. To **override** a moral value a person has to *give a moral reason why a* prima facie *principle that would normally govern does not have priority in a special circumstance.*

Somehow universal norms must be applied without either distorting the universal norms themselves or doing violence to legitimate local customs, mores, and interests. At the applied level of consideration where a specific situation is the focus of our attention, a justified universal norm's "appropriateness refers only to the particular features of this situation. . . ." (Farrell, 1993, p. x), and some of these local features may involve other principles that provide a good reason to override the assumption that all things are equal. In short, **application discourse** asks: *When all things are considered, which of the* *universally valid* prima facie *norms previously justified under the* ceteris paribus *condition seems most appropriate in "this" case right now?* Clarity at the level of background ideals, *other things being equal,* is not synonymous with clarity about the best means for applying those ideals in specific concrete situations, *all things considered.* Unlike justification discourse, application discourse requires a complete description of the entire context in order to determine which features of the specific case are the most morally relevant in the current situation, as we work our way down from ideals to the concrete immediate present. Application involves "a semantic analysis of the terms used in the norm [that is being applied], which are in turn ultimately dependent on an even more extensive (exhaustive) description of the situation" (Farrell, p. xi). Thus, before we can determine how to resolve a particular conflict, we need not only to know the details of the conflict, but also to agree about the appropriateness of the background theory we are using to frame and give meaning to the actions and local rules that we interpret as being relevant to the conflict. (We will return to this issue throughout the text.)

Since theoretical clarity about ideals does not tell us exactly what to do in each case, a skeptic might say, "Surely ethics does not need me to develop a theory. Why not just allow me to join a good profession and then follow its code religiously? Wouldn't that serve me well and also be admirable from the moral point of view?" The short answer is that moral life is not that simple. As we shall see, value diversity and shifting technological developments have complicated professional practice and thus professional ethics. By themselves, codes and procedures only give us rules and principles to follow, and they cannot guarantee that people will make the right choices if they have not developed a sophisticated background understanding of the purpose of principles and rules and the way they ought to be interpreted. To see why professionals need to explore the theoretical foundations of morality, Chapters Two and Three will review both a normative model of how professions and professionals ought to function as well as some of the ways modern professional practice has led to administrative actions that are both morally banal and horrendous. To make this discussion cogent, we will first have to explore the deep interconnection between individual moral agency and the institutional structures that serve as a background for each individual's decisions.

REFERENCES

ANZALDUA, GLORIA. (1987). *Borderlands/la Frontera: The new mestiza.* San Francisco: Spinsters/Aunt Lute Book Company.

ARISTOTLE. Nicomachean ethics. W. D. Ross (Trans.). In Richard McKeon (Ed.) (1941), *The basic works of Aristotle* (pp. 957–59, 1022–29). New York: Random House.

COHEN, SIMON BARON. (1995). Charlie and the four sweets. Cited in a film production of KCET/Los Angeles. Roger Bingham, Carl Byker & Sandra Medof. (1995). *The social brain*. Roger Bingham (Director). Princeton, NJ: Films for the Humanities and Sciences.

COOPER, DAVID; BURNS, SHEILA; LEITH, CHARLES; & PELTON-COOPER, MARY. (1998). Body memory and the possibility of change. *Tijdschrift voor Pesso psychotherapie* (2): 8–34. (The Dutch journal for Pesso Boyden System Psychomotor Therapy-PBSP-H. Colleniusstraat 28, 9718 KT, Groningen, Netherlands.)

DORNES, MARTIN. (1996). Is there an unconscious without an unconscious fantasy? In M. J. Howald (Ed.), *Proceedings of the third international PBSP—conference* (pp. 35–56). Basel, Switzerland: Pesso Vereinignung Association.

FARRELL, JOHN. (1993). Translator's introduction. In Klaus Gunther (1996), *The sense of appropriateness: Application discourses in morality and law*. John Farrell (Trans.). Albany: State University of New York Press.

GRANDIN, TEMPLE. (1995). *Thinking in pictures and other reports from my life with autism*. New York: Doubleday.

GUNTHER, KLAUS. (1993). *The sense of appropriateness: Application discourses in morality and law*. John Farrell (Trans.). Albany: State University of New York Press.

HABERMAS, JURGEN. (1993). *Justification and application: Remarks on discourse ethics*. Ciaran P. Cronin (Trans.). Cambridge, MA: The MIT Press.

_____. (1996). *Between facts and norms: Contributions to a discourse theory of law and democracy*. William Rehg (Trans.). Cambridge, MA: The MIT Press.

_____. (1998). A genealogical analysis of the cognitive content of morality. In Ciaran Cronin & Pablo De Greiff (Eds.), *The inclusion of the other*. Cambridge, MA: The MIT Press.

JOHNSON, MARK. (1987). *The body in the mind*. Chicago: University of Chicago Press.

KOHLBERG, LAWRENCE & TURIEL, ELLIOT. (1971). Moral development and moral education. In G. Lesser (Ed.), *Psychology and educational practice* (pp. 412ff.). New York: Scott, Foresman.

LAKOFF, GEORGE & JOHNSON, MARK. (1980). *Metaphors we live by*. Chicago: University of Chicago Press.

MACINTYRE, ALASDAIR. (1981). *After virtue*. South Bend, IN: University of Notre Dame Press.

MOODY-ADAMS, M. MICHELE. (1997). *Fieldwork in familiar places*. Cambridge, MA: Harvard University Press.

REHG, WILLIAM. (1996). Translator's introduction. In Jurgen Habermas (1996), *Between facts and norms: Contributions to a discourse theory of law and democracy*. William Rehg (Trans.). Cambridge, MA: The MIT Press.

SACKS, OLIVER. (1995). *An anthropologist on Mars*. New York: Alfred A. Knopf.

SMITH, ADAM. (1982). *The theory of moral sentiments*. Indianapolis, IN: Liberty Fund.

TURNER, VICTOR. (1974). *The ritual process*. Ithaca, NY: Cornell University Press.

WILKINS, BURLEIGH. (1970). The "is-ought" controversy. *Ethics* 88 (2): 160–64.

_____. (1994). The moral *prima facie*, obligation to obey the law. *Journal of social philosophy* 25 (2): 92–96.

Chapter   Two

Moral Agents, Situational Control, & Professionalism

∿ Moral Agency in Applied Ethics

For Study: Why are moral dilemmas especially problematic in ethics? Why can't codes of ethics and decision procedures solve the problem?

While it is often clear what is right—for example, you should never torture babies for the fun of it—it is sometimes not clear at all. Complex options can leave moral agents feeling like they have to face insurmountable dilemmas. Angeles (1981) defines a ***moral dilemma*** as *"a situation in which mutually exclusive moral actions or choices are equally binding"* (p. 64). Since we also want to consider conflicts in social settings, we will also use the term *dilemma* to refer to situations where groups of people who are reasonable can be found on both sides of a conflict. Thus, we will define a ***social moral dilemma,*** as *a value*

*conflict that is so complex that reasonable members of a community can dis-
agree with each other about the proper solution.* For example, a dispute over
whether to torture babies for fun or profit would not be labeled a "social moral
dilemma" because we do not find reasonable people on both sides. Only a sadistic psychopath might be confused about the moral status of this issue. On the
other hand, disputes over issues like capital punishment, abortion, employee
rights, affirmative action, and premarital sex do represent social moral dilemmas. The dilemma is caused by the fact that a person with an open mind can
find right answers only if he or she seriously considers the arguments of all reasonable people on both sides in a dispute. The fact that there is a social dilemma
does not necessarily mean both sides are equally right; it only means that for the
people who can see the reasons behind both sides, either side could be right.

We can see now why codes of ethics are especially useful. They create
prima facie obligations that ought to guide professionals when they consider the
many dilemmas that can arise in professional practice. Because business practice is becoming increasingly complex under the conditions of globalization,
many large corporations are imitating the professions by also adopting codes of
ethics. Obviously, morality is important in all institutional settings, and codes of
ethics can help people remain careful and thoughtful. But, are codes enough?
The accountants who participated in fixing the books in the 1990s to help corporations like Enron hide debt were covered by a code of ethics (see p. 63f), and
yet it didn't stop their unprofessional behavior. Because codes only give general
principled guidance, over the years, there have been many attempts to design instruments that can help people maintain ethical integrity on both the theoretical and practical level. Model *decision procedures* have become standard items
in applied ethics tool kits, because they are supposed to *help us achieve a clear
focus on all the relevant factual and moral variables in dilemma situations.* The
decision procedure that follows is typical of these tools of applied ethics. They
are to be used as part of a dynamic deliberative process. Thus, decision makers
should go back and forth between the steps of the procedure, making adjustments as ethical deliberations unfold (e.g., in order to modify preliminary assumptions, to add an important fact, or to appeal to an additional ethical or
moral principle that was not recognized the first time through).

A Model Decision Procedure

Background (Description of the current and past situational variables.)

I. **State the specific dilemma,** then place it at the proper level of ethical con-
    sideration by discussing what **general type of dilemma** is involved. That is,
    does the dilemma only involve a conflict between personal interests or does
    it involve duties of station, principles, and/or theoretical disagreements?

What level of justification will be needed to solve the dilemma; for example, can it be resolved by appealing to rules or is there also a dispute about principles or theories?

A. Does the dispute have a historical context? What are the key empirical facts: who, what, where, when, how? What do we know now without further investigation? What do we still need to know that would help define the problem? What are the major assumptions being used about how to interpret data? At what level of reasoning or moral development are the parties in the dispute?

B. On the basis of these initial background considerations, who are considered to be the significant stakeholders? (A *stakeholder* is a *person (or institution) whose interests will be affected by a decision that is going to be made.*) When trying to identify stakeholders it is useful to think of things like goods, rights, claims, duties, interests, and so forth. Have all stakeholders been given access to the decision-making process? Why not?

Ideal Theory (What moral principles should guide prescriptions about what ought to be, other things being equal?)

II. **Your Major Moral Orientation** (which has helped you characterize the general dilemma): Is your position faith-based or are you a utilitarian, natural rights theorist, social contractarian, etc? Think about your ideal goals. What would an ideal state of affairs look like, other things being equal? Identify the major rules, values, principles, and theoretical assumptions that define an ideal state of affairs, both with regard to what is morally right and to what is essential to the good life.

A. Name all values and principles that are used to characterize an ideal situation, including those of your major opponents. For example, list relevant codes of ethics and principles such as integrity, beneficence, rights, respect for persons, profit, justice, etc., but also be sure to name any personal values involved in characterizing the good life.

B. How far off from the ideal are current arrangements? In what direction should current policies be moving us? Would the same conflict arise in an ideal state of affairs or would it be different? If different, what has caused the current conflicts?

C. Do these considerations require you to reconstruct your original description of the dilemma, or were your initial intuitions about the nature of the dilemma adequate?

Implementation (All things considered)

III. Specify the **possible reasonable alternatives.** All major alternatives should be listed, including those that represent some form of compromise between extremes.

IV. Determine whether there are any **absolute moral/ethical boundaries** that act as side-constraints on the kinds of strategies that can be used. For instance:

    A. Are there absolute values that trump all other considerations? Are there moral limits on how one should make profit/loss calculations? Are both quantitative and qualitative variables being used to establish priorities?

    B. Have all stakeholders been given an opportunity to argue their case?

    C. What are the short-term and long-term, positive and negative consequences of the major alternatives? Have they been measured against each other? What kind of resolution is most likely to help us avoid similar problems in the future?

V. **Compare** all the values and possible **alternatives** to see if a clear decision emerges. That is, see if there is one principle or value, or combination, that stands out as being so compelling that the proper alternative suddenly seems clear, for example, correcting a simple defect in a product that is almost certain to cause loss of life.

VI. **Make your decision.** Select the best alternative according to your moral/ethical framework. Could you give a moral account that would justify this solution to other reasonable people?

This decision procedure gives us a general idea about how complex the interrelationships are in applied ethics. We must shift back and forth between levels of abstraction and between descriptive and normative considerations. But, can a well-designed decision procedure make people use principles in the right way? Not necessarily. Decision procedures are helpful in identifying relevant abstract principles and states of affairs, but because many people do not know how to calculate in the abstract manner required by this kind of procedure, they may well make immoral decisions even while using this kind of reasoning device. As discussed in the next few chapters, well-meaning people can abuse good techniques when they are blinded by an unsophisticated moral orientation. As mentioned in Chapter One, it is difficult to understand the difference between justification discourses (which aim to give legitimacy to background ideals, other things being equal) and application discourses (which aim to rationally apply the ideals in local contexts, all things considered). When people lack the capacity to keep these two related but distinct activities logically separated, then errors in judgment can occur that will lead to the kind of oppression in the name of universal values that worries some critics of universal morality. For instance, as we shall see, those who primarily use narrow instrumental reasoning to make moral decisions will not understand how to apply abstract ethical principles with appropriate sensitivity to local contexts. They tend to assume that justification discourse and application discourse are the same, thus they distort the purpose of valid universal values by favoring their own local perspective during the application steps. Sometimes attempts to apply universal values can be so clumsy as to contribute to gross evil. As Wilkins (1992) points out with regard to the My Lai Massacre, "all the evidence suggests, that Lt. Calley was an ordinary man, is he then simply an example of what has been called 'the ordinariness of evil'?" (p. 99). As we shall see in Chapter Four, Calley had a military code of ethics, but it didn't prevent him from becoming involved in a war crime.

So, it is not sufficient to simply hand people a decision procedure with a list of justified principles and rules. We also need a virtue ethics that will emphasize the importance of developing those emancipatory capacities (see Chapters Four through Seven) that are so essential for practical wisdom. Since we are attempting to construct a moral background that ought to guide all professional (and nonprofessional) codes of ethics, everyone is a stakeholder. But, who can participate in this investigation and what kinds of institutional contexts are required to facilitate this work?

Background Definition of Moral Agency

> **For Study:**   Why are knowledge and intentional behavior necessary conditions for responsible moral agency?

Any responsible agent should be able to participate in investigating this issue. Generally, people believe that a necessary condition for responsible agency is intentional action. We say an act is *intentional* when someone has *the conscious ability to conceive of a goal and make a choice to act on the conception.* In short, a person must knowingly make a choice to do something. To be consistent with this common-sense notion, let's define *moral agents* as *people who are held responsible because they know the difference between the notions of right and wrong and have the capacity to intentionally act on this knowledge.* The fact that someone is a moral agent does not mean they will always do the right thing. It only means that we hold them responsible because we believe they are able to do the right thing. Some moral agents may be more competent than others, but all of them must satisfy the minimum requirements for agency. A famous motto in ethics, *ought implies can,* draws attention to the logical connection between an agent's responsibility and his or her capacity to act. The motto reminds us that *it is not logical to tell people they ought to do something if, because they lack knowledge and capacity or are externally constrained, they can't do it.* Thus, ethical theory, if it is going to be practically useful, must take into consideration the empirical research that reveals what ordinary good people can and cannot do. Actions can be called *immoral* only when *moral agents who could have chosen to do their duty intentionally violate a known moral rule or refuse to accept responsibility for their actions.*

By contrast, people who *lack knowledge and/or the capacity to choose their behavior* are called *amoral* (e.g., babies, the retarded, the insane, the comatose, etc.). Rather than hold them responsible, we must excuse the behavior of people who are amoral, because they are not considered capable of moral actions at all. For instance, a two-year-old boy can pull a trigger and kill someone, but because he lacks knowledge of cause and effect, his motive is neither moral nor immoral. If we punish young children, it should be to educate them rather than give them something they "deserve" because they intentionally violated moral principles. However, as children learn to discern right from wrong, to grasp the consequences of behavior, and to control their emotional impulses, we gradually reconceptualize their standing in the moral community. Slowly, we start holding them more and more responsible until they are welcomed as enfranchised moral agents with the full array of rights and responsibilities. Once they are part of the moral community, praise and blame are meted out according to what they deserve as moral agents and not just as tools for educating children.

We have to consider both who and what may be responsible for any given action. Since individual agents live and work in institutional settings, it would be useful to examine how institutions both encourage and discourage moral behavior. Writers in applied ethics have been devoting more and more attention to discussing the significance of the institutional structures that affect the behavior of moral agents. Although individuals still ought to be held accountable, many people argue that institutions also ought to be held accountable when they put too much immoral pressure on individual agents. For instance, Goodpaster (1984, pp. 306–11) argued that corporations should be given many of the same responsibilities that we give to human moral agents, since their policies and procedures are often responsible for setting the stage within which individuals have to function.

To see how important this interconnection between institutions and individuals can be, we will review a few psychological experiments that seem to challenge the idea that individuals are free moral agents who can be held solely responsible for what they do. Then we will review the ideal structure of professional institutional settings to see how a well-designed institution can create a good moral environment for its members. After discussing how professions ought to function, Chapter Three will look at some research into moral failures that will help clarify why people in professional settings will need both a background moral theory and a code of ethics to supplement their intentions to be moral.

Moral Agency versus Situational Control

For Study: Why is situational control incompatible with the prescriptions in moral theories that tell people what they ought to do? Why does Jones's experiment support Zimbardo's experiment in terms of helping us understand the need for self-critical dialogue on the part of moral agents? How should a moral agent respond to institutional pressure?

As we saw in Chapter One, the introjection of cultural values (or encultura-tion) is one common form of control used in all cultures to raise new members. This kind of control is morally good. However, although it is necessary to place children under this kind of situational control, in democracies we expect adults to eventually develop a capacity for individual freedom of choice. If their environment continues to control them, adults lose the moral freedom needed for individual responsibility. Psychologists use the term *situational control* to refer to occasions when *features of the environment seem to shape and control individual adult behavior to such an extent that the individual seems to have lost the ability to act in the usual voluntary or free manner we would expect from good moral agents.* For instance, in the famous 1971 social psychology experiment at Stanford University, Dr. Philip Zimbardo showed that the types of pressures placed on people in prison settings could make both good middle-class college students and professional psychologists develop radically new behavior patterns in just a matter of days. That institutional pressures could make these good people (who are supposed to be fully enfranchised moral agents) drift into increasingly unacceptable moral behavior is alarming. Experiments of this kind clearly prove that there is a powerful causal connection between institutional pressures and the ability of individual moral agents to take responsibility for their actions. If we are going to develop an adequate account of moral agency, we will have to come to terms with this causal relationship.

Example: The Zimbardo Prison Experiment

Zimbardo conducted his fascinating experiment in the basement of a Stanford University dorm. He converted the hallway and rooms into a miniature prison environment and staffed it with paid student volunteers who were randomly assigned to role-play either guards or prisoners. Zimbardo and his graduate student research assistants adopted the roles of prison administrators. The goal was to see how living in a simulated prison would affect a group of average, normal, healthy, college males who had never been in trouble with authority. The plan was to run the experiment for two weeks, but because of the escalating brutality of some of the guards and the suffering of prisoners, the experiment was called off after only six days. All quotations in the following summary of the experiment, unless otherwise indicated, are a direct quotation from Zimbardo's (1971) slide/tape presentation of the experiment.

The research subjects selected to be prisoners were arrested by the city police in the early morning, blindfolded, and then processed at the Stanford County Jail. After being transported to the mock prison, they were searched, systematically stripped naked, deloused, and issued a uniform consisting of a dress, no underclothes, a prison number, loosely fitting rubber sandals, a woman's nylon stocking to be used as a cap, and a heavy chain bolted on to the right ankle. They had to wear this uniform day and night in order to enhance the illusion of being a prisoner.

The guards were allowed to do whatever they thought would maintain law and order in the prison. Their uniform consisted of starched khaki shirts and pants, a big billy club borrowed from the police, a whistle, and reflecting sunglasses to hide their eyes and "promote their anonymity. We were, of course, studying not only the [effect of the institution on] prisoners who were made to feel anonymous but the guards as well."

There were nine guards and nine prisoners. Guards worked eight hour shifts three at a time. There were three cells with three prisoners in each one. To encourage interactions between guards and prisoners, the guards would line the prisoners up and have them count off several times every night and day. When prisoners laughed during the first count, they were forced to do pushups. On the second day the prisoners rebelled and barricaded themselves in their cells. Using fire extinguishers and reinforcements, the guards broke up the rebellion and placed prisoners in solitary confinement and deprived them of privileges.

(Noises of the prison riot; the sound of the fire extinguisher) Prisoner: "NO! NO! NO! NO!" (The fire extinguisher) "NO! NO!" Guard: "Put handcuffs on him." Prisoner: "NO!" (Chaotic random noise) Prisoner: "They're gonna take our beds!" (Noise and shouting) Guard: "Against the wall." Prisoner: "Don't let 'em in!" Prisoner shouting: "They took our clothes! They took our beds! They took our clothes!" Guard: "Hands off the door! Off the bed!" (Chaotic noise) Prisoner: (shouting) "Fuck this experiment! Fuck Dr. Zimbardo!" Prisoner: (shouting) "Fucking Simulation!" Prisoner: (shouting) "Fucking simulation! Fucking Simulation! Fucking Simulation! It's a fucking simulated experiment. . . ."

From that point on, conditions degenerated rapidly. "Every aspect of the prisoners' behavior fell under the total and arbitrary control of the guards who were on any given shift. To go to the toilet became a privilege which the guard could grant or deny at his whim." At night prisoners had to "urinate or defecate in a bucket which was left in their cell, and on occasion the guard would refuse to allow the prisoners even to empty that bucket, and soon the prison began to smell of urine and feces." One third of the guards were strict but fair, one third were sympathetic "good" guards, but did nothing to stop the escalating brutality, and the other third set the brutal arbitrary tone of the prison. A guard nicknamed "John Wayne" became excessively brutal and arbitrary in his treatment of prisoners even mashing sausages into the face of prisoner number 416 when he went on a hunger strike.

Power, authority, and control were the cardinal virtues in this small totalitarian tribal community. The prisoners lost their sense of identity and became passive and dispirited. When a Catholic priest was invited in for a visit, prisoners introduced themselves using their numbers, not their names. Eventually, four of the prisoners had to be released early because they broke down emotionally. Others tried to "con" their way out; for example, 416 went on a hunger strike so he could pretend to get sick. When asked if they would be will-ing to give up all the money they had earned in order to be paroled, seven of the nine said yes, they would give up the paycheck in order to get out. Notice that at this point, they had become real prisoners. They were no longer the free moral agents who were volunteers in an experiment. Consider the video taped statement from prisoner 416 at the end of the experiment. He had gone on a hunger strike to try to force them to release him.

> I forgot my reasons for being there. I had come there with reasons, like it'll make me money, you know? Things like that. But I found that . . . as I found after 25 hours, I really had no life of, of my own, except what happened to me in that small white room, and umm, what happened to me as I followed people's orders and, umm, was shoved around with a paper bag over my head—whatever. I began to feel that I was losing my identity, that, that the person that I call Clay, the person who . . . who put me in this place, the person who volunteered to . . . to go into this prison, 'cause it was a prison to me; it still is a prison to me, I, I don't look on it as an experiment or a simulation. It's just a prison that was run by psychologists instead of run by the state. I began to feel that, that, that iden-tity, that the person that I was, that had decided to go to prison, was distant from me, was, was remote, until finally, I wasn't that, I was . . . I was 416. I was really my number.

Finally, Zimbardo decided he had to end the experiment early, because it had become a kind of prison in which people were really suffering. "Some boys called prisoners were withdrawing, becoming isolated and behaving in patho-logical ways. On the other hand, some of the guards were behaving sadistically, delighting in what could be called the 'ultimate aphrodisiac of power' and many of the guards who were not behaving that way felt helpless to do any-thing about it." In fact, the "good guards" were not being good moral agents. Empathy is not enough if it does not motivate action. By not confronting the cruel guards, they were letting immoral predispositions govern the institutional setting. This was one of the most important lessons of the experiment. As Zimbardo says,

> As a consequence of the time we spent in our simulated prison, we could under-stand how prison, indeed how any total institution, could dehumanize people, could turn them into objects and make them feel helpless and hopeless, and we realized how people could do this to each other. The question now is, how can we begin to change our real institutions so that they promote human values rather than destroy them?

What are the implications of this experiment for the relationship between moral agency and situational control? If we can only blame the environment for what happens, then the student subjects in Zimbardo's experiment cannot be conceived of as moral agents in the traditional sense. However, this seems like an odd consequence, since Zimbardo chose his research participants precisely because they were assumed to be good moral agents. If we give up the notion of moral agency, we will be forced to think of these young adult males as being more like amoral children. But that would be a mistake, because what happened in the Zimbardo experiment is not unique or even uncommon. Similar experiments, as well as real-life situations, have shown again and again that ordinary moral agents when put under institutional pressure will often behave just as the subjects did in the Zimbardo experiment. Consider the similarity between what Zimbardo discovered and the following summary of an event that occurred in a high school history class. All page references in the following account of "The Third Wave Experiment" are taken from the description of the experience written by the teacher, Ron Jones (1976).

Example: The Third Wave Experiment, Duty for Duty's Sake Can Be Dangerous

While discussing World War II, one of Jones's students asked him how so many German people could claim after the fact that they had not known about the Nazi Holocaust, when millions of people were exterminated. Jones decided to take a week of class time to investigate the question. On Monday, he lectured his class on the virtue of *discipline*. He had the class adopt a set of new classroom behaviors that emphasized personal discipline and obedience to authority. On Tuesday, he talked about the virtue of *community*, the joy of fitting in with a group and working with others toward common goals. To illustrate group boundaries, he created a salute for classroom members only, which they were to use throughout the day when they greeted one another. He called it the "Third Wave Salute," because students were to raise their cupped hand toward the right shoulder in such a way that the hand resembled a wave about to topple over. The students readily adapted to this form of tribal identification. On Wednesday, he talked about the virtue of *action*. He gave students specific tasks to perform and handed out membership cards. He told the class that three cards were marked with a red X and whoever got the X would have a special duty of station. They were to report anyone who failed to comply with class rules. Although the three recipients of the X were the only ones who were supposed to be secret agents, Jones found that over half the class began to inform on other class members. Students began to show loyalty to the "movement" by bullying those who didn't conform to all the rules, and students from other classes began to cut their classes to join the Third Wave Experiment. One student, Robert, assigned himself the role of bodyguard. He followed Jones around all day, opening and closing doors for him and so forth. When Robert, who was standing at attention next to Jones's chair in the faculty lounge, was confronted by another faculty member who told him students were not allowed in the room, Robert replied, "I'm not a student, Sir. I'm a bodyguard."

On Thursday, Jones talked about the virtue of *pride*. By then, the class had swollen to 80 students (eventually, more than 200 students accepted membership cards and pledged obedience to the "rules"). Jones was amazed to find the students embracing the discipline and order he was imposing on them. He wanted to stop the experiment but was not sure how to do it. If he stopped immediately, he would leave committed students like Robert hanging there, embarrassed in front of their peers. His solution was to tell all the Third Wave members that this was not just a game, that they were involved in the real thing. He announced that at noon on Friday a candidate for president of the United States would go on national TV and declare a Third Wave Movement for the entire nation. Thousands of youth groups across the country would stand up and declare their allegiance. Together, they would reform the entire nation, and usher in a new era based on discipline, community, pride, and action. He invited all members to attend a special Friday noon rally for members only. Then, when the presidential candidate spoke, they would all stand up and pledge their obedience to him.

As a result of this deception, Jones had the opportunity on Friday to introduce over 200 students to the philosophical virtue of *understanding* what can happen to people who avoid self-critical dialogue. They can be easily manipulated by Nazi organizations, cults, and al-Qaeda type organizations. His goal was to help them develop a theoretical interpretation of their concrete experiences that would place the event in a larger conceptual context. After the students were seated and silent, he turned off the lights, turned on a TV set, and then let them sit there and stare at the blank TV screen while waiting for the presidential candidate to emerge. Tension and anxiety mounted. Eventually, someone came to his senses and shouted, "There isn't any leader, is there?" Jones reports that the students gasped in shock but remained silently sitting there, unsure of what they should do next.

He then turned off the TV set and turned on a projector with a film about Nazi Germany to help them understand where they had all been heading. It began with the promises of community, discipline, order, pride in belonging to the super-race. It progressed to the big lie about the persecution of dissenters, the terror, and the final stench of death camps. He told them that in a small way, "We learned what it felt like to create a disciplined social environment, pledge allegiance to that society, replace reason with rules" (p. 26). He pointed out how he had manipulated and controlled them by playing on their social desire to belong to something important. He explained how they were no better, but also no worse, than the people who had lived in Nazi Germany. He predicted that they would continue to imitate the example of many of the German people because probably they too would blank out the fact that they had been controlled and manipulated into participating in the noon rally. He said he believed that not one of them would want to face the fact that they were willing to give up "individual freedom to the dictates of order and unseen leaders" (p. 26). Like Zimbardo, Jones had stumbled across the common phenomenon of situational control.

Zimbardo and Jones both discovered that older, professional adults are also vulnerable to situational control. By giving themselves roles in their experiments, they subjected themselves to the pressures of the new social setting they had constructed. Slowly, as their new roles began to dominate their behavior, they lost sight of the original purpose of their experiments and began to drift along with the institution's momentum. (Although we should be alert to the fact that because of their dual roles, both Zimbardo and Jones retained enough of a critical perspective that they were able to call off their experiments. Where comparison is possible, there is room for freedom even if we are being subjected to control.) Zimbardo (1975) reported:

> I and my research associates . . . were as much "subjects" imprisoned in our roles of prison staff as we were experimenters directing the events of the study. With each passing day, the immediacy of the demands and urgency of mundane decisions forced upon me as "superintendent" of the Stanford County Prison made me ever more remote from the reality of the detached, intellectual stance of "experimenter." (p. 35)

> [In a similar manner, Jones said:] "I played the role [of benevolent dictator] more and more, and had trouble remembering its pedagogic origin and purpose. I wondered if this happens to many people. We get or take a role and then bend our lives to fit it. Soon the role is the only identity other people will accept." (p. 23)

Zimbardo (1975) also reported that one of the guards, who the prisoners had nicknamed John Wayne, said, "As I am a pacifist and nonaggressive individual, I cannot see a time when I might guard and/or maltreat other living things." Yet, in spite of this pacifist self-image, within six days this person became the brutal guard who reported in his journal:

> The new prisoner (416) refuses to eat his sausages . . . I am very angry at this prisoner for causing discomfort and trouble for the others. I decided to force-feed him, but he wouldn't eat. I let the food slide down his face. I didn't believe it was me doing it. I hated myself for making him eat but I hated him more for not eating. (p. 49)

And as mentioned earlier Prisoner 416 clearly showed in the tape of the experiment that he recognized that the institution had the power to control him when he reported:

> I began to feel that I was losing my identity, that the person I call Clay, the person who put me in this place, the person who volunteered to go into this prison . . . the person that I was . . . was distant from me, was remote, until finally, I wasn't that, I was 416. I was really my number.

In each of these cases, individuals were surprised to find themselves being controlled by pressures from an institution. Rather than being responsible choosers, they seemed to become mirror images of their roles, shaped by the institutional setting rather than by their own beliefs. As Ron Jones said, "We get or take a role and then bend our lives to fit it. Soon the role is the only identity other people will accept."

Common sense says these research subjects are adult moral agents, however, they are not acting in the responsible manner that common sense leads us to expect so perhaps common sense is wrong. What should we expect from good moral agents? The Greek philosopher Socrates has been used as a model of moral agency for centuries. He not only accepted responsibility for his choices, but also had the ability to withstand pressures from institutional settings that would corrupt most of us. Rather than let institutions decide for him, he would adapt roles to fit his conscience. Because he did not abandon himself as a moral agent when he changed locations, he eventually developed a reputation for being the kind of man who always tended to act on principle no matter what his current role or station. He said, "Throughout my life, in any public activity I may have engaged in, I am the same man as I am in private life . . ." (Grube, 1975, p. 35). Thus, when institutional authorities called upon him to engage in immoral activities, he always refused because their request was contrary to the moral principles that guided his life. To be a truly responsible moral agent, one must be capable of this kind of moral authenticity. (We will discuss this concept further in Chapter Seven, when we define moral autonomy.)

Chapter Four will consider how Socratic virtues develop, but for now, it is useful to note that the behavior of Zimbardo's research subjects is not unusual. Untrained people will commonly behave in radically new ways when they are suddenly placed in an entirely new institutional setting. This proves that what we do is heavily influenced not only by our past but also by the current environment within which we are working. As social animals, none of us is immune to current social pressure. However, while people are adapting to the pressure from new roles, it is still reasonable to ask them to show a certain amount of moral courage and wisdom. Remember, all the guards in Zimbardo's experiment were apparently under the heavy influence of the same controlling situation, yet only a third of them became cruel. Obviously, individual differences do count. The fact that Socrates could remain true to his beliefs proves that individuals can accept responsibility and make intelligent choices while under pressure. Furthermore, since institutional influence and control come in a variety of forms, ranging from making simple suggestions about behavior to insisting on complete obedience and control, individuals often have options about when and to what degree they should comply. If there are alternatives from which to choose (even in closed institutions), perhaps it's reasonable to hold individuals responsible for how they choose to resist or to adapt to institutional pressures. We should not assume individuals are always totally responsible regardless of institutional pressure, nor should we assume that institutions always control all behavior. The goal in any particular situation should be to analyze the relationships involved to determine to what degree the institution is exerting improper pressures and to what degree individuals are appropriately striving to take responsibility for evaluating the boundaries set by the institution. Then we will be in a better position for handing out appropriate praise and blame.

Combining Empirical Research with Moral Prescriptions

> **For Study:** Why should we use empirical research to make certain that "ought" statements in moral theory are practically useful? Why does morality require us to judge forms of socialization? What background issues must be clarified before a moral theory can properly address practical issues?

The motto "ought implies can" draws attention to the fact that the extent of our knowledge about empirical research into human agency will influence what we think people ought to do. It will influence where we place blame and how we think we ought to design institutions. Social psychologists have shown again and again that some of our common-sense intuitions about where to place blame seem to conflict with what normal humans can do at certain times in their lives. Thus, in spite of the individual differences that showed up in his experiment, Zimbardo does not focus on blaming individuals for what happened. As a social psychologist, he has seen so much situational control that he no longer adopts the common-sense approach that holds individuals solely responsible for every event. He and his research associate Haney (1977) assert:

> History has surely established the futility of seeking the sources of evil deeds exclusively in the nature of its performers. Even the greatest iniquity and inhumanity generally have been the products of unsettling "normal," average persons whose commonplace motives and relative naivete were perverted in the service of evil purpose. (p. 201)

Extensive research suggests that the capacity to withstand institutional pressure develops rather slowly. Thus, because ethical behavior is so complex, we can expect that good people placed in bad institutions will often do unexpected things. The events we have been considering, then, should not be thought of as unusual. We are all familiar with stories about how basic training shapes the beliefs of young men and how prisoners of war in Korea were "brainwashed." The evidence is overwhelming; socialization procedures can be effectively used not only to civilize each new generation, but also to initiate new adult members into social groups, for both good and evil purposes. Although the focus so far has been on situations where adult socialization has led to harmful results, socialization of adults is not *per se* an evil activity. For instance, IBM's year-long orientation program, training in a professional school, indoctrination, and brainwashing are all instances where socialization techniques are used to get adults to adopt new behaviors. Some of these methods of socialization involve immoral situational control, but others encourage change in ways that stay within proper moral boundaries. In general, forms of socialization based on educational goals are defensible, while socialization based on forms of indoctrination are generally not defensible. Why? One reason is that indoctrination attempts to manipulate people into adopting a position. Thus, indoctrination undermines choice and diminishes a person's capacity to function as a moral agent, especially in a pluralistic world. Education does the opposite; it helps individuals become better moral agents.

Because some forms of socialization are brilliantly designed to keep people oblivious to how much their behavior contributes to evil, we obviously need some way to pass judgment on forms of socialization. But how can we judge forms of socialization if we are ourselves products of socialization? Won't any judgment simply be a mirror of the judge's own previous form of socialization? To get insight into how to judge socialization we need to think about the process itself. Consider the five steps of socialization that Haney and Zimbardo (1977, pp. 203–4) say are used to get people to take over the "dirty work" in institutions:

1.   To increase its effectiveness, a process of socialization often requires people to make behavioral adjustments slowly, in *a series of small steps over time*. Little things we are asked to do often seem unimportant, so there can be a slow, unreflective accommodation to the demands of the institution.

2.   There is typically a *lack of awareness of the causal factors* that can influence behavior and a corresponding obliviousness to one's own vulnerability to situational control. When we are not aware of our own vulnerability to outside pressures, we will not be on guard against those forces that have the potential for influencing and eventually controlling our behavior.

3.   There is *no historical perspective* to help us critically judge the context of our current role. Institutions need to be historically situated before they can be evaluated, but when the structures in the institution dominate our landscape and forbid comparative analysis, it is hard to see past them to get a historical perspective.

4.   There is an *emphasis on maintaining a narrow perspective on the group's own concerns*. Some form of "centricism" gets emphasized. (**Egocentric** means *to only be capable of understanding one's own point of view*. **Ethnocentric** means one is *only able to focus on the point of view of one's own group*.) This leads to "we versus them" thinking, with a lack of attention to them.

5. The person being socialized should be encouraged to have *a sense of perceived freedom of choice,* even in contexts where choice does not actually exist. Creating this sense of perceived freedom is crucial if we want people to develop a sense of loyalty to the institutions that socialize them. "It must be okay," we think, "because we have been doing it voluntarily."

A sixth factor can be added to Zimbardo's list:

6. Because we are social animals, there is *a natural tendency to give institutions the benefit of the doubt.* Both the content introjected and the socialization process itself are less likely to be challenged when they occur within the confines of familiar institutions. People need to be pushed quite far before they will challenge an institution that is part of a larger social system that seems rational. For example, when family members came to visit their loved ones in the Stanford prison experiment, Zimbardo said, "We systematically brought their [the visitors'] behavior under situational control by having them follow some arbitrary rules before they could talk to their 'prisoner.'" He said that the parents complained, but "their reaction was to work within the system." What system? Zimbardo's strategy was to alter appearances to remind the visitors that they were witnessing something that was sanctioned by a prestigious university. Stanford's educational prestige and the "official authoritative" structure of a well-run experimental prison combined to intimidate the visitors.

Because both the motives of individual agents and the socialization practices of institutions need to be judged, the discipline of ethics must continually focus on at least two different levels: (1) At the **micro level** we can ask *questions about individuals.* What did prisoner 416 do? What was his motive? What did he hope to accomplish? Was he being ethical? (2) At the **macro level** we should also ask questions about *the structure of the institution and the network of relationships created by its roles.* What are the rules? Are they justifiable? What relationship ought to exist between the social environment and the members of the group? Which duties ought to have priority when the demands of different roles conflict? These are questions calling for complex answers. Before we explore these questions in more detail, it would be helpful to consider the structure of institutions that have historically established the right kinds of relationships between the rules of the institution, individual members, and human values. Professional associations fit the bill. Members of professions have considerable prestige partly because they are members of a type of institution that has historically been properly structured according to the MPofV.

∾ A Normative Definition of Professionalism

For Study: Why is it useful to create a normative rather than a descriptive definition of professionalism? What conditions have contributed to the explosion of professional associations in the modern world?

All professional associations ought to be structured so that they encourage behavior that is morally required by the profession's code of ethics. Since a profession's code of ethics prescribes how professional practice ought to be conducted, to evaluate the adequacy of general professional practice we will need to investigate the rationality of the background norms used to justify codes of ethics. This means that an adequate definition of professionalism will be normative, since it will point to the general ideals that influence the prescriptions given in professional codes. A normative definition is useful, since it will make us more sensitive to the differences between moral and immoral professional practice and explicitly explain the vision that ought to inspire people to adopt a professional life.

Background: The Structure of a Profession

To remain consistent with the goal of communicating with as many people as possible, we will begin our exploration of professionalism by discussing a few common beliefs about professional practice. Then, using metaphorical extensions, we will be able to work toward a fairly noncontroversial normative definition of professional practice that should make sense to the average member of society. When I ask students to describe a noncontroversial example of a work-related interaction that involves a professional, they unanimously agree that visits to the doctor represent a paradigm case. They also unanimously agree that lawyers, nurses, engineers, and teachers are all professionals. When I ask for a noncontroversial example of a work-related interaction that should not be described as involving a professional encounter, students can reach agreement only if they focus on the bottom of the social-economic-prestige hierarchy. For instance, they all agree that a ditch digger, hamburger flipper, and bag boy at the grocery store are not professionals, but they argue about a waitress and waiter, a shoe-repair person, professional athletes, actors, politicians, etc. There is always someone who says, "I think a waitress can be professional." When asked why, it quickly becomes clear that for some people whatever you do for a living is professional as long as you plan to pursue it as a career, are committed to quality work, and are skilled.

Since so many students want to say, "It is possible for anyone to be professional," it will be useful to contrast this all inclusive approach with the more traditional definition that reserves the term for the noncontroversial categories of doctor and lawyer. Since students agree that these two professions represent the paradigm case of professional practice, we will start by exploring the structure of these two professions. Then we can treat the assertion, "A waitress can be professional" as an attempted metaphorical extension of these paradigm cases. This will help us to understand what standards of practice have to be met by those who want to extend the usual meaning of "professional" to cover those types of work that have not traditionally worn the label.

Origins of Twentieth-century Professions

Traditional professional associations have been around for a long time; for example, the Hippocratic Oath is over two centuries old. One traditional feature of the paradigm case of professionalism is that a socially recognized professional association such as the American Medical Association or the American Bar Association regulates professional practice. To practice medicine as a doctor, you must be licensed by the medical profession, or to practice law as an attorney, you must pass the bar exam. The existence of national organizations draws attention to the fact that professionals are part of a broad institutional context that includes a partnership with society. How many professional associations does a society need? There has been an explosion in the number of new "professional associations of all kinds [that] began in the mid-nineteenth century, at first more rapidly in England and then burgeoning in the United States" (Adams and Balfour, 1998, p. 37). Various technological, epistemological, and socioeconomic changes that helped create the conditions for the modern age are primarily responsible for this explosion.

One of the primary changes has been a shift in how people address the fundamental questions in their life. As mentioned in Chapter One, modern man has entered a postmetaphysical period that has shattered the traditional ways in which communities have been able to create consensus and thus legitimacy. In the contemporary Western world, much to the chagrin of many, we no longer rely on a shared metaphysics. Modern societies are now composed of a variety of subgroups that have different ways of understanding themselves according to different background metaphysical assumptions. We live in an age of *pluralism* where *numerous worldviews now occupy the public sphere*. People find it more and more difficult to assume without question that their lives can have shared social and cosmic meaning. Under these conditions, most people in industrialized societies listen to a voice that says, "The world is so confusing; I don't know what to believe. I wish I could find a wise professional to advise me."

The loss of metaphysical certainty has combined with the sharp rise in scientific and technological innovation that enhances the need for expert advice at the same time that it makes the advice of older, wiser people less technologically reliable. That is, increased complexity calls for increased specialization, so people feel less and less competent to govern all aspects of their own lives, let alone the next generation's. The average citizen doesn't dare make any important decisions without consulting an expert. Thus, modern societies are increasingly marked by the presence of specialized spheres focused on specific social tasks involving the economy, medicine, law, crime prevention, educational systems, modes of communication, religion, politics, and so on. Because many of us are not only confused about technology but also about the meaning of our lives, increasingly we have to hire professionals not just because they have skills that serve our ends, but also because we need advice about the ends themselves.

Figure 2.1   Advancements in science and technology have not only complicated our ethical choices, but they have also forced us to rely on a variety of experts as we attempt to govern our lives.

Under these conditions, society finds it useful to support professional institutions that can serve the fundamental needs of community members. Thus, **professions** are *state-supported organizations that have been given the privilege of autonomous, monopoly control over the delivery of services essential for promoting certain vital social values.* "State-supported" refers both to the legal protection and to the financial support provided by the legislative and administrative arms of state and national governments. Tax dollars are used to help professional schools in universities, and to pay for tuition, fund research, police malpractice, and prosecute those who practice without a license. A profession's special legal standing in society gives individual professionals powerful advantages in the marketplace, considerable prestige, and fair job security. However, access to this kind of special status is a socially sanctioned privilege and not a right (Bayles, 1981, p. 11).

Social privileges are always given conditionally as part of a reciprocal arrangement that is supposed to benefit everyone in the relationship. If a social privilege is abused because it is used purely to promote private ends, the privilege ought to be revoked. Most professionals are well aware of this point. They understand that in exchange for their profession's privilege of monopoly control over delivery of an important social service, society expects them to be extremely conscientious in carrying out their professional duties. Students (and some professionals themselves) often ignore this background expectation because they fail to consider the overall historical moral context that justified the existence of modern professions in the first place. However, most professionals are extremely conscientious in caring out their obligations under the relationship of mutual trust that exists between society and the profession. So, under these conditions, what kind of normative expectations should a society insist upon before it lends its support to professional associations?

Four Criteria of Traditional Professions

> **For Study:**   What are the characteristic features of a normative definition of professionalism? What does it mean for a professional to have an extra-strong moral commitment?

Several overlapping criteria are found in all attempts to define traditional professional practice. First, to become a member of a profession, a person must master the **esoteric knowledge** of the profession. This information is *so theoretical and technical that the general public does not easily acquire it.* For example, lawyers must complete the required course work for law school and pass the bar exam. This is not something an individual can do by herself during her spare time. The esoteric knowledge gives professionals special standing as theoretical and practical experts. Since the first few meetings with a professional focus on diagnosing the nature of the client's problem, a professional has to have a theoretical understanding of his area and how the various cases ought to be resolved. Theoretical understanding provides a broad background that makes it possible to diagnose the nature of a problem even when the case turns out to be unique rather than ordinary.

We have to hire professionals not just because they have skills that serve our ends, but also because we need advice about the ends themselves. Thus, in our pluralistic world professionals will need background esoteric knowledge that clarifies how the social values served by the profession ought to fit into the world as a whole. Professional education must emphasize acquiring cognitive and technical skills, background theoretical knowledge, and the moral sensitivity needed to function as a diagnostic expert in a pluralistic social milieu. That there is a concern for the broader picture becomes obvious when we notice that regulatory agencies have designed the licensure exams to include theoretical and moral questions in addition to the more technical questions about the details of professional practice.

Second, why should a society officially recognize a profession with laws and licensing procedures that allow the profession to exercise fairly autonomous, monopoly control over the delivery of services? One reason is that professions have explicitly dedicated themselves to serving *social values* that are *tied to essential human needs*. For instance, consider the important social value served by the following professions: physicians promote health, lawyers promote justice, accountants promote the stability of the market with reliable economic reports, engineers protect the structural integrity of public facilities, police promote public safety and justice in the streets, teachers pass on the tribe's knowledge and values to the next generation, and ministers tend to our spiritual needs. These values are so important to the members of society that they do not want to risk allowing incompetent people to offer services. Society is willing to give each professional association monopoly control over the delivery of services in exchange for the promise that the profession will promote these vital values in ways that serve the interests of society. When it looks as though professions are only serving their own interests, people begin seeking legislative changes that force professions to respect the priority of the public's needs.

Third, to exercise moral control over professional practice, professions need a way to standardize practice, communicate new techniques to professionals, and ensure that only people of integrity and competence become members of the profession. To regulate this aspect, every profession will need a *national organization* (with state chapters) that can *set standards for education and entry into the profession, create a code of ethics, investigate malpractice charges, encourage research to enhance the profession's ability to serve society, sponsor educational programs to keep members up to date, advise legislatures about the delivery of professional services, and in general police themselves as an autonomous organization—self-policing is essential, since it is difficult for members of the public to judge incompetence when they lack the esoteric knowledge.*

So far, these three criteria seem to leave the waiter and waitress on the sidelines. But there is a fourth criterion of traditional professionalism that anyone in any line of work may be able to satisfy. Camenisch (1983) notes that all professions claim in their codes of ethics that their members have an *extra-strong moral commitment* to serve those values to which the profession is dedicated (pp. 10, 33). There is something embarrassing and almost repugnant about a doctor who does not care when delivery of health care is compromised, a lawyer who is comfortable with arbitrary legal practice, a teacher who does not care if students learn, and, by metaphorical extension, a waitress who does not care if the food she serves is contaminated. One reason people feel it is an honor to be called a professional is the implication that the person has an uncommonly strong commitment to the quality of his or her work. We admire people who are uncommonly dedicated to what they do, even if it is something fairly ordinary like waiting on tables.

In fact, we expect professionals to be so committed to the values their profession serves that it seems inappropriate to think they joined the profession for purely financial motives. Professionals ought to be just as concerned with the delivery of adequate professional services as with their own financial well-being. Since the extra-strong moral commitment to professional values is supposed to take priority over personal financial interests, this special priority is always addressed in the codes of ethics by placing emphasis on the broader obligations to the public good. As an example of this kind of dedication, consider the following statement from the code of ethics of the International Federation of Accountants:

> A distinguishing mark of a profession is acceptance of its responsibility to the public. The accountancy profession's public consists of clients, credit grantors, governments, employers, employees, investors, the business and financial community, and others who rely on the *objectivity* and integrity of professional accountants to maintain the orderly functioning of commerce. . . . A professional accountant's responsibility is not exclusively to satisfy the needs of an individual client or employer. The standards of the accountancy profession are heavily determined by the public interest. (*Guidelines on ethics* . . . 1991, p. 6)

This kind of high moral tone is found in all professional codes of ethics. The accountant's code serves as a useful example because the myth that capitalism's market philosophy must favor individual egoism is very popular with students. Many students assume that the business world is a place where personal financial motives ought to always trump concerns about ethics. Many professionals in the business world, however, would disagree with the narrow agenda behind personal gain at all costs. Most of them fully understand how the entire system of business depends on ethical standards like honesty in contracts, objectivity in choosing buyers, fair competition, objective financial statements, and so on. The loss of faith in corporate accounting practices that contributed to the decline of the stock market in 2002 is a perfect example of how the entire economic system depends on the integrity of the professionals who work in the system. If accountants had remained professional and avoided conflicts of interest, then the public trust would not have been sacrificed to greedy self-interest, and the 2002 Congress would not have had to call for an independent external agency to monitor accounting practices. We can allow autonomous self-governance of the professions only if professionals are willing to honor the promise to serve society. Later, we will discuss some of the forces in modern society that can undermine the kind of moral integrity required for professional practice. But first, it will be useful to analyze the structure of professional codes of ethics.

Ideal Theory: Universal Morality and the Professional Code of Ethics

> **For Study:**   How can the professional duties of station created by codes of ethics lead to apparent conflicts with universal moral values? What is the best way to correlate codes of ethics with the universal moral principles that cover everyone? What are the reasons that support the idea that society ought to trust professional associations with autonomy and monopoly control over important social values? What kinds of conflicts can occur among the various obligations that fall on individual professionals?

If we were to treat professional codes and their special duties as separate, independent moral systems, then professionals would be covered by two unrelated moral systems: first their professional code, and second, the system of universal morality that covers everyone. Then we would need another moral system to resolve conflicts that might arise between the two. Rather than create yet another morality, it is more useful to remember the levels of justification discussed in Chapter One.

Codes are justified by higher-level moral theories. Thus, one logical solution is to treat codes of ethics as lower-level *specifications* of how particular professional institutions are supposed to help serve some of the universal human values in the system of morality that applies to all of us. Under this conception, *codes of ethics are not separate moral systems; they are part of a general strategy for specifying how universal values ought to be implemented in local contexts.* The codes specify how a group of people who have accepted professional duties of station are supposed to help implement some of the major values of the broader society (which also ought to be governed by universal principles of morality). Thus, as part of a general theory about how to apply universal values, it is useful to give professionals extra strong duties and privileges with regard to serving certain values only because it is a necessary step for helping the profession protect the broader social value it has promised to safeguard. For instance, a stronger obligation to maintain confidentiality applies to professionals than to ordinary citizens because extra strong confidentiality is needed to help the professional's association meet its responsibilities to the community's broader moral values. So, professionals do not have a special duty of confidentiality for its own sake, as though confidentiality were an independent value from a separate sphere of professional morality. They have the duty to maintain confidences because it is a necessary secondary duty for carrying out the first priority of the profession: to promote some higher value for the good of society. Maintaining confidences is one of the best ways for professionals to help promote universal moral values such as justice, equal opportunity, due process, etc., while helping people meet their needs.

These special privileges and duties of station created by codes of ethics complicate the lives of individual professionals. There will be times when professionals experience what will appear to be a conflict between universal obligations and professional obligations. But by viewing professional duties of station as part of an applied ethics strategy that serves higher universal values, the professional may be able to work out some of these conflicts without betraying either system. For example, what should a defense attorney do when she knows her client is guilty of murder? The code says she must not tell, but the normal duty of citizens is to come forward and tell what you know. Other things being equal, keeping the confidence of a killer does not seem to carry much weight when compared to the public's interest in convicting that person. Only when we see keeping the confidence as necessary for protecting the universal value of justice as due process, does confidentiality take on enough importance to balance out the normal duty to report crimes. Such complex cases create dilemmas precisely because they are not simply conflicts between higher and lower values or between competing moralities, they are conflicts about how to *implement* competing universal values within the same morality.

Clearly, if a professional is involved in a moral dilemma, we must analyze how his duty of station under his code of ethics affects the situation. But part of that analysis is to ask why the society allowed the profession to have such duties of station in the first place. For example, a lawyer must keep confidences spoken by a client, not only for the client's personal benefit but also for the integrity of the system of justice that protects everyone. In a similar manner, a priest must keep confidences in order to serve society's spiritual needs. Obviously, it is difficult to judge the adequacy of specific professional decisions without paying attention to the broader obligations that help create the social context for those decisions.

Because codes of ethics promise that the professions are more than economic associations out to further the financial interests of their members, a fairly explicit "contract" between the society and the profession is stated in the code. Thus, the code gives members of society some reason to trust the profession to look out for society's interests. This is the basis for asking society to give professions *independent control* or **autonomy** in setting standards and policing their own members. Professionals argue that autonomous control is appropriate because professions screen their members to be certain that they have the extra-strong commitment and adequate training. Furthermore, only the members of a profession have the esoteric knowledge needed to recognize shoddy and unethical practices. So, combined with moral commitment on the part of the national association, the profession is perfectly positioned to regulate professional practice by sponsoring the investigative bodies needed for self-policing. Of course, if professionals forget about their moral obligations to the larger society, the profession may begin to function more like a self-protective agency than a self-policing agency. In that case the society will eventually have to intervene from the outside. Thus, there are both moral and prudential reasons for self-policing. We will explore these different kinds of reasons in greater detail in Chapter Seven.

The areas that need to be policed involve the full array of moral and ethical relationships that come with professional practice. These include broad issues like the profession's relationships with both society and general universal values, as well as more immediate issues that concern the individual professional's relationships with clients, other professionals, the profession, the society, universal values, and his or her own personal values. Because the code has to specify how professional practice relates to all these different levels of obligations, some of which involve groups outside of the profession, it makes sense for society to insist that ethicists from outside the profession serve on self-policing committees to represent the broader interests of everyone. For instance, outside ethicists might have been more sensitive to the obvious conflict of interest that came to light in 2002 when it became clear that some corporations were hiring accounting firms to serve as both independent auditors and as business consultants. The professionals in the accounting industry should have blown the whistle on his kind of practice.

Client/Professional Relationships

> **For Study:**   Why does the relationship between professionals and clients have to be conceived of as something other than a purely economic relationship? What norms ought to regulate the relationship?

Somehow professionals and clients must find a way to trust one another. All codes recognize that professionals are supposed to have a special moral relationship with clients that will be compromised if economic concerns are allowed to dominate their interactions. Thus, to protect the integrity of their public obligations, professions need to resist the economization of relationships that is generally occurring in Western societies. Rather than allowing relationships to be structured according to professional standards, *economization converts all relationships into ones based purely on financial incentives, in effect allowing market forces to determine the quality of the interactions between client and professional.* The way in which HMOs have been accused of distorting the relationship between doctors and patients is a good example of economization. Clients have a different status than customers who are buying goods from a salesperson. The reason clients approach professionals is that they need help with vital human needs, so they are not equal economic traders in a marketplace. For instance, a doctor in good health with esoteric knowledge would have unfair advantages if the relationship with his patients were based only on economic self-interest. There has to be a different model that can characterize the proper role of a professional in a client's life.

Because the relationship with clients is based on the client's dependency, some might expect the professional to solve client problems *by making decisions for them.* But this ***paternalistic model*** of professional practice takes too much control away from the client. It assumes the professional always knows best how to serve the client's values. On the other hand, if we reverse the relationship of dependency by focusing on the fact that the client is hiring the professional, we might assume that the professional should simply *function as the agent of the client.* But this ***agency model*** takes too much control away from the professional. It implies that he or she should simply follow orders of a consumer of his or her talents. This model violates the expectation that professionals are responsible for making independent professional decisions. A professional should never blindly follow orders, since professionalism recognizes that other social obligations exist in addition to the obligation to please the client.

In short, in order to fulfill all the obligations defined in their code of ethics, professionals think of themselves as working *with* clients, not just for them. The best model for professional practice focuses on establishing a balanced relationship that respects the autonomy and responsibilities of both parties. Professional and client are supposed to work as partners to solve the client's problems within the boundaries set by the profession's code of ethics. This requires a ***fiduciary relationship,*** which means one *based on mutual trust.* This model reinforces the traditional view that professional practice has a moral dimension that requires more of professionals than is demanded by the narrower concept of market relationships in business settings. We have a right to expect professionals to feel a moral concern about the standards of excellence needed to deliver a valuable service to society while in a fiduciary relationship with a client who needs the service. (In theory, at least, a waitress or waiter could share in the moral aspect of this special relationship, although the level of need being served and the esoteric knowledge required are greatly diminished.) Camenisch (1983) worries that powerful forces are at work to undermine the strong fiduciary and moral commitment we expect from professionals.

> Retaining this moral dimension even only as an expectation will not be easy in view of a general skepticism about the actual moral distinctiveness of the professions, a widespread doubt about the possibility of altruism in any human agent, and a supposedly pluralistic society in which the very existence of generally applicable moral standards is being questioned.

> [We should strive] . . . for retention in our view of the professions of a moral element in keeping with which members of the traditional professions claim to be prepared to enter into fiduciary relationships with their clients, to be trustworthy allies in the society's and in their clients' pursuit of certain highly valued goals, and to be prepared to subordinate their own self-interest to the needs of their clients to a degree not usually found among other economic agents. . . . (pp. 32–38)

For the sake of continued discussion, we will assume that the traditional moral commitment expected from professionals is on the rebound. One can hope that a series of scandals (like the involvement of so many lawyers in Watergate and so many accountants in the economic crisis in 2002) have embarrassed professional associations and their schools, so that they will take steps to become more stringent in teaching new members about the type of moral commitment we expect from professionals. Certainly the codes of ethics of the various professions still claim that each profession as a whole has this extra-strong commitment. Since they promise dedication, we should continue to hold them to the promise.

Implementation: Professional Practice and Discretionary Decisions

> **For Study:**   Why do professionals need discretionary power to use their esoteric knowledge to make decisions? What is the proper way for a professional to justify using discretionary power?

Given that unique cases always involve special circumstances, codes of ethics cannot possibly cover every contingency that might arise in professional practice. Thus, professionals must exercise *professional discretion,* which means they need *leeway to use their esoteric knowledge to figure out the best means for carrying out the goals of their profession in specific cases.* Because there are often several different options that might satisfy the needs of a client, the professional has to be given the opportunity to help the client choose in each case which option is best; for example, should we use surgery, radiation, chemotherapy, or should we wait and see? There are, of course, dangers in allowing room for discretionary judgment. In a pluralistic world, unrestricted use of discretion could encourage arbitrary or relativistic judgments to enter professional life. Pollock-Byrne (1989) points out in *Ethics in Crime and Justice* that many people blame the use of discretion for much of the unethical behavior that occurs in the criminal justice system:

> The very nature of policing necessarily involves some amount of discretion. Even courts have seemed to support police discretion over full enforcement. . . . This opens the door, however, for decision making outside the confines of legality. Unethical police behavior often arises directly from the power of discretion. Because police officers have the power to select and entrap suspects, they can also make that decision unethically, such as by taking a bribe in return for letting a suspect go. . . . Discretion is an important element in the criminal justice practitioner's role and plays a part in the creation of ethical dilemmas. Discretion in criminal justice has been attacked as contributing to injustice. (p. 84)

One solution to this concern is to place a sharper emphasis on the professional nature of discretionary judgments. Discretion is supposed to allow tough professional decisions, not substitute personal preferences for principled professional judgments. Thus, professionals should be able to explain to others the reasoning behind their use of discretion. If you cannot give a responsible account to other members of your profession that justifies how you used your power to make a discretionary decision, then maybe you weren't making a professional decision at all. That is, although there is room for autonomous use of individual initiative in professional life, the initiative must still make sense to others in the profession. Thus, Pollock-Byrne's example of taking bribes should not be characterized as an example of abused discretion but as an example of corruption. In this context, ***corruption*** occurs when someone *uses professional powers for personal gain at the expense of the values the profession is supposed to serve.* This kind of corruption is more apt to occur when people become confused about the types of moral obligations that come with their jobs. In the modern world, people live and work in social settings that have many layers, and professionals must be sensitive to how all of these layers are related.

A commitment to justice, health, education, or other important values can be served in many ways. One way is to be a good citizen and lobby for the creation of institutional structures that promote these human values. Professions are an example of this kind of institution. However, citizens can do more than lobby for just laws. They can also join one of the professions and thereby make a conscious personal contribution to one of these important values. In this sense, entering a profession is a moral choice. Conscientious professionals should review and judge the norms their profession serves and work for reforms when they think the code of ethics is giving prescriptions that conflict with the larger moral point of view. The point is, professionals cannot simply turn their moral responsibilities over to their profession. When they become professionals, they take on additional moral duties, one of which is to help police the profession to make certain that professional practice remains consistent with broader moral values. This means that they have an obligation to be active critical members in their own professional organizations. As the "good" guards in Zimbardo's experiment discovered, all that scoundrels ask of us is that we say nothing; so committed professionals must be outspoken. Without critical self-reflective dialogue among the members, self-policing will not occur.

Professional Practice Must Be Compatible with Morality

> **For Study:** How might conflicts between a profession and a society be resolved?

A skeptic might say, "Surely ethics does not need me to develop my own moral theory. If professions are governed by codes, why not just allow me to join a good profession and then follow its code religiously?" As we shall see, value diversity and shifting technological developments have complicated professional practice to such a degree that the option of simple obedience is no longer sufficient. There will be times when each of us is called upon to use personal moral discretion to judge professional practice itself, as well as the profession's place in the larger moral world.

For instance, what happens when professional values conflict with the larger values of society? Other things being equal, society's values have priority. However, since professions generally serve major human values, it is possible for a corrupt society to be in conflict with the universal values that define a profession's mission. For example, how could lawyers in a Nazi culture serve justice? Or how could doctors supervise the torture of prisoners and yet claim to be professionals? When this kind of special case arises, ethical people in a profession may have to rebel against their unjust society by giving their primary allegiance directly to the universal values that would normally justify both the society and their profession. We will consider these kinds of conflicts in more detail in the next chapter.

For now, it is only necessary to note that professional practice evolves over time as it adapts to new technological innovations and to the pressures of pluralism. This means individual professionals cannot always rely on traditional codes in all cases, because the codes may not be up to date. For instance, consider the moral confusion professional health-care workers may feel in the face of the advances in technology that have created the need to redefine "death." In the days before technology, life was simple in the sense that we couldn't do much to prevent death. But today, we can keep vital organs going for years with the aid of machines. The time has passed when we could count on

> a person with a fatal heart attack [to] lose consciousness, stop breathing, become motionless and unresponsive, and have no detectable pulse all at approximately the same time. All the vital signs of life would vanish together. Now, however, medical technology has forced us to choose which signs of life are sufficiently important that their loss constitutes the death of the patient, while other signs of life persist. (Younger, 1996, p. 2)

In response to this technological change, all fifty states now accept loss of brain function as a criterion for being legally dead. Once brain function has ceased, organs can be removed and transplanted and machines can be turned off. Now imagine that you are a nurse or doctor in charge of a "dead" person whose body is being maintained so that its organs will be in good shape for later harvesting. Nurses and doctors "must attach them [these dead people] to breathing machines, monitor them for heart rhythm and blood pressure, give them fluids and nutrition, and when indicated, administer antibiotics and other medications. . . . [the hearts of these dead patients] are even candidates for full resuscitation should they suffer cardiac arrest" (Younger, p. 4). Never before have members of the health-care profession been required to treat dead people exactly as they treat living people, including washing the body and cutting and combing the hair. Many health-care professionals find this whole scene very confusing. There is no way a code of ethics can anticipate such changes ahead of time, so a code will need revision. Professionals must be sophisticated enough to work out for themselves the proper response to extraordinary conditions until a code is revised to give specific guidance for the new situations. Since new or unique conditions can arise at any time, individual professional moral agents need to prepare themselves for the morally unexpected, and that will require a theoretical understanding of morality.

This shift away from the good old days of professional certainty mirrors similar shifts in the complexity of the modern era that are slowly undermining the metaphysical consensus that holds traditional communities together. All of these shifts are exacerbated by globalization's tendency to undermine the control of the nation-state, the traditional final court of appeal. The presence or absence of a clear background consensus affects professional judgments and the way people interpret and apply ethical codes. Thus, by themselves, codes and procedures cannot guarantee that people will make the right choices if they have not developed a sophisticated background understanding of the way all of us, including professionals, make judgments in the context of advancing technology, increased multiculturalism or value pluralism, and globalization. To see why professionals need to explore moral foundations as part of professional education, Chapter Three reviews some of the ways modern professional practice has led to administrative actions that were banal and even morally horrendous when professionals allowed themselves to remain ignorant of moral complexity.

REFERENCES

ADAMS, GUY B. & BALFOUR, DANNY L. (1998). *Unmasking administrative evil.* Thousand Oaks, CA: Sage.

ANGELES, PETER A. (1981). *Dictionary of philosophy.* New York: Harper Collins.

BAYLES, MICHAEL D. (1981). *Professional ethics.* Belmont, CA: Wadsworth.

CAMENISCH, PAUL F. (1983). *Grounding professional ethics in a pluralistic society.* New York: Haven.

GOODPASTER, KENNETH E. (1984). The concept of corporate responsibility. In Tom Regan (Ed.), *Just business: New introductory essays in business ethics* (pp. 306–11). New York: Random House.

GRUBE, G. M. A. (Trans.) & COOPER, JOHN M. (Ed.). (1975). *The trial & death of Socrates.* Indianapolis, IN: Hackett.

Guidelines on ethics for professional accountants. (1991). New York: International Federation of Accountants.

HANEY, CRAIG & ZIMBARDO, PHILIP G. (1977). The socialization into criminality: On becoming a prisoner and a guard. In J. L. Tapp & F. J. Levine (Eds.), *Law, justice, and the individual in society: Psychological and legal issues* (pp. 198–223). New York: Holt, Rinehart & Winston.

JONES, RON. (1976). You will do as directed. *Learning*. May/June. pp. 22–26.

POLLOCK-BYRNE, JOYCELYN M. (1989). *Ethics in crime & justice.* Pacific Grove, CA: Brooks/Cole.

WILKINS, BURLEIGH. (1992). *Terrorism and collective responsibility.* New York: Routledge, Chapman and Hall.

YOUNGER, STUART J. (1996). Brain death: Another layer of confusion. *Center views* 10 (3), Spring, 1–5. Center for Biomedical Ethics, Case Western Reserve University School of Medicine.

ZIMBARDO, PHILIP G. (1971). Stanford prison experiment narration. The quotations in the text from the Zimbardo Prison Experiment come primarily from a 50-minute taped slide-show presentation of the experiment. For information about the slide show with its synchronized taped narration and sound effects portraying the dramatic features of the experiment, write to: P. G. Zimbardo Inc., P.O. Box 4395, Stanford University, Stanford, CA 94305. The study was funded by an Office of Naval Research contract (N00014-67-A-0112-0041) to Philip G. Zimbardo and carried out in 1971. A 20-minute videotape of the study with some postexperiment interviews is also available at the same address.

ZIMBARDO, PHILIP G. (1975). Transforming experimental research into advocacy for social change. In M. Deutsch & H. A. Hornstein (Eds.), *Applying social psychology* (p. 34ff). Hillsdale, CA: Lawrence Erlbaum.

Chapter   Three

Muddle, Drift, Banality, & Subjectivism versus Morality

∽ The Morality of Muddle

> **For Study:** Why is it morally dangerous when professionals who are good people remain confused about the nature of moral dilemmas? Why are some of the first reactions to pluralism not helpful? Why is conceptual bigotry incompatible with philosophical ethics?

What should we think about a professional like Judge Douglas, who debated with Abraham Lincoln about the morality of slavery? Were professionals who owned slaves simply evil men, or were they perhaps legitimately confused? Lincoln (cited in Oates, 1977, p. 116) claimed that they were so simpleminded about slavery that they treated disputes about it as though they were on the same level as concerns about "the cranberry trade." What about more

73

contemporary cases of professionals who participated in obviously evil deeds, such as the doctors who supervised experiments in Nazi Germany's death camps, or the American doctors who allowed the infamous Tuskegee syphilis experiment to continue for years and years after the discovery of penicillin (which could have cured all of the participants in the experiment)? Professionals who were mainstream members of their society committed these acts. As we shall see, even after the cases came to light, some of these doctors continued to see themselves as dedicated professionals who were only trying to make a contribution to humanity. How can this be? Many people assume that only serial killers or malevolent people deserve to be called evil. We do not like to think that people with good reputations and good intentions are also capable of contributing to evil. After all, one might argue, evil refers to "... those instances in which humans knowingly and deliberately inflict pain and suffering on other human beings" (Adams and Balfour, 1998, p. xix). Very few policymakers ever intentionally harm others in this way. On the other hand, in their book *Unmasking Administrative Evil*, Adams and Balfour demonstrate that the public policy landscape is full of examples of unintended evil done by mainstream members of society, many of whom are professionals. They argue that, with regard to modern institutional practice,

> ordinary people may simply be acting appropriately in their organizational role— in essence, just doing what those around them would agree they should be doing—and at the same time be participating in what a critical and reasonable observer, usually well after the fact, would call evil (p. xx).

> Because administrative evil wears many masks, it is entirely possible to adhere to the tenets of public service ethics and participate in a great evil, and not be aware of it until it is too late. (p. 4)

The idea that professionals and people who are pillars of their community can cause much of the evil in the world needs to be carefully examined, because if it is true, it constitutes a very strong reason to reevaluate the traditional approach to professional ethics. Ethical codes must address everyone who might commit evil deeds (including good people), and then suggest ways to minimize the occurrence of evil. Adams and Balfour argue that we need to reconstruct the foundations for professional ethics to get beyond "superficial critiques and lay the groundwork for a more ethical and 'democratic' public administration, one that recognizes its potential for evil and thereby creates greater possibilities for avoiding the many pathways toward state-sponsored dehumanization and destruction" (p. 5). This is a worthy agenda, but before we can reconstruct the approach to professional ethics, we need to better understand how good people can become so confused that they drift into supporting unethical policies.

Reactions to Pluralism

Pluralism has a double edge. It can stimulate a search for greater understanding and motivate advances in philosophical thought, but it can also create barriers that interfere with our ability to communicate new ethical insights to people who are living with conceptual confusion. People need time to adapt to fundamental changes, but the pace of modern pluralistic life does not give us that time. Sabini and Silver (1982) argue in *Moralities of Everyday Life: The Morality of Muddle* that on the whole, people in our pluralistic culture are a morally mixed-up lot. Life has accelerated to the point where there are so many value options from so many different lifestyles, that average moral agents feel unsure of themselves; they have lost their moral confidence. Social scientists have recorded several morally inappropriate but common reactions to the escalating value pluralism in the contemporary world.

Bigotry

First, pluralism contributes to a form of **conceptual bigotry.** Sometimes *people simply refuse without good reason to acknowledge that competing value alternatives might have some legitimacy.* Having so many choices seems to frighten some people so much that they react by viewing complex moral issues from only one side. Bigots often commit the **black/white fallacy,** a form of *dualistic thinking in which the possibility for compromise is denied.* If *there is no middle ground on complex issues, then competing points of view are either black or white since shades of gray do not exist.* Whenever one side (their side) is completely right, the other side must be completely absurd. Thus, the bigot cannot be serious about dilemmas because, to him, the complex issues are not complex; they are black and white. Logic books say this kind of thinking is inappropriate because it assumes the existence of a false simplicity in human affairs. It denies the existence of both personal and social moral dilemmas by ignoring the fact that there can be good reasons why moral dilemmas worry people who are willing to look at both sides of an issue.

    Why are people tempted to commit the black/white fallacy? One reason is that it helps us avoid the discomfort of having to make a tough choice. One way to simplify choice is to portray one of the sides in a dispute in simplistic, absurd terms. For example, when people make simplistic statements like, "Abortion is wrong because it is the murder of little babies," or conversely, "Abortion is okay because a woman has a right to control her own body," they are ignoring the complexity of this issue. In both statements, a tough moral choice is turned into a simplistic choice by ignoring the considerations that are important to a reasonable member of the opposition. But bigots are not interested in discourse about the truth; they are interested only in getting others to adopt their values. For the sake of stability, they may even favor authoritarian ways of resolving value differences. To them, authoritarian strategies seem justifiable, since they have already defined their opponents as either evil or foolish. From the MPofV, however, authoritarian solutions to the kinds of dilemmas created by pluralism are especially unfortunate, since solutions that are dictated by power stifle the moral dialogue that could lead to creative and rational ways of resolving the value conflicts.

Future Shock, Decidophobia, Cynicism, & Nihilism

Some other reactions to pluralism are so extreme that the behavior actually appears a bit neurotic. For instance, pluralism can create a kind of debilitating mental numbness in people who have not experienced much change in their lives. Alvin Toffler (1971) calls this psychological reaction *future shock,* since it results from *too much change so fast that it cannot be integrated into one's life-world*. The person who says, "I don't understand what the world is coming to" may be suffering from a bit of future shock. Pluralism is less likely to cause future shock in young people. They are so accustomed to value changes that some of them have a contrary tendency to assume that because nothing is permanent no value can deserve the kind of respect that lasts for generations. To the young, moral values may seem like fads or personal tastes that come and go.

Sometimes the neurotic overreaction can appear as *decidophobia* (Kaufman, 1973), which is *an irrational fear of making decisions*. Because pluralism allows for so many legitimate value differences, people may be afraid that either there is no right answer at all, or if there is a right answer, they will fail to see it. Thus, they are paralyzed by indecision. Decidophobes tend to procrastinate until someone else tells them what to do, until the problem solves itself, or until it becomes unmanageable. Advice columnists can make a living by helping people who suffer from a bit of decidophobia.

With the increased publicity about cases of corruption around the globe, some people adopt the stance of *moral cynicism,* in which they argue that morality is just a political tool. They claim that in the crunch of actual conflict no one really uses principles, since everyone only tries to get their own way. *Cynics* believe that *even if there are higher ethical values there is no need to figure out what they are, since people will ultimately always act on selfish interests*. Some cynics even argue that "right" really only means what is in the interest of the person who has the most power. Some of the prisoners I taught (mentioned in Chapter One) had adopted this point of view. They thought only a fool like Socrates would put restrictions on himself by worrying about what is right. This attitude has spread into some of the city streets. As Morris Massey (1976) says in his popular videotape "What You Are is Where You Were When," the "now" value for many young people today is: "Don't not do it, just don't get caught if you do do it."

Sometimes a person who seems cynical may actually be suffering from *nihilism,* a *psychological and/or philosophical state of mind in which a person has lost the ability to believe in any values at all, whether religious, political, moral, or social.* Nihilists argue that ethical terms are worthless, irrational, meaningless, and absurd. Cynicism and/or nihilism should not be confused with healthy philosophical *skepticism,* which maintains *that knowledge in some areas of inquiry may not be possible.* The skeptic intentionally refrains from giving allegiance to any position unless it can be supported with very strong evidence. This willingness to doubt the truth of statements is valuable, since it motivates people to question values and search for alternatives. However, nihilists and cynics take a path different from the skeptics. They do not strive for greater sophistication in their ability to analyze values. Why bother if moral knowledge is either impossible, useless, or a secret attempt to assert power?

Confusion Leads to Moral Drift

> **For Study:**   What are the distinguishing characteristics of the phenomenon of moral drift? In what way does the tendency for people to drift seem to indicate they are not adequately prepared for moral responsibilities in a pluralistic world?

The confusion about morality that we see in the reactions to pluralism can lead to an unfortunate and even dangerous kind of muddled thought. Social psychologists have studied a phenomenon known as *moral drift,* which occurs *when people make a series of small decisions without paying attention to the overall goal toward which those small decisions are gradually carrying them.* In their study of the morality of muddle, Sabini and Silver use Stanley Milgram's (1963) Yale Authority Experiment to illustrate moral drift. Milgram asked a number of research subjects at Yale University to participate in an experiment that was ostensibly designed to study learning. In fact, it was designed to study the research subjects' obedience to a malevolent authority figure. The research subjects were assigned the role of "teacher" and were told to deliver electrical shocks to a "learner" every time the learner made a wrong response to a question. The learner was in another room and could not be seen by the teacher. As far as the teacher knew, some learner who was hooked up by wires to a voltage machine would suffer a shock every time the teacher flipped a lever on the machine. Each time a question was missed, the teacher flipped another lever, slowly moving up a scale of increasing voltage (from minimal volts up to 450 volts, which is lethal). At the end of the scale, clear signs warned that the voltage was reaching a point where it could be lethal. In actuality, the "learner" was really an actor who read a prepared script. He was not hooked to the machine, and he did not receive any shocks. He merely gave rehearsed standardized responses that were correlated with the different levels of shock—that is, he would protest at first, then shout, then moan, and finally after 300 volts were supposedly delivered to him by the teacher, he would become silent as though unconscious or dead. Remember, the "teacher" was a research subject who did not know the "learner" was not actually hooked up to the voltage machine.

Forty psychiatrists agreed ahead of time that the majority of subjects would go beyond 150 volts, but that only the rare sadistic sociopath would go all the way to 450 volts. What surprised everyone was that although a few subjects refused to keep delivering increasingly severe shocks, an amazing 62 percent of the subjects in the experiment continued escalating the severity of the shocks until they reached the lethal level. This means the subjects were willing to risk doing tremendous harm to innocent people on orders from an institutional authority figure—a Yale scientist. Many of the subjects who went all the way up the scale showed a great deal of stress, but they nonetheless continued to escalate the shocks on orders from the psychologist conducting the experiment. One who went to 180 volts said: "He can't stand it! . . . you hear him hollering? . . . what if something happens to him? . . . I mean, who is going to take the responsibility if anything happens to that gentleman?" (Milgram, p. 376). When the researcher said that he would take responsibility, the subject said "all right" and continued to deliver the shocks.

By focusing only on each small step and by refusing to challenge the experimenter's institutional authority, the subjects in the experiment clearly displayed moral drift. They drifted up the scale to the lethal level of shock without ever explicitly making the significant moral choice to deliver a potentially lethal shock. It is important to recognize that when each small decision is considered in isolation, it is not in itself an evil action. After all, the subjects had volunteered to participate in an experiment at a prestigious university; they had not intended to electrocute anyone. If the researcher had told them to go from zero up to a lethal shock in one move, many more would have refused because the immense consequences of the choice would be obvious. But, given the series of small steps, they never had to confront the overall pattern of what they were doing. They drifted along, trusting the institutional authority, taking responsibility for their tiny actions, but refusing to take responsibility for the pattern being created by their overall behavior. In a sense, they were simply following their duty of station (doing their job), which is precisely what malevolent authority figures in bureaucracies want their employees to do.

Milgram's research surprised many people. On the surface, it appeared to show that ordinarily "good" people are prepared to abandon their commitment to human values in order to obey a malevolent authority figure. If this interpretation were accurate, it would be startling and controversial. However, we must be careful as to how we portray what occurred in this research. Milgram's (1974) own analysis attributed the results to a variety of factors (pp. xii–xiii). He argued that because the subjects had given up their decision-making role in order to carry out another person's wishes, they no longer felt responsible for their actions. In addition, their obedience was influenced by other variables, such as their belief that the experiment would serve a useful purpose, the sequential nature of each small step, their interest in the technical side of the experiment, and their general tendency to be polite rather than to withdraw from an activity for which they had volunteered.

I think the factor of institutional prestige also deserves considerable weight in this case. As mentioned in Chapter Two, as social animals, we tend to give institutions (and their officers) the benefit of the doubt. Why should Milgram's subjects think anything was amiss? They were naturally focusing their attention on their duty of station as volunteers participating in a benevolent experiment. They assumed the background against which they evaluated their choice was exactly as it was reported to be—a scientist in a respected research institution was doing research to benefit mankind. Other things being equal, it is reasonable to trust a research scientist at a respected Ivy League university. It makes sense to assume he will be careful to obey the principles that regulate research on human subjects. These background expectations colored their interpretation of the foreground (what was happening at the moment). Moti Nissani (1990) drew some similar conclusions about the experiment. He said his research on *conceptual conservatism* shows that *once people have committed themselves to seeing their behavior in a certain light, it is very unlikely that they will readily change their mind and rethink what they are doing.*

> Even when we deal with ideologically neutral conceptions of reality, when these conceptions have been recently acquired, when they came to us from unfamiliar sources, when they were assimilated for spurious reasons, when their abandonment entails little tangible risks or costs, and when they are sharply contradicted by subsequent events, we are, at least for a time, disinclined to doubt such conceptions on the verbal level and unlikely to let go of them in practice. (p. 1384)

Since the subjects had decided they were participating in valuable research, it was very hard for them to reconceptualize what was happening and entertain the notion that the researcher was either evil or incompetent. As support for this interpretation, Nissani points out that this kind of behavior changes to a degree when the background is altered. In a follow-up experiment, the obedience rate dropped from 62 percent to 48 percent when the subjects were told the study was being conducted by a private research firm— which compromised the prestige that comes with a nonprofit university. And it dropped to 40 percent when the experiment was altered to expose the subjects to an instance of betrayal and clear injustice on the part of the researcher, in order to give them reasons to question his moral integrity (Milgram, 1974). (Of course, 40 percent is still too high, given that moral agents are supposed to take responsibility for their participation in institutional activities.) This kind of research has important implications for applied ethics. Since people obviously have a difficult time reconceptualizing what they are doing, the background context must be designed to ensure that they start their tasks with adequate universal ideals and practical information about what is really going on. It is rather careless or banal for moral agents to simply assume authority figures can always be trusted. It is also rather banal to just drift along in situations calling for moral wisdom. To flesh out the background conditions that ought to be of concern to any moral theory, we will have to investigate in greater depth the way carelessness or banality can contribute to evil.

∼ The Specter of the Banality of Evil

> **For Study:**   In what sense is the banality of evil inconsistent with responsible moral agency? Is reference to banality an excuse for some forms of immoral behavior or an explanation of those forms of immoral behavior?

Let's begin by considering the significance of something called the ***banality of evil.*** Hannah Arendt (1963) used this term to characterize *evil that results from motives that are not in themselves wrong in a proper context but that seem excessively thoughtless, trite, or careless as moral motives in complex contexts that require a careful evaluation of right and wrong.* Although Arendt was a philosopher, she went to Jerusalem as a reporter for a major newspaper to cover Eichmann's trial for Nazi war crimes against humanity. She said she was fully prepared to find a moral monster at the trial, but instead she found a man whose motives seemed excessively banal given the background context of the Holocaust.

> When I speak of the banality of evil, I do so only on the strictly factual level, pointing to a phenomenon which stared one in the face at the trial. . . . Except for an extraordinary diligence in looking out for his personal advancement, he [Eichmann] had no motives at all. And this diligence in itself was in no way criminal; he certainly would never have murdered his superior in order to inherit his post. He merely, to put the matter colloquially, never realized what he was doing . . . In principle he knew quite well what it was all about . . . He was not stupid. It was sheer thoughtlessness—something by no means identical with stupidity—that predisposed him to become one of the greatest criminals of that period. (p. 287)

Whether or not you agree with Arendt's assessment of Eichmann, her views about the ethical predicament facing banal people raises some profound questions: Can people participate in massive evil for motives that may not, in themselves, be evil? Arendt's strange experience of watching Eichmann defend himself against the charge that he had committed crimes against humanity convinced her it was possible for people to engage in evil almost inadvertently. In an ultimate absurdity, Eichmann claimed that as a good Kantian, he lived by universal ideals and performed his duty for duty's sake, regardless of consequences (we will explore Kant's theory in detail in Chapter Nine). According to this perverted interpretation of Kantian ideals, he impartially applied the law to all persons equally without making local exceptions. He said, "I was doing my duty; that is a virtue, isn't it?" The answer is yes and no. It all depends on how one balances conceptions of duty at the various levels of justification. Moral life is not simplistic, and it seems banal in the modern world for a person to approach moral choices as though there is no need to distinguish between levels of ethical and moral duties. The students in the Ron Jones experiment in Chapter Two were young and inexperienced, thus we expect a bit of banality and assume they will one day transcend such silliness. But Eichmann was a colonel in the military, and his inability to distinguish between levels of duty was not a virtue, it was a level of banality that amounted to evil.

Some people claim that Eichmann's case demonstrates that attempting to find universal moral values will always lead us into oppressing people, since a focus on the universal blinds us to the harms that occur at the local level. What should we make of the accusation that concern for universal values contributes to moral evil? Did overly principled universalistic thinking cause Eichmann's participation in the Holocaust? On the contrary, Eichmann's approach to ethics was based on treating universals as though they are concrete rules that need no interpretation. Under such conditions, "a universalist ethics then appears as an abstract, obstinate rigorism blind to facts and of service to immoral intentions at any moment" (Gunther 1993, p. 6). This is a fault of Eichmann's banal mentality, not a fault of universal principles *per se*. As mentioned in Chapter One, universal principles are not concrete maxims for action. By their nature, they need to be impartially applied in context-sensitive ways with due regard for the ideals contained in the universal principles. This is why we cannot simply rely on codes of ethics and decision procedures. Those who use them must have enough sophistication to properly interpret and apply their principles in local contexts.

Thus, rather than blame universal values, in Eichmann's case it is much more appropriate to attribute blame to a lack of true universalistic thinking. He was a bureaucrat, not a dedicated ideologue focused on faulty universal ideals. Since the bureaucracy he served was organized for evil, he wound up serving evil while thinking of himself in idealistic terms. However, although he mouthed a commitment to universal ideals at his trial, Eichmann was content in practice to focus narrowly on the level of his own bureaucratic role. Governed as he was by his personal ambitions and duties of station, he never bothered to evaluate his own local context against true universal values. What bothered Arendt was that Eichmann participated in the Holocaust—the extermination of millions of people—and yet he was motivated almost exclusively by a concrete desire for personal advancement in the Nazi S.S. hierarchy. She was dumbfounded to discover that when banal people never carefully judge either their own motives or their duties of station, they can inadvertently help maintain and promote horrendous evil without meaning to do so. This looks hopelessly trite, trivial, thoughtless, and careless to an external witness. Eichmann's exclusively egocentric focus seemed to blind him to the larger social context of his actions. Although he helped maintain evil in the Nazi life world, if he had worked for the U.S. post office, the same motives might have allowed him to retire with a gold watch for dedicated service.

Eichmann's case represents an extreme example of an unfortunately common problem. There are obvious similarities between Eichmann's approach to his job and some of the people in Zimbardo's Prison Experiment, Jones's Third Wave Experiment, and Milgram's Yale Authority Experiment. That is, because many of the subjects in these experiments had motives that would not be considered evil in a different, proper context, they were surprised when they realized later just how much they had contributed to the maintenance of an institution that promoted immoral behavior. All agreed with hindsight that they should not have cooperated with the institutions that controlled them, but at the time, they remained banally oblivious to the broad ramifications of the many small steps they took that led them astray. By the time they understood their situation, they felt powerless to stop what they were doing. For instance, one of the "good" guards in the Zimbardo Prison Experiment eventually came to realize that he didn't like his role. Yet he seemed too confused to do anything about changing the types of relationships being sponsored by the institution. In fact, as Zimbardo points out, the passivity of these "good" guards helped maintain the brutal tone of the prison environment in spite of their feelings of revulsion. The fact that they did not speak up seems rather irresponsible, given the context. As mentioned above, all that scoundrels want from us is our silence. So, *it is not enough to recognize that something is morally wrong, to truly be good moral agents, we also must know how to confront wrongful behavior.*

Arendt is not trying to excuse Eichmann; she is merely pointing out that banality occurs. Intentional or not, when banal motives contribute to evil in the world, the people with these motives are still to be blamed. Banality can function as an excuse only in situations where we expect it. For instance, since children lack understanding, cannot delay gratification, and cannot accept the personal sacrifice for which morality sometimes calls, when they act in banal ways, we forgive them because we expect it. But we also don't give them much responsibility. Adults, on the other hand, are not supposed to act in a careless or trite fashion as though they are children. So, in this text, the concept of banality is not used as an excuse; it is only used to help us understand those situations in which agents claim they did not have evil intentions even though they carelessly participated in situations that were immoral.

Illustrations of the Banality of Evil

> **For Study:**   Why is it banal to exclude qualitative data from research results and decision making when human beings are involved?

Because it is hard to believe that decent people can do evil things for fairly trivial reasons like carelessness ("trivial" and "careless" must be judged in context), we need to look at a couple of other famous cases that illustrate the moral danger of allowing professionals or citizens to take a banal approach to morality. Although the following examples are extreme (which is one reason the people who participated in the evil were amazed and chagrined to find themselves doing what they were doing), such instances may be far more common than we would like to believe, albeit in less extreme forms.

Example: The Greek Soldiers

In 1977, Amnesty International studied soldiers who had become torturers in Greece's political prisons, documenting how evil authorities can brutally socialize good, simple people into roles that call for sadistic behavior. How does a corrupt regime induce ordinary soldiers to torture their fellow countrymen? Do they put out advertisements saying, "Needed at local political prison: burly sadistic men to torture prisoners; good fringe benefits and opportunities for innovative work"?

In this example, it is important to stay focused on the fact that the soldiers in the Greek political prisons were conscripted; they were not sadistic volunteers. Many came from "respectable, middle-class and working-class families throughout the countryside, and there is no doubt that their relatives and friends felt shocked and bitter at what had become of the promising young men they had known" (p. 35). They were socialized to become torturers, and many of the soldiers themselves felt profound guilt when society confronted them after they had been "liberated" from army duty. In the end, when some of the soldiers went to trial, even the prosecutor did not know whom to blame. He said in his closing address:

> The subordinate ranks were . . . conscripted. They were not, as some people have tried to pretend, volunteers. After they had every trace of individuality and humanity crushed out of them at KESA [a special army unit], after their lowest instincts had been aroused, after they had been threatened, terrorized and misled, they were let out like wild animals from their cages and set on their brothers to tear them to pieces. Most of them, not having the strength to resist, followed their orders. Some adjusted and identified themselves (with the procedures), after which they acted on their own, varying the repetitive monotony by personal initiatives. How can we today, members of the tribunal, go deeply enough into this to find out who are the guilty? (p. 35)

It is interesting to note that many of the soldiers who passed through KESA were from small villages. They had a good tribal heritage but little experience making value choices in the wider community. They entered the army with a naïve, narrow understanding of political reality, believing that if they followed orders everything would be fine. In short, they lacked crucial experience about how to save themselves from moral corruption. At the time, being young, naïve soldiers, they did not understand the broad ramifications of the many small steps they were required to take during the brutal training that was designed to make them feel that brutality was the norm. By the time they understood what was happening, like the "good" guards in Zimbardo's experiment, they felt powerless to stop what they were doing.

In a later chapter, we will consider how fundamentally important it is for all moral agents to begin life with a good, secure tribal heritage. However, as illustrated by the behavior of these young men, we need more than a good beginning. Thus, we will also explore the kind of virtues that tribal youths must develop if they are to transcend to a level that can prepare them for a more cosmopolitan existence that will not betray their local heritage.

Example: The Nazi Doctors

While the Greek soldiers were mostly naïve village boys (similar to Jones' high school students), what should we make of banality when it is found in the ranks of professionals? A different degree of dangerous banality occurs when idealistic professionals think noble intentions can justify anything they do. This form of banality is documented in Lifton's study of the Nazi doctors who participated in the Holocaust. Because he was so perplexed by the whole affair, Lifton chose to investigate how professionals in one of the proudest medical traditions in Europe could have conducted grisly experiments on human subjects. He traveled to Europe and interviewed some of the doctors who served in the death camps. His research led to conclusions that were compatible with what Arendt had to say about the banality of evil. He reports that many of the doctors felt that the horrible experiments on humans that took place in the concentration camps were serving a noble end. In the context of the eugenics movement fashionable in the 1930s, these "doctors came to see themselves as vast revolutionary biological therapists" (Lifton, 1986). The killing itself came to be projected as a medical operation. In short, the doctors viewed themselves as scientific idealists at the same time they presided over torturous killings.

Because these doctors seem more consciously evil than the people in our other examples of banality, I hesitate to call their behavior banal. However, aspects of their situation and character do seem to fit the description. As Lifton points out, the doctors used standard psychological forms of self-delusion to avoid confronting the immediate consequences of their actions. One technique was "psychic numbing," which results from talking compulsively about the kind of *quantitative data* that *is collected while taking detailed measurements to carefully gather technical information.* This narrow focus helped them avoid confronting the reality of the massive suffering they were causing at the local level (sometimes referred to as "collateral damage"). In fact, Adams and Balfour (1998) argue that much of the blame for many instances of twentieth-century evil can be laid at the feet of the kind of fetish for scientism that was displayed by the Nazi doctors in Lifton's study. The doctors' capacity for wise moral deliberation was corrupted by their glorification of **instrumental** or **technical rationality,** which is *"a way of thinking and living (a culture) that emphasizes the scientific-analytic mindset and the belief in technological progress"* (p. xx). Technical rationality is supposed to be a value-neutral approach to choosing the most efficient means to specific goals. A worthy utopian goal perhaps, but in reality it is absurd to strive for value neutrality in a moral context. Technical rationality leads one who desires objectivity to focus so much attention on selecting the most efficient means to a goal that no one stops to evaluate the morality of the goal being served (which, of course, is not a value-neutral stance).

Since suffering belongs in the category of **qualitative data** it involves sub-jective states of experience that include personal feelings, values, and the meanings we give to the world. To those who want to pretend that they can be computerlike in their objectivity, qualitative data seems to involve arbitrary subjective variables that they feel ought to be ignored. Indeed, Lifton reports that the doctors continually emphasized being "hard-headed" and "scientific." But from a moral point of view, when human subjects are involved, it is banal to adopt such a narrow perspective. That is, when the "object" being studied is actually a "subject"—a human being—the qualitative features of the research (such as suffering) *are* the most morally relevant data. In pursuit of information to support their vision of a grand ideal, the doctors ignored the most relevant of moral variables. In this context, it seems excessively banal to claim that one is dedicated to a moral ideal while showing such scant regard for selecting the appropriate moral means for pursuing the ideal.

Another way to characterize the behavior of some of the doctors, including Eichmann, is to associate it with Aquinas' notion of **affected ignorance.** As Moody-Adams (1997) defines it, this involves "choosing *not to know what one can and should know*" (p. 101). Examples of this phenomenon include things like intentionally remaining in the dark about certain agendas, so as not to have to deal with them. For instance, when a CEO or board member says "I didn't know what was going on," it is often because they didn't want to know. When a president allows subordinates to keep him in the dark for the sake of "plausible deniability," he's still to blame for choosing to be ignorant. Also, the use of euphemisms to describe actions is often a way of staying ignorant of the moral dimension of one's actions; for example, "we had to sacrifice the laboratory animals," rather than "we killed the animals in our research." Or, "there was some collateral damage," rather than "we had to kill some innocent civilians." Another obvious example is the way in which those who benefit from oppression manage to downplay and trivialize the suffering of the oppressed (p. 102), often to the degree that they wind up blaming the victims. I consider affected ignorance to be a fairly severe category of banality. It is a trite approach to moral life that is sometimes designed to mask one's responsibility for participating in criminal behavior.

The practical wisdom called for by applied ethics develops slowly. We all begin life inexperienced and thus prepared to be morally banal, until we learn the skills that can help us through crisis situations. Without the education they get from practical moral experience, people are vulnerable to either choosing inappropriate means for implementing their ideals or standing by in confusion while things they disapprove of take place under their noses. Like most other important complex activities, moral expertise requires practice. The point is to keep trying to do the right thing even though we know we may never be perfect. Each attempt to adjust to new situations should generate new insights that will make us more competent in the future. Thus, in a sense we need moral fire drills that are appropriate for the complex world in which we now live—fire drills that not only give practical insights but also will help us develop the confidence and courage to act when the time comes. Creating opportunities for fire drills is often the job of ethics officers. Otherwise, as Zimbardo pointed out in Chapter Two, we will remain vulnerable to the situational variables that can socialize us into doing the dirty work in institutions.

Administrative Evil Is Incompatible with Professionalism

> **For Study:** In what way does reducing reason to technical rationality interfere with our capacity for practical moral wisdom? Why is such an approach ultimately inconsistent with professionalism?

The reductionist technical approach to rationality that was adopted by the Nazi doctors was the hallmark of a movement called logical positivism that became dominant in the administrative theory that was developed during "the Progressive Era, the period from 1896 to 1920" (Adam and Balfour, 1998, p. 33). Theorists of that period claimed that social progress would be inevitable if we could only learn to apply technical skills to social problems as efficiently as we applied them to solving economic and engineering problems in the nineteenth century. This entire approach was based on the nonempirical theoretical assumption that objectivity required a quantitative focus and would be compromised if qualitative normative considerations entered into administrative decisions. Thus, several generations of social scientists were wedded to the highly problematic belief that facts and values could be logically separated to such a degree that all opinion and interpretation could be logically separated from scientific fact. For instance, a typical economics text argues that "the tools of economics—objectivity, simplification, modeling, and logic—if well learned will serve you for life (Walton and Wykoff, 1991, p. vii). Furthermore, objective economics can distinguish between opinions and analysis and remain "clear, objective, and balanced" (p. vii). The goal of the economics teacher is to teach "objectively" and remain "politically neutral" (p. viii). This ideology of objectivity is misleading since it implies values and interpretation corrupt reason, when in fact there is no rationality that is not a species of interpretation. We will explore this issue in Chapter Six.

Work in the philosophy of social science has thoroughly challenged this entire approach to objectivity. In fact, when thoroughly evaluated, this approach to objectivity begins to look irrational. Reductionist views of rationality encourage people to ignore kinds of data needed for rational considerations of social policy. As Adams and Balfour argue, the optimistic belief that objectivity was only a matter of clear logical analysis was a narrowly focused mindset that created an atmosphere emphasizing immediate short-run technical solutions to problems while ignoring long-range value analysis. The way administrators and professionals can ignore harm done to innocent people by staying focused on so-called objective, practical, short-term technical gains is truly banal. This style of thought leads to administrative evil because "reason reduced to rationality" (p. 141) of an instrumental, technological kind

> tends to drive the consideration of ethics out of the picture altogether, much less the rational calculation of how much good legitimately can be traded off against evil. Because administrative evil is masked, we typically do not see ethics in the situation at all, which means that we do not even see a choice about which we might calculate degrees of good. (p. xxiii).

This mindset facilitates the creation of various ***moral inversions,*** situations where "*. . . something evil has been redefined convincingly as good.* [An inversion makes it possible for ordinary people to] . . . easily engage in acts of administrative evil while believing that what they are doing is not only correct but, in fact, good" (Adams and Balfour, p. xx). To prove their point, the authors bring forth an array of historical cases (and examples from social psychology research) that show how easy it is for good people to drift into cooperating with morally dysfunctional institutions when they have not developed a broad moral radar that can help them see beyond the technical aspects of social, political, and economic situations. Excluding moral judgments from rational deliberations in this way seems very close to being a form of affected ignorance.

To their credit, Adams and Balfour are careful to point out that there is a difference between the banality of civil servants like Eichmann and the intellectual rationalizations of professionals like Albert Speer, who was Hitler's chief architect and minister of armaments. Speer claimed that his chief failure as a moral agent during the Holocaust could be traced back to his exceptional professionalism. He argued that as an architect, he was so dedicated to the values of his profession that he became oblivious to the extent of the damage in the wider world around him. Adams and Balfour use his protestations as an excuse to criticize the way professions have come to rely so heavily on technical rationality that ethical considerations get marginalized during professional deliberations.

I think Adams and Balfour are correct to condemn the way the narrow use of instrumental reason eliminates ethics from deliberations, but they should have done more to explicitly criticize the nonnormative interpretation of professionalism that can allow a man like Speer to claim with a straight face that he was "being too professional." According to the normative definition of professionalism outlined in Chapter Two, it's more accurate to say Speer's failure resulted from a lack of professionalism rather than too much professionalism. People who cannot see beyond the confines of their own job (or do not have autonomy to make discretionary calls) are not professionals. Such a myopic orientation fits better with technocracy than professionalism. While it is true that professionals have esoteric knowledge, specialized skills, and special privileges and duties, these traits are not the only marks of professionalism. Professionals also have a duty to integrate their special knowledge and skills into a proper social and moral framework.

As mentioned in Chapter Two, all professional codes of ethics begin with a preamble that acknowledges the profession's broad social responsibilities to further important social values in ways that benefit humanity. Professionals ask for, and are given, the privilege of exercising considerable autonomy or discretionary leeway in deciding how to carry out their profession's noble work. In exchange for monopoly control over the important social value being served, society holds all professions responsible for teaching their members to be sophisticated decision makers in all areas where the professional must interact with society (and humanity). This means that professionals must not only be theoretically and technically competent; they must be morally competent as well. To hide behind the mask of affected ignorance, technical scientism, or duties of station is banal given what we now know about moral failures on the part of otherwise good people. Professionals have chosen to be members of an organization that has promised to promote an important human value, and they have to balance their professional tasks with the many other obligations that fall on them as members of humanity. All moral agents are accountable to all the social organizations to which they belong, and this goes double for professionals like Speer and those who think of themselves as professional administrators.

The Virtue of Understanding

For Study: Why do we need to develop an abstract level of transcendent understanding before we will know how principles ought to function in the modern multicultural world?

The reactions to pluralism mentioned previously are obviously unsatisfactory, but are there more effective ways to deal with the moral confusion caused by pluralism? We are all going to have to develop the kind of broad background theoretical understanding that can provide some conceptual coherence to our experiential encounters with value diversity. This is what philosophers are striving for when they engage in metaethical discussions to clarify the modern context within which we make value judgments. However, because citizens in a liberal democracy designed for a multicultural world have to use abstract, complex concepts, there is a danger that moral principles will be distorted when conventional-thinking people try to apply them. For instance, Eichmann's use of Kantian philosophy to defend himself at his trial is disturbing. Eichmann focused exclusively on narrow concrete motives and ignored ideals, and the doctors focused exclusively on abstract ideals and ignored immediate concrete consequences, so both were excessively banal (and evil) from the moral point of view, and both deserve to be held morally accountable for their actions because that kind of banality is a moral fault. We assume that when adults are so careless, they are either not being conscientious moral agents (and thus can be blamed), or they have failed to develop reasonable skills for moral agency (and thus have been irresponsible). But it is still startling when we find that some members of professions can be so morally careless.

No matter how well intentioned, people cannot be trusted to make impartial and yet empathic decisions for others in a theoretical vacuum. When we fail to distinguish between levels of abstraction or notice that universal moral duties are logically different from the local duties attached to our legal stations, we can become so hopelessly muddled as to distort the application of ideal principles. Finding fault with the bureaucratic, narrow use of instrumental reason does not imply that people who use it are intentionally lying or attempting to deceive others. Instead, the moral drawbacks of this form of banality refer "more to a lack of care in considering the relevant facts, to an absence of sensitivity to the particular circumstances, and to an insufficient aptitude for choosing the appropriate course of action in view of the particular situation" (Gunther 1993, p. 4). Habermas (1991) argues that the inability to understand these important conceptual distinctions results in harmful "deficiencies" (p. 180) in moral thinking that can lead to the kind of oppression in the name of universal values that worries many of the critics of universal morality. (We will explore these deficiencies in Chapters Six and Seven). Obviously we will need a metatheory that can help all of us become more sophisticated in dealing with complex moral situations. Unfortunately, some of the early attempts to make metaethical sense of moral complexity simply added to the morality of muddle.

∼ Matters of Taste versus Moral Values

> **For Study:**   What is the difference between a matter of taste and a matter of ethics? Why is it a problem for a moral value to be arbitrary but not a problem if a matter of taste is arbitrary? Why are some moral theories cognitivist in their approach?

If we are going to avoid muddle and drift, we first have to develop a clear conception of the logical characteristics of moral values. In the first place, there are various types of values that can be introjected, and most of them are not moral values. When there seems to be no public justification for certain preferences, we say they are subjective and based on personal feelings. A very common type falls in the category of personal tastes. There may not be an objective reason for a taste—for example, either you like the taste of chocolate or you don't. Some of these are also private in that they only directly affect the person who has them. Thus, we will define *matters of taste* as *subjective values that are so private they do not pose a threat to other people; thus they only need to be judged from the point of view of the person who has them.* Where taste is concerned, we can simply agree to disagree; they are not inherently intersubjective. Can we resolve all value conflicts by assuming all values have the logical structure of subjective tastes?

Subjectivism: A Reductionist Metaethical Theory

For Study: Why are subjectivism and its derivative theory of emotivism inadequate metatheories?

In a pluralistic culture, when one person or group says that something is good or right and others say that it is bad or wrong, how should we resolve the dispute? Disagreements can concern the taste of chocolate, dress codes, drug use, sexual norms, or honesty in business. People develop different feelings about all these topics. What should we do about such diversity? According to *subjectivists*, there isn't much we can do because *all value statements are merely expressions of the internal feelings of some individual.* Since internal feelings are private, that makes all the value statements expressing them ultimately subjective or personal. From the subjectivists' point of view, there's no objective intersubjective context that can be used to argue for the validity of any values. Thus, there is no way to establish rational priorities between values—no way to say that someone is right and their opponent is wrong. Thus, we find subjectivists saying things like, "Hitler was right from his point of view, and his victim is right from her point of view." According to the subjectivist, no matter what you believe about anything, you are 100 percent correct from your subjective point of view.

A metatheory that says every choice about values is 100 percent correct because someone has a subjective point of view is not helpful. If the statement was at all useful, then we could just flip a coin to settle all value disputes, since any result is as good as any other when all options are 100 percent correct. Because subjectivism reduces all values to an arbitrary level, it is too simplistic to be of much help in making sense of a complex world. A *reductionist* approach to values *attempts to take sophisticated complex material and re-duce it to a type that can be described in simpler terms.* While it is important to describe things in the simplest terms possible, the simplicity must do justice to the complexity of the phenomenon being explained or it will be an invalid reduction.

Subjectivism's reductionism is faulty because it destroys the possibility for rational ethical disagreement. For instance, if my neighbor feels it is right to torture babies for the fun of it, and I feel it is wrong, does the fact that we both have subjective feelings about the issue have to imply that we are both 100 percent correct? Are we merely disagreeing about arbitrary personal preferences? We need to be careful here. If I really believe all values are merely subjective personal preferences (that is, personal feelings resulting from having values introjected into us), then there will be no objective basis from which to condemn the sadist for having a preference for torturing babies. Because simple subjectivism entails that there is no way that we can rationally argue about the moral status of the sadist's actions, the subjectivist sadist can smugly state, "Look, we just have different subjective feelings, that's all. So leave me alone." Unfortunately, this kind of moral muddle is not just a characteristic of some young people who have discovered that value diversity is confusing. It has also penetrated the thinking of some of the professionals in universities.

For Instance:

In 1966 I was asked by one of my logic professors what area of philosophy I intended to choose for a specialty. I told him that I was interested in applied ethics. He scoffed and said, "If you want to do ethics, then go to the English department." This advice was quite disconcerting. My B.A. was in English, and I had switched to philosophy precisely because I wanted to study the practical implications of normative ethics. I told him that a previous professor had said that normative ethics was a very abstract and theoretical attempt to find rational grounds to justify universal values like those that inspired the Declaration of Independence. While these kinds of universal values may seem self-evident on the theoretical level, other things being equal, it is not always self-evident how they ought to be applied in local circumstances, all things considered. Thus, it is impressive when we see someone like Socrates who has the theoretical capacity to understand universal moral values and the practical wisdom to conduct his concrete daily activities in a manner consistent with those ideals. Since I wanted to learn how to combine these two levels of wisdom in my own life, and since applied ethics investigates the best means for applying rationally based universal ideals to concrete local circumstances, it seemed that applied ethics was the right field to study.

My logic professor smiled both at my youthful idealism and my naiveté. He assured me that normative philosophy could not possibly be based on rational universal foundations. He said that once ethics is boiled down it amounts to no more than a series of subjective emotional preferences. Anyone interested in getting a teaching position in philosophy had better not advertise themselves as being interested in applied normative ethics. Universities are not going to be interested in hiring such people because professional schools are removing subjective ethics courses from their curriculums in favor of training in practical research, logical analysis, and the technical skills required for competent practice. [This was, of course, pre-Watergate advice.]

Emotivism

> **For Study:**   What does it mean to say that emotivism is a noncognitivist position? Why is it reductionist?

By studying the logical characteristics of my professor's version of subjectivism, we can get a better feel for why this reductionist approach to morality is mistaken. Looking back, it is clear that my professor was a strong advocate of a logical positivist metaethical position called *emotivism,* which is a version of subjectivism. He claimed that A. J. Ayer (1952) had "proven" that *all value statements are merely expressions of emotion, and therefore all moral claims could only have the logical status of emotional exclamations like "Hooray for our team!"* This "statement" merely expresses an emotion about a team; it does not express a claim that could be true or false. It is simply meaningless to ask about the truth of such an emotional utterance. Emotivists then go on to make the radical claim that *all* value statements have this same logical structure. Emotivists are called *noncognitivists* because of their belief that *ethical judgments lack the kind of cognitive content that can be proven to be true or false.* This means that all public arguments about the moral status of torture (or any other moral matter) are essentially only projections of private feelings about the topic. Since there is no cognitive public content that can support moral claims, arguments cannot be devices of reason used to prove an ethical claim to be true or false. It follows that ethical arguments can only play a role in morality as verbal devices used to sway emotions.

Given his point of view, it makes sense that my professor would recommend the English department as the place to study applied ethics. To him, applied ethics can amount to no more than learning how to tell dramatic stories that will cause other people to share the subjective feelings of the speaker. Since telling effective emotional stories is not the philosopher's task, he was telling me that I should not waste my time trying to convince others that moral claims are right or wrong. Because there are no background rational foundations that can support moral claims, philosophers can only use logical, analytical skills to investigate how value terms function when ordinary moral agents use them to express their own personal feelings. Of course, his emotivist theory implies that almost everyone who does take a stand on a moral issue is confused about what he or she is really doing, since most people think their ethical arguments have some cognitive content. The metaethical claim that the entire content of our moral judgments amounts to no more than an expression of our emotions has earned emotivism the facetious title of the "Boo-Hooray" theory of ethics.

My logic professor's emotivist theory seems reasonable when applied to concrete emotional utterances that amount to no more than a cheer for a team, but this theory seems less reasonable when applied to statements that assert moral claims. For instance, the theory reduces a complex moral claim like "Torturing babies is wrong" to the level of an emotional expression that simply says, "Boo for torturing babies." This is definitely not compatible with common-sense beliefs about how moral language functions. Most people want to say that because torturing babies really is wrong, the statement that asserts this fact is a true statement. To them, emotivism is a faulty reductionist approach because the simplicity of a cheer for a team does not do justice to the complexity of their moral claims. As Habermas (1991) says, "the 'ought' character (*Sollgeltung*) of norms and the claims to validity raised in norm-related (or regulative) speech acts [are] the phenomena a philosophical ethics must be able to explain" (p. 44). We do not explain the ought phenomena by reducing moral claims to something they are not—that is, speech acts functioning at the level of simplistic, private, emotional grunts.

So long as we focus only on tastes, subjectivism is not a confusing metatheory, but it is also not morally interesting. However, the fact that *some* values may only be judged subjectively does not prove that *all* values are subjective. Even if two values both originated as a result of introjection, they may still be logically different. For example, if a person had been "value programmed" to be a sadist, that introjected value should not be placed in the same category as his personal tastes. There is nothing private about such a preference. By definition, the practice of torture requires the unwilling participation of another person, so the value is, as a matter of logic, of concern to the public. Introjected values cannot be treated as matters of taste when they have serious public consequences because we cannot agree to disagree about sadistic practices in the same way that we can about tastes. So, the validity or cognitive status of a value judgment does not depend on its causal origins or the fact that it is found in an individual; it depends on whether or not there are independent reasons that would justify the judgment in public debates. The problem in ethics, then, is to find a way to distinguish between those values that are truly universal moral standards and those values based on taste that may be claiming the status of universal moral values even though they cannot satisfy the logical characteristics of a rational universal morality. What are those logical characteristics?

Logical Characteristics of Public Morality

> **For Study:**   Why is moral experience logically linked to social phenomena rather than to personal preferences? What are the four characteristics of morality? Why does subjectivism misdescribe the moral motives of people like Socrates? Why does the social dimension of morality require us to think of moral agents as people who are capable of argumentative discourse? Why is impartiality essential to morality?

As mentioned in Chapter One, ethical and moral claims are public statements needing intersubjective validation. This means, in the first place, that there must be a moral community to whom moral claims are addressed. The members of that community expect people to give reasons for making such claims, reasons that will make sense to the community. In the second place, people who make moral claims are generally prepared to offer rational arguments designed to prove their claims. This simple fact proves that tastes and moral values belong in different bags. Thus, I am not willing to agree that the sadist and I are both 100 percent correct about our separate judgments regarding sadism. I believe my moral condemnation of sadism has cognitive content that will make sense to other moral agents, including the sadist. Philosophers who advocate **cognitive moral theories** believe there are *universal standards that are supported by good reasons that will make logical sense to any rational being in any geographical location.*

Habermas (1991, pp. 46–50) draws on P. F. Strawson's (1974) attack on reductionist empirical approaches to metaethics to prove that there is a type of public moral content that is presupposed by the actions of real moral agents and which is ignored in subjectivist descriptions of morality. This public content is the basis for saying that there is cognitive content in moral claims that can provide a rational foundation for morality. There are four basic characteristics to this public content. First, moral agents feel a similar *moral indignation* when they're wronged during a violation of moral norms. Indignation is only appropriate if the wrong violates previously agreed upon public standards. Habermas (1998, pp. 3–7) points out that for any set of public standards to function as "a morality" in the social life of its community, there must be "a shared recognition that the norms have obligatory force for the members of the community." What does it mean to say that *moral oughts* have *a special obligatory force?* It means that to conceive of ourselves as members of the moral world, we must see ourselves as obligated to obey the prescriptions of that world regardless of our personal preferences. Membership in morality is not a matter of private choice; we don't get to choose whether or not moral duties apply to us. For example, "You ought to tell Jane the truth" is a moral statement meant to regulate your future conversations with Jane. It implies that you ought to tell her the truth whether or not you personally prefer telling the truth. In this sense, members of the moral community can rightly expect that people ought to give public ethical obligations priority over their own personal, private inclinations, and we feel moral indignation when a person violates that public expectation.

Second, the fact that *people can use excuses* to convert an apparent moral transgression into an action that does not violate moral norms shows that there has to be an excusable public dimension to an action before we can think of it as belonging to the category of the "moral." The logic of a moral claim requires that members of a moral system reject the idea that claims could be arbitrary. Moral judgments are public claims about what everyone in similar circumstances ought to do, and the public expects those who make moral judgments to have **good reasons** for their claims that *will make sense at the intersubjective level of public understanding (or as Smith says below, will be to the "good-liking" of others).* What kind of reasons do we have an obligation to provide? In the words of the Scottish communitarian, Adam Smith, we should remember that

> A moral being is an **accountable being.** An accountable being, as the word expresses, is a being that must give an account of its actions to some other, and that consequently must regulate them according to the good-liking of this other [emphasis added]. (Cited in Hope, 1984, p. 159.)

Since an excuse is given to another person as an account of behavior, obviously the excuse has to be to the "good-liking" of the other if it is to be accepted. This will help us decide if the reasons offered are good reasons. Before exploring the third and fourth characteristic, we'll explore this second characteristic of moral excuses in detail.

The Logic of Moral Excuses

Excuses repair apparent disruptions to the public's conception of the moral status quo. They help reestablish the integrity of the public sphere by placing an apparent harm in a different public context that makes the harm forgivable. There are at least two kinds of excuses that can be used to repair a disruption in the moral fabric of a social setting. First, consider the case of a slap in the face. If I slap your face, you will feel a sense of moral indignation unless I can give a good excuse that converts the action into one that does not violate agreed upon public standards of behavior. No one would accept "Excuse me. I felt a strong personal urge to slap you" as a moral excuse. This weak attempt at an excuse lacks intersubjective validity. An excuse has to have public content based on commonly agreed upon standards of what counts as a good reason, or the excuse will not work. So, I need to say something like this: "Oh no. You misunderstood. That was no ordinary slap." This excuse attempts to get others to see the action in a different light so that their initial moral indignation dissolves. Would you still feel moral indignation if I said, "You have to excuse me. I slapped you to wake you up so we could flee this burning building"? This excuse should work; in fact I would be very surprised if you did not accept it. Moral agents know how to give acceptable excuses when they are members of the same moral community because community members know what others will forgive and what they won't forgive. This simple fact shows that there is public cognitive content in moral interactions; they are not only based on personal feelings.

A second way that excuses work is by pointing out that the apparent violation of norms does not really belong to the category of moral actions at all. There cannot be a violation of the public's moral norms unless the actors in a situation are responsible members of the moral community. For instance, suppose you angrily report to me that your money was stolen while you were swimming in my pool. I may agree that your money has been taken, but I might disagree that someone stole it. If I say, "Yes, your money was taken, but it wasn't stolen. Unfortunately, the baby ate it," then I expect your initial moral condemnation to shift into something such as: "A baby! Oh, then there was really no theft at all, but I'm still irritated that my money is gone." An amoral person who is not capable of moral behavior cannot disrupt the integrity of a moral setting even if he can cause accidental personal harm. Harm by the incompetent is more like an accident of nature than a disruption to the moral relations that hold the community together.

Let's return now to the third and fourth characteristics that define the public content of morality. The third is that *moral emotions make sense only within the context of a community that shares in the intersubjective condemnation of some behavior.* This entails that there has to be a public or social dimension to human affairs that transcends the personal dimension. Violations of our moral integrity must involve an impersonal kind of indignation. The whole point is that morality has very little to do with private feelings and everything to do with a public expectation about background norms that determine what is right and wrong for everyone. In fact, moral emotions make no sense when looked at solely from the point of view of personal preferences. Why should I feel indignation just because I didn't get what I wanted? Why should anyone else care? Only if I feel I have a right to get what I want, and believe others will agree I have that right, do moral emotions start to make sense. In Habermas's (1991) terms, the moral is not personal; it involves the "suprapersonal, namely a generalized normative expectation that both parties hold" (p. 48). Intersubjective norms go above and beyond the personal and lead to the same kind of emotional feelings in all communities. That is, from the first person point of view, members of a moral community feel shame and guilt when they violate moral norms. From the perspective of the victim who has been violated by an immoral action, victims everywhere feel indignation, violation, or resentment. From the third person perspective (e.g., when a community member is not directly affected but is an interested moral observer), we find abhorrence, indignation, and contempt from those who witness the moral transgression.

The fourth characteristic of public morality focuses on the fact that moral claims would lose their moral force if they did not logically entail that a moral agent can give an impersonal defense of his or her moral claims. Moral claims have ***moral authority*** only if *all competent agents in the language community have reached an intersubjective agreement that the moral values in question should apply to everyone.* My claim that an action is wrong does not get its authoritative validity from the fact that *I personally* don't like what happened. Instead the claim has authority when I can show others that they too have good reasons to condemn the action. "This means that indignation and reproaches directed against the violation of a [moral] norm must in the last analysis be based on a cognitive foundation" (Habermas, 1991, p. 49) that can be used to prove the validity of the claim.

To summarize, the subjectivist is right to assert that some values treated as moral values don't seem to have any good reasons behind them, because sometimes personal preferences or tastes get treated as moral values. But he is wrong to assume that all of our moral claims have foundations that are as arbitrary as those of tastes. He would do better to challenge the logical credentials of the tastes that are masquerading as moral values, than to reduce truly valid moral values to the level of tastes. If he fails to protect the logic of moral claims, then he will convert the practical moral question, "What ought I to do?" into two other questions that do not mean the same thing, mainly: "What do I want to do?" and "How can I do it?" (Habermas, 1991, p. 49). This shift obliterates the intersubjective nature of moral claims. The essence of moral discourse is lost in this kind of reduction because the question is converted from an intersubjective inquiry about the normative moral expectations for my community, into a private question about how "I" should use instrumental reason to get what "I" want. (We will return to the reductionist nature of instrumental reason in Chapter Six.) When the subjectivist makes this move he ignores the fact that moral claims have meaning not only because we feel strongly about them but also because they make sense to others as well. To make sense to others there have to be public reasons for the claims that can convince everyone else to feel strongly as well.

It will be useful for later discussions if we take the time to explore why it is sometimes difficult to understand ethical claims made by those from a different social group. The web of moral feelings (made up of emotions like indignation, resentment, or gratitude) is logically linked with local social contexts without which the feelings have no intersubjective meaning. In other words, someone observing a moral interaction will not understand it unless the observer can adopt the intersubjective attitude of the moral agents being observed. For instance, playing off Sartre's famous World War II example, a teenage male may find a conversation between mothers—about the grief his mother feels at the prospect of his leaving home to join the army—to be fairly mysterious. He may inadvertently hurt his mother's feelings by acting over-joyed at the prospect of going off to defend his country. If his mother tries to talk him out of his choice, he may feel she is merely trying to restrict his free-dom, even though that consequence has nothing to do with her intentions. If her actions are being described by some other teenage male serving as an ex-ternal observer, then his external, third person description of her emotional state will probably distort what she is experiencing (because the observer lacks a procedural understanding of the context of motherhood). On the other hand, if someone who has never been raised to believe he has a duty to serve his country tries to describe the son's emotional state, then probably that descrip-tion will also distort what he is experiencing. To understand the web of emo-tions that make up the perspective of each of these people, we have to share, to a degree, the social context that they have each experienced.

This means that if the attitude needed for the MPofV is portrayed as that of an *impartial, nonparticipating, external observer,* then it will be an inappro-priate perspective for analyzing the nature of moral feelings. The analysis would have some of the same failings that we would expect to find if someone was analyzing the actions of moral saints from the personal, egocentric view-point of a child. An egocentric person has a difficult time grasping the logic of intersubjective contexts because people who are **egocentric *can only under-stand their own point of view*** (see Chapter Four). Thus, the egocentric are not properly positioned for understanding the moral motives of people like Socrates, Mother Teresa, or Abraham Lincoln.

Moral understanding presupposes an understanding of interpersonal re-lations that began to develop on the procedural level when we were being so-cialized to become members of a moral community. The reason that most so-cial scientists who study moral relations from the outside can understand the moral behavior of their research subjects is not because they have taken up a value neutral point of view as impartial external observers. They understand because they were themselves raised in moral settings and understand the na-ture of intersubjective moral content. Even when an anthropologist disagrees with the moral content she is studying, as Moody-Adams (1997) says, "there must be some moral common ground shared . . . in order for there even to be a genuine moral disagreement" (p. 119). The common ground may be a qualita-tive awareness of how intersubjective moral norms must function before they can play their role in the social life of the group being studied. Moody-Adams argues persuasively that cross-cultural understanding is possible only because cultures are not closed systems that cannot be accessed from the outside (p. 57). She exposes the many unempirical assumptions used by those who want to claim that cultures are incommensurable wholes, which cannot be compared with one another. (Especially interesting is her treatment of the dis-pute between Mead and Freeman regarding the culture of Samoa (p. 48ff), and her critique of the claim that there are cultures without morality. We will return to these issues when we discuss descriptive cultural relativism in Chapter Six.)

Whether or not we know how to interpret the social actions of people we are observing is not a matter of private choice. Our moral feelings and actions get their content from the public life-world that gives them intersubjective contextual meaning. We learn this kind of meaning procedurally, so we can understand others only if they have been in a similar intersubjective space as we have. Most people have some understanding in common since everyone belongs to a language community. There are of course, exceptional cases. Just as you would not ask Temple Grandin for advice about your romantic relationships (she says she does not understand such emotions, so the dating life-world is a mystery to her), you would not ask a sociopath or an egocentric child for moral advice about the nature of social life. People who lack the procedural understanding of the feelings behind morality literally cannot understand the social phenomenon of morality and will misdescribe it.

In a similar way, subjectivists are trying to describe intersubjective moral values from the outside using criteria for personal tastes that distort what they are trying to describe. This happened recently at the 1998 national meeting of the Association for Social Economics when a paper was presented that claimed all of Mother Teresa's actions could be characterized as attempts to maximize her own utility because she wanted to go to heaven (Kwilecki and Wilson, 1998). The fact that Mother Teresa said that she no longer acted only on that kind of motive was ignored or dismissed as an example of moral confusion. One might wonder who is confused, the external observer or the person who is living the life?

Most philosophers now understand the reductionist errors behind metaethical attempts to explain away the cognitive possibilities in morality. But, this entire attempt to reduce ethics to taste illustrates how confusing ethics in the modern world has become. If philosophers, who are in the daily business of trying to make sense of all of this, can become so muddled in their own thinking, then it makes sense that ordinary busy professionals might also experience a degree of muddle when they encounter the exceptionally complex value disagreements that are so characteristic of modern-day professional practice. As we have seen, failure to understand these complexities can have devastating consequences when it occurs in a social setting governed by an immoral ideology like Nazism.

Conclusion

In the modern context of pluralism, adequate understanding of the relationship between universal ideals and practical local information is difficult to achieve. In this chapter we have uncovered two basic reasons why so many people seem to be poorly prepared for moral life in pluralistic cultures: (1) People who are muddled or confused lack moral confidence. Thus, they are ready to turn over responsibility to authority figures, hoping that the authorities are not themselves muddled or evil moral agents. (2) People who lack moral confidence tend to focus narrowly on duties of station, the level of ethical consideration most closely related to their immediate situation. But, when people stay focused only on concrete commands, they are making themselves vulnerable to the banality of evil. In complex situations they may treat others in immoral ways without explicitly meaning to be immoral. While dedication to duty of station is an important virtue, other things being equal, it can also keep people from developing the broad understanding needed to judge the background moral context of their immediate situation.

This is a serious issue, but can we do anything about it? What if philosophers are in love with a moral point of view that is beyond the capacities of average civil servants and professionals? The complexity of modern, pluralistic life has led the developmental constructivist psychologist Kegan (1995) to assert that "our current cultural design requires of adults a qualitative transformation of mind every bit as fundamental as the transformation from magical thinking to concrete thinking required of a school-age child or the transformation from concrete to abstract thinking required of the adolescent" (p. 11). In other words, he claims that pluralistic cultures make demands on us that challenge the capacities of our minds to such a degree that to adapt will require an alteration in the "complexity of our consciousness" (p. 5). Without the alteration we will not be prepared for the demands placed on us by the moral point of view.

Clarifying and teaching the virtues needed for this shift in "consciousness" is, however, not an easy task. Because the contemporary postmetaphysical climate is so confusing, educational institutions increasingly retreat from that task by adopting curriculums that emphasize specialization and technological excellence. As a consequence, even professionals are not being prepared to understand the big picture. Although interdisciplinary work is often talked about, it is seldom realized. (For a good example of an exception to this rule, see Alvarez's (1998) account of how cooperation between scientists from ten different disciplines helped to solve the mystery of the mass extinction that included the end of the reign of dinosaurs.) Because "there is no place to look to consider what is being asked of the adult as a whole" (Kegan, p. 6), people are especially confused about how to proceed in addressing multicultural moral issues. Without a shared metaphysical foundation that can justify including everyone in our moral and political conversations, we can expect an increase in the various kinds of "isms" of exclusion that downgrade the moral status of those who are different. To avoid embracing these "isms," continuous moral education must be built into professional practice. Thus, we need an ethical foundation that embraces the sense of solidarity, commitment, and participation found in local communities, but also encourages the kind of thinking that can enable people to transcend themselves from within. We must learn to see beyond the boundaries of our own conventions to embrace the inalienable right of all people to control their own destinies. In Chapter Four we will explore psychological research that can help us understand what kind of developmental changes can contribute to this kind of personal transcendence.

REFERENCES

AMNESTY INTERNATIONAL (1977). Chapter 111: The soldiers. In *Torture in Greece: The first torturer's trial 1975.*

ADAMS, GUY B. & BALFOUR, DANNY L. (1998). *Unmasking administrative evil.* Thousand Oaks, CA: Sage.

ALVAREZ, WALTER. (1998). *T-Rex and the Crater of Doom.* Newport Beach, CA: Books on Tape. Text version. Princeton, NJ: Princeton University Press.

ARENDT, HANNAH. (1963). *Eichmann in Jerusalem: A report on the banality of evil.* New York: Penguin Books.

AYER, A. J. (1952). *Language truth and logic.* New York: Dover.

GUNTHER, KLAUS. (1993). *The sense of appropriateness: Application discourses in morality and law.* John Farrell (Trans.). Albany: State University of New York Press.

HABERMAS, JURGEN. (1991). *Moral consciousness and communicative action.* Christian Lenhardt & Shierry Weber Nicholsen (Trans.). Cambridge, MA: The MIT Press.

———. (1998). A genealogical analysis of the cognitive content of morality. In Ciaran Cronin & Pablo De Greiff (Eds.), *The inclusion of the other.* Cambridge, MA: The MIT Press.

HOPE, VINCENT. (1984). Smith's demigod. In V. Hope (Ed.), *Philosophers of the Scottish enlightenment* (pp. 159ff). Edinburgh, Scotland: University Press.

JONES, RON. (1976). You will do as directed. *Learning.* May/June. pp. 22–26.

KAUFMAN, WALTER A. (1973). *Without guilt and justice: From decidophobia to autonomy.* New York: P. H. Wyden.

KEGAN, ROBERT. (1994). *In over our heads: The mental demands of modern life.* Cambridge, MA: Harvard University Press.

KWILECKI, SUSAN & WILSON, LORETTA. (1998). Was Mother Teresa maximizing her utility?: An idiographic application of rational choice theory. Association for Social Economics Conference. January 3–5, 1998. Chicago.

LIFTON, ROBERT. (1986). *The Nazi doctors.* New York: Basic Books. All the quotations are taken from a review article on Lifton's research in *Time,* June 25, 1979.

MASSEY, MORRIS. (1976). What you are is where you were when. Farmington Hills, MI: Magnetic Video Library.

MILGRAM, STANLEY. (1963). Behavior study of obedience. *Journal of abnormal and social psychology* 67, 376ff.

———. (1974). *Obedience to authority.* New York: Harper & Row. As cited in Moti Nissani. (1990), A cognitive reinterpretation of Stanley Milgram's observation on obedience to authority. *American psychologist.* December. pp. 1384–85.

MOODY-ADAMS, M. MICHELE. (1997). *Fieldwork in familiar places.* Cambridge, MA: Harvard University Press.

NISSANI, MOTI. (1990). An experimental paradigm for the study of conceptual conservatism and change. *Psychological reports* 65: 19–24. As cited in Moti Nissani. (1990). A cognitive reinterpretation of Stanley Milgram's observation on obedience to authority. *American psychologist.* December. pp. 1384–85.

OATES, STEPHEN B. (1977). *With malice toward none: The life of Abraham Lincoln*. New York: Harper & Row.

SABINI, JOHN & SILVER, MAURY. (1982). *Moralities of everyday life*. Oxford: Oxford University Press.

STRAWSON, P. F. (1974). *Freedom and resentment*. London: Methuen Co.

TOFFLER, ALVIN. (1971). *Future shock*. New York: Bantam Books.

WALTIN, GARY M. & WYKOFF, FRANK C. (1991). *Understanding economics today*. Boston: Richard D. Irwin.

Chapter   Four

Descriptive Ethics: Cognitive & Moral Development

In the past sixty years, developmental psychologists have provided us with a wealth of information on the capacities, both emotional and cognitive, that people need to develop before they can participate fully in the adult world. While this kind of developmental research cannot settle philosophical puzzles, it can help us understand the motto "ought implies can," since the research teaches us about the kinds of capacities moral agents can develop under different conditions. A practical understanding of developmental material will be very useful once we reach the point of applying principles to construct concrete social policies. We will begin with a brief review of two leading theories of human development to get some insight into the variety of ways that people can fail to understand each other.

∼ Cognitive Development

> **For Study:** What is the major difference between concrete and formal operational abilities? Why is the latter necessary for understanding a theory or creating a hypothetical consideration?

If being able to adapt to pluralistic environments is necessary in modern society, then any change in consciousness that can help people avoid muddle, banality, and drift will indeed be an improvement. Since the last chapter ended with a reference to Kegan's concern that adapting to pluralistic environments may require a new change in consciousness that is beyond the abilities of average citizens, we should begin with a look at the some of the cognitive transformations Kegan (1994) was referring to. Is there any psychological evidence that people can develop the necessary skills?

According to the French psychologist Jean Piaget (1967, 1932, 1973), human intelligence develops through four sequential levels that improve our ability to solve problems. In order to move up to a higher level of thinking, we must first master the developmental prerequisites of earlier levels. Piaget argues that without developmental transitions we are more apt to experience the kind of unpleasant *disequilibrium* that comes from *being out of sync with our environment*. The attempt to avoid disequilibrium is the general psychological explanation offered by developmentalists as to why organisms are motivated to develop new skills by transcending their previous orientation. (To *transcend* means *to develop capacities that help one go above and beyond one's previous perspective*.) The changes are improvements insofar as they strengthen people's ability to develop a higher level of thinking that helps them remain in a state of equilibrium with their environment. The new skills are virtues because they help us avoid confusion and error when making judgments and provide us with the ability to solve more complex problems.

Figure 4.1 illustrates the sequence of levels or stages within which the developmental skills are normally mastered. The chart is a modification of one that Kohlberg and Mayer presented at a mid-1970s government sponsored conference on "Psychology and the Process of Schooling in the Next Decade." As mentioned in Chapter One of this book and as illustrated by Temple Grandin's developmental history, the earliest stages are crucial for developing the prelinguistic procedural knowledge that serves as a foundation for the development of all the later skills. The prelinguistic **sensory motor** stage is the first level of development. Children are amoral since the cognitive abilities needed for moral agency haven't yet developed. The next level is a *preoperational* stage where children can talk about their experiences but are still basically amoral. Because they lack causal and logical understanding, they assume that things just happen. This kind of magical thinking doesn't encourage them to figure out rational strategies for controlling their environment, thus, they don't

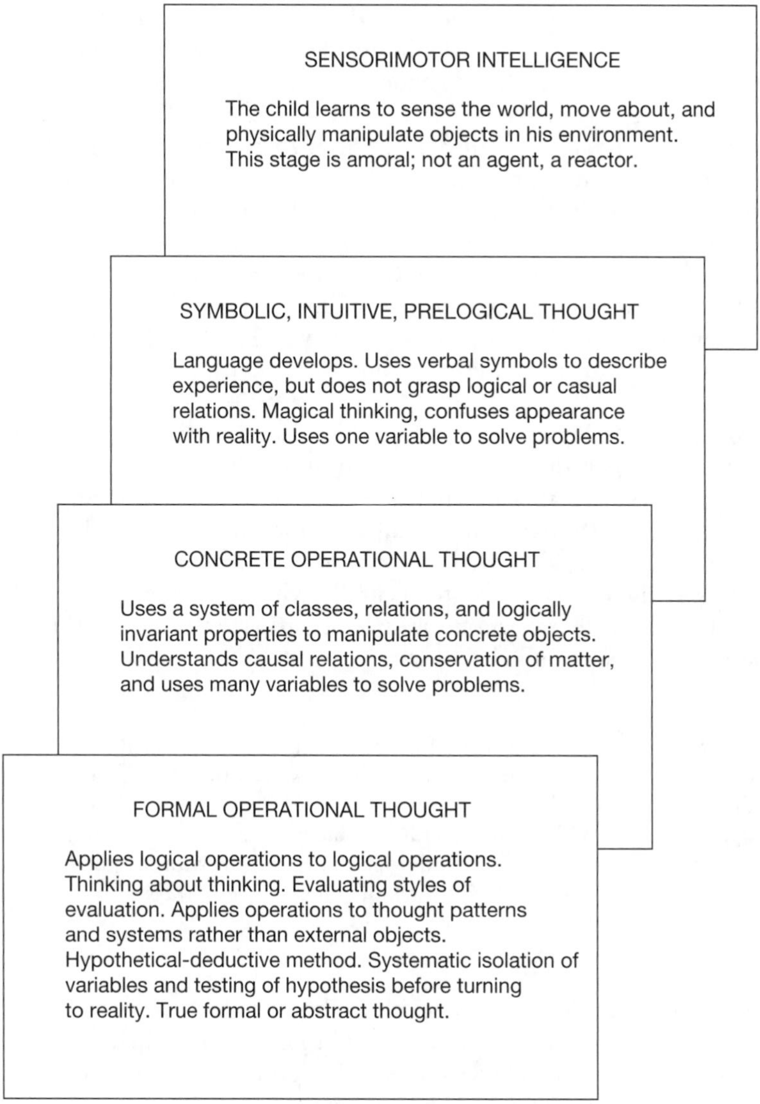

SENSORIMOTOR INTELLIGENCE

The child learns to sense the world, move about, and
physically manipulate objects in his environment.
This stage is amoral; not an agent, a reactor.

SYMBOLIC, INTUITIVE, PRELOGICAL THOUGHT

Language develops. Uses verbal symbols to describe
experience, but does not grasp logical or casual
relations. Magical thinking, confuses appearance
with reality. Uses one variable to solve problems.

CONCRETE OPERATIONAL THOUGHT

Uses a system of classes, relations, and logically
invariant properties to manipulate concrete objects.
Understands causal relations, conservation of matter,
and uses many variables to solve problems.

FORMAL OPERATIONAL THOUGHT

Applies logical operations to logical operations.
Thinking about thinking. Evaluating styles of
evaluation. Applies operations to thought patterns
and systems rather than external objects.
Hypothetical-deductive method. Systematic isolation of
variables and testing of hypothesis before turning
to reality. True formal or abstract thought.

Figure 4.1   Cognitive development.

bother to ask questions about strategies and their approach to problem solving
relies on one-shot thinking; that is, they guess or they simply obey commands
without engaging in much analysis. Since we're primarily interested in capacities for moral agency and philosophical reflection, we can skip over these early
stages and focus on the capacities that develop at the two later stages. These
two are especially important for understanding the intellectual side of moral
development.

The third level is the stage of *concrete operational thought.* Between seven and eleven years of age children develop increasingly sophisticated strategies for adapting to the demands of the concrete external world. The major intellectual advance at this level is the increased *ability to think logically in causal terms about standardized solutions to common concrete problems.* Because the new mental operations are only used to solve external problems, children are still not in a good position to develop much critical self-awareness about their own habitual use of these strategies. They tend to interpret statements in a fairly concrete way based on their experience of past events, showing little ability to conceive of new ways of doing things. Thus, when governed by this concrete mental orientation, people will have a difficult time understanding norms that are different from those advocated by their historical traditions.

A major shift begins to appear at about eleven years of age. During this time the *formal operational* capacities that *make it possible to think on a theoretical level* begin to appear. That is, while concrete operational thought is used to manipulate the external world, at the formal operational level thought *can be used to manipulate hypothetical possibilities and mental operations themselves.* This formal ability to mentally withdraw from the world for a time, so as to critically reflect on the style of our participation in it, is the root of creativity. As Richmond (1970) says,

> A formal operation is a mental action in which the statements themselves are combined to produce new statements. The result of this is a further release from the world, for the adolescent is now performing operations on the results of other operations. . . . With formal operations, the given environment can be treated as one of a number of possible conditions. . . . He begins with the possible and proceeds towards the real. Thus, formal operations reverse the relationship between the real and the possible. (p. 58)

At the concrete level the direction of thought was always outward away from the self. We simply used what we had to manipulate the external world. However, a crucial change takes place at the formal level. Formal operational thinking should be characterized as "thinking about thinking," "using logic on logic," or "evaluating evaluations." In short, formal thought brings with it the capacity to reverse directions and reflect on the process of reflection itself, so as to ask questions about hypothetical possibilities for thinking and evaluating that do not yet exist. This is the self-critical reflective capacity needed for the MPofV.

This ability to reverse directions and think about that which does not yet exist on the concrete level is the foundation on which all theoretical disciplines must rest (including science, which involves predicting the future, and ethics, which involves prescriptions about how the future ought to be). So, although concrete experience historically precedes formal thought in individual development, from the point of view of the logic of a theoretical discipline, the formal or hypothetical is prior to the concrete in terms of innovative thinking. As mentioned in Chapter One, the imagination can use formal operational abilities to metaphorically extend previous experience into new domains. Neither the scientific theory of relativity nor the ethical theory about inalienable rights could have been conceived of by a concrete operational thinker. In other words, formal thought gives us the capacity to think about hypothetical ideals before we experience them or know how to deal with them on a concrete historical level.

Some of Piaget's critics claim that he underestimates how soon children can begin to use formal operational thinking. They point out that he does not give enough credit to the effect that an educationally enriched environment can have on development. For instance, L. S. Vygotsky (1962, pp. 116–17) argues that Piaget only studied "child thought apart from the influence of instruction," and that this "excludes a very important source of change and bars the researcher from posing the question of the interaction of development and instruction peculiar to each age level." He argues that the development of thinking skills depends on environmental stimulation, so we should expect some variability in the time needed for their development. Enriched environments will speed up the developmental process, whereas deprived environments can slow it down and may even destroy it.

Vygotsky's point is supported by recent research (Hart and Risley, 1995) into family communication patterns at three different socioeconomic levels in America. They compared professional families, working-class families, and chronic welfare-assisted families. The goal was to generate data that would help explain why Head Start programs (designed to give at-risk children exposure to academic training prior to first grade) were not as successful as the program sponsors had originally hoped they would be. The study amounted to an in-depth description of the amount and style of talk between parents and children from these three different groups, focusing on children between one and three years of age. They wanted to know what kind of background verbal experiences children were bringing to their Head Start experience and what kind of verbal environment they would be returning to after the Head Start intervention. They discovered that there were fundamental differences between the families that would impact on the child's later ability to manipulate verbal symbols, a crucial academic skill. In short, when the families classified as professionals were compared with the families classified as being on chronic welfare, there was literally no overlap in the number of words spoken between adult and child or of the style of verbal interactions (i.e., positive encouragements versus negative discouragements).

This means that the least verbal professional parents still spoke more often to their children and used more positive affirmations that encouraged their children to respond, than did the most verbal of the chronic welfare-assisted families. By projecting their research over a four-year life span to cover the time period prior to entering kindergarten, they estimated that after four years children in professional families would have heard nearly 50 million words addressed to them (most of them encouragements), versus about 30 million for the average working-class child and 15 million for the children from welfare-assisted families (with many more words of discouragements). To overcome that gap and "keep an average welfare child's experience equal in amount to that of an average working-class child would require that the [welfare] child be in substitute care comparable to the average in a professional home for 40 hours per week from birth onward" (p. 252). No Head Start program can give children that much attention in a few hours per week.

On the other hand, in the sample from working-class families there was such wide variability in both the amount of talk and style of talk that the most verbal working-class family outscored most professional families and the least verbal working-class family was lower than most welfare-assisted families. This study shows that the amount and type of exposure to verbal symbols is immensely diverse and is an essential part of different cultural patterns. Thus, it is expecting a lot of a Head Start program to assume that a few hours of academic exposure a week can completely make up for fundamental differences in environmental stimulation. Head Start can help, but it is not a substitute for parental investment in teaching children to learn to use symbols. Vygotsky is undoubtedly right, then, that children from families who provide high verbal and logical stimulation will undoubtedly progress faster than some of those from Piaget's standardized research sample. However, these differences do not change the main point, namely, that prior to the development of formal operational abilities, we find very little evidence for the self-reflective and, thus, self-critical thought needed for the MPofV.

Blending the Concrete and the Abstract

> **For Study:** Why do we need formal operational skills to make sense of ideals? At what level of ethical deliberation is empirical research crucial?

As argued in previous chapters, in a complex pluralistic world we cannot have an adequate understanding of moral life if we do not also develop an understanding of the background theories used to justify our concrete ethical norms. Every concrete policy decision presupposes moral ideals, and an exclusive "concrete focus" on practical issues can deflect attention away from critical inquiry into the nature of these background ideals. For instance, some time ago in a letter to the nationally syndicated advice columnist, Ann Landers, someone pointed out that the Declaration of Independence states: "We hold these Truths to be self-evident, that all men are created equal. . . ." The writer then said that he did not believe this was true and asked Ann Landers for her opinion. She responded that she also did not believe it, because people have un-equal abilities and many people are born handicapped in many ways and need special help. As we shall see in the next chapter, Ann Lander's reply may have been an expression of what has been called the "women's voice" in ethics, with its special emphasis on caring for those who are not equals because they need our help.

While it was probably useful to point out that many people are in need of help because of physical disabilities, I was nonetheless surprised by her re-sponse to the writer's overly concrete interpretation of the background ideal of moral equality on which the Declaration of Independence was based. I as-sumed that she would take the opportunity to point out that the document addresses several different conceptual levels in morality. The Founding Fathers were not fools. They were all well aware of the day-to-day concrete inequali-ties among men, yet they ratified the Declaration of Independence with its claim that all men are created equal. Why? A theory about universal ideals was being used to explain to all of mankind why the complaints against the king of England were justified. Eighteenth-century liberal philosophy was antihierar-chical and the antiroyalist Jefferson (the primary author) believed that regard-less of their obvious material inequalities, all men were in fact moral equals who should be treated with dignity. Jefferson was not claiming that all men were equal in concrete physical terms; he was talking on a different conceptual level, one where reference to moral equality makes sense. Moral equality and inalienable rights provide the theoretical moral background against which we are supposed to "see" the concrete inequalities in the foreground. As long as we focus exclusively on the concrete or practical (the immediate foreground), we will continue to fall short in our attempts to reform institutions so that they properly implement the ideals that are derived from formal operational reflec-tion about how social, political, and economic relations ought to be structured.

I do not want the reader to think that I am asserting that concrete empir-ical data is not important in ethics. On the contrary, once we reverse directions in ethics and move from justifying ideals, *other things being equal,* to applying ideals to practice, *all things considered,* then the data generated by empirical research in the social sciences becomes crucial. The empirical nature of scien-tific methodology gives social sciences considerable practical authority, because it keeps the applied sciences focused on what works. When members of these disciplines become experts in the application of theoretical research, they often work as consultants to give concrete advice about how to achieve goals.

When questions are raised about fundamental values, however, empirical data and/or technological skills alone cannot answer the questions. As men-tioned in Chapter One, value judgments are prescriptive, not descriptive. They involve judgments about what *ought* to be the case, so they cannot be reduced to judgments about what *is* already the case. Thus, empirical research alone cannot validate ought claims. Moral norms can only be justified with rational arguments that are grounded in background normative theories. This means moral agents will need formal operational abilities before they will be able to engage in any extended abstract discussion of ideal possibilities.

∾ Moral Development

For Study: In what sense is Kohlberg's research focused primarily on the way people reason about morality rather than on how they behave in real situations? What is the difference between form and content in morality? What motivates people to change the form of their thinking about ethics?

Piaget's (1932) initial research on the development of moral thought has been elaborated on and extended by other developmentalists, most notably by the educational psychologist Lawrence Kohlberg. In a series of longitudinal cross-cultural studies, Kohlberg (1970s, 1971, 1973) identified three levels of moral development, which he divided into six sequential stages. His method was to interview the same research subjects at three-year intervals for over 30 years by having them write out solutions to moral dilemmas. Then, according to the type of reasons they offered to justify their solutions to the dilemmas, he categorized the subjects' reasoning into common stages. The following is a typical dilemma used in Kohlberg's (1971) research.

> In Europe, a woman was near death from a very bad disease, a special kind of cancer. There was one drug that the doctors thought might save her. It was a form of radium for which a druggist was charging ten times what the drug cost him to make. The sick woman's husband, Heinz, went to everyone he knew to borrow the money, but he could get together only about half of what it cost. He told the druggist that his wife was dying, and asked him to sell it cheaper or let him pay later. But the druggist said, "No, I discovered the drug and I'm going to make money from it." So Heinz got desperate and broke into the man's store to steal the drug for his wife. Should the husband have done that? Why or why not? (p. 156)

Both the *form and content* of answers to these questions can be different. For instance, people can agree that Heinz should not steal (same content) and yet give different types of reasons for their conclusion (different form). That is, one person might say, "Don't steal or else you might go to prison." The form of his reasoning is action guided by concern for self, that is, avoidance of personal pain. Another might say, "Don't steal because theft hurts people." The form of reasoning is action guided by concern for others. While the content in these answers is the same (both say don't steal), the form of the reasons given to justify their recommendation is so different that Kohlberg thinks the logic of the answer has shifted to a different type or level. What is important to Kohlberg is whether or not the form of reasoning is egocentric (focused on self), ethnocentric (focused on the group), or is governed by universal principles (focused on norms that transcend the contingencies of local circumstances).

Kohlberg believes that *different types or levels of thinking* represent different *forms* of argumentation, and those forms develop naturally during direct confrontations with real day-to-day ethical conflicts. That is, in order to avoid slipping into moral disequilibrium, people are forced to develop new forms of thinking when their old strategies can't solve new complex conflicts. But, there is a debate in the literature between learning theorists and cognitive developmentalists like Piaget and Kohlberg over the significance of the form and the content found in human development. Kohlberg claims that shifts in the *form* of thought cannot be taught as specific *content* by methods that emphasize simple habit formation through conditioning (the bag of virtues approach mentioned in the review of tribal ethics). On the other hand, Skinnerians advocate a learning theory model that places emphasis on learning the *content* of the concrete rules programmed into us during conditioning. Kohlberg agrees that we need such content to work with, but he claims that the level of one's thinking (the *form* of mental life) determines the type of content that can be learned as well as how it will be understood and used. While this is a fascinating debate, we cannot pursue the issue here. Obviously, both form and content are important, but at this point we are primarily interested in the types of reasoning that people show when they think about ethics. We can wait for psychological research to determine the exact details of how these skills develop.

It is important to remember that the subjects in Kohlberg's study are solving hypothetical dilemmas. Their answers reflect the highest ideals available to them when they are sitting at a desk deliberating calmly about how they think they ought to behave. So this research is designed to show that the way we *think* about what we ought to do can change over time, but it is not designed to explore how people behave under stress. Actual behavior in stressful situations might well be different, since factors such as fear, depression, and desire, which do not have their full impact on us when we are only *thinking* about dilemmas, are likely to affect our behavior in real-life situations.

Some research subjects did not change much and others changed considerably, but the changes in form always followed the same pattern. We should also keep in mind, however, that no one was ever wholly in one stage. Most subjects gave answers that had the characteristics of at least three different stages (which is to be expected since subjects are in developmental transition). Kohlberg (1970s pp. 8–15) placed a subject into a certain category only if at least 50 percent of his answers had the form characteristic of that stage.

Kohlberg's research is supported by an impressive array of longitudinal, cross-cultural, and experimental evidence in the social sciences. As the leading theory of moral development, his theory has been criticized by competing theorists (See *Ethics*, 1982). Critics claim that he focuses too much on justice, is culturally biased in his definitions, ignores the "feminine" themes of responsibility and care that are important to women, tends to devalue conventional morality, overestimates the role of reasoning in morality, lacks validity and reliability in his research methodology, and is vague in his characterization of the two highest stages. Some people go so far as to say that his moral-stage theory is useless and should be disregarded.

I think a few of these critics make some good points, but most are misguided. Kohlberg's work must be viewed in the wider context of the developmental constructivist tradition in psychology. The tradition has its critics, but it is hardly a dead theoretical approach. Furthermore, other researchers in the cognitive tradition have also observed subjects go through similar developmental changes (for instance, Gilligan, 1982; Kegan, 1994; and Loevinger, 1976). These researchers may quibble about the details and number of stages, but they are very much in agreement about the levels of development. The point is, somehow we have to make sense out of human development, and viewing growth in terms of sequential stages seems to help clarify a great deal of information, especially in educational settings. Although many of Kohlberg's critics raise interesting methodological problems that need to be addressed, they do not undercut the fundamental point of his empirical findings: People display different forms of reasoning, they appear in a sequential pattern, and later stages are transcendent developments that build on earlier ones.

However, because Kohlberg's original study began with 50 males between 10 and 15 years of age, we have to give special attention to the criticism that his research may have committed the standard man problem, making it less significant as a universal theory for all development. For instance, Carol Gilligan (1982) argues that both Piaget's and Kohlberg's research carries on a tradition in psychological research of focusing almost exclusively on studies of males. It is only in the last couple of decades that fascinating research studies on how women come to know about the world have received serious attention in academic circles (see Belenky et al., 1986). Thus, these critics claim that because women were not included in the research until after the structure of the stages was determined by the study of boys and men, the typical description of moral development in Kohlberg's research is sexually biased. That is, it emphasizes the content areas that are of primary interest to men—justice and individual rights, and downplays the content areas that are of interest to women—mainly relationships and care. This bias will lead to distortion when interpreting the answers that women give to the dilemmas. Since boys seem to focus on care for relationships primarily at stage three of level two, a Kohlberg researcher is apt to categorize a mature woman's form of thinking as being at stage three if she focuses on relational issues. Her reasoning about care and relationships, however, might be far more sophisticated than the young stage-three boy's reasoning about the same content. In order to add gender balance to the account of moral development, I will integrate material from Gilligan's research into Kohlberg's research during the following review of Kohlberg's conclusions. All references to Gilligan are from her 1982 book *In a Different Voice* unless otherwise indicated. In the next chapter we will consider the issue of gender differences in ethics in greater depth.

Level I, The Preconventional

For Study: What does it mean to say that Level I is egocentric in focus? What plays the role of moral authority at the preconventional level? Why do some people say Level I is not really a level of morality? What is one way to respond to this criticism?

Gilligan's research reveals that while women and men focus on different content (males on justice and rights, women on relationships and care), they nonetheless share the same common forms of intellectual development. After

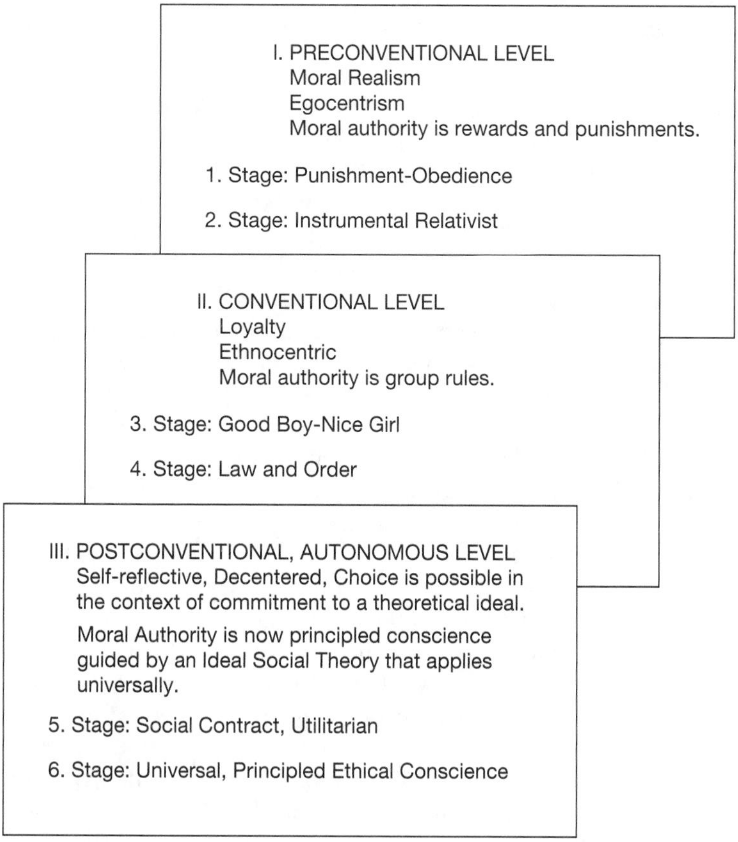

I. PRECONVENTIONAL LEVEL
Moral Realism
Egocentrism
Moral authority is rewards and punishments.

1. Stage: Punishment-Obedience

2. Stage: Instrumental Relativist

II. CONVENTIONAL LEVEL
Loyalty
Ethnocentric
Moral authority is group rules.

3. Stage: Good Boy-Nice Girl

4. Stage: Law and Order

III. POSTCONVENTIONAL, AUTONOMOUS LEVEL
Self-reflective, Decentered, Choice is possible in the context of commitment to a theoretical ideal.
Moral Authority is now principled conscience guided by an Ideal Social Theory that applies universally.

5. Stage: Social Contract, Utilitarian

6. Stage: Universal, Principled Ethical Conscience

Figure 4.2   Moral development.

an initial amoral stage of moral infancy, male and female children both must move through an initial egocentric orientation (Level I) called the **Preconventional Level.** At this level of moral awareness, the child's egocentrism leads to what Piaget (1932) calls *moral realism,* which is the *child's tendency to treat moral events as though they are independent of the intentions of people.* That is, children assess blame by focusing attention on the amount of real physical damage done to themselves, and they ignore what the other person intended. "Ought" statements and words like "good" and "right" are defined by references to personal desires for rewards and by deference to the powerful authority figures who make the rules that determine who gets rewards and punishments. For instance, Gilligan found that females who had this egocentric orientation focused primarily on personal concerns and survival.

> From this perspective, *should* is undifferentiated from *would,* and other people influence the decision only through their power to affect its consequences.... The self, which is the sole object of concern, is constrained by a lack of power that stems from feeling disconnected and thus, in effect, all alone (p. 75).

At Level I, then, what plays the role of *moral authority* in one's life is not moral conscience or commitment to social norms but *deference to whoever happens to control rewards and punishments.* As Napoleon reportedly said, "God (or right) is on the side of the army with the most legions." In a fairly straightforward way, then, subjects at this level do not display a fully developed "social" nature. This is compatible with Peters (1973) argument that "before one can choose a rule, one must first learn what it means to follow a rule" (p. 46). That is, people cannot develop into truly social beings until they take the first step, which is to develop a procedural understanding of what it means to follow the social rules that have been imposed on them. This is the initial task that must be mastered by egocentric children, and of course we must eventually transcend this orientation. If we all remained egocentric in our orientation toward rules, then society would resemble a gang of pirates rather than a community of committed moral agents.

There are two stages at Level I. The first stage is the **Punishment-Obedience orientation,** where research subjects say you should steal the drug to save Heinz's wife only if she has power (which shows deference to authoritative rules and power for its own sake). In the second stage, the **Instrumental Relativist orientation,** subjects say Heinz should save his wife only if she has instrumental value from his relativistic point of view. One thirteen-year-old said: "But the husband wouldn't want it [for the wife to die], it's not like an animal. If a pet dies you can get along without it—it isn't something you really need. Well, you can get a new wife, but it's not really the same." (Kohlberg, 1971, p. 168). At this second stage they also recognize that others have competing interests, so they begin to negotiate deals to get what they want. This helps them understand that rules not only are concrete commands of authority figures but can also be useful instruments for protecting self-interest.

Some critics claim that it is a mistake to refer to this first level and these first two stages as *moral* orientations, since they are so clearly concerned with personal agendas rather than the intersubjective moral point of view. The response to this critique is that because young people actually use the terms "right and wrong" and "good and bad" in these early years, then this style of usage must be included as one of the orientations that it is possible to adopt. In addition, since we also see some adults who occasionally display only this orientation, we cannot view it as exclusively an orientation of a premoral stage of childhood.

Obviously, a type of intersubjective ethical consciousness does develop in competent social agents, but why? Kegan's research can help us understand how it develops and why the preconventional child has trouble understanding morality prior to its development. Like Piaget and Kohlberg, Kegan claims his research proves that the transcendent move to intersubjective understanding is just a natural step in social development. Kegan's (1994) research begins with a focus on the principles of mental organization that evolve as people learn to give meaning to experience—including their thinking, feeling, and social-relating. He argues that to adapt to pluralism all people will have to move through five orders of consciousness that are related to shifts in what they are able to treat as the "subject" and the "object" of their epistemological relationships. In the **subject-object relationship,** "*'Object' refers to those elements of our knowing or organizing that we can reflect on,* handle, look at, be responsible for, relate to each other, take control of, internalize, assimilate, or otherwise operate upon. . . . *'Subject' refers to those elements of our knowing or organizing that we are identified with, tied to, fused with, or embedded in. We have object; we are subject*" (p. 7) (emphasis added).

In the very young child, the first principle of consciousness is called the **principle of independent elements.** This way of thinking leads to illogical egocentric judgments because the child is so attached to the moment that each impulse is viewed as an independently existing element in his world. However, as the parent helps the child create meaningful categories for its experiences, the child develops a higher second principle of consciousness. The independent impulse that is the subject of her early experiencing becomes an object of reflection in her more mature second-order experiences. In other words, she develops the **principle of durable category,** which gives her the ability to think of her impulses as being of a type. This means the child can categorize impulses as types with a name for later observation and reflection (i.e., I'm angry just like I was last week; I'm happy again; etc.). "Now the durable category (not impulse but ongoing preference or need; not appearance but concrete reality) becomes the new subject of her experiencing . . . She controls impulses; she reflects on appearance and distinguishes it from reality" (p. 29). Both the first and second principles are so preoperational and egocentric in focus, however, that they are not very interesting from the moral point of view. To become a social being, the child has to master the agenda that comes with adolescence or what Piaget refers to as concrete operational thinking.

Level II, The Conventional

For Study: Why does Adam Smith believe the "integrity" of citizens is a necessary prerequisite for having a functional community? What plays the role of moral authority at the conventional level? Why is the integrity that develops at this level crucial for the development of community?

This new level of moral development can be clarified by considering one of the chief virtues of tribal life, that is, the moral virtue of integrity. Smith (1982) says *integrity* refers to a person's *emotional commitment to legitimate ends or rules of conduct* (p. 162). Since this character trait develops during the normal socialization process in tribal settings, philosophers in traditional ancient societies assumed average citizens all possessed this kind of commitment. Thus, Plato's main reference to this character trait simply states that good ordinary citizens possess "self-control and integrity—which is acquired by habit and practice, without the help of philosophy and reason" (Plato, 1961, 82b). Although people who are alienated from their community might think that a motive like integrity needs special justification, people in traditional cultures assumed that every normal person would automatically have a deep-seated commitment to social norms. It will be instructive, then, to consider a philosopher from a traditional culture who is sometimes mistakenly treated as a radical libertarian individualist by those who ignore his historical context. As a good Scottish communitarian, the philosopher and economist Adam Smith accepted the "fact" that moral commitment was part of the natural order. *Communitarians* believe that *commitment to community has priority over individualism.* Since Smith believed true self-interest was logically connected to concern for community, he would be appalled at the behavior of some contemporary CEOs. He says (1982) that

> The regard for . . . general rules of conduct, is what is properly called a sense of duty, a principle of the greatest consequence in human life, and the only principle by which the bulk of mankind are capable of directing their actions. . . . If [a person] has been virtuously educated, . . . the motive of his actions may be no other than a reverence for the established rule of duty . . . (p. 162) Without this sacred regard to general rules, there is no man whose conduct can be much depended upon. It is this, which constitutes the most essential difference between a man of principle and honor and a worthless fellow. [For Smith, this sense of duty supports all our other duties.] . . . without this principle . . . what would become of the duties of justice, of truth, of chastity, of fidelity, which it is often so difficult

to observe, and which there may be so many strong motives to violate? But upon the tolerable observance of these duties, depends the very existence of human society, which would crumble into nothing if mankind were not generally impressed with a reverence for those important rules of conduct. (p. 163)

In Smith's philosophy, duties and virtues are not simply theoretical fictions. They are based on the intersubjective moral emotions that help determine the identity of every citizen. Learning the qualitative meaning of these emotions is not a matter of personal choice or academic lectures, it is a natural part of being nurtured and socialized in a stable family/tribal setting. In other words, just as we do not privately decide what language we first learn to speak, we do not decide to develop moral emotions—in normal social settings both develop on a procedural level during socialization because they serve the intersubjective needs of the community's members. Smith also argues that the ordinary reverence for general rules of conduct (Plato's reference to integrity), which we find in average citizens, presupposes that citizens will also have developed the virtue of *self-command* (Plato's reference to self-control). In Smith's system self-command is *the capacity adults have to restrain their selfish inclinations in order to do what is right or to allow their benevolent feelings to have priority.*

A very young child has no self-command, but, ... [In] the great school of self-command [the intersubjective playground], it studies to be more and more master of itself, and begins to exercise over its own feelings a discipline which the practice of the longest life is very seldom sufficient to bring to complete perfection. (p. 145)

According to traditional philosophers, then, a mature person not only obeys traffic laws because he doesn't want a ticket (the child's motive of fear), but also because he is committed to them on a procedural level as a member of the social group. To become a person capable of the traditional kind of integrity discussed by Plato, Socrates, and Smith, adolescents have to develop the ability to make the durable category of "my interests" move from subject to object, so that they can reflect on their interests with a new "subject" who is made up of the "relationships" between "their interests" and those of "others." This requires us to develop a third principle of consciousness that gives us the capacity for **cross-categorical meaning making.** This capacity will free us from having to rely on rigid boundaries predefined by closed durable categories of personal egocentric experience (Kegan, 1994, p. 359). This ability to create new broader categories made up of abstract properties from previous categories is crucial on two levels. First, to understand morality we must be able to construct social ideals. "'Ideals' always involve making imaginatively real the not yet-real and bringing the filled categories of 'current actuality' into relation with these unfilled categories of 'real possibilities'" (p. 362). Second, we need to be able to see ourselves as being members of relationships that transcend the self, or as Adam Smith would say, we need to become identified with the norms of the group and transcend our personal impulses. Thus, adolescents have to learn to give priority to the relationships that are the subject of their new social identity (Kegan, p. 41). This makes the intersubjective relationships that make up the conventional self the new subject of experience, and the elements of one's old personal interests the objects of experience. Now the person is capable of a level of introspective, self-critical reflection on those personal aspects of the self that can conflict with the relational self. Those who can judge their selfish interests in this way have a more complex social identity, which makes "their social-relating capable of loyalty and devotion to a community of people or ideas larger than the self" (p. 29).

The major triumph of this third order of the mind, then, is that it allows the group's or another's point of view to matter to us. The developmental constructivist believes that, in fact, we create our sense of being as a social self in the sphere that is made up of our own point of view and the point of view of the other: "The individual really becomes a part of society because society has really become part of the individual" (p. 126). As mentioned, this way of organizing experience is all that is needed to be a good member of a traditional society. "It is just this order of mind that indeed allows one to be socialized into a "discourse community" (p. 288), and thus understand the intersubjective nature of norms.

If caring for others or recognizing that their perspective counts are prerequisite capacities for full moral understanding, then the tribal heritage that imposes rules on us must also, in some sense, provide each of us with a sense of commitment to a *social* identity that can help us transcend our initial egocentric focus on personal desires. So, as family groups impose rules on young members, they must at the same time affirm in the young members a sense of unconditional worth as group members. In return, new members will then learn to care about the social rules and come to understand that others who belong to the group have the same unconditional standing as members. If these elementary lessons are not learned, then people may lack the procedural knowledge that they will need to build on if they are going to be able to transcend to a more abstract level of moral understanding.

People become full social beings only when their *identity is inherently linked to the values of group membership*. To move up to the conventional level, then, where one becomes a loyal member of a group, a major shift toward a more **ethnocentric** form of consciousness has to evolve. Obedience to social norms is no longer based only on awe of power (stage-one fear) and/or self-interest (stage-two manipulations) as it was at the preconventional level. From the ethnocentric point of view, *satisfying the expectations of peer groups and/or the community is perceived as valuable for its own sake, regardless of the immediate consequences to self.* To understand this change, think about the difference between a mercenary soldier who fights for pay and a patriotic soldier who fights out of love of country. People now focus on questions like: Was he loyal? Is he one of us? At this level, what plays the role of *moral authority* in one's life has shifted to *a general respect for the rules of your group*. Because people can empathize with the point of view of the group, for the first time true self-sacrifice becomes something one can choose. Gilligan's (1982) review of the research shows that this orientation becomes the dominant theme in the socialization of many young women.

> The woman at this point validates her claim to social membership through the adoption of social values. Consensual judgment about goodness becomes the overriding concern as survival is now seen to depend on acceptance by others. Here the conventional feminine voice emerges with great clarity, defining the self and proclaiming its worth on the basis of the ability to care for and protect others. (p. 79)

There are two stages at Level II. At the **Good Boy–Nice Girl** orientation (stage three), subjects may say that Heinz should steal the drug even if he might go to jail, because it is natural and right for a husband to be loyal to his family. Heinz shouldn't be blamed, because any nice person (a social being) would do the same. Or conversely, he should not steal the drug because "nice" people do not steal. There is, in short, heavy emphasis placed on "conformity to stereotypical images of majority behavior" [everyone is doing it] (Tapp and Kohlberg, 1977, p. 91). People in stage three can clearly differentiate between instrumental values based on needs of the self and social values that serve the needs of the group, and they begin to feel more loyalty to the group's needs. At previous levels these two types of values are not clearly differentiated.

In complex societies people often belong to a number of groups that can be in conflict. Thus, to establish priorities in their life, at the **Law and Order Orientation** (stage four) people begin to give their legal community the highest moral priority. Other groups to which they may belong become morally subservient to the larger society as it is expressed in *positive law* (that is, *law that is passed by a recognized legislative body*). People have learned to differentiate between acts based on having nice social motives (peer groups) and acts based on civic or legal duty. So people may say that Heinz should not steal because stealing violates the community's laws. If they say that he should steal the drug, they will refer to a legal obligation for which he is responsible—for example, the husband's legal duty is to protect his wife.

Level III, The Postconventional

> **For Study:**   How is independence at Level I, stage two different from independence at Level III? What plays the role of moral authority at the postconventional level? How does each level illustrate the process of decentering? What is the difference between positive and negative rights and supererogatory actions?

Finally, under conditions of pluralism and after one has mastered the conventional skills that are prerequisites for becoming a member of a community, it is possible to develop a third orientation of *postconventional consciousness* that *allows people to transcend beyond the ethnocentric level*. People begin to display a capacity to critically reflect on and improve the social norms that had previously shaped their social identity. This is the level where people achieve full moral agency as autonomous choosers. They finally have the capacity to critically judge (and thus to affirm or reject from a moral point of view) the rules that have been governing them. Kegan (1994) says the problem with the third-order cross-categorical consciousness that regulates thinking at the conventional level is that it is both capable of, and subject to, socialization, but is not "able to reflect critically on that into which it is being socialized. [Thus,] It is responsive to socialization [but] not responsible for it" (p. 288). So, the third order lacks the internal virtues needed to subject its own inferences to systematic self-criticism (p. 286). This makes the third order of consciousness inadequate for dealing with social life in places that have evolved a pluralistic mode of existence, because pluralistic cultures do not enclose us in a warm tribal embrace, instead they bat us back and forth between competing ideologies (p. 105).

When claims about truth or morality have to reach across cultural boundaries, then people will be forced to accommodate the added intersubjective cultural complexity by shifting to yet another, higher level of consciousness. Kegan (1994) argues that a fourth order attempt to find a universal solution to cross-cultural conflicts is the trademark of eighteenth-century philosophy. The fourth order's **systemic way of knowing** is guided by its own vision (p. 173), in the sense that it is a critically self-reflective theory about relationships. Pluralism causes new kinds of social conflicts that give rise to the need for a philosophy based on the vision of a self-legislating autonomous citizen who can become aware of the standard person problem and take steps to avoid it. He has the capacity to be critical of his own heritage even while he embraces it. This requires a theory or a philosophy. Our loyalty is transformed from obedience to what our community has deemed to be of value to the process of critical self-reflection that creates what is of value (p. 169). Kegan's work explains the conceptual change that Adam Smith (1982, p. 147) struggled to clarify in the six revisions of his book on the moral sentiments. It is at this fourth level, that Smith's notion of an actual, moral spectator takes over in a person's mind and evolves into a self-critical, rational, principled moral conscience (see the discussion of Smith in Chapter Five).

Kegan (1994) says that the new expectation upon us "is to develop the capacity to organize our knowing in a way that can originate value" (p. 191). Thus, at the fourth order we try to do what is right by exercising our capacity for critical self-evaluation as though we are a social system that is self-governing (p. 122). However, as Kegan says, "at any given moment, around one-half to two-thirds of the adult population appear not to have fully reached this fourth order of consciousness" (p. 191). No wonder then that so many lack Socrates' ability to remain committed to moral principle in the face of concrete institutional pressures. Most people are still trying to transcend to a universal philosophy that can deal with the confusing pluralism that has challenged the status quo of their community. Kegan concludes that, "insofar as we can come to any preliminary conclusions [from our research, it] is that the experience of being in over one's head as an adult—even a relatively privileged, well-educated, middle-class adult—in contemporary culture is a widespread phenomenon" (p. 190). This, of course, leads to the morality of muddle that was discussed in Chapter Three.

This fourth order of consciousness ushers in what Kohlberg calls the **Postconventional, Autonomous, Principled Level** of moral development. At this third level, *abstract theory begins to play a dominant role in one's interpretation of moral experience.* There is a movement away from the unreflective concern with maintaining the status quo for its own sake in favor of giving one's allegiance to abstract principles that have validity and application apart from the contingent authority of established groups. When we say people choose their own principles, however, the emphasis should be placed on the logic behind having commitment to a universal social principle, not on the idea of simply being committed to one's own personal agenda. This level at which true social criticism becomes possible should not be confused with the preconventional person's egocentric tendency to complain about the norms he sees as external constraints on his personal desires. Since the preconventional person has not experienced the conventional orientation, he lacks qualitative understanding of social relations and thus the point of having commitment to valid intersubjective principles. That is, his egocentric emotional ignorance amounts to a psychological incapacity that deprives him of the ability (and thus the freedom) to truly choose moral rules that have the proper intersubjective focus. In contrast, postconventional freedom combines a new rational theoretical understanding about new possibilities with regard to universal values with the previous level's conventional capacity to care about and be loyal to social norms. Together these two developments give people a new capacity for impartiality that allows them to simultaneously critically judge (both the rational and social emotional quality of values) and yet experience a feeling of loyalty to what is being judged.

An element of impartial concern for doing what is right has entered into one's orientation, thus this is the orientation of greatest interest to philosophers. Since Piaget's formal operational thinking abilities are fully developed, the question "What is it that I ought to do?" is now seen as referring to an ideal state of affairs that goes beyond personal and group preference. People recognize that moral claims must be impartially justified in a universal court of appeal, so the **moral authority** in one's life has become *the guiding ideal principles of an abstract theory that prescribes how we all ought to ideally treat each other.* (In anticipation of a debate yet to come, I would like the reader to notice that this is a rational self with emotional commitments, not merely a rational self that maintains a stance of logical or analytic value neutrality.)

I think this ability to care about abstract principles results from the developmental process called *decentering*. Normal developmental decentering *moves us from egocentric children's capacity to care about those who provide for them, through ethnocentric caring about the family or tribe, to a universal perspective where we care about the abstract ideals of humanity in a manner similar to our concern about the norms of the tribe.* In this sense, moral development is about transcending human limitations (imposed first by self-interest and then by tribal needs) by universalizing that which is found in self-interest and in family or tribal life—mainly, the ability to care for self, for others, and also for the social norms that make a community possible. It is the transcendence of narrow ego and ethnic concerns that makes philosophical ethics inspiring. However, there will always be tension between the personal desire to favor one's self or one's tribe and the impersonal concern to do the right thing. For the MPofV to work in each of us there will have to be "transformations in the motives of ordinary people" (Nagel, 1991, p. 1083). People will have to become postconventional in their orientation.

Since the phenomenon of decentering suggests that the emphasis on priorities shifts from the personal to the impersonal as we pass through the stages of development, the goal of a moral society should be to encourage people to develop the ability to care (which is initially learned on the family level) and then to universalize this ability so as to care for everyone. But we must remember that ethical sensitivity goes both ways. While moral saints do not reject their family heritage (they universalize it to include all of humanity), they also do not lose sight of concrete commitments to individuals. In other words, one ought to care deeply about decentered background ideal principles but should not lose sight of what these principles mean for concrete human relations at the local level. It seems to me that this was one of Albert Speer's greatest failings (Hitler's munitions minister, see Chapter Three), when he claimed he was so dedicated to the principles of his profession that he failed to pay enough attention to concrete consequences for real people.

Level III also has two stages. First, there is the **Social Contract, Legalistic Orientation with Utilitarian Overtones** (stage five). We begin to see an emphasis on changing laws to promote theoretical notions of social utility or constitutional rights. Thus, Heinz should steal the drug if that will promote the greatest amount of happiness for all concerned. Alternatively, Heinz should not steal the drug because the social contract, which benefits everyone, cannot allow individuals to set aside laws for their own purposes. At this stage people have realized that personal opinion and local laws are often arbitrary, so they emphasize procedural rules of justice to help achieve impersonal consensus. Interests are characterized as naturally conflicting, so the conflicts need to be resolved in accordance with some notion of a just contract designed to promote the common good. This implies that obligations have a contractual nature based on social consensus about human happiness.

At this level there is a tendency to conceive of obligations as *negative duties* that tell us to *avoid doing things that are harmful*. That is, we are negatively constrained with the phrase "Thou shalt not do x." As long as we don't do anything that violates the social contract or another person's natural rights, we have no other specific duties to others (i.e., no duty to take positive steps to help them). There is, of course, a general obligation of charity, but this positive contribution to the general welfare is classified as an exceptional virtue, that is, as a *supererogatory act,* which means *to go above and beyond the call of duty.* This means that a stage five thinker might believe it makes sense to say that a person has a right to life (so we have a negative duty to refrain from killing them) but that no one has a *positive duty to do something to help a person satisfy this right, for example, help them stay alive* (Kohlberg, 1973, p. 638). So, if you choose to save someone's life without being obligated by contract, then you are acting in a supererogatory fashion. Kohlberg says that stage five does not have a complete integration of rights and duties because to save a life is charity rather than a duty (I am not my brother's keeper).

In the **Universal Principled Ethical orientation** (stage six), decisions are based on principled conscience in accordance with ethical principles that are meant to be universal and consistent at all levels. Rights and duties are completely integrated, because, if it makes sense to say that someone has a right to life (a legitimate moral claim), then everyone in a position to help has a duty to render assistance. This kind of general duty of conscience to take positive steps to promote all rights (not simply negatively refrain from violating them) gives us more duties and thus fewer opportunities for supererogatory actions. To go above and beyond the call of duty, a stage six thinker would have to do something that was fairly extraordinary, like giving up his own right to something to help someone else who does not have a greater right. For example, if I choose to give you my turn on the kidney dialysis machine, or I jump on top of a live grenade to save others, only then am I being benevolent in the supererogatory sense of going above and beyond the call of duty. At stage six, then, there is a general duty to give assistance to those in need when anyone is in a position to do so. None of Kohlberg's research subjects reached this level. He constructed it on the basis of the writings of morally admirable people (Mother Teresa, Martin Luther King, Jr.) and philosophers like Kant and Rawls. Is there evidence that this kind of cosmopolitan moral perspective will become more widespread during the twenty-first century?

In the first place, cultures have to be careful to nurture such attitudes during the process of political will formation. As Habermas (1994, p. 47) says, the "political self-consciousness of a nation" is a fragile thing, vulnerable to the forces of history that threaten to drive us back into ethnocentric hatreds. Once it's ruined, it's "ruined for good" (p. 47). On the other hand, I think Kegan's (1994) research indicates that under normal conditions the direction of the evolution of human consciousness is toward expanded positive duties. Barring war or global catastrophe, it is natural to decenter and include greater numbers of people under the moral umbrella. But, even so, Kegan says the level of consciousness needed to truly understand the subtleties of abstract eighteenth-century philosophy are not yet widely available to the twenty-first–century citizens. Thus, those postmodern philosophers who strive to meet the challenge of diversity by insisting that adults should transcend the search for universal morality appear to be pushing for an agenda that will cause even more confusion. (We will cover postmodern philosophy in Chapter Six. For now, it is enough to know that *postmodernism* refers to a *metaethical position that encompasses a variety of post-Enlightenment theories all of which reject the concept of universal foundations for human knowledge and ethics, emphasize contextual interpretation and the deconstruction of universal concepts, and downplay the Enlightenment goal of finding universal norms.*) As Kegan says, "what we call 'postmodernism' is not just a different way of thinking, it is identifiable on the continuum of the evolution of consciousness; what postmodernism is "post" to is the [eighteen-century philosopher's] fourth order of consciousness." [However,] "if a great many of us are working with dignity and difficulty at the gradual transformation from the third to the fourth order, how can we be expected to appreciate or understand a critique of the limits of modernism?" (p. 317). Although many are still using third-order modes of thought, the facts of human evolution are clear. "For the first time in human history, three mentalities exist side by side in the adult population . . . the traditional, the modern, and the postmodern. . . . [thus] nearly all of us, are in over our heads" (p. 385). However, even without complete understanding we have no choice but to adapt to multiculturalism and the twenty-first century thrust toward globalization. This necessity explains why there is an advantage to the postmodern fifth order of consciousness. It promotes a type of learning which encourages the

> willingness and ability of each party to understand and respect the position of the other. . . . [it leads to] new thinking about the possibility of developing solutions that preserve the most precious features of each other's positions. In situations of protracted conflict, especially in the international arena, such changes could be of historic and life-saving proportion. (p. 317).

It is not easy to transcend to this kind of consciousness. When postmodern critics of modernist universal theories label social arrangements as "privileging," "valorizing," "hierarchizing," "advantaging," "normatizing," or "generalizing" to indicate that others are the captives of a particular, repudiated ideology, the critics are showing that they themselves have not yet transcended to the fifth order, because "a language that was created originally to proclaim the withering of the authority of absolutism is being used to advance contending brands of absolutism" (Kegan, 1994, p. 337). When philosophers themselves can't seem to get it right, the skeptic has good grounds for claiming that it is not realistic to expect the massive shift in the consciousness of the population that will be needed for most people to grasp the significance of this level of philosophy. The MPofV, however, does not have to wait for postmodern philosophers to get it right. The insights from the MPofV can be utilized at the application level to help avoid the oppression in the name of universals that worry postmodern critics. We will return to this issue in Chapters Seven and Ten.

Using the Developmental Model to Interpret Events

> **For Study:**   Why should differences in the patterns of thought at various levels of schooling be considered support for the developmental approach to morality? Why does Kohlberg believe that the way one thinks influences how one behaves in situations like My Lai?

Because these shifts in style of thought show up continually in studies of the general population, it should be a useful model for making sense of some of the value diversity in the world. For instance, the model can be used to explain the way people are socialized to think about the law at various educational levels. Levine and Tapp (1977) asked the following kinds of questions of hundreds of students in primary grades, middle school, and college, as well as of teachers, law students, and inmates in prison: "What would happen if there were no rules?" "Are there times when it might be right to break a rule?" "Why should people follow rules?" "Why do you follow rules?"

If developmental studies accurately describe the cognitive transitions in real life, we should see these transitions mirrored in the answers people give to these questions at the various levels of schooling. We would expect more preconventional responses from the primary school children but expect middle school students and high school students to conceive of laws in a conventional manner—that is, as a necessary means for creating social expectations and a sense of identity. And among college and law school students, we would hope to see the emergence of a postconventional understanding of law. At least some college students would indicate that obedience to the overall system of law is based on its contribution to the good of humanity (human welfare and justice rather than a need to conform for its own sake). What Levine and Tapp found in their studies fits these expectations:

> The adult data were strikingly consistent with developmental patterns. [Mainly, that most people do not develop beyond a conventional attitude toward social rules.] Most youth by preadolescence emphasized a conventional, system-maintenance view of rule guidelines that matched adult modes of thought. Across these samples, no one, regardless of age or situation, inferred that rules are needed to protect rights, establish legitimate claims, or guarantee freedoms—reasoning that would have demonstrated aspects of an ethical legality (p. 169).

To the question "What would happen if there were no rules?" none of the primary and middle school students showed postconventional answers, and most of the subjects gave conventional, system-maintenance answers. While 88 percent of the graduating law students, 90 percent of the teachers, and 56 percent of the prisoners could not even imagine social order without external rules and/or assumed anarchy would result, nonetheless 8 percent of the college students and 16 percent of the prisoners did begin to show signs of postconventional thought (p. 169). (No explanation was given as to why prisoners were more sophisticated than college students. Perhaps it was due to the fact that prison populations are older and perhaps have had more conflicts to resolve.)

To the question, "Why do you follow rules?" 60 percent of primary school students gave answers that indicated they wanted to avoid negative consequences, and none of them mentioned social conformity or postconventional considerations. On the other hand, while 25 percent of college students still said they obeyed to avoid negative consequences, 33 percent now indicated that they obeyed laws for some postconventional principled reasons, and 46 percent of teachers mentioned postconventional concerns. The data suggests that there is, indeed, a movement away from preconventional personal considerations and toward postconventional principled understanding of rules. While most adults remain in the conventional, system-maintenance mode, a sizable number of adults begin to express postconventional concerns about theoretical ideals as their reason for following rules.

Kohlberg's major theoretical contention is that a person's cognitive structure will influence his moral behavior in real-life situations. We should expect, then, to see some correlations between observable behavior and styles of thought when people are forced by circumstances to make moral choices or confront moral dilemmas. Thus, the developmental model should also be able to shed light on some aspects of real moral tragedies. In this light, Kohlberg and Scharf (1972) analyzed instances of mass violence and reached conclusions strikingly similar to Hannah Arendt's theory about the banality of evil. They focused most attention on the My Lai tragedy, where American soldiers rounded up the inhabitants of a Vietnamese village and then massacred the captives—primarily babies, women, and old men. In their analysis of the massacre, Kohlberg and Scharf focused on the reasoning styles of three principal characters who were at the scene of the massacre: Paul Meadlow, a private who admitted he was involved in the massacre of civilians; Lieutenant William Calley, the officer who was subsequently court-martialed by the army for ordering Meadlow and others to fire on the civilians; and private Michael Bernhardt, who refused to obey the orders to shoot at Vietnamese civilians. According to Kohlberg and Scharf, Meadlow appeared to function primarily at the preconventional level: You obey orders not because you respect them, but to avoid getting into trouble.

During basic training if you disobeyed an order, if you were slow in obeying orders, they'd slap you on the head, drop-kick you in the chest and rinky-dink stuff like that. If an officer tells you to stand on your head in the middle of the highway, you do it.

Why did I do it. . . . We was supposed to get satisfaction from this village for the men we lost. They was all VC and VC sympathizers. I felt, at the time, I was doing the right thing because, like I said, I lost buddies. I lost a damn good buddy, Bobby Wilson.

Nowhere in Meadlow's interview does he refer to principles of human welfare. We do consistently see references to his own personal concerns, his desire for satisfaction, and his interest in not getting in trouble. To him doing the right thing means "I acted on these personal motives." The fact that he grieves for lost buddies shows he is not a sociopath, but only an egocentric person would think that his personal grief justifies killing babies to get "satisfaction." Meadlow seems excessively banal, which is one of the marks of the simplistic preconventional level of thinking. Lieutenant Calley, on the other hand, is much more conventional in his orientation. He is concerned about being a good officer, a regular fellow who will be accepted into the system. He also had a tendency to defer responsibility to those higher up in the system.

I was a run-of-the-mill average guy. I still am. I always said the people in Washington are smarter than me. If intelligent people say Communism is bad, it's going to engulf us [sic]. I was only a Second Lieutenant. I had to obey and hope that the people in Washington were smarter than me.

Calley shows little comprehension that an order needs to be evaluated by higher criteria or that the military code does allow for this option (it forbids soldiers to obey illegitimate orders). Like most conventional thinkers, he does not look beyond the norms of his immediate social position. If legitimate authorities give an order, a good soldier carries it out, even if it might lead to the death of innocent people. What seems to be the most relevant moral consideration in Calley's conceptual framework is the fact that there was an order or a concrete rule, not the consequences for people who are not part of the social group, and not the order's compliance with abstract principles. He said his intention was simply to go in and destroy the enemy.

Q. Were you motivated by any other fact besides that they were the enemy?

A. Well, I was ordered to go in there and destroy the enemy. That was my job on that day. That was my mission I was given. I did not sit down and think in terms of men, women and children. They were all classified the same and that was the classification we dealt with them, enemy soldiers . . . I felt, and still do, that I acted as I was directed . . . and I do not feel wrong in doing so.

Calley's apparent lack of insight into the moral dimensions of what he did might just be an element of his trial strategy, but I doubt it. His remark is completely in tune with what we might expect from a "run-of-the-mill average guy," if Hannah Arendt's analysis of the banality of evil in Chapter Three accurately reflects a stage in development. It also fits perfectly with the results of Daniel Goldhagen's (1996) analytical case histories that studied the motives of ordinary Germans who participated in the Holocaust. As summarized by Habermas (2001), "Goldhagen's study is inspired by the idea that evil is not to be understood as sheer aggression as such, but rather as the kind of aggression which the perpetrators believe themselves to be justified in committing. Evil is *distorted* good" (p. 34). This is the only explanation that fits with the strange phenomenon of seeing ordinary citizens who murder proudly posing with their dead victims. This is a human phenomenon found throughout the world (as illustrated by some acts of terrorism and the evidence of ordinary people posing for photographs at lynchings of African Americans in America). Clearly people must be able to engage in horrendous acts while thinking of themselves as somehow being justified. This is the perplexing cognitive state that needs explanation and which causes so much discomfort in those who like to think that evil can only be committed by a person with a deranged mind. Unfortunately, ordinary tribal virtues can also contribute to this kind of evil when a banal person steps outside the boundaries of his own familiar domain. Notice how Calley's banal approach to interpreting moral behavior in the previous quotation shows no sensitivity to how certain differences between people ought to make a difference in how we treat them. Babies are different from adult soldiers and that difference ought to make a difference.

In contrast to Meadlow and Calley, Bernhardt's thinking displays clear elements of a postconventional consciousness that can help him see relevant moral differences. He is not only willing to accept responsibility for his own actions as a moral agent, but is also able to recognize that a concrete social rule or command from an authority does not alleviate him of the responsibility of choosing whether or not to obey the concrete command. He is trying to maintain a sense of personal moral integrity at the same time that he is trying to figure out how to create a place for himself in a terrible time of war.

If I recognize something is right or wrong . . . this is the first step to actually doing right. And this is the thing. I can hardly do anything if I know it is wrong . . . Since My Lai . . . I have had to follow my own way because nobody else's has been right . . . Now this is what I try to do: I try and apply logic to it rather than anything else; logic to say, "Is this right, or should I do this."

For Bernhardt there are universal standards and principles that have priority over any particular command or law. For him, what is most relevant in a situation is abstract principles as they apply to the local situation. For instance, with his universally based moral consciousness something like the "ethnic cleansing" conducted by the Serbian army from 1997 through 1999 would not only be evaluated on the basis of tribal commitment but would also have to pass the test of a higher moral authority. As Habermas (2001) says, "an intercultural discourse on human rights provides the terms in which a truly decentered perspective must prove itself" (p. xix). Bernhardt continues,

> The law is only the law, and many times it's wrong. . . . My kind of citizen would be guided by his own laws. These would be stricter than in a lot of cases, the actual laws. People must be guided by their own standards, by their self-discipline.
>
> I was telling Captain Franklyn about an old woman that was shot. I couldn't understand why she was shot because she didn't halt. . . . I told him that she was shot at a distance. They said to shoot her was brigade policy. . . . Nothing needs an excuse to live. The same thing goes for bombing a village. If there are people in the village, don't bomb it. . . . When I saw them shooting people I figured, "Well, I am going to be doing my own war and let them do their own war," because we just didn't agree on anything.

Another person at My Lai who shared Bernhardt's belief that the killing was an immoral war crime almost came into direct conflict with other United States soldiers. Warrant Officer Hugh Thompson observed the massacre from his helicopter. At one point he and his fellow crewmembers landed and saved about ten villagers. In a confrontation with Calley during the rescue, he pointed to his helicopter and said, "You see my guns? If you open up, they open up [on you]" (Thompson, 1999, p. 64).

The fact that the world is populated with people who bring strikingly different moral capacities to the same situation raises some serious ethical problems that will have to be dealt with in a theory of application discourse. Should rules and codes of ethics be designed for the Meadlows among us? Or the Calleys? Or the Bernhardts? Can any code of ethics ever be adequate when members of a profession can show such marked contrasts in their moral perceptions? There are many who would argue that people like Bernhardt and Thompson are wrong because they disrupt the functioning of just systems that require obedience. How can we have an efficient army if soldiers are allowed to confront each other like this? A confrontational approach to military service is far removed from the traditional approach summarized in the British saying, "Ours is not to reason why, ours is but to do or die."

Would it be contrary to the greater social good to ask professionals in the military to think like Bernhardt or Thompson? With time to reflect, people tend to favor the outcome that results from a postconventional orientation over Calley's conventional blind obedience. For instance, Thompson was eventually (about 25 years later) given a medal for his conduct and recognized as a moral hero. Calley, on the other hand, was court-martialed, convicted, and punished (even though he was released from his sentence at an early date). People remain conflicted about the whole issue, partly because they want obedience to authority without question and partly because they want to hold individuals responsible for whom they choose to obey.

A study of history shows us over and over again that while many people get away with engaging in the evil behavior that is encouraged by institutional authorities, many others don't. We may eventually be held accountable by our victims if not our peers. Greek soldiers who became torturers were put on trial, Calley was tried by his peers, Eichmann was tried by his victims, and many other people of lesser renown have been judged to be morally responsible even though they tried to argue that they were under heavy institutional pressure to act as they did. It is clear, according to the historical record at least, that we want to treat adults as autonomous moral agents who can be held individually responsible, even when they have been commanded by apparently legitimate institutions. We want adults to accept this responsibility because we do not want a society where we will need a police officer on every corner or one where we have to fear that the majority of citizens will unite to ethnically cleanse a minority. On the other hand, some critics of mainstream Western society argue that many of our moral failures are the direct result of this tendency to focus on individual responsibility and autonomy. They argue that we should stop focusing so much on individual rights and individual choice because this focus distorts the reality of our social existence and leads to a decline in morality. That is, some fear that emphasizing autonomy and individual responsibility may give comfort to those who favor egocentric personal agendas.

At this point, we should take a closer look at the idea that rational people can be held responsible for what they do because they have the capacity for autonomy. If we can make sense of individual autonomy and rationality in a way that also supports commitment to community and universal values, then we will be in position to use these values as powerful tools for judging the adequacy of professional institutions and theories of morality. This kind of investigation will require us to analyze the role of reason in human affairs. As we shall see in Chapter Six, reason can be used in different ways—some of which give top priority to morality, some of which don't. Before we turn to an in-depth analysis of the role of reason in judging autonomy and morality, however, it will be instructive to analyze the way in which the life experiences of different groups can affect their orientation to morality. For the sake of achieving a clear focus, the next chapter will primarily consider how gender differences in ethics can affect one's moral perspective. However, the conclusions we draw from the differences in perspective between men and women will also help us understand how the life experiences of other groups can also give them their own insights into morality.

REFERENCES

BELENKY, M. F., CLINCHY, B. M., GOLDBERGER, N. R., & TARULE, J. M. (1986). *Women's ways of knowing*. New York: Basic Books.

Ethics, special issue on moral development 92 (3), April 1982.

GILLIGAN, CAROL. (1982). *In a different voice*. Cambridge, MA: Harvard University Press.

HART, BETTY & RISLEY, TODD. (1995). *Meaningful differences in the everyday experience of young American children*. Baltimore, MD: P. H. Brookes.

HABERMAS, JURGEN. (1994). *The past as future*. Max Pensky (Trans. & Ed.). Lincoln: University of Nebraska Press.

———. (2001). *The postnational constellation: Political essays*. Max Pensky (Trans. & Ed.). Cambridge, MA: The MIT Press.

KEGAN, ROBERT. (1994). *In over our heads: The mental demands of modern life*. Cambridge, MA: Harvard University Press.

KOHLBERG, LAWRENCE & MAYER, ROCHELLE. (1970s; no specific date was given). The concepts of developmental psychology as the central guide to education: Examples from cognitive, moral, and psychological education. In Maynard C. Reynolds, (Ed.), *Proceedings of the conference on psychology and the process of schooling in the next decade: Alternative conceptions*. Washington: A publication of the Leadership Training Institute/Special Education, sponsored by the Bureau for Educational Personnel Development, U.S. Office of Education. For a sample of criticisms and Kohlberg's response, see *Ethics, special issue on moral development* 92 (3), April 1982.

KOHLBERG, LAWRENCE. (1971). From is to ought: How to commit the naturalistic fallacy and get away with it in the study of moral development. In T. Mischel (Ed.), *Cognitive development and epistemology* (pp. 151–235). New York: Academic Press.

———. (1973). The claim to moral adequacy of a highest stage of moral judgment. *The journal of philosophy* 70 (18), October 25. pp. 630–46.

KOHLBERG, LAWRENCE & SCHARF, PETER. (1972). Bureaucratic violence and conventional moral thinking. A paper given at the 49th Annual Meeting of the American Orthopsychiatry Association, Detroit, MI. April 5–8.

LEVINE, FELICE J. & TAPP, JUNE L. (1977). The dialectic of legal socialization in community and School. In J. L. Tapp & F. J. Levine (Eds.), *Law, justice, and the individual in society* (pp. 163–82). New York: Holt, Rinehart & Winston.

LOEVINGER, JANE. (1976). *Ego development*. San Francisco: Jossey-Bass.

NAGEL, THOMAS. (1991). *Equality and partiality*. Oxford: Oxford University Press. Cited in Steven M. Cahn. (2002). *Classics of political and moral philosophy* (pp. 1080–98). Oxford: Oxford University Press.

PETERS, R. S. (1973). *Reason and compassion*. London: Rutledge & Kegan Paul.

PIAGET, JEAN. (1932). *The moral judgment of the child*. London: Kegan Paul, Trench, Trubner & Co.

———. (1967). *Six psychological studies*. New York: Random House.

———. (1973). *The child & reality*. New York: Viking Press.

PLATO. (1961). Phaedo. In Hugh Tredennick (Trans.), *Plato: The collected dialogues*. New York: Pantheon Books.

RICHMOND, P. G. (1970). *An introduction to Piaget*. New York: Basic Books.

SMITH, ADAM. (1982). *The theory of moral sentiments*. Indianapolis, IN: Liberty Fund.

TAPP, JUNE L. & KOHLBERG, LAWRENCE. (1977). Developing senses of law and legal justice. In J. L. Tapp & F. J. Levine (Eds.), *Law, justice, and the individual in society* (pp. 89–105). New York: Holt, Rinehart & Winston.

THOMPSON, HUGH. (1999). The massacre at My Lai. *Newsweek*. March 8. p. 64.

VYGOTSKY, L. S. (1962). *Thought and language*. Cambridge, MA: The MIT Press. For a very good discussion of these issues, see Michael S. Pritchard. (1991). *On becoming responsible*. Lawrence: University Press of Kansas.

Chapter   Five

The Role of Voice in Ethics, With the Focus on Gendered Interpretations of Morality

∼ The Plurality of Voices versus Universal Morality

> **For Study:**   Why is it important to pay attention to "voice" in moral theory? Why must a universal morality account for all voices? Why is it difficult to deal with differences if we assume there is only one standard voice for a group? How is interactive dialogue supposed to help us understand differences?

When we interpret moral theories, it is important to be sensitive to the "voice" with which various groups speak. Members of the same group speak with the same *voice in so far as they share similar life experiences in the same life-world.* If we ignore the different voices of those who are affected by public policy we will be vulnerable to the standard person problem. For instance, it is banal to assume that well-meaning representatives who understand only the standardized voice of privileged members of one gender can choose for others from another gender who are fundamentally different in their life experiences. This is especially true in a public sphere, where power relationships are not designed for the benefit of the weaker group. In general, the public world of competition is not based on the kind of mutuality that is present in relationships that do empower all members. In fact, relational theorists Miller and Stiver (1997) argue that dominant groups maintain their dominance by employing a "power-over" (p. 49) or dominant-subordinate system in which the lack of mutuality generates systematic "relational oppression." The style of language which is controlled by the dominant group contributes to the maintenance of racism, classism, heterosexism, etc. These "isms" of exclusion intrude into the public sphere to create disconnections between groups and individuals rather than connections. These kinds of disconnections are experienced as relational ruptures that limit the authenticity and growth of those who live in groups marginalized by the dominant-subordinate systems of power.

In some ways this is similar to Foucault's (1976) concerns about the way voices of various disciplines create their own discourses of truth that lead to what he calls "disciplinary coercion." "The disciplines may well be the carriers of a discourse that speaks of a rule, . . . a norm. The code they come to define is not that of law but that of normalization" (p. 1114). This leads to a society of normalization that controls people through scientific knowledge and disciplinary mechanisms tied to the disciplinary "language of truth," since those who deviate from the disciplines' conception of the normal are labeled and marginalized. In so far as professional jargon creates this kind of disciplinary power over others it contributes to voices in ethics that lead to disconnection rather than connection. Foucault would argue that professions of this kind pose a serious threat to human freedom. In a universal morality we must make it possible for marginalized voices to be heard, rather than forcing people to normalize by adopting the dominant group's language of truth.

As we saw in Chapter Four, during developmental transitions males and females both first encounter social rules as external constraints, then they embrace them as a source of identity, and finally they develop a capacity to criticize and reform them so that they will evolve with the individual's developing principled conscience. However, while women and men appear to share these same forms or perspectives during their intellectual transitions, Carol Gilligan (1982) claims that typically the content they emphasize in their respective ethical orientations is quite different. As discussed below, the content of the voice men use to extend their procedural understanding of moral experience to the more abstract theoretical levels is different than the content found in the voice of women. Since males have been the dominant voice in the construction of Western moral theory, we will find that Western theory is dominated by male metaphors while the metaphors representing the woman's point of view have received less attention. This is a serious matter, since this difference in representation in the literature threatens to undermine the claim that universal morality can be sufficiently impartial to account for the voices from all life-worlds.

This same concern applies to other voices that develop due to experiences of religion, race, creed, age, vocation, class, education, etc. It is not easy to account for all relevant voices. For instance, although feminist philosophers should be exceptionally sensitive to inadvertent but false standardization, the movement has been undergoing a fascinating and instructive form of self-criticism that provides a clear example of how the standard man (person) problem can arise even among people who are united in their universal opposition to oppression. For instance, Chesler (2001) argues that while the feminist movement empowered women and opened an opportunity for them to be taken seriously in the public sphere, it also carried forward racism and patriarchal views that had already been internalized during the socialization process (p. 442). She argues that feminists are really no better or worse than other groups and that the time has come to move away from the idealized image of women contained in the relational model. In fact, there is a dark side to the emphasis on relational caring. Women need to acknowledge and own the aggression and competition which is inevitably also found in the relational style. She believes that in the next phase of feminism, women must learn to compete and disagree with other women without feeling betrayed by disagreements. It is precisely because they care so much that disagreement starts to feel like betrayal. The task facing the women's voice in the future is to integrate negative emotions such as envy and anger in with their caring, so that the negative can be made compatible with respectful and ethical relationships even when there are disagreements (p. 480).

Furthermore, women of color have been pointing out for some time that the perceived interests of privileged white women are not universal and in fact may represent special needs of a privileged group of women that conflict with the more basic needs of women who are differently situated. They charge that the failure to recognize that different women speak with different voices has lead to a betrayal of women of color as well as others from less-privileged socioeconomic classes. We must realize that all women (and men) are not raised in a uniform, nurturing community (even if it is oppressive). All are not provided with the same stable linear heritage. As mentioned earlier, many grew up in what Gloria Anzaldua (1989, p. 20) calls life in the *borderlands*, which is *the space between cultures.*

Borderland experiences of oppression are not available to privileged people who occupy the cultural center in a society. Some argue this means those in the borderlands are in a privileged position for understanding oppression, as can be seen by comparing a slave's moral insights with that of the master. To the master the slave is invisible, leaving the master with only one point of view. But to survive, the slave learns to understand at least two positions, her own and the master's. The slave, then, has broader understanding. For a look at the voice coming out of the experience of slavery, see McGarey's and Lawson's (1992) argument that by "listening to the voices of former slaves . . . [we can] gain a better understanding of . . . [moral] concepts" (p. 2). Those who have been oppressed have a different view of how ordinary moral terms work to structure human relations. For these reasons, women in the borderlands are rightly suspicious of those white women who only understand the position of privileged women and yet claim to speak for all women. Because white feminists have acknowledged this problem in the recent literature, feminist writing has taken on a different tone. However, while acknowledging the new focus in the discussions, Maria Lugones (1991) points out that there is a deeper step that has yet to be taken. She says,

> Difference makes the kind of difference that makes inappropriate the theoretical division of labor between those of us who work on difference and those of us who don't.

> White women used to simply and straightforwardly ignore difference. In their theorizing, they used to speak as if all women *as women* were the same. Now white women recognize the problem of difference. Whether they *recognize* difference is another matter. As white women are beginning to acknowledge the problem in their theorizing, it is interesting to see that the acknowledgment is a noninteractive one, or at least there is no clear emphasis on interactive acknowledgement (p. 38).

If Lugones is right, then the standard person problem is indeed deeply embedded in the human situation. In other words, it is not easy to become what she (1987) calls a *"world-traveler."* This is her name for those who are *willing to accept the fact that others may have their own complete worldview and are thus willing to show respect for the other's humanity by trying to see the world from their perspective.* While privileged white feminists are well meaning and concerned about respecting differences, the response of many of them to the criticisms leveled by women of color is often to avoid real change by staying focused on the theoretical problem of difference. Thus, Lugones claims that while Lorraine Bethel's (1991) question in her article "What Chou Mean We White Girl?" was actually a call for dialogue, many women treated the question as an interesting theoretical problem about how to adjust feminist theory to explain the phenomenon of difference. As a result, important aspects of the universal values of liberty and equality of participation have not been adequately implemented in the feminist movement, since the necessary practical dialogue between the different voices didn't materialize on the substantive level. That is, discussion continued, but in a theoretical vein that failed to engage the lives of many women.

What is the best way to facilitate a real interactive dialogue between people who are different but whose lives will of necessity affect each other? Rourke (1993) argues that it is not enough to merely recognize differences; *one must also learn how to talk across differences.* As a lawyer, she argues that the institutional norms that guide law practice should be redesigned so as to facilitate real communication between lawyers, judges, and clients. To help people to express their actual perspective, the legal profession must make it possible for all participants to enter into the kind of dialogue in the legal system that can reveal real differences and promote mutuality. This would be in keeping with people's fundamental basic need to be seen and heard. For instance, gifted therapists argue that successful professional interventions require the professional to **witness** the other's experiences so that they *convey to a client "that they understand something of his or her experience in the way he or she experiences it* (Kegan, 1982, p. viii)(emphasis added). The ethical professional must learn to communicate in a way that does not force clients into using a language that mutes a client's own voice to such a degree that she disappears.

Professional codes ought to explain in detail the moral necessity for dialogue between clients and professionals, so that all members of professions will take this moral requirement seriously. Of course, in practice clients are dependent on the esoteric knowledge of professionals, and in light of this, they may show little inclination to act as equals in specific interactions with professionals. But professionals should not make this reality worse than it is by using their position of expertise and power to hinder the development of interactive dialogue. Instead they should use their esoteric skills to further such dialogue even if it takes some special effort to learn to communicate across differences. Different professionals from the same profession can show different degrees of sensitivity to this issue.

For instance:

I once witnessed the following exchange between two doctors during an institutional review board discussion of an informed consent form. One doctor commented that "Patient consent is a farce. I can get a patient to consent to anything I want." He is right on a concrete level, especially in paternalistic doctor-patient interactions. However, the ideals behind informed consent point to what *ought* to be, not to *what is* in some clinical interactions. To become concrete realities ideals must be implemented in concrete interactions, and that will require the cooperation of the professionals in the particular medical setting. In the same conversation, another doctor pointed out, "If you approach the issue of consent properly, clients will not consent to just anything. The idea of informed consent involves the values of honesty, patient and professional autonomy, standards of medical practice, and a mutual dialogue that should be educational for both us and our patients." Which doctor is being more sensitive to the moral norms that ought to regulate the dialogue between professional and client? The doctor who is most sensitive to levels of abstraction is more likely to intelligently integrate universal norms, duties of station, and personal needs in his professional relationships so as to facilitate dialogue across differences. The first doctor focuses too much on the empirical fact that doctors can easily sabotage the abstract ideal of informed consent if they refuse to cooperate with the ideal. In a literal sense, he is blinded by the power and influence that comes with his professional perspective and the dependency sick people feel in his presence. The voice with which he speaks will interfere with attempts to seriously consider the tentative voice of the patient, because in Miller and Stivers terms, he is employing the "power-over" system to interpret the dynamics of the relationship.

Because we are fallible humans, a group of well meaning people cannot solve this practical problem for all others. Thus, we must find a way to give real power and voice to all people, especially those who are different. This will not be easy, since by definition it is difficult to understand a different point of view. Even if two groups agree on background universal norms, they may disagree about how the universal norms should be translated to fit local contexts. For instance, the title of the May/June 1994 issue of *ACADEME* was "Black Colleges at the Crossroads." The articles in this issue provide a good example of the kinds of disputes that can occur at the level of implementation when we try to use abstract universal concepts to shape specific institutional structures without being sensitive to the differences among people's situations. Thus, even though Constantine's (1994) research seems to prove unequivocally that black colleges are more successful than predominantly white colleges in helping African American students develop the skills needed to function as free citizens in a democracy, some people want the colleges abolished because they see them as being in conflict with the formal requirements of moral and legal equality.

How to find a proper balance between the ideal formal demands of equality and freedom during the concrete distribution of social goods as a means to these ideals is a recurring theme in contemporary philosophy. If one views the problem from a purely abstract, theoretical point of view (other things being equal), we can assume that all voices are the same and that we obviously ought to all be treated the same way in every instance. But, if we view the attempt to apply ideals with sensitivity to historical situations (all things considered), then we have to take the unique situation of various groups into consideration. Exceptions at the application level may have to be allowed, even if only for a time. To figure out which exceptions are justifiable, will take real dialogue among all the groups with their different life experiences (we will return to this issue in Chapter Ten). As the feminist ethics debates illustrate, creating opportunities for real dialogue among people with different voices in ethics is not going to be easy. We can explore this difficulty in detail if we take a closer look at how differences in experience can create different voices in men and women. Since about 50 percent of the population in any culture is either male or female, it is useful to begin with a look at differences between these large groups.

∼ The Focus on Gender in Moral Development

> **For Study:** Why would the women's voice in ethics disappear if women were removed from research?

What are the significant differences in morality that are supposed to show up when the two genders speak about moral concerns? Typically, the women's voice focuses on care and social responsibility as ultimate moral values, in contrast to the typical male voice that places emphasis on impartial justice and individual rights. Sichel (1991, p. 13) argues that early research indicated that while both genders use both of these voices at times, there was a predominance of care language in the reports of women. Of course, there are some women who approach morality in ways that do not appear to be different from men, and in recent studies of men and women who do take up one orientation or the other 50 percent of the women still focused on care, but the other 50 percent were now focusing on justice. On the other hand, nearly all the men *who focus* are still focused on issues of justice (Held, 1989. She did not mention how many have no focus at all). It seems, then, that women are beginning to shift their orientation, while men are remaining the same. However, it is more important to note that the interesting consequence of these differences is that "if women were eliminated from the research sample, care focus in moral reasoning would virtually disappear" (Held, p. 222). Held also argues that although Gilligan has recently weakened some of her initial claims, the relational ethics of care is still a legitimate voice that needs to be accounted for in a complete moral theory. To see the importance of this difference, we need a more detailed analysis of each voice.

The Traditional Men's Orientation

For Study: What are the primary features or traits of character behind a typical male voice in ethics? What does it mean to say that men typically see morality as a means to facilitate their success dream, while women are more likely to see morality as being a lifestyle question itself?

To illustrate the male voice in ethics, Gilligan chose the definition of morality given by a young man named Ned.

> Morality is a prescription, . . . the idea of having a concept of morality is to try to figure out what it is that people can do in order to make life with each other livable, [so we have an] equal share in things. [Without this] . . . the individual has no chance for self-fulfillment of any kind. Fairness, morality, is . . . prerequisite to the fulfillment of most individual goals. If you want other people not to interfere with your pursuit of whatever you are into, you have to play the game (Gilligan, p. 98).

Like most males, Ned presupposes that moral agents are separate but equal individuals whose primary concern in life is to pursue private goals. These assumptions fit with the individualistic emphasis we find in philosophically liberal societies which emphasize autonomous agency. Social separation is accepted as a basic given in adult life—the problem for the individual is to figure out how to live with others. Relationships are important, but they are a means for facilitating the primary end—the individual's "success dream"

(Levinson et al., 1978, pp. 93ff). Thus, in Ned's words, morality is conceived of as a game of reciprocity each must play to protect each individual's right to pursue "whatever you are into." The right to freedom, privacy, and the negative obligation to avoid interfering in the life plans of others receive primary emphasis. The individual's primary concern in ethics is to be protected from external interference, and individual rights are supposed to provide that protection. The first priority in life is to choose a conception of the "good" life where self-fulfillment is possible, and then be willing to accept obligations to obey rules that protect everyone. Thus, moral rules are seen as a very important means for supporting the right to pursue personal goals. In its simplest form, the morality of doing one's duty is not an end in itself. Morality is a set of negative constraints that is a means to protecting private agendas.

The popular rugged individualist version of this approach argues that no one has positive duties to help others satisfy their goals (unless, of course, one has voluntarily taken on some positive duties of station by entering into explicit contractual commitments—e.g., marriage). For instance, we have positive duties to feed our own children, since in conceiving them we contract to care for them, but no one has positive duties to care for orphans. It is, of course, morally virtuous to help orphans, but that is simply charity of the supererogatory kind. It is virtuous to choose a lifestyle that helps others, but it is not a duty to do so. Betty Sichel (1991, pp. 3–4) argues that the following features are central to this male way of viewing ethics. First, the male voice emphasizes the abstract, the general, and the universal. Second, it advocates emotional detachment and viewing relationships in subject-object terms as opposed to subject-to-subject relationships. Third, it sees moral dilemmas as primarily involving justice issues of autonomy and individual rights. While men and women both share these three traits, males are more likely than females to emphasize them. Sichel is not saying that these are bad traits, only that they seem to dominate the focus of the male gender.

The Women's Orientation

> **For Study:** What are the characteristics of the women's voice? How does the woman's perspective change the way we are apt to conceptualize an ethical issue? Contrast the different way that men and women typically treat issues of charity and duty with regard to helping needy others.

When asked to define morality, Diane (a woman in her late twenties) said,

> [Morality is] . . . trying to uncover a right path in which to live, and always in my mind is that the world is full of real and recognizable trouble, and . . . is it right to bring children into this world when we currently have an overpopulation problem, and is it right to spend money on a pair of shoes when I have a pair of shoes and other people are shoeless? It is part of a self-critical view, part of saying

"How am I spending my time and in what sense am I working?" I think I have a real drive, . . . to take care of children, . . . to take care of the world. When I am dealing with moral issues, I am sort of saying to myself constantly, "Are you taking care of all the things that you think are important, and in what ways are you wasting yourself and wasting those issues?" (Gilligan p. 99).

In contrast to the male's background emphasis on autonomous individuals who have private ends, women's development occurs in a web of relationships and intimate connections. Her responsibility is to maintain the connections by caring for others and helping those in the web develop. Indeed, most women measure their self-worth by their ability to form and maintain relationships that foster the social growth of themselves and others at the same time (Miller and Stiver, 1997). If a person's personal gain leaves intimate others behind, it does not contribute to the person's sense of self-worth.

Thus, Diane defines morality as a sense of feeling a need to take care of the world. This reflects a feeling that she has immediate responsibilities to help needy people she encounters. According to this conception, morality is itself a lifestyle choice, not merely a means to make other choices possible. For instance, one of Diane's primary concerns is whether she should create the ultimate relationship between mother and child in a world where relationships cannot be properly maintained. In general, because women emphasize interventions designed to meet the different needs of unique individuals, they are less focused on complying with rules and are more likely to search for the best exceptions to the rules to alleviate the needs of people who are seen as exceptions.

For Instance:

When I coached Little League baseball with both boys and girls on the team, on family day we would let younger siblings play. If a five- or six-year-old brother or sister had three strikes, the older boys on the team would insist, "That's it. Three strikes and you are out." The older girls on the team would often plead with me to suspend the rule and make an exception because the children were so young. They insisted that it was not fair to treat tiny kids the same as everyone else. Being an older, less rule-obsessed male, I always let the little kids have more strikes, which caused considerable consternation in some of the male ball players.

In traditional households, women learn to define themselves in terms of a relational network, at the same time that they are being discouraged from participating as individual decision makers in a world controlled by competitive males (Gilligan, 1982, Miller and Stiver, 1997). When we combine this competitive disadvantage with the fact that generally young girls model on their mothers (who seem to be selfless to the young), we get a unique nest experience that teaches women to think that "the moral person is one who helps others: goodness is service, meeting one's obligations and responsibilities to others, if possible without sacrificing oneself" (Gilligan, p. 66).

Betty Sichel (1991, pp. 7–10) argues that the different life experience of girls changes the way women conceptualize moral issues. First, women are more likely to emphasize the uniqueness of each person. This leads to an emphasis on listening, trying to see the other person's side, and to paying attention to the particularities of the form of life within which each person is embedded. Second, this requires a concrete focus on the particularities of the immediate foreground—what is the situation of "this" person right now, right here? Third, since no one can ever be another person, women recognize the need to rely more on a tacit understanding of another and less on explicit public definitions of types. Thus, women are more likely to listen to others with their whole being, as a mother does to her child. Fourth, since the relationship to the other is the center of focus, women strive to be responsive, to communicate, to avoid betrayal or isolation, and to care for the other's needs given their unique situation.

Possible Causes of Gender Differences

> **For Study:**   Some people think that gender differences are caused by different nesting experiences. What kind of early experiences might cause men to focus on autonomy and rights and woman to focus on relationships and care?

What causes these gender differences in one's orientation to the world? Perhaps they arise because males and females typically begin life under normal but different "nesting" conditions, which give them different body-based experiences. We do not have the space to fully explore the possibility that there are fundamental differences in formative early experiences, but a brief survey of some of the current literature suggests that there are differences that may be fairly crucial. For example, Chodorow (1978) and others argue that in the first three years of their lives when children are choosing their gender identity, in modern industrialized societies both male and female children are primarily raised by women. The phenomenon of the absent male creates some significant differences in the life experience of boys and girls.

Studies show that parents naturally treat little girls differently than little boys. Girls are touched more often (both at home and in the nursery), held for longer periods of time, comforted longer, are not as severely punished and are not discouraged from expressing emotions. This teaches girls that it is safe to seek intimacy by moving toward the mother, or toward day care and nursery school nurturers, in order to bond with them. There is less emotional need to separate and individuate when it is so pleasant to be "in" relationship. Because girls are also often systematically discouraged from acting independently or autonomously, a girl's developing self is defined by her relationships with adult women who are physically present to act as role models. Where one is encouraged to stay close and be like the caregiver, there is less need to strive to earn attention by stressing your individual accomplishments. Little girls learn that their natural task in life is to duplicate the most intimate relationship of all by becoming mothers themselves.

Traditionally in industrialized cultures, boys learn early that they are on their own and that intimacy is dangerous. To become male, boys must separate early from the female nurturers that surround them. Although little boys want the same love and affection that girls get, they cannot become "males" if they model themselves on women, so the female nurturers unconsciously push them away while encouraging the girls to remain close. This has to happen for the boys to become men, but it hurts on the procedural level of emotional development. (Perhaps we need more male nurturers so that little boys do not need to withdraw or define themselves negatively as "I'm not her."). Studies show that boys are not comforted as long, and they are more often shamed for showing the emotions that are associated with vulnerability. They are told: "Big boys don't cry." "Be tough." "Stand on your own two feet." "You have to decide what you are going to be when you grow up." The stereotype is that boys should go out and look for a life and girls should stay close to home (see Figure 5.1).

Figure 5.1   Cultures with absent fathers deprive both girls and boys of prolonged daily interactions with male role models.

For Instance:

I saw these stereotypical gender differences between boys and girls clearly modeled during a family's interaction outside my office window. A woman (I assume the mother) was pushing a baby buggy with the aid of her daughter who could barely reach the handle of the buggy. A little boy, who was about two years older, was running in circles around the buggy as they walked down the side walk. Suddenly the boy cried out, "I can tackle you!" and then he swerved toward the little girl. She cried out, "Mom!" and looked up for protection. The mother said, "Billy stop. You can't tackle her." He said, "Yes I can" and continued to bear down on the girl. The mother said, "You may not tackle her, she doesn't want to play." The boy swerved away at the last moment and continued on his circular path—perhaps looking for the absent father, his success dream, or the Holy Grail. But why did he want to tackle his sister in the first place? Was he jealous of her closeness to mom? We don't know, but the image fits Chodorow's theory.

In fact, in American culture at least, boys are systematically socialized to retreat from emotional expression, which forces them into "emotional ignorance and isolation" (Kindlon and Thompson, 1999, p. 3). Thus, when boys are "shamed by school problems or stung by criticism," they only know the fight-or-flight option. They either "lash out or withdraw emotionally (p. 3). If "emotional literacy involves recognizing the look and feel of our emotions" (p. 4–5), then the average teenage boy is emotionally illiterate. "Some boys don't even have the words for their feelings," (p. 4) since children learn the meaning of experiences only if the older generation helps them conceptualize them by talking about and naming the experiences. But, when we raise boys and girls in stereotypical ways, we systematically teach them that some feelings have meaning for their gender and others are not to be mentioned. In general, boys have been told to ignore their internal states and just to do things in a stoical manner—the strong, silent type. In general, girls have been told they can have their internal feelings, but they should leave the public arena to the boys. Thus, historically, both genders have systematically been banished from access to different but important parts of human experience, and this causes further disconnection between the genders (Miller and Stiver, 1997).

According to Wheeler and Jones (1990) boys develop a shame barrier between their publicly displayed and praised, rugged individualist self and their unconscious, dependent self that wants to live "in" emotional relationship with others. They are given public rewards if they behave like "men" who are strong, silent, stoical, and striving to be successful, and they are shamed if they admit (even to themselves) that they feel vulnerable and might want above all else to live in an intimate caring relationship with others. A polarity then develops between an inner, receptive, private self that must remain hidden (e.g., involving all those needs to be supported, held, protected, express spontaneous emotion, and receive unconditional love), and an external public self that is self-reliant and productive. To avoid the sense of shame that would come over them if they let the inner self out, they either repress their feeling states or they create a few narrow excusing conditions that will allow displays of vulnerable emotions. For example, they don't have to be ashamed if they show emotion momentarily at a funeral, when a baby is born, when their country is attacked, when they are drunk, or during sex. This model can be reversed to explain how girls have historically been confined in the private realm of the family so that as women they were shamed when they tried to break out and join the public realm by seeking careers. These historically disparate nesting experiences may have contributed to the development of differences in voice between some men and women.

One thing is clear from the survey data: In varying degrees men and women do focus on different ethical content. It might be possible to transcend some of these differences. The power we have to let reason critique reason itself, to turn feelings on feelings, and to make comparisons between traditions holds out the possibility that we may be able to engage in a rational search for new experiences that can usher in successively transcendent ethical conceptions. A sexual heritage, a tribal heritage, and a philosophical heritage are all stages in the process of natural human development that can (and ought to) lead to new transcendent points of view. But how can we truly understand and assimilate another orientation? I will explore this issue in more detail in the chapter on autonomy.

A Mature Ethics Requires Both Genders

> **For Study:** In the search for a transcendent point of view in ethics, what are the different tasks that fall on men and women?

Gilligan cautions that from the perspective of moral agency and individual responsibility, the woman's orientation may not necessarily be a positive development given the social context in which women find themselves. Because women have historically been a disenfranchised group, too often what emerges from their traditional experience "is a sense of vulnerability that impedes these women from taking a stand" (Gilligan, 1982, p. 66). The "intimidation of inequality" (p. 95) can combine with their relational orientation to make them too selfless. When this happens, it is difficult to fully exercise the right to take a place in the social world as an active, responsible moral agent. Gilligan says,

> The essence of moral decision is the exercise of choice and the willingness to accept responsibility for that choice. To the extent that women perceive themselves

as having no choice, they correspondingly excuse themselves from the responsibility that decision entails. Childlike in the vulnerability of their dependence and consequent fear of abandonment, they claim to wish only to please, but in return for their goodness they expect to be loved and cared for (p. 67).

There is another side to this issue that also needs to be addressed. In a talk at the Midwest American Philosophical Association meetings in the late 1980s, Claudia Card warned that we must approach the woman's perspective cautiously, since it is always possible that it represents what Nietzsche called a *slave morality*. Nietzsche believed that the downtrodden often designed moral systems that expressed their own lack of power. Slave morality *convinces the oppressed that they are actually better off and superior to those who oppress them, and in this way it justifies their own inferior position and gives them a kind of passive power over the oppressor.* Catherine MacKinnon (1989) expresses a similar worry about the ethics of care by reminding us that the care ethic was developed in a world of male power and may not be what women would choose if they were not oppressed. But, I think a care ethic would be a slave morality only if the final conception of this voice insisted that passivity and self-sacrifice were *the* major virtues. Mature women, however, coordinate their emphasis on care for others with an equal emphasis on honesty and the personal obligation to take care of oneself and to become an active moral agent who exercises choice.

Gilligan's research shows us that because the developmental path of men and women is different, in their respective search for transcendence they have different tasks. Men start attached to mother, learn at an early age to separate and be independent, and then develop a universal ethical orientation that recognizes that they are alone and vulnerable in a hostile world. They emphasize justice, rights, obedience to rules, and treating everyone equally before the law. This orientation works well when the goal is to regulate interactions between strangers in the public sphere. So, one important new task for males is to learn how to care and be responsible for others in need.

Women start attached to mother, learn to bond in a caring intimate relationship with female nurturers, and develop a contextual ethics that affirms the value of creating these intimate relationships. Thus, they emphasize becoming dedicated to caring for and maintaining intimate relationships in general. This is an ethics ideally suited for protecting the intimate contacts found in the private realm of the family. Since intimacy is usually local and contextual, the woman's voice focuses less on abstract universal obligations to mankind and more on serving those with whom they have actual contact. For instance, Noddings (1984) argued that because caring requires an ongoing relationship, then we cannot have obligations to starving children in Africa in general since there is no ongoing relationship with them. This lack of cross-cultural concern indicates that the special task facing some women is to learn to separate and become autonomous enough that they can choose to follow the abstract postconventional aspects of care that are needed in a pluralistic world filled with strangers. Miller and Stiver (1997) argue that what women need is a connected social world that also fosters greater autonomous, authentic use of all their capacities—not by acting as men, but by blending independence and respect for strangers with their unique capacity to care for intimate others. Men, in a corresponding way, need a world that allows them to care and be responsible for others without feeling ashamed and without running the risk of losing the autonomy that they have already worked so hard to achieve. Full development for both genders would therefore seem to entail developing the ability to integrate individual rights from the public sphere with the capacity to accept responsibilities to care for others from the private sphere. Since both genders need to communicate across their differences, let's look at the way decentered development can facilitate communication.

Development Improves Communication Between Voices: The Example of Race

> **For Study:** Why should the development of racial understanding facilitate dialogue across differences? Why is the ability to engage in dialogue across differences so important in a universal morality?

Research into how people develop their cultural and racial attitudes shows that the ability to engage in dialogue improves as people decenter during moral development. We cannot assume, however, that everyone shares a common experience of cultural diversity that will tell them what is important. Since each person in a diverse environment has their own unique cross-cultural experiences, they will each have their own multicultural identity. Thus, to a degree, each person has a unique individualized form of procedural knowledge tied to his or her own experience of race, sex, culture, religion, and so forth. "We need to be sensitive to the wide range of personal differences in how people experience and interact with their own multicultural society" (Pelton-Cooper, 1997, p. 8), so we should be cautious when making assumptions about how various social factors might have affected particular individuals (or subgroups). We may have some stereotypical information about one of the groups to which an individual belongs, but that does not prove that any particular individual will share his group's stereotypical patterns.

We also have to be cautious about drawing universal conclusions about *all* women or *all* men just because we see some common patterns in many of them. For instance, while gender issues may be a central issue in the identity development of many Caucasian woman, a particular woman of color may be far less concerned about gender issues if racial discrimination has played a more central role in her development. Just as we try to show respect for particular aspects of personality development in individuals, we must also try to show respect for the unique aspects of a person's (or subgroup's) multicultural identity development, especially for those who were raised in the borderlands.

This is an important consideration for anyone who wants to engage in interactive dialogue with people who are different. In trying to figure out ways to work with college students, with different racial backgrounds, Sue and Sue (1990) reviewed a number of multicultural identity models and attempted to provide a conceptual framework for stages of development with regard to the growth of race consciousness. Initially, most models were intended to describe the developmental process experienced by people of color who were raised in a predominantly white culture. However, Sue and Sue noticed that the members of the dominant white racial group also followed a similar sequence in the pattern of their development of race consciousness as they progressed toward a more nonracist, multicultural personal identity. So, Sue and Sue constructed the following five-stage model to describe the transitions in race consciousness that they observed in members of the dominant groups.

First, the most elemental stage in orientation to race is characterized by the child's minimal awareness of herself as a racial being. Lacking accurate knowledge about differences and racial groups, children adhere to egocentric stereotypes about them and cannot imagine that the stereotypes might be considered distortions of reality by others. As they get older, they begin to use denial and compartmentalization to live with the contradictions about racial groups that egocentric knowledge usually entails. For instance, one might believe that differences among people should not be important, and yet at the same time believe discriminatory treatment is justified because minority persons are somehow inferior. Such contradictory values are held in compartments because logically they cannot be integrated. Because people like to feel that the parts of their belief system are harmonious, they are motivated to avoid looking too closely at the compartmentalized discrepancies.

A second stage of dissonance develops, however, when people are forced by circumstances to acknowledge such inconsistencies. When confrontations with the reality of racism break through denial and compartmentalization, feelings of guilt, shame, anger, and depression can arise. If one recognizes one's own role in perpetuating racism, guilt feelings may intensify, which may lead to a defensive rationalization of one's racist values. The negative feelings associated with this stage sometimes prompt a retreat into specialized cultural subgroups that promote and help maintain both the rationalization and a return to denial.

If development continues, however, we see the emergence of a resistance and immersion stage, in which one's general sense of justice begins to help one focus on the need for antiracist action. At first, the emerging multicultural identity begins to resemble "White Liberal Guilt," since people either tend to over identify with oppressed groups and work hard to be accepted as a "good" white person, or they tend to adopt the stance of paternalistic protector. "White guilt" can motivate antiracist action, but it can also fuel a kind of reactive anger toward minorities if the guilt does not seem to be sufficiently appreciated. At this stage, the primary motivating factor has become the desire for approval from the oppressed group.

The dissonance experienced both by seeking external approval and by over identification with a group whose life experience is significantly different can help promote the development to a fourth more introspective stage. Since authentic identity cannot be defined by external forces, people begin to realize that their multicultural identity must emerge from an internal integration of their own values and goals. In this stage, people learn to move beyond guilt and defensive reactions, and to seek direction by autonomously integrating their experiences and values so as to create a new relationship with those who have a different voice. Now authentic communication can begin, since one's own voice is no longer governed from without.

At the final stage, an integrative awareness develops where people are able to tolerate internal conflict created from knowing their culture grants them unfair privileges because of their skin color, but at the same time they can feel a deep commitment to fight unjust racial inequality. They are able to take some personal responsibility for participating in a system that perpetuates racism without becoming immobilized or controlled by reactive negative feeling. If they seek out minority individuals for friendship, it is because they like the individual. They are no longer trying to prove something, or support a belief in their own racial tolerance. They are able to enjoy an increased, genuine appreciation for cultural diversity without feeling disloyal to their own heritage. "They seek appropriate opportunities to promote healthy multicultural development in their communities and support the political eradication of racism" (Pelton-Cooper, p. 9). Obviously, this last stage has strengths that would facilitate actual authentic interactive dialogue. Having moved beyond defensive reactions, people are willing to allow others to be different (and even hostile) without feeling it is a threat to their own identity.

This model can also be used to judge the appropriateness of the kind of dialogue that is perpetuated by the structure of professional life. Does a profession's structure encourage participation of all people in ways that show universal respect for different voices? Or does the profession develop the kind of professional jargon that makes the esoteric knowledge of the profession hopelessly obscure to those who are not members of the profession? Professional jargon forces clients to adopt a position of dependency and mystifies the power-over nature of such a relationship. This hinders clients' ability to express their version of their needs and supports the stance of paternalism taken by some professionals.

Trying to accommodate different voices is going to complicate moral theory and the application of moral theory. But if they are going to be logically consistent with their expressed mission, universal theories are going to have to be complex enough to account for all the voices with which people speak. Jaggar (1991) points out that many feminists are beginning to have doubts whether anything as simple as a male/female difference in voice can be sustained, since there appears to be many different voices and experiences in both genders. This is an important insight that complicates the search for a transcendent conception of practical reason. Since we are interested in everyone, not only groups of people, this is a problem that has many permutations. If we are going to share a world, however, the extra complexity does not negate the need for a universal theory that can help us with disputes that arise between perspectives. Thus, it would be instructive to consider any theory that could successfully unite the stereotypical voices that represent the male and female perspectives. This kind of theory would give us an example of the kind of moral progress we should be looking for in a universal philosophy. It may not be a final theory (since other voices also must be integrated), but the theory would be more enlightened than if it arose only out of the individual heritage of one gender. Is there a philosophical tradition that has attempted to combine both the woman's relational concerns and the individualistic concerns of men? Annette Baier (1991) argues that the Scottish moralist David Hume is a man who comes close to being a women's philosopher.

> Hume lived before autonomy became an obsession with moral and social philosophers, or rather lived while Rousseau was making it their obsession, but his attack on contractarian doctrines of political obligation, and his clear perception of the given-ness of interconnection, in the family and beyond, his emphasis on our capacity to make others' joys and sorrows our own, on our need for a "seconding" of sentiments, and the inescapable mutual vulnerability and mutual enrichment that the human condition, when thus understood, entail, make autonomy not even an ideal, for Hume (p. 295).

Baier is pointing us in the right direction, but like Hume, she seems too willing to take an empirical approach to ethics. This makes her too much opposed to autonomy as a moral ideal. I would like to see her struggle to find a proper place for autonomy in the moral world (which I will attempt in the next two chapters). But, since Baier thinks Hume, who is a Scottish communitarian philosopher, is on the right track, let's look at the Scottish tradition more closely and see if it can properly blend the voices from both genders. Since another philosopher from that tradition, Adam Smith, has generally been associated with the individualistic men's voice in economic theory, it will be instructive to see how the Scottish Enlightenment accommodated both the "caring concerns" from the women's voice and the "individual rights" concerns from the male voice. In modern political philosophy these differences are often contrasted in the debates between representatives of liberal individualism and communitarian republicanism.

Blending the Voice of Liberal Individualism with Communitarian Republicanism

> **For Study:** Why does the Scottish communitarian tradition seem to have elements of both the male and the female voice in ethics? In particular, what is the primary virtue that humans see and approve of with their special moral sense? Why is classical liberal philosophy sometimes criticized for being overly individualistic and supportive of evil behavior? Why has it been associated with negative rights theory? Why do liberal critics think that unrestricted communitarianism is dangerous for individual rights? How might one use the developmental model to bring these two traditions closer together?

The background conditions that set the stage for the Scottish communitarian perspective on individual rights seems more compatible with both the male and the female voice than does the liberal individualistic perspective that has evolved out of Locke's social contract theory. Members of the Scottish Enlightenment were careful to contrast their approach with what they called the *selfish school of morality* behind the theories of Hobbes and Locke (Wills, 1978, p. 215). Since Hobbes and Locke began with an assumed background of original self-rule, they naturally emphasized the male voice's concern with the utility of having a moral theory that would protect an individual's interests in pursuing his own preferences. In contrast, theories constructed during the Scottish Enlightenment assumed morality was based on man's social nature. Since males in such tribal settings typically speak with a voice that places a strong emphasis upon positive obligations to their community, perhaps the tendency in much individualist philosophy to deny that we have positive duties to be benevolent is primarily a characteristic of pluralistic cultures in which men have been torn from their tribal roots.

The Scottish communitarian Hutcheson had a powerful impact on both David Hume and Adam Smith. Hutcheson (1961) argued that everyone has a *moral sense,* which *is a faculty of perception that allows us to naturally see and approve of benevolent relations and disapprove of selfish ones.* This sense is like an aesthetic sense in that it leads to disinterested approbation of moral behavior. We take pleasure in witnessing benevolent acts even when we are not the recipients of the benevolence. Thus, where moral sense rules, the basis for social intercourse can be a bond of affection, rather than mutual gain through bargaining and contracts. When one lives in a society where the main focus in moral life is benevolence toward others, one will develop procedural expectations that make positive obligations to help members of the community seem like the natural responsibilities of any worthwhile life.

Scottish communitarians are not obsessed with competition and the struggles between strangers for a place in a hierarchy of private profit. They emphasize the possibility for a kind of personal success that does not have to be purchased at the expense of relationships, but instead, will contribute to community relations. The Scottish philosophers were free to think of rights as social conventions that created the opportunities to exercise our highest faculties by interacting with others in a benevolent manner. Thus, the individual rights to life and liberty were justified prerequisites for the possibility of benevolent community life (Wills, p. 213). "Good men" in Scottish society would insist on these moral rights not because they want protection from others, but because they wanted the right to participate in benevolent relations with their fellows. These are rights of inclusion, not rights that keep others back. Communitarians judge all social institutions in this way, including the marketplace, exchange of goods, competition, etc. Each is judged according to how it affects the opportunities for cooperative interdependence (i.e., market relations would be morally justified because, in creating a need for commodity exchange in a community, they provide an opportunity for benevolent interactions).

The male voice takes on a natural interdependent social connotation when viewed from the context of moral sense theory. That is, as every "good" Scottish communitarian knows one cannot seek fulfillment of the "self" unless one is part of a social web that allows us to exercise our highest faculties. Since our moral sense is the source of the highest form of pleasure for a communitarian, the most fulfilling life is benevolent social life. Thus, even when a person is motivated only by "self" fulfillment, his moral sense will moderate any natural tendencies to be greedy in interpreting what "self" means. Committed social life based on benevolence rather than private satisfaction of interests will be the source of his greatest pleasure. This emphasis on community involvement supports what is known as the *republican* view of the political process. *The rights of citizens are positive political liberties that guarantee "the possibility of participating in a common practice,* through which the citizens can first make themselves into what they want to be.... [so a right] both enables and guarantees the integrity of an autonomous life in common based on equality and mutual respect" between members of the political order (Habermas, 1999, pp. 241–42) (emphasis added).

This version of communitarian republicanism is often contrasted with an overly narrow version of liberal individualism, which defines the citizen as an egoist in competitive market relations with others. Political rights are conceived of as negative individual rights "that guarantee a domain of freedom of choice within which legal persons are freed from external compulsion" (Habermas, 1999, p. 241) so that they can pursue their private interests. Communitarian critics claim that liberal emphasis on individualism causes moral decay, because it undermines prerequisite virtues for community life. For instance, in their criticism of administrative evil, Adams and Balfour (1998) place the blame for much of this kind of immoral behavior on liberal individualism, technical rationality, and the lack of an adequate historical consciousness in administrative literature. They reject the Enlightenment liberal tradition, which is represented by the six foundational principles listed in Chapter One. They claim that this liberal tradition has ushered in an extreme form of abstract individualism whose emphasis on individual liberty and procedural justice has undermined the value of equal participation in community life. That is, liberal individualism leads to a kind of selfish libertarianism that insists people have negative duties to avoid harming others but that no one has a natural positive duty to help others or to make sacrifices for the common good. If positive duties to help people do exist, it is only because certain free individuals have explicitly consented to bind themselves by taking on such positive duties. For example, no one has a positive duty to save another person from drowning, unless someone has voluntarily accepted a job that gives him a duty of station to save drowning people, for example, a lifeguard. This shows that liberal democracy is "not designed to address the real conditions of people's lives that enable—or disallow—them to act as citizens in a democratic state. . . . [It] is the core value of individualism, married as it has been with technical rationality, that stands as a primary roadblock in finding a basis for public service ethics" (Adams and Balfour, p. 172).

In other words, critics claim that the liberal male emphasis on individualistic personal freedom distorts human relationships in so far as it undermines the positive duties that members of a community naturally have to one another. When individual freedom has top priority and our only obligation is to avoid harming others, it becomes permissible to abandon vulnerable members of the community. Because individualism undermines the development of the concrete sense of empathy for others that is taught and sustained by commitment to community, it eventually destroys the possibility of a caring community. The welfare liberal's attempt to counteract this tendency by providing the material means to freedom will not work, since liberal theory itself does not support an obligation to guarantee the equal right to the means for freedom.

As a counter to this individualistic emphasis, Adams and Balfour (1998) advocate restructuring professional ethics so as to place it on a communitarian foundation. They argue that "a new basis for ethics is needed that does not demand individual conformity to the procedures of technical-rational solutions to social problems, but that instead engages administrators as citizens in an ongoing effort to promote and sustain an inclusive democratic polity." (p. 160). This call is compatible with the woman's voice emphasis on maintaining the caring relational network that nurtured us when we were vulnerable.

I think there are problems with the way this entire debate is often formulated. We do not benefit from an ethical analysis that portrays one tradition in glowing terms while focusing on all the errors of the opposite tradition. Of course, the description of communitarian ethics given above sounds attractive, since it is compatible with our earlier characterization of mature professionalism (and moral agency). Remember, a professional has to be someone who has the capacity to use discretionary power in a fiduciary relationship that requires mutual accountability for how the discretion is to be used. And critics of liberal philosophy are right to point out that this philosophy can be abused. But, as we shall see in Chapter Eight, it is not at all clear that the logic of the liberal tradition is inconsistent with the strengths of the communitarian point of view. As Nussbaum (1999) points out,

> liberal thinkers, such as Mill, Hume, Smith, and Rawls, have an evidently social and other-inclusive psychology, building affiliation with and need for others into the very foundations of their accounts of human motivation and denying that individuals can satisfy their basic desires independently of relationship and community. (p. 1139)

~ Adam Smith, A Liberal Communitarian

> **For Study:**   What elements of Smith's ethical philosophy might lead one to modify the masculine interpretation of laissez-faire principles (self-command, sympathy, impartial spectator, dignity, etc.)? Why is it possible that Smith might not have wanted to make a distinction between duty and virtue so as to contrast meeting an obligation with acting in a supererogatory fashion? What kind of impartial spectator is Smith talking about in the sixth edition of his *Theory of Moral Sentiments?*

Let's consider the Scottish communitarian with the most liberal philosophy. Adam Smith is often given an individualistic twist that he would probably reject. He is best known in Western culture for his famous assertion in *The Wealth of Nations* (1981, p. 456) that the best way to help a nation prosper is to allow businessmen to pursue their own interests in a competitive marketplace free of government regulation. Pursuing self-interest in a free laissez-faire market will maximize the social good just as though a benevolent "invisible hand" (p. 456) were directing the outcome. Smith's apparent emphasis upon the individualistic pursuit of self-interest free from government regulation seems to fit nicely with the liberal economic tradition that emphasizes protecting negative rights to economic freedom among autonomous equals who are pursuing private agendas. A modern statement of this practical philosophy says,

> pure *laissez-faire* capitalism implies *unimpeded, absolute individual discretion on the part of property owners to use, trade, or sell their property without government regulation, even in emergencies, wars, catastrophes, and so forth.* [emphasis added] . . . laissez-faire capitalism lets business do what it wants outside of such

criminal conduct as assault, theft, and murder, and precludes the great bulk of government regulatory measures many citizens now take for granted. (Machan, 1984, p. 204)

Would Smith be happy with this interpretation of economic philosophy? One must interpret his work against the background of his communitarian moral heritage. Smith rejects the model of the egoistic self-interested individual that has been attributed to liberal economic philosophy. His economic person is a decentered Scottish communitarian keenly aware of the importance of human relations to his sense of well-being. The individual not only can sympathetically understand the lot of other economic agents, he can exercise *self-command* over his selfish impulses. Self-command is Smith's (1982, p. 145ff) way of referring to *the capacity to restrain selfish inclination in order to do what is right*. If Smith believes that economic agents do not need government regulation, it is because he assumes that they are already regulated by an *"impartial spectator"* or a "man within" their own breast (Smith, 1982, pp. 129–31). This is Smith's way of talking about our formal operational *ability to observe and judge our own behavior from an impartial perspective, as though we were outside of ourselves*. To understand the social, caring nature of this abstract sounding concept, we must look more closely at Smith's theory of the moral sentiments.

How do moral agents develop self-command? The way in which Smith's (1982, pp. 146–56) account of the impartial spectator develops is very similar to Kohlberg's and Gilligan's account of how the formal levels of moral reasoning develop. That is, in the early editions of his text, Smith says we exercise self-command to gain the approval of external others (like the stage-two child). But in later editions of his book, he says we begin to exercise self-command to gain the approval of our own conscience (like a stage-six mature adult). Consider the following statement from the first edition of Smith's *The Theory of Moral Sentiments*.

> We must imagine ourselves not the actors, but the spectators of our own character and conduct, and consider how these would affect us when viewed from this new station . . . We must enter, in short, either into what are, or into what ought to be, or into what, if the whole circumstances of our conduct were known, we imagine would be the sentiments of others, before we can either applaud or condemn it. (Smith, cited in Hope, 1984, p. 159)

In this first edition of his work Smith is pointing out that conscience is guided by the attitudes of our fellow members in the community. It represents a fairly low level of moral development. By the time the sixth edition of his work came out, however, Smith's theory had evolved to the point where he contrasts this first primitive conception of self-command with a much more mature conception of principled empathic conscience. Thus, Hope (1984) points out that the rudimentary stage of the virtue of self-command, found in the child or the man of weak character, depends on the feelings of actual spectators. The higher stage, reached by the man of constancy, depends entirely on conscience (p. 158).

As we saw earlier, Kohlberg's developmental research shows that this higher conscience develops only after people pass through two previous stages of (1) forced obedience and (2) voluntary identification with the social order. So, the sixth edition's "man within" may refer to an autonomous conscience, but it is the conscience of a communitarian man that has learned to fully understand and sympathize with social existence, it is not the conscience of a purely self-interested economic agent. Of course, Smith did not have access to the modern developmental theory that can make sense of principled empathy. Thus, according to Hope, Smith was always uneasy with the elevation of the inner "impartial spectator" to the level of an abstract *ideal observer* (who might be emotionally detached from community feelings). He continually emphasized that ethics must be based on the sympathy felt between "real" people (which is, of course, another emphasis we find in the women's voice). Smith also seemed uncertain about how to characterize the relation between conscience (which should be principled and universal) and convention (which remains local and exclusive), having a tendency to equate the two at times, but apparently not feeling comfortable with the equation. Perhaps this tendency was due to a tension between his communitarian roots with its emphasis upon "intimate" human relations and his later recognition that morality must ultimately become universal in some transcendent sense if it is going to work for people from more than one tribe. Hope (1984) summarizes Smith's dilemma as follows:

> If conscience is conventional, the ordinary man can be conscientious, but duty is the slave of fashion. If conscience requires perfection, duty is freed from public opinion, but the ordinary man cannot be conscientious. His confusion is indicated, perhaps, by his reference in the second edition to "this inmate of the breast, this abstract man, the representative of mankind," the latter phrases suggesting someone who is not real, yet somehow epitomizes real attitudes (p. 161f).

While this could be seen as tension that results from an attempt to accommodate both the women's and the men's perspectives, or between communitarian concerns and the concerns of a transcendent cross-cultural ethics, Hope chooses to give a male voice interpretation of Smith's problem. He says that

> Smith unfortunately, confuses mere dutifulness with virtue, of which, indeed, it forms a part, and hence precludes the possibility of being more than dutiful . . . [H]e should recognize the difference between mere dutifulness and true virtue,

between meeting an obligation and acting supererogatively. There is no inconsistency between conscience agreeing with a minimum laid down by convention while advocating that more be done. How much more the individual does is up to him and his natural virtue. (p. 161f)

But, perhaps as a good communitarian speaking in a more relational caring voice, Smith did not want to make use of the male voice's emphasis on a minimum captured by negative duties, leaving all other actions in the category of the supererogatory. The fact that a moral spectator is impartial does not mean he has to be conceived of as being blind to the interdependent, emotional nature of social life. The impartial spectator develops in the breast of real social people who are sensitive to everything that is relevant to a complete ethical judgment. Smith says that a complete judgment is informed by "the whole circumstances of our conduct." To a communitarian, protecting the relational context of conventional social life is an important part of the circumstances. It is possible then, that Smith may have wanted benevolence to be a duty rather than a supererogatory act, because he saw benevolence as being at the heart of a conventional relational ethics based on sympathy for the other rather than as being a supererogatory virtue that takes us beyond individualistic conceptions of negative duty. A transcendent male voice sympathetic to Smith's problem would try to explore the logic behind an ideal observer who accepts the view that we have positive duties to maintain a caring or sympathetic conventional order.

For Smith, true self-interest is tied to perfecting our nature, and he says, "To feel much for others, and little for ourselves, to restrain our selfish, and to indulge our benevolent affections, constitutes the perfection of human nature . . ." (cited in Lamb, 1974, p. 675). For a man to achieve this sense of self, he must benefit from a rich moral heritage. This is not an individualistic social atom pursuing private profit and hiding from duties to care for others behind his negative rights. This is a mature social being who accepts his duty to protect the quality of social relations. Thus, it is possible to see both an individualist in Smith who might speak with Ned's masculine voice, but it is also possible to see Diane's more relational and caring voice in Smith. As a tribal social being, a Scottish gentleman would be more concerned with his place in the community than with a private individualistic goal.

It seems clear that the voice one uses to interpret Smith does matter. In popular Western economics, the elements of Smith's philosophy that recognize our interdependence have been marginalized, leading people to believe that it is morally correct to pursue private interest at the expense of the public good. Perhaps it is due to the tendency of male writers to focus on those features of his philosophy that are of special interest to the individualist male voice, but this is not the best historical interpretation of Smith. Even more important, it is not the best prescriptive use of Smith's rich philosophy. An impartial spectator with a heritage built on human sympathy will emphasize our interdependent social nature and our need to support and maintain the network of relationships that make a community of autonomous beings possible.

So, liberal philosophy does not have to be individualistic in an egoistic sense. Conceiving of individual human beings as bearers of human rights does not mean that we must now conceive of individuals as beings who exist outside of communities and have no positive duties to others. It is possible to make sense of liberal philosophy without adopting such a naive ahistorical interpretation of moral agency. In the liberal tradition, moral agents are supposed to be mature individuals to whom it is "self-evident that all people are created equal" no matter which life-world they inhabit. Members of liberal democracies have to go through the same developmental stages as everyone else; they are not to remain egocentric children. I will argue in Chapter Six that liberal notions such as self-governance make no sense unless people are raised in communities that teach them what governance is all about. Because self-governance in the Jeffersonian sense does not develop unless people develop a procedural foundation for understanding social life, the logic behind liberal concepts is consistent with strong positive duties and commitment to community.

Let's reconsider the communitarian charge that liberal principles destroy the social conditions needed for their own existence. What should we make of this criticism? In the first place, it is true that because liberal philosophy evolved as a way to help us transcend hereditary hierarchies and deal with a multicultural world, it has to make use of abstract, complex, postconventional concepts. Thus, there is indeed a danger that liberal principles will be distorted when egocentric and ethnocentric people apply these postconventional concepts in local situations. To take this concern seriously, we only need to revisit the way Eichmann used Kantian philosophy to defend himself at his trial (see Chapter Three). However, I believe that similar dangers exist for any theory in the modern world, including communitarian approaches. That is, technologically focused, banal, communitarian administrators are just as likely to engage in administrative evil as their liberal cousins. Consider the fact that the liberal emphasis on human rights and individualism were not dominant characteristics of the fascist regimes that perfected administrative evil in the twentieth century. Appeals to the fatherland and the good of the community, however, could be heard everywhere.

As we saw in Chapter Two, the Zimbardo Prison Experiment and the Milgram Yale Authority Experiment show how easily our social nature lends itself to compliance with administrative authority. This human tendency is supported by developmental literature. In healthy communities people naturally move away from egocentrism and toward the greater social compliance that is a normal feature of an ethnocentric focus. This is a necessary human development, since communities cannot thrive unless their members develop a deep sense of commitment to social norms. Unfortunately, in a multicultural environment, this healthy social development also contributes to sustained tribal conflict. Much of the evil done in the twentieth century has been motivated not by individualistic desires to further a personal agenda, but by a conventional commitment to a social reality that transcends egocentric versions of individualism. Thus, the motives of people who participate in administrative evil do not of necessity have to be individualistic motives at all. Evil of the ethnic cleansing variety is ample proof that harm conducted in the name of furthering tribal values is just as devastating as harm conducted for individualistic reasons.

One problem with privileging community norms above individual rights is that it leads to a kind of cynicism about the possibility that there could be transcendent cross-cultural moral values that protect individuals. It implies that if a tribe chooses to practice something like slavery, ethnic cleansing, or clitoridectomy (sometimes called female circumcision, but better described as FGM—female genital mutilation [Burstyn, 1995, p. 32]), well, that is just their local custom and everyone from the outside should respect their cultural choice. Notice the dilemma this poses for the therapist, educator, or human rights advocate. What should they do when a young woman pleads for sanctuary because she does not want to be mutilated by a traditional tribal practice? Must

Figure 5.2 Can oppressive tribal practices be evaluated from the outside?

we tell her that each tribe has to pick a story and stick to it no matter what? Since her tribe just happens to pick a story that sanctions FGM, should she stop whining and get on with being a good member of the tribe? As historical practices of tribal abuse clearly illustrate, simple loyalty to a community's values will not prevent administrative evil. Too often, under the guise of promoting community values, people adopt some sort of *ism of exclusion,* that is, *a philosophy that allows administrators to marginalize, exclude, oppress, or ignore those with whom they disagree.* The strength of communitarian philosophy lies in its sharp focus on the need to develop the strengths of our conventional nature, its weakness is that it may be too contextual in its focus. The approach works best in a republican setting that treats "everyone" as an equal member of a supportive community. But, in the modern world we have to interact on a daily basis with strangers who often seem to be quite alien. The sense of solidarity that naturally develops between members of a homogeneous republican community might be missing. The critics of communitarianism agree that the virtues espoused in communitarian ethics are necessary prerequisite skills for moral agency, but they worry that these virtues are not sufficient for dealing with the kinds of cross-cultural (class, racial, gender, religious) disputes between strangers that are so characteristic of intersubjective life in the contemporary world

> under conditions of irreducible pluralism, consensus concerning basic values and notions of the good life has permanently receded beyond the horizon of possibility, and hence neo-Aristotelian appeals to tradition and community as a basis for coordinating social action simply fly in the face of historical reality. (Cronin, 1993, p. xx)

Without some serious conceptual elaboration, then, I doubt that an appeal to communitarian virtues will eliminate most of the administrative evil that is done to strangers who exist outside the borders of the public servant's community. To address this problem, modern communitarians have made use of metaphorical extensions that encourage people to think of everyone as belonging to one global community, for example, the family of mankind. It requires a major conceptual reorientation in the direction of postconventional consciousness for people to transcend to a level where they can feel commitment to a "world community." The need for this transcendence shows that an adequate communitarianism is going to have to use concepts that are just as abstract as the universal human rights found in liberal theory. This need for postconventional consciousness leaves communitarians as vulnerable to abuse by banal civil servants as does the liberal tradition. Somehow we need "to find a middle ground between the abstract universalism with which Kantian ethics is justly reproached and the relativistic implications of communitarian and contextualist positions in the tradition of Aristotle and Hegel" (Cronin, 1993, p. xi). In other words, neither theory can save us from ourselves unless we learn to work with both theories to generate a position that combines the

Figure 5.3   Do we first have to belong to a group to be protected from bias? Individuals may need rights against "isms of exclusion" to be protected across cultural boundaries.

strengths of each to make it difficult for banal people to misapply universal principles.

Both liberal individualism and communitarian republicanism represent voices that seem adequate when they are interpreted in such a way that they focus attention on protecting vulnerable people from abuse, and both seem inadequate when they are interpreted in such a manner that attention is directed away from helping vulnerable populations. The point, it seems to me, is to figure out a way to design institutions so that administrators (as professionals who are working at the application level) will understand that they have a duty to help empower all the people affected by administrative decisions. The research on human development is vital for helping us understand the dimensions of this problem. The specific developmental history of a population that is affected by policy decisions must be taken into consideration when preparing to intervene in people's lives. Rather than advocating paternalistic approaches and running the risk of imposing inappropriate local agendas on people who are different from themselves, professional administrators should be creating opportunities for discourse that will empower all people affected by social policies. The most fundamental practical need in a pluralistic world is to find a way to make shared power and real interactive dialogue between different people a practical reality. After all, "nothing better prevents others from perspectivally distorting one's own interests than actual participation" (Habermas, 1991, p. 67).

Conclusion

At the higher stages of development, men and women will need to experiment both with abstract perspectives (like the "impartial benevolent spectator") and with different ways to live on a concrete relational level. To achieve a transcendent vision an attempt must be made to characterize abstract individuals as social and social people as individuals. Just as Gilligan says some women have trouble accepting the moral responsibility that comes with the background of autonomy presupposed in the male world; some men have trouble remembering that they are obligated to care about meeting the needs of others in this relational world.

In this regard, the worldview of the Scottish moralists is more likely to keep us focused on the full range of social values than is the Lockean liberal tradition, because it draws our attention to a proper reverence for community while it acknowledges that individuals ought to be autonomous in the sense of being self-governed. Our ability to exercise self-command, and thus govern ourselves, comes from the development of formal operational abilities in a caring social context that teaches us empathy—Smith's idea of sympathy. As we will see in Chapter Six, rationality requires us to integrate the concerns of all affected voices. Is this possible, even in principle? It may be that the world is full of logically different types of moral values, so that establishing some kind of unanimous consensus is impossible. Nagel (1991) claims this might be the case, when he asserts,

> My general point is that the formal differences among types of reason reflect differences of a fundamental nature in their sources, and that this rules out a certain kind of solution to conflicts among these types. Human beings are subject to moral and other motivational claims of very different kinds. This is because they are complex creatures who can view the world from many perspectives—individual, relational, impersonal, ideal, etc.—and each perspective presents a different set of claims . . . Conflicts between personal and impersonal claims are ubiquitous. They cannot, in my view, be resolved by subsuming either of the points of view under the other, or both under a third. (p. 60)

Nagel's position raises interesting questions about pluralism. Obviously morality is complex, and any tradition that focuses exclusively on any one aspect of the complexity is going to be deficient. Moral education needs to focus on promoting all the human virtues. It must provide opportunities to relate to and to be cared for by others, to exercise moral judgment and think reflectively, to stimulate our moral imaginations, to hypothesize about ideals, and to practice using the virtues. The voices of men and women and the plurality of other traditions (religious, ethnic, economic, and so forth) make up pieces of this complex world, and may represent worldviews that are so different that it might be impossible to unite them. For instance, in the above quotation from Baier, we see that she does not think the male virtue of autonomy is especially important as an ideal. And yet, Kant, who was responding to Hume's philosophy, made autonomy the foundational concept for his entire ethical theory. Why would he do this after having read Hume's philosophy? If we are going to understand the current debates in ethics, then we will need a detailed analysis of the concept of autonomy, for it occupies center stage in many of the debates.

Since autonomy is supposed to be based on our capacity to reason, however, we will first have to explore this latter concept in more detail. The next two chapters take up the task of trying to find room for both rational autonomy and relational sympathy in an account of practical reason.

REFERENCES

ADAMS, GUY B. & BALFOUR, DANNY L. (1998). *Unmasking administrative evil.* Thousand Oaks, CA: Sage Publications.

ANZALDUA, GLORIA. (1989). *Borderlands/la Frontera: The new Mestiza.* San Francisco: Spinsters/Aunt Lute Book Company.

BAIER, ANNETTE. (1991). Hume, the women's moral theorist? In Tom L. Beauchamp (Ed.), *Philosophical ethics* (pp. 290–95). New York: McGraw-Hill.

BETHEL, LORRAINE. (1991). What chou mean we white girl. Cited in Maria C. Lugones. (1991). On the logic of pluralist feminism. In Claudia Card (Ed.), *Feminist ethics* (pp. 35–44). Lawrence: University Press of Kansas.

BURSTYN, LINDA. (1995). Female circumcision comes to America. *The Atlantic monthly* 176 (4), October. pp. 28–35.

CHESLER, PHYLLIS. (2001). *Woman's inhumanity to woman.* New York: Nation Books.

CHODOROW, N. (1978). *The reproduction of mothering.* Berkeley: University of California Press.

CONSTANTINE, JILL. (1994). The 'added value' of historically Black colleges. *ACADEME* 80 (3), May/June. pp. 12–17.

CRONIN, CIARAN P. (1993). Translator's introduction. In Jurgen Habermas, *Justification and application: Remarks on discourse ethics.* Ciaran P. Cronin (Trans.). Cambridge, MA: The MIT Press.

FOUCAULT, MICHEL. (2002). Two lectures. In Steven M. Cahn (Ed.), *Classics of political and moral philosophy* (pp. 1102–15). New York: Oxford University Press.

GILLIGAN, CAROL. (1982). *In a different voice.* Cambridge, MA: Harvard University Press.

HABERMAS, JURGEN. (1991). *Moral consciousness and communicative action.* Christian Lenhardt & Shierry Weber Nicholsen (Trans.). Cambridge, MA: The MIT Press.

———. (1999). *The Inclusion of the other: Studies in political theory.* Ciaran P. Cronin & Pablo De Greiff (Eds.). Cambridge, MA: The MIT Press.

HELD, VIRGINIA. (1989). Liberty and equality from a feminist perspective. In Neil MacCormick & Zenon Bankowski (Eds.), *Enlightenment, rights and revolution* (pp. 214–28). Aylesbury, England: Aberdeen University Press.

HOPE, VINCENT. (1984). Smith's demigod. In Vincent Hope (Ed.), *Philosophers of the Scottish enlightenment* (pp. 150–65). Edinburgh, Scotland: University Press.

HUTCHESON, FRANCIS. (1961). Concerning the moral sense, or faculty of perceiving moral excellence, and its supreme objects. In Daniel Sommer Robinson (Ed.), *The story of Scottish philosophy* (pp. 42–53). New York: Exposition Press.

JAGGAR, ALISON. (1991). Telling right from wrong: Toward a feminist conception of practical reason. A conference paper delivered at the August 1991 meeting North American Society for Social Philosophy, in Colorado Springs, CO.

KINDLON, DAN & THOMPSON, MICHAEL. (1999). *Raising Cain: Protecting the emotional life of boys.* New York: Ballantine Books.

KEGAN, ROBERT. (1982). *The evolving self.* Cambridge, MA: Harvard University Press.

LAMB, ROBERT BOYDEN. (1974). Adam Smith's system: Sympathy not self-interest. *Journal of the history of ideas* 35, October–December. pp. 670–84.

LEVINSON, DANIEL J.; DARROW, C. N.; KLEIN, E. B.; LEVINSON, M. H.; & McKEE, B. (1978). *The seasons of a man's life.* New York: Alfred A. Knopf.

LUGONES, MARIA C. (1991). On the logic of pluralist feminism. In Claudia Card (Ed.), *Feminist ethics* (pp. 35–44). Lawrence: University Press of Kansas.

———. (1987). Playfulness, world-traveling, and loving perception. *Hypatia* 2 (pp. 3–20).

MACHAN, TIBOR R. (1984). Should business be regulated. In Tom Regan (Ed.), *Just business* (p. 204ff). New York: Random House.

MACKINNON, CATHERINE. (1989). *Toward a feminist theory of the state.* Cambridge, MA: Harvard University Press.

McGAREY, HOWARD & LAWSON, BILL (Eds.). (1992). *Between slavery and freedom: Philosophy and American slavery.* Bloomington: Indiana University Press. For another interesting voice see Bill Lawson. (1992). *The underclass question.* Philadelphia: Temple University Press.

MILLER, J. B. & STIVER, I. P. (1997). *The healing connection: How women form relationships in therapy and in life.* Boston: Beacon Press.

NAGEL, THOMAS. (1991). The fragmentation of value. In Tom L. Beauchamp (Ed.), *Philosophical ethics* (pp. 58–63). New York: McGraw-Hill.

NODDINGS, NEL. (1984). *Caring: A feminine approach to ethics and moral education.* Berkeley: University of California Press.

NUSSBAUM, MARTHA C. (1999). *Sex and social justice.* Oxford: Oxford University Press. Cited in Steven M. Cahn. (2002), *Classics of political and moral philosophy* (pp. 1136–61). Oxford: Oxford University Press.

PELTON-COOPER, MARY M. (1997). Multicultural identity models, a valuable resource for program planning. *Michigan journal of college student development* 1 (1), May. pp. 7–9.

ROURKE, NANCY. (1993). Talking across difference. *AMINTAPHIL* conference on radical critiques of the law in Youngstown, PA.

SICHEL, BETTY A. (1991). Gender, thinking and moral development. *ISDA Journal* 4 (1): 1–15.

SMITH, ADAM. (1981). *An inquiry into the nature and causes of the wealth of nations,* Vol. 1. Indianapolis, IN: Liberty Fund.

———. (1982). *The theory of moral sentiment.* Indianapolis, IN: Liberty Fund.

SUE, D. W. & SUE, D. (1990). *Counseling the culturally different: Theory and practice.* New York: John Wiley.

WHEELER, GORDON & JONES, DANIEL E. (1990). The male self: A developmental journey for men. Cleveland, OH: A workshop at the Cleveland Gestalt Institute, Case Western Reserve University.

WILLS, GARRY. (1978). *Inventing America.* New York: Vintage Books.

Chapter   Six

Metaethical Search for Moral Rationality

To foster moral dialogue between heterogeneous strangers, professionals with a multicultural practice will need to transcend their traditional ethnocentric worldview and adopt some kind of postconventional, rational strategy. This will be as difficult as it sounds. Philosophers have been striving without much success to reach a consensus about how to rationally approach cultural differences throughout human history. Why should we be optimistic about finding a solution now? If there is a contemporary metatheory that can help us to communicate across differences, will it be a theory that can be understood by all the different voices in our multicultural world? As a way to get started in answering these questions, we will take a quick historical survey of some of the traditional metaethical attempts to explain how universal moral values can or can't be rationally justified.

~ Traditional Naturalist and Absolutist Metatheories

> **For Study:**   According to naturalists, how do we discover absolute moral values? In what sense are the absolutes supposed to be transcendent? How can absolutist naturalists account for the value diversity in the world? At which level do they expect to find a final consensus on moral values?

Historically, people treated norms as though they were similar to the properties in objects referred to in descriptive statements. "The sunset is beautiful" was interpreted to mean that the sun was an object that possessed the natural property of beauty, just as the descriptive statement "the rock is round" meant the rock had the property of roundness. This makes sense only if one assumes values exist as properties that can be perceived by moral agents. Eighteenth-century Scottish philosophers went so far as to claim that humans have a special "moral sense" (like a sixth sense) that enables them to "perceive" natural moral properties—for example, properties like benevolence. Because all men of good character possessed this moral sense, the farmer was as capable as the scholar of apprehending moral truth (Wills, 1978, pp. 184ff). Other philosophers, such as John Locke, argued that humans had a special capacity, the divine light of reason, which made it possible for them to reflect on events in the world and discover the moral values existing in nature. Because these approaches shared *the common assumption that values are objective properties that in some sense exist naturally in the world,* their position in ethics has generally been called *naturalism.* If moral norms are natural properties in a rational world, then rational people will perceive the values that are true of the world and irrational people will perceive something else, perhaps their own subjective preferences or the demons that dominate their culture's worldview.

People who adopt the naturalist perspective in morality are usually called *absolutists,* because they *believe that the objective moral norms to be discovered in nature are universals that transcend local customs.* Sometimes *transcendence* refers to *a metaphysical capacity to achieve a point of view that is outside or above human history—for instance, in the sense of a revelation from a creator God that is outside of space and time.* But, as mentioned in Chapters Three and Four, the term can also be used to refer to *personal* or *cultural transcendence,* where *one builds on one's own history to go beyond it to a new higher level of understanding.* Habermas (1996) refers to this as the idea of *transcendence from within* (p. 14), since one uses the virtue of critical self-reflection to broaden one's own point of view while in dialogue with others. In other words, we do not have to go outside of history to transcend, instead we can simply *move from one perspective to a second perspective that represents a broader context for understanding.* If there are moral values that are rational and truly transcendent, then no matter what culture we are from, if we master the reflective virtues we should be able to transcend to the broader level of understanding.

In the eighteenth-century's **Age of Enlightenment,** the search for transcendent absolutes stimulated intense philosophical investigation. Whether philosophers of the Enlightenment relied on God, a divine light of reason, an appeal to natural laws, or moral sense theory, the goal was the same: *to transcend social and cultural idiosyncrasies by grounding moral judgments in universal, absolute values.*

Absolutists are, however, well aware of the descriptive fact that there is concrete diversity in terms of local cultural values. They not only expect such diversity but they may also encourage moral agents to be sensitive to it, since local customs and environmental circumstances influence the intelligent application of absolute principles. Absolutists cannot, however, accept such diversity at the level of foundational moral values. They expect that as we move up to increasingly abstract levels of ethical consideration, rational people will develop a consensus about which principles ought to serve as rational background universal norms to regulate cross-cultural discussions. MacIntyre (1988) argues that the plurality of philosophical traditions proves that Enlightenment philosophers were overly optimistic in their faith that reason would lead us to a set of transcendent universal norms that can serve as a foundation for rational discussion.

> Both the thinkers of the Enlightenment and their successors proved unable to agree as to what precisely those principles were which would be found undeniable by all rational persons. . . . Nor has subsequent history diminished the extent of such disagreement. It has rather enlarged it. Consequently, the legacy of the Enlightenment has been the provision of an ideal of rational justification which it has proved impossible to attain. And hence in key part derives the inability within our culture to unite conviction and rational justification. (p. 6)

Because of the considerable formal agreement behind the MPofV, I am not yet ready to abandon the Enlightenment's optimism. For one thing, I am impressed by the fact that whenever there exists a reasonable balance of power, so that one side in a dispute cannot use force in an attempt to "ethnically cleanse" the other side, reasonable people always eventually conclude that all sides in the dispute must try to justify any normative claims being made in a way that will make public sense. They also agree that other things being equal, agreements should be reached through negotiations that are fair to everyone involved. In light of contemporary research into moral development, however, it will be useful to modify the Enlightenment search for absolute values so as to emphasize the style of the search rather than the results. The goal would be to find increasingly better transcendent "truths," which in their own turn would need to be historically transcended. But perhaps the idea of transcendence is itself overly optimistic. According to cultural relativists, we should give up completely on the search for transcendent absolutes because they believe the search is a waste of time.

The Cultural Relativist Reaction

> **For Study:**   Why do cultural relativists reject absolute values? What level of tran-
> scendence are cultural relativists willing to accept? What are the different levels at
> which we can use practical reason, and of these, which one is favored by relativists?

Cultural relativism is a metaethical position that claims *moral values can only
be judged relative to the particular culture within which they arose.* In terms of
Kohlberg's developmental theory, this form of relativism represents a considerable advancement since it is a temporary stage between stage four and five that
helps us move away from the conventional level's ethnocentrism. Before we
can develop an adequate theory of morality, we must free ourselves from the
belief that conventional beliefs are right just because they are ours, and relativism helps in this transcendent move. Relativists have become aware that social values evolve within ways of life and that they do not necessarily possess
absolute truth. They then follow up this insight with the claim that *all* social
values only make sense in the context of the way of life that created them. This
metatheory takes the subjectivist's major insight about the arbitrariness of
some individual values and elevates it to a cultural level. They argue that moral
values are cultural ethical norms that can transcend individual preferences, but
only within a culture. Thus, value disputes between individuals and subgroups
can only be resolved by appealing to the authority of the values that are universal to a particular culture. The advantage of this move is that it appears to
give cultural relativists a way to make reasonable ethical judgments at least
within a specific culture.

The cultural relativist agrees that there are good reasons to keep public
intersubjective prescriptions distinct from private preferences or feelings. There
is no reason to assume a personal feeling can work on an intersubjective level
just because an individual feels strongly about it on a personal level. We can
clarify the difference between the way cultural relativists and subjectivists
approach moral values by distinguishing between the different level of practical
rationality each uses to define what constitutes a good reason for a moral choice.

Practical reason is the name for *the mental capacity to make practical
choices that are supported by good reasons.* There are basically three different
levels at which people use their practical reasoning abilities to discover reasons
for acting: First, there is pragmatic or strategic rationality; second, there is ethical rationality; and third, there is moral rationality (Habermas, 1993, p. 2ff).
At the *pragmatic level, rationality is used in a strategic way to determine the
best means for attaining given goals.* The ability to think strategically is important for pursuing success regardless of the nature of the goal. Strategically
speaking, what counts as a good reason is determined solely by reference to the
preestablished fixed goals of some person or group. This pragmatic use of reason is referred to as instrumental rationality in economic theory. In a sense,

Figure 6.1   Pragmatic or strategic reasoning is used to figure out the best means to reach a fixed goal, or to get what you already want.

then, pragmatic or instrumental rationality is similar to a person (or group) trying to rationally decide what dessert will be best for him (or them). When making this kind of decision, the only factors relevant are personal (or group) preferences. As Habermas says, since what is rational is determined by reference to one's own fixed preferences, what a person rationally ought to do is "relativised" (Habermas, 1993, p. 9) by the person's subjective wants. When this level of reason is used by an egocentric person, "other persons are accorded merely the status of means or limiting conditions for the realization of one's own individual plan of action" (pp. 5–6).

Since strategic choice is based on the contingent attitudes and preferences of only one person (or group), this use of rational skills is not adequate for making sense of the impersonal or suprapersonal type of decision making that emerges at the level of ethics. Until we move beyond the egocentric level, and take up "a radical shift in perspective and attitude, an interpersonal conflict cannot be perceived by those involved *as* a moral problem" (p. 6). In fact, the strategic level's idea of a good reason begins to look arbitrary to the people who learn to adopt the more complex intersubjective point of view.

There is something about the ethics of a culture that demands more of its group members than that they simply learn to use strategic reasoning. As we saw in Chapter Four, children cannot become social beings until they learn to think in the ethnocentric fashion that allows them to care about group norms. Habermas (1998) argues that this intersubjective level of ethical consciousness develops in conjunction with the development of the capacities for noncoercive dialogue about the good life. "Ethical insights result from the explication of the know-how that communicatively socialized individuals have acquired by growing up in a particular culture" (p. 25). This is the level of Aristotelian virtue ethics, with its concerns about the authenticity of a life defined by social standards. At this intersubjective level of *ethical rationality,* new questions about the nature of social existence have emerged. *The rationality of choices is not fixed only by preexisting preferences. Preferences themselves must be reevaluated in light of concerns about self-realization as a social being.* In other words, commitment to an authentic social life that involves intersubjective ideas about mutual respect begins to dominate preferences. Ethical reasoning involves "an individual life history that is always already embedded in inter-subjectively shared traditions and forms of life" (Habermas, 1993, p. 26). At this level, practical reason leads to "insights that bind the will, . . . [so] the freedom to choose, in the sense of rational choice, is transformed into the freedom to decide upon an authentic [social] life" (p. 27). In short, a new qualitative understanding of intersubjectivity has taken over rationality, so that what counts as rational has taken on an "us" quality that transcends mere consider-ations of "my" preferences.

> Practical reflection can lead to insights of this kind only when it goes beyond the subjective world to which the actor has privileged access and pertains to the con-tents of an intersubjectively shared social world. In this way reflection on shared experiences, practices, and forms of life brings to awareness an ethical knowledge to which we do not have access simply through the epistemic authority of the first person singular. (Habermas, 1998, p. 25)

That intersubjective understanding is intuitively obvious to average citi-zens who function at the ethical level of reasoning helps explain why the label "sociopath" is so appropriate in cases where people do not understand the suprapersonal nature of the social world. This pathology reveals itself in ego-centric speech acts that sound absurd to conventional people. For instance, in a court case a sociopathic woman explained to the judge why she stole welfare checks from old people by using a level of ethical reasoning that seemed to say, "It is right for me to take someone's check *because I need it,* and it is wrong for someone to take my check *because I need it*" (Kegan, 1994, p. 41). In another case a judge could not understand the motives of an adolescent thief, so he asked: "Before I sentence you, . . . I just have to ask you: how can you steal from people who trusted you so?" "But, Your Honor," came the sincere reply, "it's very hard to steal from people if they *don't* trust you" (p. 39). Given the way theft violates intersubjective expectations, it does not make rational sense to evaluate the ethical, moral, or legal validity of theft by appealing solely to one's own needs or convenience. However, these types of egocentric evalua-tions seem completely logical to people who suffer from social pathology. They are capable of narrowly focused strategic rationality, but that is all they are ca-pable of. This is why Kegan says that sociopaths are often reported to be both extremely clever and extremely naïve at the same time. In pursuing self-interest, they make excellent use of strategic reasoning to evaluate the means to their egocentric ends. They are not distracted by social concerns like shame, guilt, or loyalty, so they can be extremely focused—looking very clever. On the other hand, when evaluating their statements we see the egocentric signs of a kind of preoperational thinking (see Chapter Four) that ignores the logic of intersubjective relations in all evaluations. This makes them miscalculate the reactions and concerns of other people, making them seem extremely naïve about how the social world really works.

Because strategic reasoning based on *personal feelings* cannot clarify the nature of good reasons at the intersubjective level of ethical behavior, the cultural relativist recognizes that we must base ethical standards on something that is essentially more social than private feelings. Can the relativist solve this problem by simply relying on *common public feelings* to explain the intersubjective level of ethics? On the surface, this approach seems reasonable, since feelings shared by all of us do not seem to be inappropriately personal. In fact, there is a long tradition in conventional morality that emphasizes how important it is for each person to share the fundamental values of their own society. Lord Devlin's (1971) version of relativism takes this approach. He argues that the values embodied in the norms of a society are ultimate, not because they are necessarily the most rational or the most satisfying to an individual, but because shared norms are a necessity for saying we have a society at all. Devlin defined morality as nothing more than the body of common feelings that holds a society together. In a famous attack on liberal individualism, he argued that since society's standards of right and wrong have been introjected into each Englishman, *morality amounts to no more than the rules that are consistent with the feelings of the average man in the street*. We'll call this relativistic approach to judging values the ***reasonable man (person) standard.*** As Devlin says,

> English law has evolved and regularly uses a standard that does not depend on the counting of heads. It is that of the reasonable man. He is not to be confused with the rational man. He is not expected to reason about anything and his judgment may be largely *a matter of feeling*. It is the viewpoint of the man in the street. . . . It is what Pollock called "practical morality" which is based not on theological or philosophical foundations but *in the mass of continuous experience half consciously or unconsciously accumulated and embodied in the morality of common sense* [emphasis added]. (p. 38)

The strength of Devlin's approach comes from its acknowledgement that society's historical intersubjective context is important. He accepts the reality that much of who we are as persons is a function of introjected social values that make each individual a mirror of the general culture. His reasonable person standard is in tune with our conventional desire to have people conform to society's norms for the good of the whole. As we saw in Chapter Four, it is normal for people to develop a conventional sense of tribal integrity that will lead

them to respect social traditions for their own sake. Even when aspects of social tradition are arbitrary, they can still have intrinsic value to one's way of
life, so people of integrity will respect them for that reason. As Devlin says, if
a man "wants to live in the house, he must accept it as built in the way in which
it is" (p. 33).

Taking Devlin's metaphor a step further, we can say, if you want to live in
the house, you have to wear the cloth that go with the house. This is a useful
metaphor because it implies that at this level of value consideration, there is both
an element of inevitability about the values that come with the house (many of
them are introjected tastes and thus not easily changed), and there is an element
of arbitrariness (there may not be any reason for some of the values other than
tradition). At the level of *ethical rationality,* then, the search for good reasons is
*concerned with intersubjective questions about what kind of life is best for
everyone in a particular community given their historical feelings.* In a sense, we
are looking for a rational evaluation of the clothes we ought to be wearing in the
house into which we were born. As Habermas (1996) says, the standard of
judgement is based on "the form of life of the political community that is 'in each

Figure 6.2   Practical reason at the ethics level requires members to critically evaluate how to
structure their particular society to create a good life for all members.

case our own'" (p. 108). Decisive reasons for adopting some social style "must be acceptable to all members sharing 'our' traditions" (p. 108) or we will judge the style to be irrational and unethical. The key point, however, is that reason's public role is contextually restrained by the social tradition within which the evaluation of dress styles emerged. At this level, Devlin is right: The man in the street is the judge of what is reasonable.

Relativists are good at explaining how we are shaped by the life-world in which we were raised. As formulated by Devlin, however, this relativistic approach to moral values is too arbitrary. For instance, Devlin goes so far as to point out that because "there is no logic to be found in this" (p. 45), we should not expect rigorous standards of consistency when we establish laws to implement the feelings of the man in the street. That is, since feelings can shift over time, the man in the street can have different feelings about fairly similar cases. To illustrate his point, Devlin points out that because the reasonable men in the streets of England in 1955 feel differently about male homosexuality than they do about lesbianism, it is not an objection to the reasonable man standard that the former sexual preference is illegal in England while the latter preference is not. It is all relative to what the reasonable man is feeling. Legal scholars are quite alarmed when they see arbitrary discrimination of this kind, but on Devlin's account, their alarm is misplaced. He believes that there is no logical moral basis from which to criticize arbitrary discrimination, since the best and only standard that we have is "the *feelings* of the man in the street."

Because this standard undermines the belief that there must be a rational basis for law, Dworkin (1971) has challenged the standard by reminding us that *"Feelings do not justify moral positions, moral positions justify feelings"* (p. 63) (emphasis added). This motto applies at both the personal and social level. Just as the subjectivist's personal feelings cannot work as a justification for ethics, so too the common social feelings of a group cannot work as a justification at the level of morality. There is nothing in a feeling that can guarantee it will be to the "good-liking" of others. So, while shared social feelings are important to the members of a particular community, by themselves they do not provide a good reason for action by some other community with different feelings. Clearly, ethical rationality is not adequate for dealing with complex multicultural societies. For that level of complexity we will need a universal morality. Justice between groups requires the feelings of people to be supported by intersubjective reasons (moral positions) that make sense to all the people affected, no matter what their local cultural heritage or personal feelings.

Cultural relativists assert that it is impossible to satisfy the universalist demand that we discover good reasons that will be acceptable to all cultures. Many of them adopt the doctrine of *descriptive cultural relativism* that claims *different cultures are governed by incommensurable belief systems, making cross-culturally valid universal moral values impossible.* These theorists talk as though morality itself has been shown to be ethnocentric to the core. But, can descriptive cultural relativism itself be proven? Is it really an empirically valid theory, or is it simply a position of faith based on nonempirical assumptions? Moody-Adams (1997) offers a devastating critique of descriptive relativism's empirical credentials. She thinks the doctrine rests on a series of problematic, unexamined, and nonempirical assumptions about the nature of cultures. She argues that cultures are not static closed systems, and that relativists simply assert rather than prove that there are incommensurable differences between them. Their claim is so problematic that it is not even close to being an empirical fact (pp. 14ff). If anything, history teaches us that cultural evolution is continuous and always based on cross fertilization that results from cultures mutually stimulating each other.

Furthermore, the assertion that cultures are incommensurable appears to be based on a selective use of attention because it ignores the equally plausible assertion that there are deep value similarities in all forms of human existence. Which of these assertions a person adopts is based more on the way a person likes to interpret experience than on any particular empirical observations. In other words, two different people traveling to the same exotic cultures can each come back with two different but reasonable interpretations of their common travels. One may focus on surface differences and assert, "It is amazing how different people are everywhere." The other may focus on deep similarities and assert with equal accuracy, "It is amazing how no matter where you go, people are all the same." Whose experience is empirically more valid? It all depends on what you are looking for and the layer of human existence you are looking at.

The Need to Transcend Cultural Relativism

> **For Study:**   Why is it a logical mistake for a descriptive cultural relativist to make prescriptive statements about how we should judge other cultures?

Many philosophers have serious reservations about moral relativism primarily because it cannot help us resolve cross-cultural moral disputes. When people ask, "How should we resolve ethical disputes between different cultures?" what can the relativist say? Not much. Some cultural relativists argue that we must remain silent in the face of such disputes. Others are bolder. They assert that we "ought" to remain silent, because any cross-cultural judgment is bound to be ethnocentric. Others become even more prescriptive and claim that it is wrong to make cross-cultural moral judgments. The assumption is that we shouldn't condemn what looks evil in another country, since we would only be judging from our culture's perspective. At the end of Chapter Five we saw how human rights advocates experience major discomfort when confronted with cultural practices like ethnic oppression or FGM (female genital mutilation). Normative relativism seems to imply that those who fight such practices are being insensitive and totalitarian with regard to respecting local customs (Burstyn, 1995). For the sake of cultural autonomy, the relativist might argue, people from other cultures should refrain from making moral protests from outside the culture they are observing.

Notice the subtle shift from descriptive statements to prescriptive statements that takes place when relativists condemn those who want to make judgments that go beyond cultural boundaries. When a cultural relativist shifts to saying *we "ought to" refrain from cross-cultural judgments because all moral values are relative,* she has moved from the strong position of descriptive relativism to the weak position of ***normative relativism.*** The shift is logically inappropriate because the statement "It is wrong for one culture to morally judge another" is a moral judgment that crosses cultural boundaries. Is this moral judgment relative as well, or is it logically different from the other cross-cultural moral judgments it is condemning? If the judgment is relative to its own culture because it is a local ethical value, it has no special transcendent status as a moral judgment for those from other cultures. In fact, it contradicts its own claim that cultures shouldn't make cross-cultural judgments. It is very difficult to make sense of a cross-cultural judgment about not making cross-cultural judgments. If the relativist holds, on the contrary, that it is a valid transcendent moral judgment, then it refutes its own thesis of normative relativism because it shows we can in fact make cross-cultural moral judgments.

Normative relativism shares other logical problems that are found also in subjectivism. The mere fact that there are different value positions in the world does not tell us anything at all about the validity of any particular value position. Culture A may be different from culture B, but why do we have to suppose that they are both "right" in some sense? Why not assume one may be better than the other, or that both could be wrong? Even if all moral judgments are tainted by ethnocentricism, why assume they are all equally tainted? It makes sense to say, "Don't be so ethnocentric," and thus it also makes sense to believe there are degrees of ethnocentrism. If it is possible to be less ethnocentric, then perhaps some cultures have values that are closer to being absolute than the values found in other cultures. Finally, although some relativists presuppose a kind of cultural determinism that assumes the choice of moral values is beyond the reach of ordinary citizens (Moody-Adams, 1997, p. 21ff), history indicates that in fact, many people learn to question the arbitrary aspects of their own cultural values. Anyone can wonder if there may not be better ways to live simply by imagining what it would be like to reverse the way they are now living. In fact, one of the best ways to gain greater moral insight is to make and defend cross-cultural judgments.

Relativism's great strength as a metaethical theory comes from its emphasis on paying attention to context. We cannot adequately judge an action or value unless we understand its historical, cultural context. Relativism's weakness lies in its controversial assumption that the importance of context proves it is not possible for one context to be superior to another in some transcendent moral sense. Cultural relativists start out by observing that "different cultures have value systems that contain some differences." As a descriptive piece of data their point is well established. But absolutists respond to this data by saying, "So what?" It is one thing to notice that values vary from culture to culture; it is another thing to prove there is not even one universally transcendent value that *ought* to be used to judge the other values in all cultures. The important issue is whether it makes sense to look for rational standards for evaluating the validity of various cross-cultural comparisons. This issue takes us back to the eighteenth century's Enlightenment project.

Moral Rationality

> **For Study:** Why would Mill object to Devlin's cultural relativism? Why is moral rationality needed for the MPofV?

The relativistic consequences of Devlin's reasonable man standard are especially worrisome to universalist philosophers like John Stuart Mill (1859, 1971). He argued that unreflective use of popular public sentiments by public officials would violate basic individual rights to freedom of lifestyle by imposing popular but arbitrary public feelings on individuals. Mill said,

> nine-tenths of all moralists and speculative writers . . . teach that things are right because they are right; because we feel them to be so. They tell us to search in our own minds and hearts for laws of conduct binding on ourselves and on all others. What can the poor public do but apply these instructions, and make their own personal feelings of good and evil, if they are tolerably unanimous in them, obligatory on all the world? . . . The public of this age and country improperly invests its own preferences with the character of moral laws . . . until it encroaches on the most unquestionably legitimate liberty of the individual . . . (p. 19).

Mill would probably ask Devlin: "Whose introjected feelings best represent the man in the street?" In a pluralistic culture, "society" is a vague term, since it is not clear which group should get to have its preferences represent society. Mill thinks ethical positions about what clothes to wear in the cultural house should emphasize preserving individual choice rather than imposing some favored communal or cultural dress code. He fears that the dominant social feelings might turn out to be no more than mass prejudices. If a feeling cannot be justified by sound reasoning it may represent a popular feeling, but also one that could be evil.

Mill is trying to shift the debate to a higher level of rational consideration. The question to be addressed at the cross-cultural level involves the constraints of justice that must be observed by all life-worlds. To move to this cross-cultural level of moral consideration, we have to reconceptualize what can count as a good reason. At this third level, reason must now be impartially based *and* universal in scope. This requires a type of *moral rationality* that *assumes people can function at the highest order of decentered intersubjectivity.* Habermas (1993) argues that we only "approach this moral outlook once we begin to examine our maxims as to their compatibility with the maxims of others" who have social agendas different from our own (p. 6). A person with moral rationality is prepared for a practical discourse that breaks "with all of the unquestioned truths of an established, concrete ethical life, in addition to distancing oneself from the contexts of life with which one's identity is inextricably interwoven" (p. 12). The rationality behind the MPofV is the only level of value consideration where rationality can be expected to support universal, cross-cultural prescriptions (Habermas, 1996, pp. 60ff, 108–10). This level uses a *rational person standard* that emphasizes *basing moral decisions on reasons that are universal because they can be accepted by everyone affected after critical public debate.*

Figure 6.3 Practical rationality used to justify universal principles that regulate everyone functions at the level of moral theory.

Is the rationality behind the MPofV just a culturally relative manifestation of the ideology of our Western period in history, or does it have universal normative significance for all periods in history? Moody-Adams (1997, pp. 62–69) argues that there is no more reason to adopt historical relativism than there is to adopt relativism about contemporaneous cultures. Both forms of relativism are empirically suspect, which leaves us with decentered rationality as the best hope for developing an impartial perspective on which to base cross-cultural morality. Because the MPofV developed as a way to deal with cross-cultural conflicts, it is attractive to philosophers from many different cultures. It gives all people the obligation to avoid bias when making moral judgments about those who are culturally different. Thus, it offers protection to everyone from pernicious attacks by technologically dominant cultures. However, the MPofV also contains an inherently problematic moral agenda. To avoid bias one must learn how to adopt a universal perspective that can critically judge the adequacy of one's own cultural, historical context. Thus, this point of view is not a value neutral position, since it puts cultures that don't want to critically reflect on their own values at risk. Furthermore, in our secularized and/or multicultural historical context, reason now has to find a way to bear the burden of being the most important moral virtue without appealing to metaphysical foundation. Is it up to the task?

Postmodern Philosophy

> **For Study:**   Why do postmodern philosophers believe that the pursuit of universal values "or a grand metanarrative" is incoherent and, in fact, may contribute to the oppression of minorities?

According to some postmodern contemporary philosophers, rational transcendence is a hopelessly compromised notion. Since in the history of philosophy the "modern" era began with the early Enlightenment philosophers of the seventeenth and eighteenth centuries, "postmodern" philosophy is supposed to represent an orientation that repudiates or goes beyond the aspirations of this "modern" Enlightenment period. Thus, *postmodernism refers to a metaethical position that encompasses a variety of post-Enlightenment theories all of which reject the concept of universal foundations for human knowledge and ethics, emphasize contextual interpretation and the deconstruction of universal concepts, and down play the Enlightenment goal of finding universal norms.* In the first place, they argue that because differences in background culture and personal experience will always cause people to "project" different interpretations of events into the world, striving for impartial universal principles is conceptually incoherent. People are "always already" prepared to see the world in a certain way according to their own linguistic heritage. This simple fact proves that there can never be a transcendent impartial perspective that gives some particular interpretation of rationality privileged access over all the rest. Because the ideal of a transcendent perspective cannot be achieved, Flax (1990) argues that we must abandon "'truth' enunciating or adjudicating modes ... [since there can never] be a perfectly adequate unified theory of the 'whole'" (p. 4).

Walzer (1994) argues that universalist philosophers have become so confused that they have reversed the process of history. They think "minimalism precedes maximalism; [as though] once we were thin but have grown thick" (p. 13). He is pointing out the obvious historical fact that people first become members of a tribal culture with its "thick" theory about how to live, and only after that do they begin to engage in abstract reflections about "thin" transcendent principles of justice that can apply to everyone—such as the universal human rights in the Declaration of Independence. But because we are "always already" thick, our choices about thin transcendent principles are "always already" infected through and through by our previous socialization into our own thick, local or parochial worldviews. Thin principles of justice are, then, simply biased abstractions that reflect the story of our own thick cultural existence. Thus, moral principles are not and cannot be impartially based, because they "always already" presuppose a thick taken-for-granted background that reflects the stereotypes of any privileged group that has historically controlled the evolution of any set of principles, legal norms, or political policies. Because of the general skepticism about the possibility of consensus on impartial universal principles, critics like Lyotard (1984) argue that

> the grand narrative has lost its credibility, regardless of what mode of unification it uses, regardless of whether it is a speculative narrative or a narrative of emancipation. ... the principle of uni-totality—or synthesis under the authority of a metadiscourse of knowledge—is inapplicable. (Cited in Glass, 1993, p. 2)

This legitimate skepticism about the possibility for impartially based transcendent rationality is often allied with another criticism that is quite alarming. Just being committed to universal values will supposedly eventually lead to the oppression of minorities. This is a standard theme in postmodern philosophy. As Foucault (1988) says, "All my analyses are against the idea of universal necessities in human existence. They show the arbitrariness of institutions and show which space of freedom we can still enjoy and how many changes can still be made" (p. 11). For Foucault, so-called universal norms are simply an expression of the desire for power; that is, they are used in the service of the need to control others. He argues that the best way to avoid the desire for power is for each group to only represent its own interests in the political sphere. To try and help other groups in the name of universals will invariably lead us to misjudge their interests and contribute to their oppression. In short, any attempt to find a privileged ideal observer perspective is politically dangerous; because it lulls people into thinking they can be objective, leading them to overlook the inherent bias behind all so-called universal ends. When so lulled, banal civil servants can then support oppressive policies while thinking of themselves as honorable patriots serving absolute truth.

As an alternative, some critics recommend the adoption of a postmodern *particularist* story that will help us explicitly *reject universal assumptions, acknowledge the relativity of all interpretations of reality, and accept the fact that different cultural groups will always be embedded in incommensurable ways of life.* In a strong statement of this kind of thesis, Dancy (1992) points out that particularists understand that "there is no room for [universal] moral principles, and that it is bad faith to try to make moral decisions by appeal to them" (pp. 462ff). Walzer (1994) argues if we choose a universal principle, it should only be that of tribal "self-determination" (p. 67). He argues that even if the impulse to promote a universal vision is well intended it should be resisted:

> sometimes, watching the tribal wars, some of us may yearn for the uniform repressiveness of imperial or even totalitarian rule. For wasn't this repression undertaken in the name, at least, of universalism—and, in the case of the communists, of a thick morality ambitiously intended to replace every sort of moral particularism? (p. 81)

History has shown us again and again that some of the fears of postmodern philosophers are legitimate. People consistently misapply the universal norms that emerge during the discourse of justification. Attempts to implement such abstract universals are especially vulnerable to the "standard person problem." In short, we can expect even the most well-meaning of practical interventions by privileged powerful groups to be tainted by the special history of the groups. As Gunn Allen (1989) says:

> under the guise of protecting the Indian from extinction at the hands of numerous interests who thought extermination the best solution to "the Indian problem," Anglo-American liberals . . . pushed for cultural rather than physical genocide. . . . although the measures favored by white liberals did nothing to stem the pernicious effects of Anglo-European dominance, the situation improved when native people themselves became involved. (p. 16)

Problems with Postmodern Particularism

> **For Study:**   What are the two primary weaknesses of particularism that undermine the ability of the oppressed to criticize the injustice of their situation?

The postmodern particularist alternative has serious difficulties of its own. In the first place, MacIntyre (1981) points out that contemporary postmodern critics of universal values share assumptions about reason that are in tune with eighteenth century theologians who denied that reason could ever give us access to ultimate ends. They assume that "reason is calculative, it can assess truths of fact and mathematical relations but nothing more. In the realm of practice it can speak only of means. About ends it must be silent" (p. 52). The critics are assuming that all uses of reason must remain at Habermas's first level of pragmatic or strategic consideration. But, this narrow conception of instrumental rationality is hardly compatible with our ability to reason at the ethical and moral levels. Since the use of reason in morality is not supposed to be in the service of any local political agenda, in conception at least, at the level of justificatory discourse everyone must participate in an ongoing struggle against the domination of instrumental reason because it "always already" serves background agendas (sometimes acknowledged sometimes not.) For this reason, Gunther (1993, pp. 137–54) argues that many of the postmodern criticisms of universal reason are really only complaints about the lack of a well-developed application discourse that can tell people how to impartially apply universal norms.

We should not allow the legitimate doubts about metaphysical foundationalism in epistemology to precipitate an unnecessarily hasty antiuniversalist movement in morality. If we reject universals we risk cutting off our moral feet, leaving those of us who are opposed to oppression with no place to stand. In fact, on the face of it, the idea that universal values must lead to oppression seems surprising, since people who abuse in the name of universal values appear to be violating their own professed belief system. As Habermas (1993) says, "nobody may be excluded in the name of moral universalisms—neither underprivileged classes nor exploited nations, neither domesticated women nor marginalized minorities. Someone who in the name of universalism excludes another who has the right to *remain* alien or other, betrays his own guiding idea" (p. 15).

While it is true that all people begin embedded in thick cultural contexts that introject values into them during their socialization, we should not automatically buy the particularist assumption that all tribal values should be given equal moral weight, as though they are all equally benign ethical systems. For those interested in fighting oppression in all of its varieties, an unqualified acceptance of all positions is self-defeating. It leads directly to what Louise Antony (1993) calls the **bias paradox** (p. 190), which means that *if all criticisms are equally biased, then "the critique of oppression" is just another bias even though the critic wants to be taken more seriously than those he criticizes.* But the critic cannot be taken seriously if there is nothing that is not an interpretation against which to judge, since competing interpretations of the world simply become arbitrary (Hiley, Bohman, Shusterman, 1991, p. 8). When all choices are arbitrary, liberation itself becomes just one more arbitrary option sitting side by side with other arbitrary options like oppression.

If those who are oppressed are to have any basis for distinguishing normal forms of cultural bias from the pernicious forms that oppress, they need more than descriptions of how context affects belief; they also need to be able to make normative distinctions between types of contexts. In the end, many postmodern criticisms of modern Enlightenment aspirations seem to be arbitrary themselves. For instance, Huntington (1995) argues that poststructuralist feminists face a contradiction similar to the bias paradox. Their approach is "stuck in the awkward position of being unable to differentiate naive from critical consciousness while nonetheless presupposing its own authenticity as contrasted with other positions" (p. 404).

Finally, those involved in the fights against oppression are rightly uneasy about the underlying passivity in some particularist accounts of political consciousness. Particularism is too closely allied with cultural determinism, which portrays people as essentially passive recipients of the worldview introjected into them by their language community. Huntington (1995) warns that we must not reduce attempts to achieve liberation "to a form of stoic awareness" (p. 43), and Wilkins (1992) argues that "it is an individual's assessment of the logic of the situation in which he finds himself, his own determination of the options which are open to him, not the circumstances themselves, which are in the final analysis decisive" (p. 92). As Habermas (1997) says, to adjust to the pressures that come with globalization, "What generally seems to be necessary is the development of capacities for political action on a level above and between nation-states" (p. 122). This will require postconventional forms of consciousness that emerge during the transcendence from within.

Pluralism and Rationality

> **For Study:**   What should we do about the fact that there appears to be a plurality of absolute values? Given a plurality of backgrounds, what kind of approach to finding rational standards is most likely to facilitate talk about ultimate values that can help us resolve our disputes?

Even though some varieties of postmodern philosophy are overly cavalier in their treatment of morality, we cannot merely dismiss postmodern criticisms of Enlightenment concepts. Another postmodern alternative for dealing with pluralism seems more promising. *Pluralism* is a metaethical position that claims *there are a number of higher but irreducible ways of living, none of which can have absolute priority over the others.* They acknowledge that people can transcend ego and ethnocentric concerns in some contexts (which is why people continue to do research and seek therapy), but they say we may never be able to establish any ultimate priorities between the major belief systems themselves. Pluralism is not the same as relativism, since "some" belief systems are better than others, but a number of them may be equally adequate. This theory asserts that there are a number of background fundamental starting points supporting different absolute belief systems that are simply incommensurable with each other. For example, MacIntyre (1991) argues that each of the protagonists in an ethical argument

> reaches his conclusions by a valid form of inference from his premises. But . . . there exists in our culture no recognized procedure for weighing the merits of rival premises. Indeed it is difficult to see how there could be such a procedure since the rival premises are—to borrow a term from contemporary philosophy of science—*incommensurable.* That is to say, *they employ and involve concepts of such radically different kinds that we have no way to weigh the claims of one alternative set of premises over against another* [emphasis added]. (p. 56f)

If contradictory abstract ideals can have the same logical status as absolute truths, then how can we deal with conflicts between them? In the first place, there are those who disagree with MacIntyre's assertion about their status as incommensurables. We have to be careful not to become so impressed with our differences that we fail to notice the extent of our similarities. Johnson (1993) argues that MacIntyre's skepticism about the possibility of universal values overstates the case, because "moralities are not radically incommensurable forms of life. The fact of our embodiment guarantees . . . a core set of universal needs and desires . . . [Thus,] prototypes of *the bully, breach of promise, the good Samaritan,* and *exclusion from the group* [are all] basic human experiences, even though they may be variously elaborated in different traditions" (p. 234). As we saw earlier, Moody-Adams (1997) takes issue with the common belief that it is "self-evident that rationally irresolvable moral disagreements are an unavoidable fact of experience" (p. 3). She argues that this defeatist approach to rationality relies on nonempirical reductionist assumptions that lead philosophers away from the complexity of real moral experience and toward a metaphilosophy that disengages from the morality of real people (p. 3ff). To keep their theories useful to ordinary people, philosophers must find a way to formulate a conception of rational moral life that blends Devlin's devotion to the common feelings essential to one's heritage with Mill's willingness to go against those feelings when they come into conflict with the higher principles that govern the conscience of rational people.

It is important to note that the incommensurability thesis is asserted, not proven. In fact, if we look in the right places we may find foundational values that are the same in all cultures. For one thing, before any system of morality can work in any culture, the agents in the culture have to learn what it means to make a moral claim using the culture's language. Thus any competent member of any language community already knows what it means to ask people to give good reasons to justify their moral claims. Even if the content of what counts as a good reason varies, the idea of a good reason has a common logical structure. This shared logical understanding keeps different systems from being totally incommensurable. Therefore, a potential normative foundation upon which to build universal moral understanding may "always already" exist as procedural understanding in each competent language user, even if only tacitly. We may only need to make use of the "sciences that systematically reconstruct the intuitive knowledge of competent subjects" (Habermas, 1976, p. 9) to bring our shared intuitive understanding to the conscious level. Since some critics claim that any reconstruction by emotionally detached male philosophers will distort moral experience, let's begin our reconstruction by considering the relationship between emotion and reason that must exist in all competent members of language communities.

Rationality and Moral Emotions

> **For Study:**   Why does practical wisdom require that we keep rational skills and emotional intelligence integrated rather than separated?

Many who try to be objective or logical seem to believe that reason requires them to characterize all emotion as a source of arbitrary preference. But of course, this is not the case. Nothing in the concept of impartiality has to imply that reason should "ignore" how people feel. If feelings are ignored when they are in fact relevant to understanding the human situation, that is not a failure due to male rationality, it is a failure of those who do not understand the level of moral rationality. We can see just how important emotional understanding is to the proper use of practical reason by considering a famous case in which a person's capacity for rationality was destroyed when he lost the capacity to integrate reason and emotion. As we shall see, the case supports the argument that we can only make sense of intersubjective contexts if we develop a conception of reason that can intelligently integrate abstract theoretical insights with the moral emotions that govern choice in local social contexts. Without emotional sensitivity to local contexts, theoretical understanding and impartiality remain abstract and useless.

As reported in the account of the "Phineas Gage matrix" by Damasio (1994, p. 62), Phineas Gage was a highly respected, socially competent, construction foreman who suffered a severe injury when an explosion blasted a pointed iron rod through his cheek and out the top of his skull. The rod, which was three feet seven inches long and one and a quarter inches in diameter at it thickest point, passed so quickly through his brain that it only damaged specific localized area where his left and right frontal lobes meet. What amazed all observers is that Gage never lost consciousness and appeared to be in control of all his rational faculties. The attending physician said: "I can safely say that neither at that time [of initial medical intervention] nor on any subsequent occasion, save once, did I consider him to be other than perfectly rational" (Damasio, p. 6). In fact, of course, as his subsequent life history clearly demonstrated, Gage was no longer the rationally competent moral agent that everyone had respected. Areas of the frontal lobe necessary for integrating logical, analytic reasoning skills with emotional preferences had been damaged. Although he could put on a good show for short periods of time, he could no longer hold down a steady job. He had lost his ability to stay committed to his plans. And although once a very competent social agent, he was now unconcerned with whether or not he hurt people's feelings during conversations. With this kind of injury, "the value system remains and can be utilized in abstract terms, but it is unconnected to real-life situations" (Damasio, p. 11). In short, Gage had lost his capacity for practical wisdom, because he had lost the ability to connect his abstract theoretical understanding with the social emotions that make moral life emotionally "intersubjective" rather than merely logical and impersonal.

Studies of more recent cases involving the **Phineas Gage matrix** reinforce the point. Because these patients look so normal to the casual bureaucratic observer, they are sometimes denied disability pensions. Knowledgeable neurologists, however, can demonstrate that although these *patients can know things in an abstract way, so that they can say the right things in interviews, they cannot properly feel or intuit on a gut empathic level the intersubjective emotional impact of their abstract decisions.* When someone can talk theoretically about emotionally laden contexts and consequences, but can no longer care about real results, can we truly say they still understand the rational consequences of their theoretical knowledge? For instance, a patient called Elliot failed to consistently follow principles in real life situations, even though he demonstrated on tests that he still "knew the rules and principles of behavior that he neglected to use day after day" (Damasio, p. 46). He scored in the normal range on standard psychological and neurological tests, including the MMPI and the Standard Issue Moral Judgment Interview (which is similar to Kohlberg's moral development interviews). In brief, on standardized tests

> Elliot had a normal ability to generate response options to social situations and to consider spontaneously the consequences of particular response options. He also had a capacity to conceptualize means to achieve social objectives, to predict the likely outcome of social situations, and to perform moral reasoning at the advanced developmental level. . . . [but these results] contrasted sharply with the defective decision-making he exhibited in real life (Damasio, p. 48f).

After he had listed an abundant quantity of reasonable options for how to solve a problem on a social test, Elliot said: "And after all this, I still wouldn't know what to do!" (Damasio, p. 49). Elliot had lost the capacity to integrate abstract understanding with emotional commitment. He could no longer care about real social situations, so he was curiously detached—hardly what we would hope to find in an ideal rational observer. "The cold-bloodedness of Elliot's reasoning prevented him from assigning different values to different options, and made his decision-making landscape hopelessly flat" (Damasio,

p. 51). It is clear that the message to be found in the Phineas Gage matrix is "that observing social convention, behaving ethically, and making decisions advantageous to one's survival and progress require knowledge of rules and strategies *and* the integrity of [those] specific brain systems" (p. 17) that allow us to integrate all of this on a practical emotional level. Cognitions and emotions are not discreet separate mental events. As Nussbaum (1999) points out, "Emotions involve ways of seeing" (p. 1149), and in a similar vein, seeing clearly in morality involves emotions. So, as a prerequisite for moral agency, we need the ordinary capacities that allow tribal members to integrate abstract beliefs about principles and rules with the social emotions that underlie commitment and loyalty to community. Small communities are perfectly structured for teaching these basic virtues to new members.

On the other hand, the modern pluralistic state places a tremendous strain on these capacities. *Multicultural states* require citizens to *daily interact with strangers who have customs and beliefs that are so different they challenge our conventional ability to feel empathy for the situation of others.* Thus, we find ordinary people who say they agree with the abstract moral principle that all people are moral equals who have the same moral rights, but then seem unconcerned when people outside of their group have their rights violated. The third person ideal observer's contempt for immoral behavior which we expect to find in Smith's man of integrity seems to be missing. In some ways, their lack of concern for others seems like Phineas Gage after his accident, but of course, their failure to integrate theoretical principled understanding with practical emotional commitment is caused by something besides neurological failure. Do pluralistic cultures, with their confusing complex philosophies, ask for more than we can deliver? Not according to Habermas. He argues that the foundational virtues needed for the necessary expansion of moral consciousness are already present in all competent members of any language community. People only need to learn to decenter to a sufficient degree that they can use their virtues on a more general level that will include those who are different.

> [All we need to do is] . . . reconstruct the Ought that has immigrated into praxis itself, and we only need to observe that in positive law and the democratic constitutional state . . . principles are embodied that depend on a postconventional grounding, and to that extent are tailored to the public consciousness of a liberal political culture. (Habermas, 1997, p. 145)

Kantian Conditions for Rationality

For Study: Why does O'Neill think that Kant's theory can be reconstructed so that it encourages rational discourse across our differences?

If the norms we need are already embodied in the legal institutions of liberal culture, then let's return to the origins of this culture to see what norms were of concern to those who fathered liberalism. Because the culture arose during the eighteenth-century age of Enlightenment when philosophers were trying to develop intuitively obvious standards for rational moral reflection, we should briefly look at a major figure from that era. Many scholars agree that the Enlightenment reached its peak in the philosophical works of Immanuel Kant. Perhaps the best option is to reconstruct Kant's emphasis on commitment to universal principles to make it compatible with contemporary postmodern skepticism. It is not an accident that Kant turned to reason to discover the norms embodied in ordinary moral institutions. Given the background of a hundred years of religious wars between people of different faiths, he believed we had no other choice. Any attempt to establish grounds for the criticism of reason in some outside authority would simply transfer all the postmodern skeptical questions to that "new" foundation. As Kant (1938) says, "It would be absurd to look to reason for enlightenment, and yet to prescribe beforehand which side she must necessarily favor . . . Allow . . . your opponent to speak in the name of reason, and combat him only with the weapons of reason" (pp. A747, B775). O'Neill (1989) summarizes the consequences of Kant's theory about how practical reason functions as follows:

> The problem of seeing which modes of thinking—if any—are authoritative pre-supposes not only the lack of a "dictator," but the presence of a plurality of non-coordinated (potential) actors or thinkers. Kant uses the imagery of "citizens" or "fellow workers" to contrast the situation with that facing the subjects of a dictator who imposes common standards. He does not suggest that reason's authority is based on a constitutional convention, but reminds us that there is a plurality of potential reasoners. (p. 16)

This intersubjective way of characterizing reason leads logically to the idea that abstract universal concepts and principles are best conceived of as insights that emerge during cross-cultural moral discourse between *fellow workers,* that is, *all those from different traditions who work together to rationally evaluate the good reasons needed to justify moral claims.* This type of rationality requires respectful inclusion of opposing traditions, that is, it accepts MacIntyre's insight that there may be a number of opposing traditions each of which works quite well for the people within it. This kind of awareness makes it rational to insist upon open, inclusive debate between such systems. By including a plurality of participants, reason acknowledges that there is a critical *intersubjective* dimension to reason itself. But does this lead to an empty acceptance of every lifestyle choice no matter how immoral? No. Reason's tolerance has a cutting edge. It cannot tolerate the destruction of those conditions necessary for us to lead rational, social lives. As O'Neill points out, according to Kant, people who are in disagreement cannot even begin to share a world if there is no cognitive order. Those who are to be fellow workers [in the search for truth] must at least refrain from basing their action on basic principles that others cannot share. Those who act on such maxims are not guaranteed agreement at all points; but if they wholly reject it, communication and interaction (even hostile interaction, let alone coordination) will be impossible. (p. 23)

In this conception of moral reason, the attempt to communicate is at the heart of the enterprise. Specific universal values can be thought of as emergent temporary agreements that serve as ethical resting points, possibly to be transcended during subsequent, more enlightening, discussions. It is, of course, quite appropriate to be skeptical of the moral standing of any particular claims that emerge regarding which values ought to have the status of being foundational, cross-cultural, universal moral norms. Because even well-meaning people make mistakes, fail to take into consideration relevant differences, and are unduly influenced by morally irrelevant differences, moral discourse between fellow workers must be ongoing, never final. To keep this kind of communicative discourse rational, what norms do we need? O'Neill claims that Kant's classical liberalism asserts not only that one must refrain from "using force" but that everyone must accept an equal responsibility

1.   . . . **to think for oneself.** Only those who think for themselves have any contribution to make to a debate or plan. . . . Parroted words cannot be taken as expressions of judgment or as acts of communication.

2.   . . . **to think from the standpoint of everyone else.** Only those who . . . strive to listen to and interpret others and to see the point of their contributions are genuinely aiming to be "fellow workers" and to avoid maxims to which others cannot agree. . . .

3.   . . . **always to think consistently.** This is . . . a never-ending task. The set of judgments that we independently form, then revise as we shift our standpoint to take account of others' standpoints, will constantly change, and so may repeatedly fall into inconsistency. (pp. 25ff)

"To think from the standpoint of everyone else" is literally impossible. But it is not impossible to make a sincere effort to empathize with all other positions to the degree necessary to try and take in the contribution of other fellow workers. Proper use of empathy presupposes the kind of decentered epistemological and moral motives appropriate to a pure use of reason. Since *pure reason* is not in the service of any political agenda; in conception at least, it *requires an ongoing struggle against ideological uses of reason.* This means reason should not be equated with the positivistic conception of strategic or in-strumental reason, which always serves background agendas, sometimes ac-knowledged sometimes not. In ethics, the concept of pure reason should be used as a regulative metaphor to help us get a sense of what it means to strive for fairness in our treatment of people. This kind of impartiality should not be a problem, since it is morally required that we try to avoid pernicious forms of personal prejudice when making policy decisions that affect others. It is also a mistake to think of pure reason as being opposed to emotion, since as we note in Chapter Nine, Kant says pure reason causes reverence and awe for the moral law. We can treat O'Neill's work on Kant as a careful reconstruction of his phi-losophy that highlights the social (intersubjective), practical character of rea-son as well as its self-reflective and self-critical aspects. These are the kinds of norms Habermas thinks are already embodied in the talk among professionals in the justice system. But, is this ideal of a self-critical perspective really avail-able to average moral agents? Can ordinary nonprofessionals step outside of their own historical space and take a fresh critical view of values in the same way as trained professionals? Gadamer (1989) warns that we are presupposing a great deal even when we attribute such skills to professionals.

> In fact, history does not belong to us, but we belong to it. Long before we under-stand ourselves through the process of self-examination, we understand ourselves in a self-evident way in the family, society and state in which we live. The focus of subjectivity is a distorting mirror. The self-awareness of the individual is only a flickering in the closed circuits of historical life. That is why the prejudices of the individual, far more than his judgments constitute the historical reality of his being. (p. 245)

A mere "flickering" of self-awareness is not very inspiring. Gadamer is claiming that individuals can never transcend their own historical situation (their prejudices), so on the surface, his emphasis seems to be more sympathetic to the cultural relativists than to those who are striving for an absolute that can transcend cultural heritage. However, although Gadamer's position gives pri-macy to history, it also allows for a conception of rational progress if that progress results from historical or cultural forces that give us access to new horizons of understanding with more sophisticated interpretations of experi-ence. Gadamer is not a relativist, because he is working within what is called the hermeneutic tradition.

Hermeneutics refers to *the practice of interpretation (of texts or stories) or the study of the methods of interpretation.* According to the hermeneutic approach to reason, the fact that I believe that one interpretation is better than the others does not mean that I am claiming to already possess an absolute truth. In talking about interpretations, I have already relinquished my hold on the absolute truth. But, I have not relinquished the ideal that it is possible to make progress. I can respect and take seriously the position of those who come from a different heritage, so long as they are being serious about being responsible, and so long as they are not being banal or making obvious mistakes of a kind that my tradition has already transcended. (If I have no acquaintance with a tradition, I cannot say that I have transcended it.) Thus, relative to where we have been, we can talk meaningfully about moral progress, but we cannot claim to know that we have reached some kind of ultimate final destination that is superior to all future possibilities.

If we have to wait for history to lead the way to new modes of interpretation, are we saying ordinary people should remain passive and simply accept their historical lot? We can't say that because we can't wait. History demands that we become active choosers. In a pluralistic world, ordinary people, like you and me, are called upon to make the most amazing judgments. The responsibilities that come with professionalism are even more intense. "Moral agency," "government of the people," and "professionalism" all mandate that we be informed responsible decision makers. At the very least, then, we should occasionally challenge ourselves to transcend our previous orientations. With their capacities for mastering esoteric knowledge, professionals must lead the way, but how?

The goal of a well-thought-out, self-critical theory, is to help us rationally choose our future actions rather than habitually react to forces without reflecting on them. But why assume people can develop such a decentered perspective, when it is a developmental achievement that requires special historical circumstances for its full development? Classroom lectures alone will not stimulate the required transformation in consciousness (although five years of using the Minnesota DIT test of moral reasoning to evaluate the impact of applied ethics courses on student's perspectives has convinced me that classroom discussions help). As Johnson (1993) points out, the locus or medium of the necessary dialectical interchange does not take place during mere intellectual debate. Development is part of a historical process that "is worked out in the struggles of concrete economic, political, social and religious traditions, and not [only] in the debating hall" (p. 235). In other words, professional practice with a multicultural clientele will begin to promote the required transcendent growth, and critical discussion can merely speed up the process. Habermas (1996) argues that "communicative rationality" is what is needed to support the moral dialogue across differences that is required to stimulate the needed transcendence from within. Luckily, ordinary modes of communication have given everyone the procedural understanding they will need to make sense of this level of moral rationality.

Communicative Rationality

> **For Study:**   What are the normative presuppositions behind communicative rationality? Why is it inherently intersubjective? Why is it well suited for analyzing the rationality of a moral theory?

A postconventional understanding of the way communicative rationality logically supports the level of moral rationality needs to develop in everyone in pluralistic settings. The goal is to develop a conception of practical reason sophisticated enough to handle intersubjective emotional commitment at the multicultural level, but concrete enough that naive bureaucrats such as Eichmann cannot misuse it. Habermas believes that the basis for this kind of moral rationality already exists on a tacit procedural level in the practical reason of all competent members of language communities. In other words, we only need to consciously reconstruct this intuitive procedural understanding to make people aware that "moral rationality" at the cross-cultural level is only a decentered version of the *"communicative rationality"* (Habermas, 1996) all people already use as good members of their life-world. Since all forms of *rational communication aiming at reaching consensus* already involve the kinds of principles Kant mentions above, Habermas (1993) argues that at least on a tacit level, we all already know that the universal norms of discourse are rational, for example, *"freedom of access, equal right to participate, truthfulness on the part of participants, absence of coercion in taking positions, and so forth"* (p. 56). (For an indepth analysis of these norms see Chapter Ten's discussion of communicative rationality.)

The logic of these rational norms of discourse is studied in the discipline of *pragmatics,* which is a relatively *new linguistic field that studies the performative aspects of speech acts rather than the grammatical and syntactical structure of language.* Using the results of research in pragmatics, Habermas (1976) argues that the only reason communication is possible at all, is that competent speakers have internalized the procedural norms that allow competent members of speech communities to reach mutual understanding when striving for consensus (pp. 1–68). Communicative rationality is based on the awareness that these norms are logically required by any communicative discourse that aims for mutual understanding. Since every language community has the same pragmatic need for its people to coordinate their public plans on a consensual basis, the rational norms behind the practice of argumentative communication are correspondingly found in all life-worlds (Habermas, 1996). In other words, although different language communities can use different grammatical and syntactical structure to communicate, the underlying practical norms that make the intersubjective activity of communication at all possible appear to be the same in all language communities. Why is this the case?

To survive in a life-world, people have to learn to evaluate their consensual agreements in terms of an "intersubjective recognition" (p. 59) of what can count as valid reasons for making public claims. This entails that competent members of language communities have all had to learn "how to base their interactions on *validity claims* that their hearers will accept or that *could, if necessary, be redeemed with good reasons*" (Habermas, 1996, p. xv) (emphasis added). It is safe to assume, then, that on a neurological level the normative language structures that support a rational basis for mutual respect have already been internalized by anyone who knows how to engage in communicative discourse in a language community. These normative skills are procedural or automatic only because we learn them very early and use them without conscious reflection. To support universal respect for mankind, then, only requires us to make explicit to everyone the universal import of the norms of communication that they always already tacitly use.

To fully understand this point, we must clarify the logical structure of the three types of claims people use when they communicate with each other (Habermas, 1991, pp. 58–60). *First*, people make assertions that involve *truthfulness claims about private preferences* (our autobiographical statements). For example, people say things like, "I'm hungry now." How do you know they are telling the truth? You have to trust them. But, trust is appropriate only if their previous claims about themselves *have been redeemed or justified with the currency of consistent behavior*. That is, when they claim they are hungry, they typically use strategic or pragmatic rationality to find food.

Second, another type of assertion involves **truth claims** about the world or universe, for instance: "The moon is a sphere." These kinds of empirical claims about states of affairs *must be socially redeemed or justified with good reasons formulated according to the standards of a culture (e.g., the scientific community or the empirical traditions of a tribe).*

The *third* type of assertion involves **value claims** about what is right or appropriate. These are *redeemed with the norms that regulate a shared social world*. For example, "No one should lie for personal gain." This moral judgment is *justified or redeemed with good reasons that come from previous intersubjective agreement about what is right and wrong*.

It is important to keep these three categories separate, because practical reason functions differently as the level of intersubjectivity becomes more complex. Thus, the **claims to rationality** in both science and morality *require us to take a position that can be judged according to agreed upon public standards versus the private preferences of one person or group*. For instance, just as a private language based on personal preferences is logically inconsistent with the idea of public communication, so a private science and a private morality based on personal preferences is logically inconsistent with the public practices of science and morality. These latter two are inherently intersubjective enterprises. To be rational in either science or morality one must understand how to offer publicly acknowledged good reasons in each of them. This understanding presupposes one has the capacities for communicative rationality.

While scientific claims and moral claims share the intersubjective logic behind the idea of good reasons, they are also different with regard to the standards used—that is, the norms that define empirical evidence versus the common moral agreements used by a language community to regulate what is considered to be right and wrong. Habermas (1991) argues that the reason some people think we can give a purely empirical justification of moral norms is that they confuse the role that good reasons play in science with the role of good reasons in morality. This confusion tends to cause people to reduce the moral question "What ought I to do?" (which contains a moral "ought") into a question about what is prudent or expedient. This is a mistake because it converts an intersubjective question about a moral ought into "two other kinds of questions: What do I want to do? and How can I do it?" Because these latter questions distort the logic of the intersubjective moral context, Habermas says concerns about social utility should not be allowed to reduce the moral ought "to the technical question of the instrumental creation of socially desirable outcomes" (p. 49).

Communicative rationality avoids this empirical, reductionist obliteration of the intersubjective nature of morality. It is far better suited for evaluating the normative content of dialogue across differences than the simpler strategic or instrumental model of reasoning used in economic explanations of how individuals pursue satisfaction of personal preferences. Because the norms of communicative rationality are clearly intersubjective, they keep us focused on the obligation to provide good reasons to others. This intersubjective focus helps us understand the rationality behind those virtues that make it possible to provide good reasons cross-culturally.

As an example of the moral rationality behind communication, let's analyze the importance of the core pragmatic norm that makes reaching a consensus through communicative language possible. To communicate everyone must rely on the same public expectation that other members of the language community will honor the norm of honesty in their speech acts. Why is this expectation rational? Because it is an inherent aspect of communicative speech without which communication will be impossible. Since all societies require communication, it is irrational to reject this norm. The publicly recognized *communicative commitment to honesty* exists in a social space over and above the mere expression of words to another; it exists in the shared understanding of how communicative speech works. For instance, as a shared social norm it *entails that we all have an intuitive understanding that in the intersubjective context of communication it is illogical to say: "Using lies and manipulations, I convinced you that my position was right."* Every competent member of a communication community intuitively understands that lies and manipulations do not convince; they deceive. Merely by engaging in communicative discourse, *speakers have committed themselves to a "suprapersonal" norm that exists on an intersubjective higher level than the private interests that can be served by lies.* Thus, they know that in general communicative speech could not exist without the trust that accompanies the assumption of honesty. Communicative rationality is based on this intuitive understanding. Because both speaker and hearer know this on a procedural level, it leads to a bond of mutual trust (and thus communicative respect) that exists between speakers and hearers. It is only this shared social expectation—that others are obligated by and will be loyal to the norms of communication—that makes continued rational interaction possible (Habermas, 1991, p. 59). Even the conman acknowledges the existence of this inherent intersubjective expectation when he is being dishonest, because he has to rely on it while manipulating it to work his tricks. His intentional violation of implicit public trust explains why those who are committed members of the community ostracize him.

Although this bond based on communicative rationality exists within language communities, there are, of course, formidable hurdles in the way of institutionalizing honest discourse across cultures. With increased globalization and the economization of relationships between groups, survival seems to call for strategic action rather than communicative action. Habermas (1996) says,

> In the case of conflict, persons engaged in communicative action face the alternatives of either breaking off communication or shifting to strategic actions—of either postponing or carrying out the unresolved conflict. One way out of this predicament, now, is for the actors themselves *to come to some understanding* about the *normative regulation of strategic interactions*. (p. 26)

In a multicultural setting, the only way to regulate strategic interactions is to insist on honest discourse on the part of professional diplomats who are committed to real dialogue. They will need to develop an approach that gives them "access to the intuitive knowledge of the [various] life-world[s]" (Habermas, 1993, p. 13) that frame the perspectives of the affected people. Because members of local communities are the only ones who can properly clarify the qualitative features of their life-world, truly *impartial moral choices* will *only emerge if affected parties get to represent themselves in the rational communicative discourses that establish policy.* In principle, then, communicative rationality requires the active participation of everyone affected, and entails an obligation of justice to include everyone with the baggage of their own unique heritage. If people can transcend to this level of understanding, they should be able to develop a sense of decentered *solidarity* with everyone because of the communicative bond. They will see each other as fellow members of an *abstract, moral, communicative community where each gets to be uniquely who he or she is* (like a Kantian kingdom of ends; see Chapter Nine).

Communicative rationality raised to the level of cross-cultural morality, explains the intersubjective logic behind our moral obligation to include everyone affected in social discussions before final decisions are reached. People ought to be given power over their own lives as a way of showing communicative respect for the fellow workers from different traditions. We must do this because the limits of the tribal ethical point of view become manifest once questions of justice arise. From the perspective of ethical rationality, moral concerns about impartial justice are reduced to being just another ethical value that might be traded away. So we either move up to the higher level of moral rationality, or we lose an important deontological or nonconsequentialist feature of moral life (see Chapter Nine). Habermas (1998) says,

> as long as duties are viewed *solely* from the ethical point of view, an *absolute* priority of the right over the good, . . . cannot be maintained. . . . [And without that priority] one cannot have an ethically neutral conception of justice. This deficit would have unfortunate consequences for equal treatment in pluralistic societies. (pp. 27–28)

Conceptions of the good life vary from group to group and any attempt to base universal standards of justice on these local conceptions will lead to the standard person problem, where one group will impose its definition of the good life on other groups in the name of justice. To avoid this kind of injustice, the moral rationality that determines universal standards of justice has to have priority over the ethical rationality that determines local conceptions of the good life. Thus, justice based on communicative rationality requires that each group speak for itself during communication about how to resolve conflicts. It is clear that the intersubjective norms that make such cross-cultural communicative action possible are far less likely to lead to abuse due to standard person problem errors than the simpler personal and group agendas that guide instrumental reasoning.

We must now turn to a reconstruction of the concept of moral autonomy, so as to give it an interpretation consistent with the modern social sciences as well as with the normative constraints of communicative rationality.

REFERENCES

ANTONY, LOUISE M. (1993). Quine as feminist: The radical import of naturalized epistemology. In Louise M. Antony & Charlotte Witt (Eds.), *A mind of one's own* (pp. 185–226). Boulder: CO: Westview Press.

BURSTYN, LINDA. (1995). Female circumcision comes to America. *The Atlantic monthly* 176 (4) October. pp. 28–35.

DAMASIO, A. (1994). *Decartes' error: Emotion, reason, and the human brain.* New York: Avon Books.

DANCY, JONATHAN. (1992). Caring about justice. *Philosophy* 67, 462ff.

DEVLIN, LORD PATRICK. (1971). Morality and the criminal law. In Richard Wasserstrom (Ed.), *Morality and the law* (pp. 55–73). Belmont, CA: Wadsworth.

DWORKIN, RONALD. (1971). Lord Devlin and the enforcement of morals. In Richard Wasserstrom (Ed.), *Morality and the law* (pp. 55–72). Belmont, CA: Wadsworth.

FLAX, JANE. (1990). *Thinking fragments: Psychoanalysis, feminism, and postmodernism in the contemporary West.* Berkeley: University of California Press.

FOUCAULT, MICHEL. (1988). *Technologies of the self: A seminar with Michel Foucault.* Luther H. Martin, Huck Gutman, & Patrick H. Hutton (Eds.). Amherst: University of Massachusetts Press.

GADAMER, HANS-GEORG. (1989). *Truth and method*. J. Weinsheimer & D. Marshall (Trans.). New York: The Crossroad.

GLASS, JAMES M. (1993). *Shattered selves: Multiple personality in a postmodern world*. Ithaca, NY: Cornell University Press.

GUNN ALLEN, PAULA (Ed.). (1989). *Spider woman's granddaughters: Traditional tales and contemporary writing by Native American women*. New York: Fawcett Columbine.

GUNTHER, KLAUS. (1993). *The sense of appropriateness: Application discourses in morality and law*. John Farrell (Trans.). Albany: State University of New York Press.

HABERMAS, JURGEN. (1976). What is universal pragmatics? In Thomas McCarthy (Trans.), *Communication and the evolution of society* (pp. 1–68). Boston: Beacon Press.

———. (1991). *Moral consciousness and communicative action*. Christian Lenhardt & Shierry Weber Nicholsen (Trans.). Cambridge, MA: The MIT Press.

———. (1993). *Justification and application: Remarks on discourse ethics*. Ciaran P. Cronin (Trans.). Cambridge, MA: The MIT Press.

———. (1996). *Between facts and norms: Contributions to a discourse theory of law and democracy*. William Rehg (Trans). Cambridge, MA: The MIT Press.

———. (1997). The European nation state—Its achievements and its limitations. On the past and future of sovereignty and citizenship. In W. Krawietz, E. Pattaro, & A. Erh-Soon Tay (Eds.), *Rule of law: Political and legal systems in transition* (pp. 109–22). Berlin: Duncker & Humblot.

———. (1998). *The Inclusion of the other*. Ciaran Cronin & Pablo De Greiff (Eds.). Cambridge, MA: The MIT Press.

HILEY, DAVID R., BOHMAN, JAMES F., & SHUSTERMAN, RICHARDS (Eds.). (1991). *The interpretive turn*. Ithaca, NY: Cornell University Press.

HUNTINGTON, PATRICIA. (1995). Toward a dialectical concept of autonomy. *Philosophy & social criticism*, 21 (1): 37–55. London: Sage.

JOHNSON, MARK. (1993). *Moral imagination: Implications of cognitive science for ethics*. Chicago: The University of Chicago Press.

KANT, IMMANUEL. (1938). *Critique of pure reason*. Norman Kemp Smith (Trans.). London: Macmillan.

KEGAN, ROBERT. (1994). *In over our heads: The mental demands of modern life*. Cambridge, MA: Harvard University Press.

LYOTARD, JEAN-FRANCOIS. (1984). *The postmodern condition: A report on knowledge*. Minneapolis: University of Minnesota Press.

MACINTYRE, ALASDAIR. (1981). *After virtue*. Notre Dame, IN: University of Notre Dame Press.

———. (1988). *Whose justice? Which rationality?* Notre Dame, IN: University of Notre Dame Press.

———. (1991). Moral disagreements. In Tom L. Beauchamp (Ed.), *Philosophical ethics* (pp. 55–57). New York: McGraw-Hill.

MILL, JOHN STUART. (1859, 1971). *On liberty*. In Richard Wasserstrom (Ed.), *Morality and the law* (pp. 10–23). Belmont, CA: Wadsworth.

MOODY-ADAMS, M. MICHELE. (1997). *Fieldwork in familiar places*. Cambridge, MA: Harvard University Press.

NUSSBAUM, MARTHA C. (1999). *Sex and social justice.* Oxford: Oxford University Press. Cited in Steven M. Cahn (Ed.). (2002). *Classics of political and moral philosophy* (pp. 1136–61). Oxford: Oxford University Press.

O'NEILL, ONORA. (1989). *Constructions of reason: Explorations of Kant's practical philosophy.* New York: Cambridge University Press.

WALZER, MICHAEL. (1994). *Thick and thin: Moral argument at home and abroad.* Notre Dame, IN: University of Notre Dame Press.

WILKINS, BURLEIGH. (1992). *Terrorism and collective responsibility.* New York: Routledge, Chapman and Hall.

WILLS, GARRY. (1978). *Inventing America.* New York: Vintage Books.

Chapter   Seven

Moral Autonomy, Accountability, & Lifestyle Choice

Philosophical moral theories must be able to distinguish between values that can function as foundational universal moral values and those popular but local values that are not foundational universal values. It is natural to experience tension between the personal point of view, which wants to favor self and family and tribe and the impersonal MPofV (moral point of view), which wants to do the right thing even when it may conflict with personal or tribal values. Other things being equal, we expect moral agents to resolve this tension in favor of the MPofV. We try to support giving morality priority with codes of ethics, decision procedures, and moral folklore designed to constrain the personal so that the impersonal will triumph. Do these institutional attempts to promote universal conceptions of justice undermine the autonomy of individual moral agents? As we shall see, while they may compromise personal autonomy, they are consistent with moral autonomy.

∿ Autonomy

For Study: When applied to humans, what does the concept of autonomy mean? Why do children lack autonomy?

Autonomy is a concept that was originally borrowed from political philosophy. Autonomous nations were not controlled by other nations. They could support themselves, were self-governed, and could develop an independent foreign policy (Feinberg, 1973, p. 15). When referring to people, then, autonomy means the capacity to be in control of your own behavior. This point should not be misinterpreted. We are not saying autonomous people ignore external events. It would be irrational to ignore factors in the environment that provide us with useful information. So, *autonomous* people are *influenced by externals,* but they are *not controlled* by them. Control of action is internal and based on the autonomous person's belief system and values. Personal autonomy is thought of as a virtue partly because it concerns consistent, conscious self-control by a stable set of beliefs and desires that we welcome, rather than control by arbitrary or inconsistent desires over which we appear to have little control (such as a nicotine fit or voices that invade the thinking of the mentally ill). According to R. S. Peters (1973), young children in Piaget's preoperational stage are not yet autonomous in this sense, because they are the victims of unexamined wishes and aversions, naive inadequate concepts, and external pressures (p. 36).

Autonomy develops in institutions that encourage emotional attachment and rational choice. Families that provide inconsistent arbitrary environments in which similar choices lead to contradictory, self-defeating consequences do not promote capacities for autonomy. For instance, households that are dominated by mental illness or severe drug abuse teach children that emotional investment and rational plans are useless at best and dangerous at worst. Since it hurts to have expectations squashed for irrational and arbitrary reasons, children raised under these conditions develop irrational coping strategies that will make them vulnerable to external control when they become adults (Middleton-Moz and Dwinnell, 1986). Since "rationality" is one of the components of morally responsible decision making, arbitrary households that punish consistent behavior are dysfunctional from the moral point of view. These considerations lead to the following definition of *personal autonomy:*

> One is controlled by an independent will with a stable, fairly consistent set of emotions and beliefs, in contrast to being controlled by (1) biological or introjected social desires that we consciously reject, or (2) social and external forces that we consciously reject.

Personal Autonomy Is Not Moral Autonomy

> **For Study:**   Why can a sociopath satisfy the minimum requirements for autonomy? What characteristics do sociopaths lack that make it difficult for them to make rational "moral" choices?

This minimal level of autonomy covers the prudential skills needed to evaluate the consequences of personal habits (like smoking) or to make economic career plans. This is autonomy at the pragmatic strategic level of reasoning discussed in the last chapter. This is not the notion of autonomy that has inspired eighteenth century philosophy. As we saw in Chapter Five, a critic of the male voice can ask, "Why should autonomy be a moral ideal?" By itself, personal autonomy isn't. It is morally neutral and consistent with choosing good or bad, moral or immoral options. As Feinberg (1986) says,

> It is important to emphasize at the outset that even a refined conception of autonomy will be at best only a partial ideal, for since it is consistent with some important failings it is insufficient for full moral excellence. No further analysis can be expected to rule out as impossible a selfish but autonomous person, a cold, mean, unloving but autonomous person, or a ruthless, or cruel, autonomous person. After all, a self-governing person is no less self-governed if he governs himself badly, no less authentic for having evil principles, no less autonomous if he uses his autonomy to commit aggression against another autonomous person. The aggressor is morally deficient, but what he is deficient in is not necessarily autonomy. He may have more than enough of that. (p. 45)

To see why we need to reconstruct the concept of autonomy, it will be instructive to look at a type of person who sometimes seems autonomous even though he is the opposite of the moral ideal. The 1994 version of the *American Psychiatric Association's Diagnostic and Statistical Manual of Mental Disorders* (sec. 301.7) defines "antisocial personality disorder" as someone who has "a pervasive pattern of disregard for and violation of the rights of others, occurring since age 15 years." People with this disorder used to be called psychopaths and more recently sociopaths. I will use the term *sociopath* since I want to emphasize that the person seems to have a personality disorder that interferes with his or her ability to understand social life at the level required by moral rationality. Many sociopaths are controlled for the most part by their own internal beliefs and personal desires and do not act on whim or impulse any more than the rest of us. Their problem with morality is not a lack of self-control; it has more to do with the narrowness of the self that is in control.

Because a sociopath is not bothered by social emotions such as remorse or guilt, his life choices are socially naive in the sense that they display an overly simplistic interpretation of human relationships. But, if they are careful to play "the social game" and not collide with external authority figures, they can even be strategically rational when choosing social means to their ends. Kegan (1994) points out that most sociopaths do not get in trouble with the law, they just break the hearts of the people who love them (p. 38). But for the sake of creating a clear contrast, let's consider an extreme case. The drifter and mass murderer Ted Bundy had quantitative rational skills, but according to psychologists who examined him and reporters who interviewed him, he appeared to have the emotional development of someone about twelve years old. He understood punishment and rewards and could think on an abstract level about quantitative matters, but because he was morally undeveloped, he could not understand the qualitative emotional side of social commitment and obligation. When we read the following statement, we can only shake our heads in disbelief. Bundy believed

> that under the correct circumstances he could select any person as a victim and that there would be virtually no attention paid to that person's disappearance. People disappear every day. It happens all the time. . . . He was always amazed and chagrined by the publicity generated by disappearances he thought would go almost totally unnoticed. There are so many people. It shouldn't be a problem. What's one less person on the face of the earth, anyway? (Michard and Aynesworth, 1983, pp. 310–11)

This kind of person has no qualitative procedural understanding of loyalty to community nor of normal human empathy (or what Adam Smith calls human sympathy). Normal members of communities care about the community, and they are outraged when community members are murdered, even when they don't know them personally. An inability to empathize, however, does not automatically mean one is sociopathic. Remember, Temple Grandin had trouble feeling empathy for many human emotions, but she at least wished she could fit in and says she always wanted to make a contribution to humanity. The sociopath goes beyond Grandin's difficulties with emotional understanding; he just doesn't care. Bundy's so-called autonomy in the face of social norms, then, is not based on human virtues but on human deficits. He seems more like a ten-year-old concrete thinker in an adult body (Kegan, 1994, p. 39). He lacks certain common moral intuitions that are based on the conventional human capacity to empathize and to understand the qualitative point of conventional life. If, on a fundamental level, a person cannot care about social life, how can he make choices in an autonomous "moral sense" when he can't understand the most important options?

To be autonomous in a sense that is morally significant, people must have some qualitative understanding of the social nature of the moral options available to them, even if for some reason they decide not to choose any of these alternatives. I am assuming, of course, that autonomous choice implies that options are available and the chooser has the capacity to evaluate them. Autonomous people are assumed to be in control of their life, and to be free to choose their own values, life plans, and principles, but their choices will not earn our respect if they are based on a deficient vision of the social world. A sociopath like Bundy cannot comprehend what it means to feel social commitment or respect for others, thus he cannot be said to have *chosen* to exclude them. He excludes them by default, not because of independent value deliberation. He may be autonomous in a banal sense, but he is not an autonomous *social* agent since he is socially blind. Without some sense of moral or social commitment, then, social life in a full moral sense is only a fantasy.

At the application level, society has to hold the Bundies among us legally responsible, as though they are fully developed moral agents. But, it is instructive to keep in mind that even though it is necessary to treat Bundy as a legally recognized autonomous agent, he is not really a morally autonomous, responsible agent. His autonomy amounts to no more than what we would expect to find in a clever, preconventional, antisocial child. The fact that people can think on a "theoretical level" gives them the capacity to turn around and criticize the institutions that nurtured them, but the critique will be poorly informed if they lack procedural qualitative understanding of social norms. In other words, intellect alone does not lead to moral wisdom; one also needs emotional maturity. The need for well-rounded development helps explain why very bright but emotionally undeveloped children, and some computer nerds who create computer viruses, seem so strange when they start talking about social issues. The social topics are merely a computational game to them; they literally are lacking important social information in their database. When we praise autonomy, then, we have people such as Socrates, Lincoln, or Mother Teresa in mind as models for our children. They understand why certain rules have intrinsic social value in addition to their instrumental value to particular individuals. Peters (1973) makes a similar point when he says that to be a moral agent, a person

> must be sensitive to considerations such as the suffering of others or fairness which are to serve as principles for him. For it is not sufficient to be aware that actions have certain types of consequences; he must care about the consequences. (p. 99) [Otherwise he will be like Phineas Gage, who was discussed in Chapter Six.]

The concept of autonomy that is inspiring is a "moral" concept, not just a personal one. So, to clarify the concept we have to explore the "moral" assumptions behind the idea of self-governance.

∿ Moral Autonomy

> **For Study:** What kind of special understanding does a person need to be morally autonomous? Why do social rules have to be self-imposed for autonomy to exist? How is that compatible with an ideal where everyone is considered autonomous?

The concept of moral autonomy must refer both to an ability to live according to moral principles (rather than live only on the basis of desires), as well as to an ability to authentically adopt or reject the principles after informed critical deliberation. The moral rules a morally autonomous person imposes on himself must also be authentically his; they cannot be slogans picked up somewhere. Actions and thoughts based solely on causal factors outside of a person's rational moral will are simply not his or her own moral actions and thoughts. A person is neither a rational agent nor a moral agent when he is forced to obey someone else's rules. In some sense of authenticity, then, moral principles and rules must be our own. Feinberg (1986) points out that

> Immoral authenticity is as real as its moral counterpart. In theory we all have a choice between the moral life and its amoral and immoral alternatives. But if we opt to govern our lives by moral principle, then insofar as our subsequent moral convictions are authentically our own, certain life policies will no longer be eligible for our choice. We cannot even consider, for example, the *satanic life-principle* that *we should inflict as much pain as we can* [Emphasis added], or the principle that we should promote our interests at all costs to those who might get in our way. Persons who opt otherwise, to repeat, may be thoroughly self-governing (autonomous), but in order for moral principles to be authentically their own, they must have moral principles in the first place. (pp. 38–39)

Authentic moral agents must not forget the logical requirements needed for a norm to be *social*. In the same manner as communication, moral choice is an inherently intersubjective social activity. We cannot deny the intersubjective logic of what we are doing and still consider ourselves to be rational "moral" beings. Morally autonomous people care about having *moral* values, but they are still willing to critically evaluate their own introjected and learned moral values. They judge principles (and the rules that follow from them) with the conscious knowledge that the moral principles are supposed to apply *universally* in all social contexts. This means that any standard they accept as a moral principle must be universal in two ways: first, in the sense that the principle applies to all moral agents (no one can have their status as a moral being arbitrarily rejected) and second, in the sense that it must make sense to think that at least in principle every morally autonomous agent could agree to follow the moral standard. Thus, in an ***ideal society*** where morally autonomous people are governed by their own choices, *concrete moral policies and laws would be justified only if it makes sense to say that they are the kind of laws and policies that, in principle, would have been self-imposed by any morally autonomous person.*

Notice that the need for a public morality requires choosers to decenter and take everyone into consideration. Egocentric and ethnocentric people cannot adopt a decentered perspective, so by default rather than by choice, local concrete concerns will dominate their decision making. They may agree that debate between all members of the moral community is important, but their definition of moral community will be excessively narrow. So, at the decentered level of morality human reason strives for universal conceptions that can be shared by all. Universals do not require people to stop being who they are, unless who they are on a concrete level is inconsistent with toleration of the right of other people to live according to a universal moral point of view. But universals do require people to care about others in a way that transcends their own concern for their heritage. We are now prepared to give a final definition of *moral autonomy.* It means:

> to be governed by social principles that are self-imposed because as a caring moral agent the chooser believes they are the kind of principles that would at least in principle be acceptable to other agents who are rational choosers of their own principles.

This conception of autonomy does not guarantee that the principles chosen will be the best available. Morally autonomous people can make mistakes when choosing. Also, morally autonomous people do not always win (remember, Socrates was executed). It only means the chooser is trying to be morally responsible and has the capacity to make the effort. Thus, morally autonomous efforts deserve our respect because the "form of the behavior" is morally admirable even when we disagree with the content of the choice made. To agree that people should respect moral autonomy as an ideal does not beg any important questions, since it is compatible with reasonable disagreements between proponents of the major theories. However, it does imply that when we intervene in one another's lives, or create new social settings, we should be paying close attention to how our choices will affect the development of moral autonomy in all people, including future generations.

Moral Autonomy Entails Moral Accountability

> **For Study:** Why are moral autonomy and moral accountability logically linked? If we refuse to give an account to those we affect, what message are we sending them?

As we saw in Chapter One, Adam Smith, the Scottish communitarian, claims that

> A moral being is an accountable being. An *accountable being,* as the word expresses, *is a being that must give an account of its actions to some other, and that consequently must regulate them according to the good-liking of this other* [emphasis added]. (Cited in Hope, 1984, p. 159)

Accountability relationships all share the same form: "Some agent" (A) is accountable to a "person affected" (PA) for the "activity that affects" (AA) him. Generally, A must be a person or agency competent to give an account of a required kind, and the PA must be a person or agency capable of receiving and understanding the account. Obviously, the nature of the account given will depend on the capacities of both the agent and the recipient as well as on the complexity of the type of activity. For instance, the account a nuclear physicist gives to a regulatory agency may be considerably more sophisticated than the account he offers to the general public, even though the activity is the same in both cases (Bayles, 1979). Liability to an occasional account is not a severe restriction on autonomy; it only asks for an explanation of how a person is exercising autonomous judgment. As mentioned in Chapter Two, all professionals who exercise discretionary power are responsible for giving an account to other professionals that will explain how the discretionary call is consistent with the professional code of ethics.

This kind of minor restriction on autonomy is required by the logic of moral autonomy itself. Moral autonomy gives all people power over their own life, but *only* their own life. Thus whenever our actions affect the interests of others we owe them an account of why we think our actions have stayed within the boundaries set by the ideal of moral autonomy. In morality there is always room for leeway to act, hence there is always room for individual judgment about how to be moral. A moral account clarifies the theory, principles, and rules that we are following. Moral agents, then, need to act with awareness that background moral autonomy implies a background of **moral accountability** as well. The obligation requires that *in principle, agents must be prepared to give those they affect an explanation that will show how their actions respect the moral autonomy of those affected.*

To refuse to give an account for public behavior is to refuse to recognize the fundamental background norm that comes with the ideal of moral autonomy, that is, that people are in principle **moral equals.** This is the background ideal of moral equality that was referred to in the Declaration of Independence, and is sometimes summarized by the phrase *everyone counts as one.* Moral equals are accountable to one another no matter what concrete material inequalities exist. This level of abstraction is sometimes difficult for people to understand. Because there are so many concrete relationships of inequality in their daily life, it is difficult for them to stay focused on the "reality" of the abstract moral equality that comes with an ideal such as moral autonomy. To make moral equality real for them, one would have to actually implement it in concrete institutions by creating a system of moral accountability that encourages people to think of one another as equals. But, because this does not get emphasized in most hierarchical systems, the ideal of moral equality lacks substance for many people.

Perhaps people can better understand the concept if they use procedural knowledge they already possess to create a metaphorical extension that transfers the substantive content in the notion of "family equality" to the concept of "moral equality." That is, in many families, having an equal right to family status does not depend on having equal power in the family. Parents are constantly trying to teach older siblings that baby brother counts as an equal member of the family, even if he is the runt of the litter. In a similar manner, the MPofV tells us that *we are all members of the moral family, with equal moral status, even while we live with the reality of unequal status in the political and economic world*. Once we accept that moral equality gives everyone a right to a place, it changes our orientation to the material relations in the world. That is, we become suspicious of all those material inequalities that seemed like unchangeable realities before we grasped the concept of moral equality. Material inequality is a fact of life, but how much material inequality is compatible with moral equality? It is clear that some forms of inequality are not justifiable (such as slavery) while other inequalities are compatible with our equal moral status (such as babies should not have a license to drive). Calls for the reform of existing institutions often start when people begin to doubt that an existing concrete inequality is compatible with their ideal status as moral equals.

The Need For Accountability Procedures

> **For Study:**   Why do concrete inequalities make accountability procedures necessary? What kind of inequality can distract professionals from their moral duty to respect moral equality?

An *accountability procedure* is an institutional device that *calls for actual accountability, so as to encourage us to remain thoughtful about our actions, just as we would be if we knew we were being watched by a third person*. We are reminded to ask ourselves, "Would I be doing this if I had to give an account to an independent rational agent who was observing my actions?" Among people who are equal in rank, this kind of third-person perspective is always present; that is, equals think of themselves as having enough status and power to be rational observers of each other. We expect our peers to be aware of what we are doing to them, so the obligation to give an account to a "real" equal is taken for granted (we can say a kind of third-person moral point of view is inherent in the nature of equal relationships). But concrete institutional inequalities in status can undermine this perspective, or make it difficult to keep it in the forefront of our attention.

For Instance:

Many years ago, I experienced the way in which real inequalities in status can contribute to a type of moral insensitivity. I was a new assistant professor at my university. I made an appointment to talk to the director of the Counseling Center after his lunch hour. I arrived at 1:00 P.M. and had to wait 45 minutes before he showed up. This was not particularly disturbing, for I assumed he was tied up with something important and would apologize (give an account) for keeping me waiting. When he arrived, however, he looked surprised to see me and said: "Oh, David. I didn't know you were my 1:00 o'clock appointment. I thought it was a student. I would have been on time if I had known it was you." There are, of course, problems with this account. If he could have made it on time for me, he could have made it on time for anyone, so he should have been on time. An appointment is an appointment. Alternatively, if there had been good reasons for his being late, he should have used the good reasons to give me the account that he owed to anyone, including a student. I think his attitude illustrates the easy way we let real institutional inequalities in status and power begin to undermine our obligations to treat one another as moral equals. When he saw it was a peer waiting for him, he felt either embarrassed or apologetic, so he gave me the type of account that he thought a peer (who shared his status on campus) would understand. To him, his concrete institutional superiority was real and grounds for treating people as unequal in terms of punctuality. By the way, I did not challenge his poor account. At the time I did not have these ideas organized into a coherent framework. I was also like the "good" guards in the Zimbardo experiment. I was morally sensitive enough to disapprove of immoral behavior when I saw it, but I had a tendency to let immoral and unpleasant behavior slide by—hoping it would soon go away. I should have encouraged him to go into more detail, so we both could develop a deeper understanding of the situation. I have often wondered: If a third person had been observing the entire affair, thus giving the director a concrete reason to believe in the reality of the ideal of moral equality, would he have been more sensitive to the equal human status of students and faculty, and thus less likely to keep a student waiting for no good reason?

The ideal of moral autonomy (moral equality) should have priority over local concrete inequalities. An ability to keep concrete relations compatible with abstract ideals helps explain why Socrates was considered by the Oracle at Delphi to be the wisest of all the Greeks. He had achieved a conceptual level that allowed him to see moral ideals as more stable and real than the shifting concrete conventions at the local level.

Unless we are careful, everyone can easily become overly impressed with concrete inequalities. Institutionalized inequalities can begin to look like unalterable facts of nature. The mere existence of unequal status has been used to justify the power of kings, the oppression of marginalized populations, and overt evils like slavery. As far back as the Enlightenment, we find Rousseau criticizing the empirical moral reasoning of Grotius, Hobbes, Caligula, and Aristotle. He claimed that they all made the mistake of trying to derive what ought to be from the fact of what is. Hereditary class structures were so common, that most people just accepted them as philosophically legitimate because they believed such hierarchies were unchangeable natural phenomenon rather than inventions of mankind. In ancient Athens, Aristotle observed the empirical reality of slavery and concluded that slavery was a natural inequality because some men are born to be slaves. Rousseau (1762, 1968) rejected this empirical interpretation of this oppressive convention.

> Aristotle was right: but he mistook the effect for the cause. Nothing is more certain than that a man born into a condition of slavery is a slave by nature. A slave in fetters loses everything—even the desire to be freed from them . . . If some men are by nature slaves, the reason is that they have been made slaves *against* nature. Force made the first slaves: cowardice has perpetuated the species. (pp. 171–72)

I think Rousseau is right when he asserts that "It might be possible to adopt a more logical system of reasoning, but none which would be more favorable to tyrants" (p. 171). In spite of his centuries-old warning, we still find that each new generation has to be reminded that "the way it has been" is not synonymous with "the way it ought to be." It is a fact of life that those high up in a hierarchy possess real concrete superiority to those below them (e.g., unequal political and economic power). Because professionals have esoteric knowledge, and are dealing with people who need their help, they too are daily confronted by their concrete superiority in knowledge and power. This can have a debilitating effect on their moral sensitivity, since real institutional superiorities of this kind can daily draw our attention away from abstract ideals. Thus, when a focus on concrete inequality is the background for one's moral consciousness, it becomes easy to forget that those below us in a hierarchy are none the less still our actual moral equals. To fight this tendency, we may need to adopt explicit requirements that call for accountability to those who are below us in institutional status, for example, through the use of student evaluations of teachers or client evaluations of professionals.

A concrete system of accountability will not, of course, stop all activities that unjustifiably harm those in whose lives professionals must intervene. Other forces are also at work. But by focusing our attention on (a) moral autonomy's special status as a moral value, (b) variables that affect moral autonomy, (c) the accountability structure in institutions, and (d) our obligations to give an acceptable account to the moral equals we affect, a system of accountability can help us lower the number of instances in which we are genuinely surprised to discover that we have harmed someone despite our good intentions. Stop for a moment and think about some situation where you did something that made you feel ashamed or guilty. Would you have been as likely to do it if you had to give an account to some third party who had been observing you? Ideally, we should develop an internal conscience to whom we feel accountable. Adam Smith (1976) said,

> In order to defend ourselves from such partial judgments, we . . . set up in our own minds a judge between ourselves and those we live with. . . . one who has no particular relation . . . to us, . . . an impartial spectator who considers our conduct with the same indifference with which we regard that of other people. (p. 129)

Zimbardo (1974) must have arrived at a similar conclusion, since after analyzing his Stanford Prison Experiment (see Chapter Two), he concluded "in the future [we will] incorporate a metaexperimenter in the role of unbiased monitor with 'detached concern.' His/her task will be to assess the impact of the treatment on the subjects as well as the impact of the progress of the experiment on the researchers" (pp. 254–55).

Zimbardo's use of a *detached observer* is innovative and in the spirit required by the concepts of moral autonomy and accountability. His recognition of the need for *an outside observer to whom he would naturally feel accountable* might be traceable to the fact that it was an outsider who caused him to finally halt his experiment (that is, someone who was not participating in the actual experiment). Although he reports (1975) he was planning on stopping the experiment anyway, he was jolted into action when his fiancée (who had accompanied him to his mock prison) looked through the observation hole at the end of the hall and tearfully told him: "It's awful what you are doing to those boys" (p. 44). This contact with criticism, which was external to the closed environment of the research setting, helped him bring moral reality back into his professional practice, where concrete inequalities had taken control of all of the participants.

It should be clear by now that ethical theories can have a fairly practical impact if we will let them guide our decisions. Theoretical ideals are transcendent moral realities that can become actual in our lives when we allow them to influence our actions and when we build them into the structure of our institutions. In pluralistic cultures, of course, we can become confused about how to proceed. Recommended ideals are not always consistent with one another, and even a consistent set may not always be uniformly implemented in the day-to-day rules by which we live. Under conditions of pluralism, transcendent norms have to be constantly rediscovered for each new generation. We have to make a continuous, conscious effort to keep evaluating them and to keep rebuilding them into the structures of our concrete daily existence.

Moral autonomy leaves considerable room for individual lifestyle differences and unique emotional attachments, but it does make a **significant normative claim** that puts boundaries on lifestyle choice. Promoting *the enabling virtues for moral autonomy should have the highest priority in any caring, individualistic tradition that recognizes our right to be independent agents with a capacity to feel social responsibility.* What is the impact of this claim? How are enabling virtues promoted? Will promoting them lead to a debilitating attempt to homogenize all people? What if people who lack autonomy do not want to develop these virtues?

Moral Autonomy and Human Virtues

For Study: What faults can make institutions dysfunctional from the moral point of view? Why are sociopaths and shame-based codependents morally dysfunctional? What kinds of virtues promote moral autonomy?

To even talk about autonomy seems a bit paradoxical. What evidence supports the idea that people can develop virtues that will enable them to act in a morally autonomous fashion? What kind of environments are needed?

> People grow best where they continuously experience an ingenious blend of support and challenge; the rest is commentary. Environments that are weighted too heavily in the direction of challenge without adequate support are toxic; they promote defensiveness and constriction. Those weighted too heavily toward support without adequate challenge are ultimately boring; they promote devitalization. Both kinds of imbalance lead to withdrawal or dissociation from the context. In contrast, the balance of support and challenge leads to vital engagement. (Kegan, 1994, p. 42)

To understand the positive side of an issue, it is often instructive to compare it with its opposite. So, let's begin by looking at the harmful effects of families that challenge but offer no support. These family structures actually inhibit the development of virtues that enable autonomous moral choice. We can define a family as *dysfunctional from the moral point of view* when *it produces children with such extreme personality styles that they cannot function as morally autonomous adults on either the rational or the caring dimension.* Claudia Black (1981) argued that dysfunctional family relationships are usually characterized by three rules of survival adopted by the weakest members of the family: (1) don't talk, (2) don't trust, and (3) don't feel. Relational models of therapy argue that when there is no mutuality and support in a family it causes a disconnection in the relational bond. This leads to skewed power relationships that can lead to verbal, emotional, and/or physical abuse unless the imbalance in power is tamed by a strong sense of empathy for weaker family members. Without the safety that comes with empathy, vulnerable family members develop a cautious inhibition that has devastating effects on family members who are still struggling with developmental tasks.

We can see this most clearly if we take a deeper look at a couple of personality disorders. Studies of sociopaths teach us the importance of providing a consistently supportive family or tribal heritage. If an abusive home life forces separation and autonomy too soon, it destroys or inhibits the development of an ability to care, sometimes leading to attachment disorder. Marshall and Barbaree (1984) (who use the term psychopath rather than sociopath) point out that

> [with regard to etiology of social pathology,] the same disturbed family interactions and parental mismanagement are observed whether the offender is from a lower-class, middle-class, or upper-class background. . . . Not only do the parents . . . use inconsistent discipline, they almost exclusively employ harsh punishment . . . [which makes] feedback irrelevant to the budding psychopath, [and] it also fails to endow the parents (and by generalization other people) with

reinforcement value. . . . [The sociopaths] learn by observation to be self-interested and aggressive, and they fail to experience affection, and are not provided with models whereby they might acquire appropriate emotional concern for others. . . . Psychopaths enter an adult world prepared to look after themselves in an exaggeratedly self-interested way. (p. 422)

Children need social support early in life to lay down the foundational structures for the crucial procedural knowledge on which later moral development depends. Once developmental stages are missed, it can be very difficult to undo the consequences. Thus, to deny early nurturance is to make a decision that might morally sterilize a segment of the next generation. While an emotionally abusive environment may still allow children to calculate and manipulate, it will not teach them to feel normal human sympathy for others. Without sympathy their calculations will be grossly one-sided. The tragic fact is that because sociopaths are emotionally flat, they are

far less responsive to stimuli or events that are emotionally provocative to others, and consequently, . . . experience boredom more frequently than others. Boredom, of course, leads individuals to seek excitement, and so we would expect psychopaths to be stimulus seekers. . . . [In studies they] showed a greater preference for frightening and dangerous experiences than did normal subjects . . . (p. 422)

At the other extreme on the caring spectrum we find people who seem to care so deeply for another (or seem so desperate for emotional attachment) that they lose (assuming they ever developed it) their ability to be independent decision makers. This moral incapacity sometimes results when a deep longing for normal bonds of mutuality get connected to a kind of shame that is caused by family rejection. Lewis (1987) argues that "shame is the affective-cognitive state of low self-esteem" (p. 191). If it is the *kind of low self-esteem* produced in dysfunctional families that teach children they are unworthy of love, it can become so strong as to be maladaptive from the moral point of view. Lewis states:

Shame is one of our species' inevitable responses to loss of love . . . In order for shame to occur, there must be a relationship between the self and the other in which the self cares about the other's evaluation. . . . This special position of the self as the target of attack makes shame a more acutely painful experience than guilt. . . . Shame is about the self; it is therefore global. **Guilt** is more specific, being about events or things. . . . Shame involves a failure of the central attachment bond. This failure evokes rage, as does the painful experience of lost attachment because one is unable to live up to the standards of an admired image. The "other" is a prominent and powerful force in the experience of shame. . . . In this affective tie, the self does not feel autonomous but dependent and vulnerable to rejection [emphasis added]. (p. 191ff)

A rejected child may develop a vulnerability to shame reactions that carry over into adulthood and are so severe *the reactions in the adult will seem childishly immature* to an observer. Sometimes the name *adult child* seems appropriate for someone who suffers from this kind of shame reaction. To avoid the acute pain of humiliation, and also the guilt that is induced by fits of humiliated rage against the loved person, shame-based persons will do almost anything to avoid rejection by a significant other. Their effort to please may overwhelm their ability to remain morally responsible. Some one who has a shame-based need for love appears to be extremely vulnerable to charming people with sociopathic personalities who will not hesitate to take advantage of their extreme vulnerability to manipulation (e.g., He said he would leave me unless I did the awful thing he wanted). Sociopaths and the victims of shame who love them are two extremes on the caring dimension who are capable of uniting in a lethal alliance, for instance, as when the mass murderer Charles Manson teamed up with his emotionally starved runaway girls.

The discussion so far has been about human traits that we all possess to some degree. There will be times when all of us find it difficult to care about other people, and there will be times when most of us care very much. But when normal human traits are carried to an extreme, they become psychological disorders that can interfere with moral function. People who suffer from these character disorders are reactors rather than autonomous choosers. It is difficult for them to stick to principled conduct, especially in situations calling for intimacy and commitment. Helfer (1978), who works with abusive adults who were abused as children, points out that he has to consistently remind his clients that childhood comes first. Until they go back and master the developmental tasks of childhood and learn to care in a reasonable manner, they cannot expect to break their dysfunctional style of relating in social situations. Unless they learn to rework their past on both a cognitive and physiological level, they will not be prepared to enter adulthood as morally autonomous agents. To review a brand of therapy that teaches the virtues for autonomy by helping clients make cognitive and physiological bodily adjustments that can adjust their emotional states, see the Pesso-Boyden system of psychomotor therapy on the website *http://www.pbsp.com.*

It is clear that when certain normal human virtues are missing, it is hard for people to function as autonomous adults. Piaget (1967), Erik Erickson (1963), Pesso-Boyden (1991), and others discuss these virtues in depth in their psychological and clinical work. We have already discussed Piaget's theory of cognitive development in Chapter Four where he characterizes the highest intellectual virtue as "thinking about thinking." Erickson studied the development of emotional virtues. He argued that those which are "basic" develop in the following order: trust or hope, willpower, purpose, competence, fidelity, love, care, and wisdom (p. 274). When we combine Piaget's cognitive virtues with Erickson's emotional virtues we have developmental achievements that give people the intellectual capacities to create their own principles as well as the motivation and existential courage to act on them. Acting together these virtues are **emancipatory** because they *help people become Socratic in their ability to care about social norms, gain theoretical understanding about them, and yet critically evaluate and choose between the available concrete and theoretical options.* It is irrelevant that these emancipatory virtues may be causally or historically related to a particular kind of socialization, because once acquired they enable people (with the help of other like-minded persons) to reflect back on, criticize, and then build on their own previous socialization.

Autonomy and Emotional Choice

For Study: Why do morally autonomous people need to be able to change their emotional preferences?

Adina Schwartz (1984) pointed out that autonomous people not only must choose the *means* to their goals but also must be able to choose the *goals* themselves. But is this possible? If goals involve ultimate foundational feelings, can we really choose them? Do we have to give up our emotional selves, who we are, to become impartial presocial abstract agents who are somehow supposed to be choosers of foundational values? These questions raise some fascinating issues that force us to take a fresh look at the relationship between feelings, cognition, and autonomous choice.

Schacter and Singer (1962) conducted a seminal experiment designed to study the relationship between thoughts and emotions. They told a group of subjects that they were going to be injected with a substance that would improve their vision. After the injection they were asked to wait in a room for about twenty minutes while they filled out a form. In actuality Schacter had injected them with a form of adrenalin that would create a visceral reaction (an emotional state). One group went to fill out their form in a room where a research assistant was waiting with instructions to act like a very happy person (call it the joy room). In another room (the anger room) a person was waiting who was instructed to act very angry. There was also the usual control group. Predictably, depending on which room they were in, the subjects interpreted their reaction to the adrenaline as either joy or anger. This looks like a pure case of situational control. None of the subjects consciously chose the quality of their feelings—they simply reacted first to the drug and then to the cues planted in the environment by the actor. On the basis of this preliminary data, one might conclude that people cannot choose their emotions; they can only have them. This seems to support Hume's famous assertion that reason is the slave of the passions.

Schacter conducted his experiment again, however, and added a new variable. He told the subjects part of the truth—that the injection would have a visceral side effect, that they would feel hot, a faster heartbeat, jitters, perhaps feel like walking around, and so on. He advised them to ignore the symptoms. This time when the subjects went into the joy and anger rooms they seemed rather immune to the emotional cues planted in their environment. Instead of imitating the quality of emotion displayed by the actors, most of them reported that they were feeling the side effects they were told to expect. Simply by changing their background cognitive state—their beliefs about what they were going to experience—Schacter was apparently able to change the foreground, that is, the quality of their felt emotions.

They were, of course, still subject to situational control because they did not have accurate information about their world, but notice what this means. Schacter's experiment clearly demonstrated that emotional "reactions" to the world are affected by previous history, biology, and current stimuli. But, he also shows that our ability "to control how we feel" about our environment is directly correlated with (a) the background belief system we use to interpret the significance of stimuli, and (b) the extent of the knowledge available to help us reflect on our current situation. If we can increase our *cognitive control* over the symbols we use to construct our knowledge, we *can increase our choice of how to feel*. With greater understanding comes increased freedom to choose emotional states and alter original foundational values. The need for accurate information and knowledge increases the importance of gaining moral experience and of living in environments that promote honest communication. As mentioned in the previous chapter, this result supports the idea that thinking is emotional and emotions respond to how we think. In so far as we can control our imagination and cognitions, we can have some autonomous control of our feelings and values.

To achieve moral autonomy, we have to develop capacities to conceive of and care about both community life and the abstract principles that ought to govern communities. Since these capacities are developmental achievements, people will always have differing degrees of both personal and moral autonomy. As James Madison (1984, pp. 112–13) pointed out during debates about how to structure the U.S. Constitution, we will always have conflicts between social factions that have different opinions about what kind of rules to impose on members of the community. It seems that actual universal autonomous agreement must always remain an ideal. But respect for the right of morally autonomous people to be different can become one of the guiding background norms for those who adopt the MPofV. This was one of the guiding ideals implemented in the U.S. Constitution. By forbidding Congress to pass laws controlling how people chose to practice religion, the Founding Fathers were protecting the right of people to be different, since freedom of worship guarantees that differences in lifestyle will exist.

Although the concept of moral autonomy cannot tell us exactly what to do, it does focus our attention on relevant human values that should play a role in establishing policies. In addition, this norm makes at least one thing explicitly clear. In this theoretical framework, moral autonomy is not just another value. Given that we are required to live in pluralistic cultures, fostering the abilities for moral autonomy is essential for encouraging responsible moral choice. It should have the highest priority in social policy (assuming we do not want to return to tribal forms of existence). Respect for moral autonomy helps us focus on some of the worst harms that ought to be avoided at all costs—harms that either destroy (e.g., starvation or brainwashing) or inhibit (e.g., learning deprivation or indoctrination) the development of the capacities for moral autonomy.

Paternalistic Interventions

> **For Study:**   When dealing with paternalistic decisions for those who lack autonomy, what kind of guiding questions should we be asking?

Even if a morally autonomous professional can decide issues for herself, she must still ask, "How should I treat clients and other people who are dependent on my decisions but who do not themselves have complete moral autonomy?" When dealing with agents who are not legally autonomous (e.g., children or the mentally impaired), most people agree that a fair degree of *paternalism* is justified. Paternalism means that *we make decisions for others, for their own good, even if they do not agree with our intervention on their behalf*. While paternalism is in direct conflict with a principle of individual autonomy for legal adults, nonetheless, practical considerations often require us to decide for other legal adults (perhaps they are ill, temporarily insane, in a state of ignorance or duress, not present to decide for themselves, etc.). When we decide for either type of individual (children or adults), we should not forget the accountability required by the background notion of moral autonomy. According to Gerald Dworkin (1971) one way to satisfy this requirement is to use the concept of *future oriented consent*. We can ask, "*What would they consent to in the future when they better understand their position?*" (p. 119). Although the safest route is to always let people decide for themselves, when practical necessities require us to be paternalistic with people who are dependent on us, we must always make our decisions on the basis of what the person will come to welcome, rather than only on what he does welcome now.

Even with this kind of guiding background conception, however, it is still not easy to make the right choice for those who are not autonomous. For example, do I decide for them on the basis of their current preferences and project into the future what I think they will come to want—that is, what they would come to want if they were rational autonomous persons who were starting with their current preferences? (But wouldn't they have different preferences if they were rational autonomous people?) Or should I try to do for them what I think any rational autonomous person would want done, whether they currently prefer that or not? (Let's set aside for the moment that in complex cases, it is possible that morally autonomous people might not be able to agree in any case. Sometimes continued debate is the only option.) It seems to me that I must do both. I must take account of their current preferences (and leave them alone if they are not immoral or insane), but I must also ask idealized questions about their future as well, that is, what their preferences would probably look like if they were autonomous, or will look like once they become autonomous. Of course, it is presumptuous on the one hand to assume we could know what people would consent to, but in many care-taking contexts we don't have much choice. When people cannot speak for themselves, practical life requires us to presume we know what they would or ought to want.

If an intervention might change a person's preferences (a developmental effect), the change ought to be for the better, from the point of view of moral autonomy. Once we are certain that the development of autonomy has not been compromised, we can then ask, based on a theory of human needs, preferences, and cultural conditions, "How would they want to be treated now, if they could make the decision for themselves?". When we are done parenting, educating, giving therapy, rehabilitating, or experimenting, will they be left with preferences that are compatible both with who they are now as well as with the ideal of moral autonomy? If not compatible with whom they are now, is that because who they are now is immoral or clearly insane or maladaptive? If not, then maybe we should not intervene. None of these questions are easy to answer, and of course particular cases would need to be historically situated. However, although the whole approach is very abstract, it is conceptually coherent to ask the questions, and trying to answer them in an honest, committed way can make us more sensitive during our interventions into one another's lives.

Moral Autonomy and Lifestyle Choice

> **For Study:**   What kinds of factors make it difficult to make ethical decisions about universal standards for the quality of life? Why do decisions about the quality of life require the participation of all affected morally autonomous agents?

It is one thing for the morally autonomous person to choose universal principles of justice at the level of moral rationality. It is another thing to choose a lifestyle at the level of ethical rationality and claim it is universally the best. Judging the goodness of a way of life is not a matter of justice (which is open to universal discussion), it is more a clinical matter that can be addressed only by those who have experienced the way of life in question.

> Whether the life-form of a collectivity has turned out more or less "well," has more or less "succeeded," may be a general question we can direct at every form

of life, but it is more like a clinical request to judge a patient's mental or spiritual condition than a moral question concerning a norm's or institutional system's worthiness to be recognized. (Habermas, 1987, p. 109)

There are a number of complications that make any universal claim about the good life problematic. In the first place, questions about the quality of life for adults are about more than universal biological needs, they also involve questions about how to interpret experience. The way a person gives meaning to experience may be unique to the individual and/or her culture. Thus, there is always an element of subjectivity and ethnocentrism at this level of value consideration. Furthermore, some phenomena are more than the sum of their parts. The content of the final whole cannot always be predicted from knowledge about the individual parts alone. For instance, in human development, emergent properties appear that seem to involve new variations on old patterns. The evolutionary biologist Niles Eldredge (1998) argues that as we come to understand more about human evolutionary theory, we realize that "what is selected for is flexibility and the ability to think" (p. 61). The big brain allows people to critically reflect and choose new behaviors rather than simply react in stereotypical ways; thus, as we learn, we adapt *and change*. This means that genetic endowment does not predetermine all of our behavior, and even if it did, the permutations available in genetic transmissions are for all practical purposes infinite. We are all, indeed, incredibly unique biological beings. The same goes for cultural determinism; we are not just passive mirrors of our culture.

The number of genetically unique offspring a single breeding couple could theoretically produce far exceeds the number of people who have so far walked this earth. Certainly we all have the same nucleotides as our building blocks, but the way each person assembles them is all his own. Then too, there is environmental uniqueness that starts at the genetic level. Other genes influence one gene's specific productivity and the influence continues at the intracellular level. It is impossible to duplicate the specific set and sequence of environments to which any person has been exposed. (Platt, 1998, p. 1)

Both genetic and environmental complexity makes it very difficult to say with precision what any particular individual needs for a quality life. Furthermore, part of the difficulty of achieving a scientific consensus in psychology and social science is that the subject matter being studied is not stationary. Psychological research is notorious for keeping research subjects ignorant during experiments, precisely because awareness of what is happening is a confounding variable. Because humans are subjects not objects, as they understand more about themselves they become increasingly autonomous and begin to evolve in ways that are individually unique. The data gathered about social reality is never only value neutral factual data, it is always permeated both with assumptions about validity and with the complications that arise because of the choices made by evolving, dynamic, unique subject participants. Knowledge changes behavior, and in accordance with that, transcendence of previous value orientations is part of the social reality of adult life. Not only can we adapt and shape our behavior to fit the demands of environment, we can decide to change the environment itself to influence our own social evolution.

At any given time, humans may be characterized as being in the process of developing new *emergent properties* and values that *appear as the byproduct of their continuing interactions with the world*. Emergent properties include things like decentered consciousness, critical self-reflection, a new sense of autonomy, and spiritual growth. Descriptive science, which is a finite human enterprise, may always be playing catch up with the emerging norms that are part of the individual's subjective evolution. Even if science does catch up, the facticity of science still can only describe norms that already are, it cannot prescribe what norms ought to emerge from the ongoing dynamic interactions between autonomous agents trying to create the good life (Habermas, 1996, p. xiii). What provides quality during one phase of life may not provide the same quality after the subject goes through various shifts in consciousness. Thus, any description of what people valued yesterday will inevitably lag behind what they may value today. Personal growth, and each person's unique make up, make predictions about how to design institutions for everybody hopelessly complex.

So, basic differences between the baby, the child, and the adult, emerge as we develop the capacity to go our own way. People cannot have a quality life if they are deprived of the opportunity to govern themselves (which includes contributing to social discussions about the meaning of life). In the modern age, a basic human need "to be respected as a morally autonomous being" has emerged. Adults have come to understand themselves as self-governed social beings that ought to have a say in formulating lifestyle options. This kind of need can only be satisfied by providing a place for everyone's active participation in the running of social, political, and economic subsystems. It appears that, unlike children, modern adults cannot find happiness if they have to be manipulated into it. Because the need for moral autonomy emerges in adulthood, it means diversity in lifestyle within the limits of justice will be a permanent and valuable part of the human landscape.

At this point, we begin to see a convergence between the universal moral values behind the concept of social justice, and the possibility for a universal ethical theory about the good life. The ancient Greek motto, "The unexamined life is not worth living," makes sense only if humans are in fact intellectual social animals who need to know themselves. It appears that in learning to know themselves, they also learn to value creating themselves. So, the motive behind moral autonomy is the democratic desire to be involved with others in creating those common norms of morality and ethics that place limits on our collective way of life. If people turn this task over to another, it is only with the faith that the other will be a representative of a social order that already has a structure compatible with the norms that they would have approved of anyway as morally autonomous people.

For Instance:

I experienced the truth of this claim during a poignant exchange in one of my ethics classes. We were discussing the rise of the concept of "autonomy as self-governance" during eighteenth-century political philosophy. A Native American woman from the Ojibwa tribe said she had no desire for autonomy. What she desired was a traditional tribal marriage in which she would obey her husband, who would make decisions for the family. I asked, "Would you obey him on all matters, or are there some areas where you would govern?" She said he would govern in all matters. I don't know if this is an accurate portrayal of traditional Ojibwa life, but she was firm in stating what she wanted. Some of her female classmates were aghast. They asked, "But what if he started to abuse you. Would you still obey?" She replied, "Oh, he wouldn't. The tribe would not permit such behavior. To maintain his place in the tribe, he would have to treat me with the respect a wife in the tribe deserves." So, her story is not actually a refutation of moral autonomy, because the respect she would insist on if she were a morally autonomous person is already built into her conception of the tribal setting. This is exactly why people want moral autonomy, so that they can create a social space that satisfies their personal needs for a social life. If the tribe is doing that, then they already have the social place they want, and moral autonomy may seem irrelevant. This correlates with the fact that concerns about moral autonomy emerge under conditions of pluralism, where conflicts cause us to doubt that social structures will be able to protect us without the guidance of our own active participation.

The Autonomous Life and the Meaning of Life

> **For Study:** Why are questions about moral and ethical meaning especially difficult in pluralistic environments?

We are the kind of creatures that we are, and we are not capable of complete happiness as adults if we find ourselves engaged only in pursuits that are meaningless from a social and cosmic point of view. But how can we find meaning in a postmetaphysical age? Are there biological, social, or theoretical limits to how humans can find meaning in life, or as autonomous beings, are we free to create whatever story we please? There is at least one limit that has interesting philosophical implications. Humans need to believe that the story that gives meaning to their life is true or right in some fundamental sense. This must be the case; otherwise, we could use strategic reason to create fictional stories for fun and these fictions would satisfy our thirst for meaning. But fiction does not ultimately satisfy precisely because everyone needs to believe there is truth to the story line of his or her life. This fact of human existence explains why pluralism causes a crisis of meaning for many people. It raises doubts about the truth or meaning of various aspects of every heritage.

Some postmodern skeptics say that concerns about truth are just an old bogus notion leftover from the Enlightenment (see Rorty, 1991). For instance, the ancients believed there were many gods, but were still able to feel fulfilled by worshiping only the one appropriate for their tribe. Why not imitate ancient man's tolerance of other gods by tolerating all stories? Then, we can just choose to believe in our own and live according to it. The postmodern message seems to be: When we worry about truth, there is always a danger that a local value will be treated as though it is universal when it is not. Then atrocities will occur when we try to reeducate or ethnically cleanse anyone who does not share the local worldview. So, stop worrying about truth. Don't give in to universalistic thinking, since it reinforces the tendency for people to impose their own "universal" vision on everyone.

This particularistic advice will be unsatisfying if it implies to people that everything they cherish is ultimately arbitrary. Tolerance for other gods was possible only because people believed that stories about all the Gods were true. But we live in a postmetaphysical age where doubt is everywhere. If there is no truth, then all stories are arbitrary and believing in a local God is not going to give meaning. If anything, we will simply feel foolish. Furthermore, the postmodern concerns about the potential for universal values to contribute to atrocities, confuses the desire to serve ultimate justified universals (justification discourse) with the lower-level decisions that need to be made about how to apply universals to concrete cases. Brutish application strategies do not refute the validity of universal values, they only point to lack of practical wisdom at the bureaucratic level. In all social structures there are neophytes who don't get it. The same debates about facts and norms can be found in all traditions, also the same need to decenter, also the same confusion about the difference between justification and application, and also the same emerging wisdom. Thus, many mistakes occur because people who have yet to achieve wisdom apply justifiable universal principles without hermeneutic sensitivity, ignoring both the levels of complexity as well as those local contingencies that a man of practical wisdom would have learned how to factor in. Lack of local practical wisdom should not stop the search for transcendent values and a meaningful life. But since we are morally autonomous people, the nature of the search for meaning should be left to individual conscience, and not be imposed by authority figures who favor their own solution.

Universal Moral Meaning in the Golden Rule

For Study: What kind of insight into the meaning of moral life can we get from a universal principle such as the Golden Rule? How do spiritual concerns fit into moral questions about the meaning of life?

Other things being equal, any local custom that is compatible with universal moral principles deserves respect as an essential element contributing to the quality of life for someone. Thus, it is always a mistake to ethnically cleanse, since it violates the right of morally autonomous people to build their own system of belief. What kind of universal principle of justice is apt to generate a consensus among morally autonomous people who are trying to construct a meaningful life? It would have to be a principle that will respect cultural differences (or we won't get a consensus), and yet contain enough moral truth that it can help people in a postmetaphysical world maintain meaning in their life. Consider the following versions of the Golden Rule, a principle that emerges in all spiritually advanced cultures. What exactly is it telling us to do with regard to the good life?

CONFUCIUS:	What you do not want done to yourself, do not do to others.
JUDAISM:	What you hate, do not do to anyone.
BUDDHISM:	Hurt not others with that which pains thyself.
HINDUISM:	Do nothing to thy neighbor which thou wouldst not have him do to thee.
ARISTOTLE:	We should behave to our friends as we wish our friends to behave to us.
ISLAM:	No one of you is a believer until he loves for his brother what he loves for himself.
CHRISTIANITY:	Do unto others as you would have them do unto you and love thy neighbor as thyself.
KANT:	Always treat humanity (whether yourself or another) as an end unto itself, never use humanity as a means only.
HABERMAS:	No norm is valid unless it meets (or could meet) with the approval of all affected in their capacity as participants in a practical discourse.

All of these versions of the Golden Rule draw attention to similar universal constraints on the choice of lifestyle, but they all also need to be interpreted. First, the early versions stated by Confucius, Judaism, Hinduism, and Buddhism, emphasize the negative duty to do no harm, which is a minimum condition for any civilization. They then invite each of us to use our own procedural understanding of personal harm as a reference point for defining what ought to be universally avoided. The principles draw people's attention to the fact that people everywhere are not so different since there are common harms that humans everywhere would like to avoid.

Second, as can be seen in the version of the principle offered by Aristotle, there is an issue involving the breadth of the principle's coverage. Is it just friends who deserve reciprocal treatment? One of the advances made in ethics over the centuries has been the steady expansion of the domain of morally relevant beings (as humanity has learned to decenter). In ancient Greece there were different moral principles for different groups. Slaves, foreigners, women, and children were not considered to be moral peers of adult male citizens. Most versions of the Golden Rule, however, emphasize that everyone counts as a moral being. For instance, in the Good Samaritan story (Luke 10:25–38), Jesus clarifies for the lawyer how to "love thy neighbor as thyself" Jesus emphasizes that a neighbor is even a person from a foreign tribe who is not normally our friend (Jews and Samaritans did not like each other). A simple metaphorical extension can turn everyone into a neighbor, so everyone should be treated as one of Aristotle's communitarian friends.

Third, there is also a positive injunction to do good deeds in the Golden Rule. Christianity, Islam, and Kant's versions all explicitly give us positive duties. Jesus' "Good Samaritan" story has the Samaritan going out of his way to help the injured traveler. Jesus says, you must love and do good "without expecting any return" (Luke 6:32–37). This is not a matter of punishment and reward, it is a matter of developing a conscience that recognizes positive obligations to others. Muslims are not showing "what they love for themselves" if they do no more than refrain from hurting people, since everyone wants more than that for themselves. Kant (1797, 1964, p. 98) says a mature agent must strive to further the ends of humanity, which requires more than the mere avoidance of harm. As civilizations advance, we see increased recognition that people expect not only that help will be given when it is needed, but also that mature people will help others thrive in ways that the others choose. A good moral agent, then, promotes good in the world by helping to meet the needs of those he encounters; he doesn't just avoid doing harm.

Fourth, in accordance with the need for spiritual growth and self-realization, Habermas's version of the Golden Rule (see Chapters Nine and Ten) encourages us to not only feel empathy for everyone, but to create a social world that is based on participatory consensus. Empathy and social participation by people affected are moral goods that ought to exist in all social settings. As a morally autonomous person I want to be treated according to my conception of the good life, thus I must treat all others according to their conception of the good life. This requires me to ask what they would like, which requires their participation in my decisions.

As the interpretations of the Golden Rule throughout history take on a decentered universal emphasis that respects the way of life of different tribes, it contributes to the growth of spiritual meaning in the world. But, in a post-metaphysical world what can this reference to spiritual growth possibly mean? I like to begin on a fairly concrete level when I think about social and spiritual values, so I will use these abstract concepts from the Golden Rule to interpret a concrete event from my past.

For Instance:

When I was a twelve-year-old boy scout, a group of us were on a hike and we came to a small pond filled with frogs. One boy (a budding sadist?) said that we ought to tie rocks to the legs of the frogs and throw them in the water to see what they will do (Figure 7.1). Some of the boys did so. We were surprised that the frogs only kicked a couple of times and then gave up and passively drowned.

We thought they would have put up much more of a fight in order to survive. Then our sadist friend said: "I know. Let's use a longer string so they are just barely beneath the surface." Option (2) turned out to be much more satisfying to the sadist (Figure 7.2). He laughed as the frogs struggled frantically but in vain to negotiate the last few inches of water that separated them from an early death and the life giving air. On the other hand, several of us felt suddenly horrified by the frog's plight. This was no longer fun, but like the "good" guards in Zimbardo's prison experiment, we didn't do anything to put an end to this gruesome game. Then to the dismay of the sadist, suddenly a little boy jumped into the water and started rescuing the frogs (Figure 7.3). Along with a number of the other boys, I felt a tremendous sense of relief and cheered him on.

This rescue by the courageous empathic little boy irritated the sadist. He threatened to beat the boy if he didn't stop, but the boy continued until he had rescued

Figure 7.1   Egocentric spirituality. Using frogs as a means only.

Figure 7.2   Passive spirituality. Good boys watching the sadist.

Figure 7.3   Universal spirituality. Empathy for all creatures—even frogs.

all those still living. Luckily, there were enough of us cheering him on that the sadist backed off. In fact, eventually he even began to help, as we relieved our conscience by cutting the string from the legs of living frogs.

Looking back I realize that on that day, I witnessed at least three different levels of spiritual development. The clinical therapist Albert Pesso (1998) says that as we grow spiritually we feel empathy for larger and larger portions of the universe. I think he is right. The egoistic sadist was very much centered in on himself and his own pleasure. This kind of person focuses on the "me" part of the golden rule, rather than on the needs of the "other," which is the proper focus of this principle. Quality of life for the sadistic boy did not automatically involve moral respect for others, an ethical commitment to his uniformed heritage (the Boy Scout code emphasizes kindness), or a desire for a deeper empathic connection with other living things. He was all about using strategic reason to figure out how to get a personal thrill. I, on the other hand, had decentered to a degree. I could feel empathy for the plight of the frogs, and I lived up to the first negative injunction in the golden rule to avoid doing harm. But I lacked sufficient commitment to doing more than the minimum. I stood by rather than acted to promote positive good in the world. Even to this day, I still think the third boy was amazing, given his tender age. Not only did he avoid doing harm, he felt enough connection to these tiny amphibians that he took positive steps to rescue them—and in spite of the presence of threats to his own well-being. He was spiritually quite advanced. A meaningful life is about more than avoiding evil; it is also about creating a better world. This boy had some of the virtues that will one day make him a man of practical wisdom as well as a man of moral courage. As Martin Luther King says, "When evil men burn and bomb, good men must build and bind. When evil men shout ugly words of hatred, good men must commit themselves to the glories of love."

Conclusion

Quality of life issues are personal, cultural, ethical, moral, and spiritual in the sense that a life full of quality will satisfy needs on all of these levels. We can use the practical wisdom found in discussions amongst morally autonomous moral agents to pinpoint some universal moral themes that ought to be included in any theory of the good life. As long as a tribal practice helps satisfy basic human needs on any of these levels, then it is contributing to the good life. Is there a universal theory of the good life? The universal is what can legitimately be universally agreed upon. Thus, if people really have **basic human needs** for place, nurture, support, protection, love, respect, and so forth (Pesso, 1991), then we should find these needs being addressed in some way in all lifestyles that are called "good". A culture that does not satisfy them should be universally condemned—especially by those whose needs are not being addressed.

There are many cultures that are "good enough," in that they can provide a social space where people can work to satisfy all these needs. However, because people also have a need to be in charge of their own search for satisfaction, a good enough institution encourages them to choose their own system of meaning. This helps explain the reticence of Erickson, Habermas, and other modern people of practical wisdom to choose for others. Moral autonomy implies that we have a positive duty to help each other overcome deficits that stand in the way of people taking charge of their own development. Adults ought to be free to experience the higher pleasures that come with emancipation.

Finally, do we need cosmic consciousness for a quality life? I think it depends on stages of development. The baby doesn't need it. The teenager primarily needs a peer group, the citizen a nation. However, perhaps we will all need cosmic consciousness as well by the end of our life. True cosmic consciousness is a decentered state of mind that does not exclude others. In the history of humanity, people who were admired for the quality of their spiritual life were all committed to nurturing the next generation and were not narrow in terms of their ability to accept different ways of life. They could see the humanity in most forms of diversity, and they could feel empathy for and offer support to both people and frogs.

Since transcendent moral and personal ideals are discovered (or created) during theoretical discussions, some people say they are only abstractions and not real. What a philosophical orientation to values helps us to remember is that all ethical and moral norms were once merely part of someone's ideal conception. It is by acting on theoretical ideals that we improve and modify the actual concrete environment. Ideals become concrete reality when people live them, but to live them consciously we have to understand the role they play in moral life. Philosophical theories help us to transcend concrete situational variables that can trap us into living unreflective, institutional lives. They can also explain why it is so important to interpret a principle like the Golden Rule in ways that are sensitive to local context. Without the intellectual possibilities generated by philosophical theories, there would be no freedom, moral autonomy would be fantasy, and Socrates' life could not inspire us to seek greater understanding. But what kinds of values are most relevant when making moral, ethical, and strategic decisions? To address this question, the next two chapters analyze the background theoretical context of six major principles that have been advocated by morally autonomous philosophers.

REFERENCES

AMERICAN PSYCHIATRIC ASSOCIATION. (1994). *Diagnostic and Statistical Manual of Mental Disorders,* 4th ed. Washington, DC.

BAYLES, MICHAEL D. (1979). Accounting for the variables in accountability: A commentary. Paper prepared for the AMINTAPHIL conference at the University of Texas, Austin, TX.

BLACK, CLAUDIA. (1981). *It will never happen to me.* Denver, CO: M.A.C.

DWORKIN, GERALD. (1971). Paternalism. In Richard Wasserstrom (Ed.), *Morality and the law* (pp. 107–27). Belmont, CA: Wadsworth.

ELDREDGE, NILES. (1998). Cited in *Time*. June 22, 1998, pp. 61ff.

ERICKSON, ERICK. (1963). *Childhood and society*. New York: W. W. Norton.

FEINBERG, JOEL. (1973). *Social philosophy*. Englewood Cliffs, NJ: Prentice Hall.

———. (1986). *Harm to self*. New York: Oxford University Press.

HABERMAS, JURGEN. (1987). *The philosophical discourse of modernity*. Frederick G. Lawrence (Trans.). Cambridge, MA: The MIT Press.

———. (1996). *Between facts and norms: Contributions to a discourse theory of law and democracy*. William Rehg (Trans.). Cambridge, MA: The MIT Press.

HELFER, RAY. (1978). *Childhood comes first*. East Lansing, MI: KEMPE National Center.

HOPE, VINCENT. (1984). Smith's demigod. In V. Hope (Ed.), *Philosophers of the Scottish enlightenment* (pp. 150–65). Edinburgh, Scotland: University Press.

KANT, IMMANUEL. (1797, 1964). *Groundwork of the metaphysics of morals*. H. J. Paton (Trans.). New York: Harper Torchbooks.

KEGAN, ROBERT. (1994). *In over our heads: The mental demands of modern life*. Cambridge, MA: Harvard University Press.

LEWIS, H. B. (1987). The role of shame in depression in women. In R. Furmanch & A. Gurian (Eds.), *Women and depression* (pp. 191ff). New York: Springer.

MADISON, JAMES. (1984). Cited in Richard K. Matthews. *The radical politics of Thomas Jefferson: A revisionist view*. Lawrence: University Press of Kansas.

MARSHALL, W. L. & BARBAREE, A. F. (1984). Disorders of personality, impulse, and adjustment. In S. Turner and M. Hersen (Eds.), *Adult psychopathology and diagnosis* (pp. 422–29). New York: John Wiley.

MICHARD, STEPHEN. G. & AYNESWORTH, HUGH. (1983). *The only living witness*. New York: Signet.

MIDDLETON-MOZ, JANE & DWINNELL, LORIE. (1986). *After the tears*. Pompano Beach, FL: Health Communications.

MILL, JOHN S. (1863, 1957). *Utilitarianism*. New York: Bobbs-Merrill.

PESSO, ALBERT. (1998). Notes taken from Pesso's lecture at a workshop sponsored by the Northwest PBSP Society. Minneapolis, MN.

———. (1991). Ego development in the possibility sphere. In Albert Pesso and John Crandell (Eds.), *Moving Psychotherapy* (pp. 51–59). Cambridge, MA: Brookline Books.

PETERS, R. S. (1973). *Reason and compassion*. London: Routledge & Kegan Paul.

PIAGET, JEAN. (1967). *Six psychological studies*. New York: Random House.

PLATT, STEVEN A. (1998). Keynote address: Honors banquet. Northern Michigan University, Marquette, MI. April. Also see: Platt, Steven A. & Bach, M. (1997). Uses and misinterpretations of genetics in psychology. *Genetica* 99: 135–43.

RORTY, RICHARD. (1991). *Objectivity, relativism, and truth*. New York: Cambridge University Press.

ROUSSEAU, J. J. (1762, 1968). The social contract. In Sir Ernest Barker (Ed.), *The social contract: Locke, Hume, Rousseau* (pp. 168–307). London: Oxford University Press.

SCHACTER, S. & SINGER, J. (1962). Cognitive, social and physiological determinants of emotional state. *Psychological review* 69: 379–99.

SCHWARTZ, ADINA. (1984). Autonomy and the workplace. In Tom Regan (Ed.), *Just business: New introductory essays in business ethics* (pp. 129–66). New York: Random House.

SMITH, ADAM. (1759, 1976). *The theory of moral sentiments*. Indianapolis, IN: Liberty Fund.

ZIMBARDO, PHILIP. (1974). On the ethics of intervention in human psychological research: With special reference to the Stanford Prison Experiment. *Cognition* 2 (2): 250ff.

————. (1975). Transforming experimental research into advocacy for social change. In M. Deutsch & H. A. Hornstein (Eds.), *Applying social psychology* (pp. 44ff). Hillsdale, NJ: Lawrence Erlbaum.

Chapter Eight

Consequentialist Theories versus Natural Rights Theory

The six foundational principles mentioned in Chapter One represent six important universal theories of morality that attempt to be compatible with the MPofV. They naturally divide into two types—consequentialist (i.e., teleological) and nonconsequentialist (i.e., deontological) theories. This chapter discusses the consequentialist approach, and contrasts it with the most popular of the nonconsequentialist approaches—natural rights theory. Keep one thing in mind during our review of the following theories: Philosophical frameworks are very complex. Thus, our discussion will only scratch the surface of the technical aspects of these theories. However, the discussion should be adequate enough to give the reader a good idea about the kind of background context for professional ethics that is provided by each theory. Since I am using the pattern laid out in the decision procedure presented in Chapter Two, the discussion of each theory will first consider background issues, then the ideal formulation of the theory, and then issues involving the implementation of the theory.

~ General Background for All Consequentialist Theories: They Need a Theory of Value

> **For Study:**   Why do consequentialists need a theory of value before they can develop a complete theory of obligation?

Variables such as rights, glory, efficiency, power, self-interest, wealth, justice, contracts, benevolence, love, hate, profit, friendship, respect for persons, duty, happiness, envy, and so forth, can all serve as reasons for acting. But which are the most relevant variables for guiding ethical and moral judgments? Theories provide foundational principles, such as those listed in Chapter One, to emphasize the factors that should have top priority. Egoism and utilitarianism are called *consequentialist* theories, because their principles tell us that what is right is what will promote good consequences. We should *evaluate various options to see how much nonmoral value or "good" can be promoted by each option. Then it is our moral obligation to promote as much of that nonmoral good thing as possible.*

Consequentialists focus our attention on the variables that are deemed most important when people treat morality as a strategic tool for fulfilling their desires. With this kind of approach, moral duties are characterized as the most strategic or prudent means for attaining some other nonmoral value like happiness or pleasure. Morality is not an important activity in its own right, it is only a system of principles and rules designed to help facilitate the pursuit of the other values that are defined by one's theory of value. As we saw in Chapter Four, this is Ned's approach; we have to be moral in order to be free to pursue our personal goals. Consequentialist theories need a well-developed *theory of value* to *clarify what nonmoral values we have a moral obligation to pursue, and to help us pick the best means to these goals.* The theory of value has priority over any theory of obligation. Since the latter serves the former, a complete theory of obligation can't be developed until we discover which nonmoral values to pursue.

Prudence: Strategic Reasoning

> **For Study:**   To a hedonistic consequentialist, what kind of value do "money" and "morality" have? Why is it difficult to compare the utility of different kinds of value?

A *prudent* person *makes wise decisions about how she should live.* Because prudent people are interested in satisfying their interests, they will search for the best theory of value to give them a proper background perspective about how to establish priorities between their conflicting interests. *Hedonism* is one very common theory of value. Hedonists claim that *above all else, people want to be happy. Since pleasure is the essential variable of a happy life, everyone ought to pursue it.* Each pleasure is like a moment of happiness and all of them together make up a happy life. There is no reason why we value pleasure. Its value is simply an obvious fact of experience. Something of this nature is called an *intrinsic good,* because *it is valued for its own sake. It is always a goal or end; it is not a means to an end.* There is no way to prove a value is an intrinsic good; the proof is in the experience of the value itself. For instance "Pleasure is good," the hedonist will say, "and that is just the way it is. If you don't believe it, try some." Likewise, experience tells us pain is intrinsically bad. It is not bad because it is not useful (in fact, a little pain may be very useful when it tells us what to avoid); it is experienced as bad on an immediate intuitive level, and that too is just the way it is. If you don't believe it, try some.

On the other hand, *extrinsic goods* are *those things we value because they are useful for getting other things that we value.* It is easy to give reasons why an extrinsic good has value—we simply point to the other goods that it leads to. Pleasure is intrinsic, and something like money is extrinsic. We want money for the sake of something else, for example, the pleasure it can buy. Extrinsic goods have *utility.* Utility is *the quality in a thing that contributes to its usefulness for getting other values.* For example, if we are hedonists, the utility of an object depends on how much it contributes either to pleasure or to the avoidance of pain. In theory, then, we can calculate a thing's extrinsic value by adding up how much utility it has. In a similar manner, *disutility* refers to *the properties in a thing that either create pain or deprive us of anticipated pleasures.* The more pain produced, the more disutility the object has. The prudent consequentialist will, therefore, try to maximize utility and minimize disutility.

How do we measure the amount of utility? We use our strategic reasoning abilities to engage in a profit and loss calculation. These are often very rough, since there is not always a clear quantitative standard (like money) that can be used to guide judgments about profit and loss. For instance, how much is Uncle Joe's life worth? The amount of his projected earnings over a life time? Or how hard his family will work to keep him alive? There is no obvious answer, so we have to rely on personal experience, intuition, and the meaning system of the people involved. We must also decide whether we should delay gratification and strive for long-term utility, or design institutions to bring immediate rewards. Another complicating factor in utility calculations is the trade-offs that need to be made between kinds of goods. For example, should we trade away some of our freedom for more money? The prisoners in the Zimbardo experiment did this. All but two of them regretted it—they were willing to give back all the money earned in order to be paroled so they could have freedom. In the future, will they give freedom more utility in their calculations?

These calculations are difficult because of the qualitative differences between kinds of pleasures. The quality of a thing's value shifts depending on how central it is to our way of life. How much weight (both in terms of intrinsic pleasure and extrinsic money) should I give to something like my love for my child? For most parents, a child is so important in their life that it seems ridiculous to even think in comparative utilitarian terms about the child's importance—it is beyond measure. These thorny issues involving the quality of pleasures can complicate issues that look relatively simple on first glance. Thus, theories of value quickly become quite complicated. Economists sometimes duck these difficult issues by leaving choice of values up to consumer preferences. But, even if we try to stay simple and assert that "good" only means any consequence that people seem to prefer based on their spending habits, complications immediately arise. It does not take much experience to realize that "what we have an interest in" is not necessarily the same as "what is in our interest." For instance, children often have no interest in school, but with our broader understanding we know it is actually in their interest to go to school. It is always possible for people to be mistaken about what is good for them; thus, before we can design strategic moral systems to further our or anyone else's interests, we need to discover what is actually in our and other people's interests. Each theory will give top priority to different values depending on their background assumptions about human nature. But, other things being equal, it is clear that rational consequentialists will emphasize doing what is in a person's *best* interest, so that the person's choices will not be self-defeating.

∼ Ethical Egoism, The Simplest Consequentialist Theory

> **For Study:**   Why is it difficult to apply even a simple moral principle in a rational manner?

The egoist's theory of value seems straightforward. What is good is what brings me pleasure by satisfying my best interests, all things considered. What is bad is what harms my interests. The theory of obligation that naturally follows from this theory of value is expressed in the foundational principle that says, we are obligated to promote our own best interest. This theory looks easy to use; it seems so uncomplicated. But, before we can even begin, we have to confront an immediate problem. At what level do we apply the foundational principle? A major principle, by itself, is already fairly abstract. If we focus on it, we are looking past the immediate foreground made up of the rules within which we live. Are we supposed to skip the intermediate levels that involve rules and apply the principle directly to each of our actions? Or are we supposed to apply the principle at the intermediate level of institutional rules, and then, as an individual, just follow the rules the principle justifies? Strategically, which approach is more apt to be in our best interest?

The impulse behind the egoist principle seems straightforward. Do whatever will promote your own best interests. But, even this simple command is not easy to carry out in a social world. To apply even a simplistic principle requires us to have already made a number of theoretical assumptions about our interests and strategies of application. One of the first questions that has to be answered is "How do I know if the ethical egoist principle itself is in my best interest?" Because these questions can be confusing, it may be useful to begin on a concrete level by exploring how one would have to modify Kohlberg's second stage "Instrumental Relativist" form of egoism in order to turn it into a Level III philosophical form of moral egoism that could conceivably convince other morally autonomous people that egoism can function as their intersubjective moral theory.

Background for Ethical Egoism: Personal Egoism Is Not a Moral Position

> **For Study:**   What characteristics have to be added to personal egoism to try to make it compatible with the moral point of view?

We have to live in institutions. What should Kohlberg's stage-two instrumental egoist focus on when designing institutions? In the first place, he wouldn't have to worry about others, since he defines human values egocentrically as "my values." A person who takes this approach to all questions about "what ought to be" is called a *personal egoist.* The strategically rational principle that governs his behavior can be stated as follows: *I ought to always do whatever will promote my own best interests.*

Although a philosophical egoist can understand that other people have their own points of view, from his perspective there is no inherent ethical reason to value satisfying those other points of view. In short, other people have extrinsic value for an egoist; they do not have special intrinsic moral status of their own. However, let's assume that our personal egoist wants to go public with his principle so that it can begin to function as a social moral principle that will obligate others. The fact that he wants to live with other people or keep them from killing him will give him sufficient reason to modify the principle.

To make his principle a matter of morality, he would have to make it universal so that everyone is given the same duties. Thus, if the theory of value says "What is good is what is in my best interest," the theory of obligation should say "Everyone ought to promote what is good—that is, what is in my best interests." Now the principle has a universal form, but it won't work. Why should all of us think we are obligated to satisfy the egoist? A prudent personal egoist must ask himself: "Is it really strategically rational to publicly lobby for institutions that only satisfy me?" He cannot constantly be on guard against attack from those who would like to modify institutions so that they benefit themselves. If he wants security, he will have to change the principle to make it more appealing to others. Furthermore, what if an egoist would like to have friends? He will have to convince others to voluntarily adopt his principle by convincing them that it is also in their best interest. This means he will have to decenter to a greater degree and modify the theory of value so that it includes powerful or useful others. A modified principle would read: "Everyone ought to act to promote the best interests of the people in my group."

In this limited form, the principle becomes an *aristocratic* or *"club" principle*. It *gives special privileges to a restricted group* and universal duties to the rest of us. Because aristocratic principles (which pretend to be moral principles) arbitrarily exclude moral agents from the benefits of the social order (often as a hidden agenda), it is very difficult to think of them as principles of a rational morality. A rational morality treats like cases alike. Rational people are going to expect an account that clarifies why they have been excluded (for example, as when we give empirical reasons for excluding children from driving privileges). Before anyone will accept being excluded from equal consideration by a moral principle, they are going to insist that they be given very sound logical reasons why they should be excluded. The problem with aristocratic principles is that they exclude certain people for reasons that seem arbitrary from the moral point of view.

Personal egoists may think the rational concern for consistency and universal application are irrelevant to their chosen way of life, but that is just one reason why their position is rejected in most philosophical literature. Before egoism will be taken seriously as a moral principle, it must satisfy the criteria of the moral point of view. This is the goal of those who advocate a philosophically based ethical egoism. They modify the principle to make it universal in application and sufficiently general. The final version of philosophical *ethical egoism* says, *"Everyone ought to act so as to promote their own best interest."* This universalized, generalized principle now has the form required by the MPofV. A morally autonomous person can now at least legitimately consider ethical egoism as a consequentialist moral option. The ethical egoist can say, because everyone in fact values their own interest, they have good reasons for adopting a moral system that tells them they have a right to promote their own intrinsic values. But, are there sufficient reasons to assume this principle is really compatible with what rational, caring people would choose?

Psychological Egoism Is Not Ethical Egoism

> **For Study:**   Why do normative egoists reject psychological egoism?

We need to be careful not to confuse the normative theory of egoism with the descriptive theory called *psychological egoism.* The psychological theory says,

"People in fact always do act in their own self-interest." Sometimes psychological egoism is used to argue for ethical egoism, but the wise ethical egoist has to be careful about accepting a theory that purports to describe human nature. For instance, suppose a psychological egoist argued that since ethical egoism is the only theory that does not contradict what people are capable of doing, it is the only theory that can be empirically recommended. A normative egoist would not find much comfort in this defense, because it conflicts with the logic of his own ethical principle. Psychological egoism makes it redundant for the ethical egoist to tell people that they ought to act on self-interest. Why do we need an ethical principle to tell people to do what they will naturally do? If psychological egoism is a true description of human nature, the ethical egoist principle appears to be reiterating nature; it is not really giving prescriptive advice.

As a prescriptive theory, ethical egoists have to explain in what sense it is possible for people to act contrary to their principle—making it necessary to give the prescriptions. There are two ways they might do this. First, they can reject psychological egoism and assert that people can in fact act in ways that will sacrifice their own interests (e.g., for the social good, for the good of someone else, or for the sake of a higher principle). This ethical egoist position would agree that altruistic behavior is possible, although it argues that altruism is morally wrong. An egoist believes sacrifices for the social good are right only if somehow the sacrifices will lead to a benefit for the egoist. This is a key point on which to focus. On a fundamental level, egoists challenge any moral point of view that requires us to care about principle, the tribe, or others as much as we care about ourselves.

A second way to deal with psychological egoism is to accept it, but point out that it does not necessarily negate ethical egoism. Psychological egoism says that people always try to act on their own self-interest, but it does not say they are always successful. Because people can fail to act on their true self-interest, an egoist prescriptive theory could be used to encourage them to stay true to their nature. The ethical principle would be used to remind us to look for the best alternative. Of course, if psychological egoism is true, once we know our best interest, we will have no choice but to act on it. Further prescriptions become redundant when there are no temptations to overcome.

The major problem with psychological egoism is that it just seems to be a poor descriptive theory of human nature. There are countless counterexamples of people who seem to act in selfless ways for others, for principles, for nations, and so forth. Psychological egoists often defend themselves by asserting that there are hidden self-interested psychological motives behind such counterexamples. But of course, if we allow theories to appeal to hidden evidence, then they can never be falsified and any crazy belief can be defended, no matter how absurd. We can leave this issue here, since even if the descriptive theory could be proven, it would not help the ethical egoist's position.

Problems with Ethical Egoism

> **For study over the next three sections:**   Why do many critics think that ethical egoism fails to satisfy the conditions of the moral point of view?

The toughest question for the ethical egoist is: Can it really be in our self-interest to live in a world governed by a universal principle that obligates everyone to act only on self-interest? The most popular egoist with students seems to be the writer Ayn Rand (1999). She makes her version of egoism seem attractive by using moral concepts from other theories, such as "human rights" and "man as an end in himself" (p. 426). She then reinterprets the concepts so that they imply only negative duties. As we will see in the section on Kant, he disagrees that this is the proper interpretation of what it means for "man" to be "an end in himself." Some critics claim that Rand confuses individualism with egoism. She popularizes her theory in novels with simplistic themes that always pitch rugged individualists (people with individual rights) against various mobs that want to control them (those who serve "altruist-collectivist doctrines" [p. 425]). The problem with this approach is that it sets up a dualistic conflict with no middle ground. Of course, individualism is to be valued, but not if it means selfishness.

So long as we are social beings who must live in a social context, it is not going to be easy to implement an egoist principle that favors selfishness. Troubling questions immediately arise. The corporate scandals coming to light in 2002 can be attributed partly to the philosophical assumption that greed is not only good, it is philosophically justified. On a more personal level, would you want to marry an egoist, or have one for a parent? Will we be able to trust anyone? Can we trust an egoist to protect all rights, or only their own? Egoism tells people they have no obligation to care for others unless they can get a reward for caring. Will we have to change the connotations for ethical terms, so words like "loyalty," "commitment," and "friendship," which entail some self-sacrifice, refer only to people who are "saps"? In short, egoist advice goes against what has inspired people for most of human history. Tribal and religious people call for self-sacrifice for a larger good; for example, Jesus says you must help others without concern for personal reward (Luke 6:35). Why do moral saints give prescriptions in their own teachings that are the opposite of egoism? Can egoism ever be in the best interest of enough people to make it work as a social theory?

If a person is really rational, he will see that a life governed by egoism cannot be in his own best interest unless he can maintain a favored economic slot (and data clearly shows that there are no guarantees of that for most of us). Would a rational egoist want some kind of social insurance policy to protect himself against the possibility that he too might slip into the ranks of the poor due to accidents, assaults, the harsh whips of inflation, unemployment, and declining welfare programs? What about slipping into the ranks of the aged? If we live long enough, membership in this group is guaranteed. Can we trust the next generation to help us out when we begin to lose our faculties if they have been told to live like egoists? Why would an egoist help anyone who cannot pay him back? Why wouldn't young powerful egoists simply use old people for medical experiments? Can someone who is only self-interested really be committed to any principle at all—even an egoist principle?

Although Hobbes (1839, 1962) is associated with social contract theory, he is also an ethical egoist who tried to explain why an egoist might remain committed to principles of justice. Hobbes had a terrible beginning in life. His mother died two days after his birth and his father was a violent drunk who fled the family when Hobbes was eleven to avoid being charged with assault. Hobbes says his mother "brought twins to birth, myself and fear at the same time" (Hampton, 2002, p. 383). This background procedural understanding of life was the dominant theme in his theory. Accordingly he argued that the motive for the social contract is fear and the desire for security. Without the social contract there would be no powerful external authority who could control other egoists, and thus life would be "solitary, poor, nasty, brutish, and short" (1962, p. 100). To avoid this terrible consequence, egoists themselves would favor an absolute police power who could force egoists to keep their contracts. Hobbes at least had a clear vision of egoism's lack of potential, since he recognized that you could not trust egoists to obey rules of justice without the threat of the sword.

The need for a police state creates a practical problem for the egoist. How can he get enough people to support such a program to make it work as social policy? Most people are not fearful egoists, so they will look at the consequences of advocating an egoist philosophy and say, "I just don't want to live that way. There are more rewarding ways to live." People with religious and family convictions often feel this way, as do those who believe tribal loyalty and duty of station are essential elements of a good life (these concepts require a level of commitment that conflicts with egoist motives).

Ideal Theory: The Enlightened Ethical Egoist's Response

> **For Study:**   What is the difference between a simple ethical egoist and an enlightened ethical egoist?

To respond to these concerns, egoists sometimes claim that rational egoists will take all of the above into consideration. The principle says to promote your *best* interests, and rational people know that the good life requires that we give priority to the higher pleasures—things like love, charity, and social commitment. These options will not be left out, since they are intrinsic goods that should be included in a rational person's lifestyle choice. Once everyone is educated to understand how humans get the richest pleasures, then we can trust that egoists using strategic reason will not make choices that defeat their own happiness. Ancient Greek philosophers often talked like this. Everyone seeks their own happiness, but since humans are social animals, the only way to be happy is to have friends, a city-state to support, and a just soul that will bring you rewards in an afterlife. This view implies that our social nature makes us the kind of animal that cannot be happy by being a simple egoist. We must have a commitment to something beyond ourselves, like our family, tribe, or community, or we will be unhappy.

Implementation: Problems Remain

The critics of enlightened egoism argue that it only pretends to represent the moral point of view (by advocating a stance that is impartial, caring, universal, general, and prescriptive), when in fact it actually represents a perspective that is the opposite of the moral point of view (by advocating a stance of being partial, self-interested, and caring only because it brings a reward). If someone is truly enlightened, the critics argue, he will probably not be an egoist at all. That is, egoism glorifies being partial in opposition to a truly enlightened point of view such as the one which advocates impartiality in ethics. A primary dilemma in moral life concerns the problem of how to get a judicious balance between being partial or self-interested and being disinterested or impersonal, that is, balancing concerns for self with concerns for people and principles. Ethical egoism glorifies one at the expense of the other, and does not give very good arguments for its choice of priorities.

There are also certain logical or conceptual problems with egoism. First of all, the theory is weakest as an ethical theory precisely where we expect ethical theories to do their best work. When there are major conflicts of interest to be resolved, ethical egoism becomes practically useless. Assume you are an ethical egoist who wants to live, but Joe will benefit if you die. Assume Joe is in a position to either save you or let you die with no penalties to Joe. Your principle of ethical egoism obligates both of you to act on your own self-interest. But is it in your interest to tell Joe this? If he asks you what he ought to do, are you going to tell him he has a duty to act on his own self-interest and allow you to die? Or are you going to do your duty as an egoist and act on your own self-interest and lie to him (tell him he is obligated to save you)? Ethical theories tell us how we are supposed to act. Surely we should be able to advocate them openly and with pride without betraying the theory or ourselves. It is a strange ethical theory that requires a moral agent to keep quiet about the ethical theory in order to act according to the theory.

This latter point is not a strong argument against egoism until we tie it back to the overall consequences that follow from living in an egoistic world. Because the only kind of rationality that gets emphasized is strategic reason, egoism implies it is in our self-interest to be deceitful or at least shrewd and calculating.

Ethical egoism has trouble explaining why anyone should do his duty when he knows no one is looking. If it is in his interest to carefully break promises, contracts, and other rules, then an egoist ought to do so. When duties are merely an extrinsic means to self-interest, doing your duty has no intrinsic moral worth.

The enlightened egoist will argue that promoting honesty protects egoists themselves. It is not prudent for egoists to promote a society that may allow them to be cheated, so they will advocate punishing dishonesty in general. This response does not satisfy the critics, however. They worry that the shrewd egoist will tell other people to be honest, but she will only pretend to be committed to her own duties. There is no reason not to violate duties when it is in her interest to do so. There will always be times when an egoist can get away with violating her duty, so it is hard to see how we can convince her to respect (in a full sense) standard ethical notions like duty, loyalty, devotion, or tribal integrity. The egoist will develop these character traits only if she thinks they will benefit her, and she will feel justified in ignoring them when it serves her purpose to do so. An occasional violation of a duty or promise will not bother the committed egoist, but it should bother others who have to live with her.

One final point: Enlightened ethical egoism is supposed to work as a social theory because enlightened egoists understand that it is in their best interest to have a community of trusted fellows. But this argument presupposes that egoists are socially sophisticated beings who can understand the long-range social implications of their and other people's behavior. To be truly enlightened, they would need to understand the qualitative social meaning of intersubjective norms like Smith's notion of integrity. For this sophistication to develop, children need to pass through the kinds of moral stages studied by Kohlberg. That is, in order to know how to function at a Socratic level of self-interest, people need to experience what it is like to live a Level II Conventional orientation to social norms where one sacrifices self-interest for the well being of the group. If we explicitly teach egoism throughout childhood, people may well fail to develop the conventional capacities that underlie the enlightened egoist's worldview. The egoist cannot teach people his theory until after they have gone through their conventional training, where they learn that egoism is wrong. This objection is not crucial, but it does seem strange to advocate an ethical theory that cannot be openly taught in childhood.

∽ Utilitarianism

> **For Study:**   In what way are egoists and utilitarians the same? In what way do they differ? Who are we supposed to make happy, according to utilitarians?

Most people who favor a consequentialist approach that focuses on satisfying interests adopt some version of *utilitarianism.* Traditional utilitarian theories adopt the same theory of value as egoism, but they reject the personal in favor of the impersonal perspective since this is more compatible with the MPofV. They agree with the background theory of human nature that says seeking pleasure and avoiding pain are intrinsic goods. But, they point out that since this is true for everyone, then from an impartial perspective everyone's pleasure counts equally. Thus, the utilitarian theory of obligation says it is our duty to distribute goods in such a way that we will promote as much utility as possible for everyone. *Our moral task is to evaluate all alternatives, then act on the one whose consequences will make for the greatest amount of happiness even if this means we have to sacrifice our own interests.*

How do we reduce pain and promote happiness? Can we just send out happiness shares in the mail? Of course not. Just as we saw in egoism, happiness is an intrinsic nonmoral value. To increase it, we must distribute extrinsic values (like money, prestige, honors, and liberties) in a way that both reduces pain and promotes happiness. Thus, the utilitarian principle can be stated in a number of different ways: *Everyone ought to always choose the option that will create the largest number of happy people.* Another version: *Always choose the option that will promote the greatest amount of utility.* Another version: *Always choose the option that will create the greatest good for the greatest number.*

It is important to keep the focus on the number of people. Some critics of utilitarianism assume utilitarians are interested in maximizing pleasure—period!—as though it were some kind of entity that exists independently of people. If this were the case, a creature that could experience an infinite amount of pleasure would be an embarrassment to utilitarian theory, for it would then make sense to distribute all the extrinsic goods in such a way as to feed the pleasure monster. This is absurd. The original point was to make everyone happy, not promote pleasure for its own sake. So utilitarians start with a background theory that says: what is important is people in general and how they are feeling. It is right to promote people's good feelings, and wrong to promote their bad feelings. It is good to have lots of happy people; it is bad to have any unhappy people. The ideal is to eliminate pain if possible and make everyone as happy as possible.

Background: How to Interpret Decentered Pleasure

> **For Study:**   Why does the existence of incommensurable pleasures make it more difficult to calculate utility? Why is the principle of utility different than a majority rule principle? How do utilitarians deal with sadistic desires?

What all of the versions of the utilitarian principle have in common is the emphasis on minimizing disutility and maximizing extrinsic and intrinsic values so as to promote general happiness. Utilitarian theory is completely decentered, so it is a mistake to apply it in an ethnocentric fashion. Everyone's good counts equally in social calculations. The pleasure or happiness of a king is no better than the pleasure of a peasant. The happiness of people in Asia is just as important as the happiness of people in the United States. The we/they approach to social problems is inconsistent with the major thrust of utilitarian theory. However, insofar as ethnocentric concerns bear on people's happiness, these concerns will also have to be taken into consideration since they amount to interests that need to be satisfied.

Because of the emphasis on maximizing pleasure or happiness, critics of hedonistic forms of utilitarianism once charged that it was a philosophy only fit for pigs. They argued that if pleasure is the greatest value in life, we might as well sit around and scratch our itches. Mill (1863, 1957) responded to this kind of argument by pointing out that the "type of agent" experiencing the pleasure is important. He said that it was unfortunate that these critics were only acquainted with pig pleasures. As for himself, Mill argued that he received the greatest pleasure from things that exercised the higher human faculties. These higher pleasures cannot be reduced to the kind of sensual pleasures that dominate the life of pigs. Of course, a quality life should begin by satisfying all those physical pleasures that make babies and pigs happy—food, gentle touching for the senses, sweets, music, and so forth. But Mill argued that as we mature, new capacities emerge. A physically satisfied pig can be happy; a physically satisfied human needs more. Given the kind of creatures we are, humans must pursue the higher pleasures found in a life filled with spirituality, intellectual understanding, beauty, moral autonomy, and love of partner, family, and humanity. It is because humans need the freedom to judge these things for themselves that it is better to be Socrates unsatisfied than a fool satisfied (12ff).

Mill was making the point that there are higher and lower pleasures in life that are *incommensurables.* As we saw earlier, values are incommensurable when *they are so radically different that there is no common standard that can be used to measure the properties of one set against the properties of the other.* A popular way to express this is to say, "you cannot compare apples and oranges." They are different in kind or quality not just different in degree or quantity. For example, Mill believes that freedom is one of the higher values. The pleasure we get from sensual joy is different in kind and not just degree from the pleasure we get from being free. Beyond a certain necessary minimum (e.g., avoiding starvation), no amount of the sensual (pig) pleasures can compensate for the loss of the higher pleasure that humans get from being free. If you don't understand this, Mill would suggest that you need training in the higher pleasures. He thought that only a judge who has experienced both types of pleasure can properly choose between pleasures that are different in quality.

By making a distinction between higher and lower pleasures, Mill greatly complicates utilitarian calculations. What is the legislator to do? If Mill is right about human nature, it is probably a mistake in the long run to trade off higher pleasures for lower ones (e.g., spending money on activities that promote intellectual virtues is more likely to maximize happiness in the long run than spending money to promote drinking, eating, dancing, and football.). So, in re-designing institutions, we have to do more than figure out how to satisfy the current interests of all the people involved; we need to decide as well if their interests are tied to higher pleasures or lower pleasures. If two interests conflict and one is higher, other things being equal, we should always take the higher.

It is important to remember that, as an ethical theory, utilitarianism is a moral philosophy about the way we ought to live while in pursuit of nonmoral goods. Utilitarians do not have to passively sit by and accept whatever interests some person wants to champion. They can use the utilitarian agenda to judge interests. Some interests are easier to promote, last longer, are more apt to lead to additional pleasure, have greater intensity and greater quality, and so forth. A utilitarian can also legitimately judge on the basis of maximizing utility in the long run. A child may want a lollipop now, but the tooth decay in the future will also affect a parent's utilitarian decision. A country may want to cut down its rain forests now, but a utilitarian will balance the next generation's interests against the interests of those who will benefit immediately from turning the forest into farmland.

Because of their willingness to judge the utilitarian value of various pleasures, it is a mistake to think of utilitarianism as a majority rule principle. The majority will not always rule; it depends on what the majority wants. For instance, from a utilitarian perspective, what the majority has an interest in may not be in the interest of the greatest happiness for humanity. When evaluating public policy or legislation, it is not enough to simply ask: "How many people want this?" A utilitarian also has to ask: "What intrinsic values are involved, what extrinsic values, are they higher or lower pleasures, what are the long-range consequences for human happiness?" In short, utilitarianism is not an economic theory where we simply try to efficiently maximize people's preferences; it is a moral theory that calls upon us to judge preferences as well as everything else that needs to be judged from the moral point of view.

A different kind of problem concerns the clash between pleasures that are proutilitarian and those that are antiutilitarian. What has more value, a sadist's interest in humiliating others or a person's interest in deciding for himself what he wants? Granted everyone counts for one, but does it really make sense to give sadistic pleasure the same weight as interests in pleasing ourselves? Narveson (1967) argues that sadistic pleasures should not be given any weight at all. They are by their nature antiutilitarian. First, they cannot be satisfied except by creating pain in another, thus sadistic pleasures cancel themselves out with the disutility used to purchase them. But Narveson claims there is a second objection that is even stronger. He says there is no reason why a utilitarian should have to give positive weight at all to an interest that is known to be opposed to utilitarianism.

> There is a sense, of course, in which the internal character of a desire is irrelevant to the utilitarian. . . . But it is one thing to say that the particular character of the

desire is irrelevant because all desires should be considered, and quite another to say that no desires of any sort should be rejected, upon consideration. The most obvious consideration there could possibly be for rejecting a desire in any system of ethics is that it is a desire for the exact opposite of the aim of the system . . . (p. 161)

A desire to inflict harm on another person is the very paradigm of the kind of desire the utilitarian is out to control. (p. 166)

To acknowledge a principle is to recognize that we must inhibit desires that conflict with it. It follows, therefore, that we all ought to inhibit desires that make us want to inflict pain. As Adam Smith would say, the sadist needs to exercise some self-command, because the sadist takes pleasure in doing the opposite of what utilitarianism obligates us to do. Thus, if anything, the sadistic individual should be punished for not being a good utilitarian rather than rewarded by having his pleasure treated as though it is equal in merit. These considerations further complicate utilitarian calculations, because it is not always easy to tell the difference between a motive that is antiutilitarian and one that is merely self-interested. If pushed far enough, would self-interest itself be antiutilitarian, as some of the relationship-oriented women in Gilligan's study seem to think?

Ideal Theory: Impartial Benevolent Calculations of Utility

For Study: Why do utilitarians advocate the "impartial benevolent spectator" device of reason?

Because it is not easy to calculate how to maximize happiness, and because it is easy to rationalize and think that our own pleasure counts more than the pleasure of other people, utilitarians often recommend an artificial device to help people adopt the MPofV when they calculate utility. The goal is to convert strategic reasoning into moral reasoning. They say we should calculate utility in the same manner as an *impartial benevolent spectator* would calculate it (Firth, 1952). The utilitarian calculation is *impartial* when it *treats like cases alike* (so everyone counts as one and everyone affected is included in the calculation). It is *benevolent* when the calculation *expresses concern or sympathy for the people involved.* (The calculator cares, she can empathize and properly weigh the pleasure and pain involved.) And it takes the view of a *spectator* when it imitates the moral agent judging from a third-person point of view with a *proper balance between interest and disinterest.* Egoism glorifies the personal, so utilitarianism has to change the emphasis to the impersonal. Moral rationality from the MPofV has entered the picture, since an impersonal interest in judging right from wrong has priority over the personal view of a biased participant who simply wants his own side to win.

The use of this device of reason provides a good example of how modern theories have tried to stay focused on the mainstream philosophical point of view that has evolved in philosophy. The theory acknowledges that a morally responsible decision involves more than purely intellectual skills. By emphasizing benevolence, utilitarian theory acknowledges that both rationality and moral emotions are important. This is, of course, a very sophisticated moral point of view. Imagine the complex set of traits needed to fully grasp and utilize this ideal spectator device. Egocentric children cannot be impartial, benevolent, or disinterested enough to function as an ideal utilitarian agent. Once reason develops one may well develop the capacity for impartiality, at least in the sense of intellectual neutrality, but benevolence or caring can only be learned through social intercourse. Of course, this is not an all-or-nothing dimension. Each of us will experience degrees of caring, and it is quite possible that our capacities may fluctuate during life's transitional phases and situational crises. As Erickson (1963, pp. 274ff) argued, children must first learn trust in a family that protects them during periods of vulnerability, afterwards they can learn to love or care for intimate others. Eventually, they will have to undergo a transcendence from within where they learn to feel respect for distant others, or else they will not calculate utility in a way that will insure *everyone* counts as one.

Implementation: Problems with Utilitarianism

> **For Study:** Why do some utilitarians advocate "rule utilitarianism?" What do utilitarians have to say about equality and the distribution of goods? Why do some people say utilitarians ask too much of moral agents?

Does the principle of utility allow us to break our agreements when it will promote more utility to do so? Attempts to answer this question have led utilitarians to emphasize two different ways to apply the utilitarian principle. *Act utilitarians* argue that *we should apply the principle of utility to individual actions.* At any given moment, act so as to promote the greatest amount of happiness. Act utilitarians think that rules should definitely be considered when we are making our calculations, but we should treat them as guidelines or rules of thumb, not as unbreakable absolutes. Although rules should generally be obeyed, there will always be cases where the spirit of the rule cannot be served by strict adherence to the letter of the rule; that is, more pleasure for everyone can be promoted by breaking a rule than by following it. For example, the general rule of thumb is that one should not lie, but in some cases it is right to tell a lie if lying will promote more happiness—lying to save a life, or lying to your senile grandfather to spare his feelings. Even when an act is covered by a rule, the act utilitarian may apply the principle of utility directly to the act itself rather than just obey the rule.

This willingness to suspend rules bothers some utilitarians. They worry that if we allow people to choose for themselves whether or not to follow a rule, they will too often break rules for self-interested reasons as children do. *Real will theory* indicates that too many *real people do not or cannot calculate utility like impartial benevolent spectators,* so people need to follow rules at the implementation level. After all, what is the point of having a professional code of ethics if professionals are free to decide for themselves whether or not to follow its rules? If all moral agents could think and act like Socrates, maybe we could allow everyone to be act utilitarians; but until then, it might be better to apply the principle of utility only to the system of rules, then those of us who are not Socratic can just follow the rules. This approach is called *rule utilitarianism* since it says that *individuals should always obey the rules that will bring the greatest happiness.* Rule utilitarians are arguing that in the long run more happiness will be promoted if individuals will stay consistent by following the levels of application. First, the foundational principle is applied to generate other principles, which are then applied to rules, and then the rules will apply to the acts of individuals. We should apply the principle of utility to actions only if a rule does not already cover the situation.

Whatever level they focus on, both act and rule utilitarians have a formidable task. To judge the rightness of an act they must be able to look into the future and predict with some degree of reliability the consequences for everyone who will be affected by a decision or rule. Then they must prescribe actions or rules on the basis of their predictions. But imagine how difficult it is to accurately predict utility in a pluralistic society. Even if we rule out preferences that are not right (e.g., sadistic ones), the diversity in preferences will still be considerable. People with different value programming will be made happy by different things in different amounts. Should these individual differences be taken into consideration? Giving everyone a lump sum of money would be easy, but everyone is not made equally happy by the same amount of money. As Aristotle pointed out 2,000 years ago, because Milo the wrestler has nutritional needs that are different from the average person, an equal distribution of food won't maximize happiness.

To help simplify our task, utilitarians argue that we should use supplementary principles such as the *principle of diminishing marginal utility* to help guide our calculations. This principle says that *the more goods a person has, the less utility a person gets out of an additional unit of the goods.* Five dollars does not mean as much to a millionaire as it does to a person who is broke, so if you have five dollars to distribute give it to someone who is poor. A loaf of bread to a welfare mother creates more utility than it does in a home where people have cake. Other things being equal, then, adopt policies that will distribute extrinsic goods in a broad-based manner, rather than allow them to accumulate in certain wealthy localities or social classes. In the long run, then, there will be pressures in utilitarian societies that will favor an egalitarian distribution of extrinsic goods.

There are two other problems with the utilitarian approach to ethics. First, notice how much it demands of us. Whether we are act or rule utilitarians, each time we act (or judge a rule) we must always do whatever will make the most people happy. This entails a heavy moral burden. For instance, in making a decision about how to spend my time, I have to consider all who will be affected by my decision. What right do I have to play a round of golf? My time could be used to promote much more utility if I worked to help the poor. I may feel thirsty and be inclined to spend a dollar on a beer. This will promote my utility, that is, quench my thirst and create a slight pleasant numbing of my nerves, but wouldn't it create much more utility to drop dollars in a church's poor box? The principle of utility is clear. So long as there are people within range of my actions, I have a duty to choose the act that will maximize the happiness of each of us. Where do I draw the line between utilitarian duty and utilitarian charity? Is there any room for individual choice in these matters?

One response to these concerns is to point out that people are happier when they decide issues for themselves. The general duty is to do what you can, but you decide how much you can do. Furthermore, since utility is promoted by letting people have a private life, they should also get to decide how much of their time they will spend in private pursuits. This makes sense, since no theory can determine ahead of time the extent of all of our moral actions. All theories rely on individual conscience in situations that require judgment. The problem still remains, however, am I or am I not always duty-bound to maximize everyone's happiness? That I have freedom to make the calculation myself does not change the extent of the burden.

The second major problem concerns the moral status of special duties. People make decisions on the basis of legitimate expectations they have about the way the world runs. If I take on **special duties** by *voluntarily signing contracts or making promises,* how long do they last? Should we nullify existing contracts and special commitments whenever doing so promises to create more utility? How would we decide when it is appropriate to nullify a contract? On the basis of utilitarian calculations, of course, but these calculations involve the touchy issue of changing the rules. Thus, we would also need some due process procedures and appeal procedures to help us avoid hasty calculations. Wouldn't this be hopelessly cumbersome and, perhaps, interfere with utility maximization by taking decision-making power away from individuals?

Furthermore, the principle of diminishing marginal utility seems to imply that we should design institutions so that there is periodic redistribution of goods. Those who are worse off will always be able to experience greater utility from periodic judicious redistributions, so society ought to periodically take extrinsic goods away from one group and redistribute them to other groups who have less. Those well off will complain, but so long as the redistribution is kept within limits their complaint would be offset by the gain in utility for those worse off. The graduated income tax is based on this notion. This seems unfair to some people. They claim utilitarian theory makes them sacrifice some of their legitimately earned income for the good of others who haven't earned it. (Is this the kind of complaint that a good utilitarian would make?) More to the point, some critics argue that redistribution violates fundamental property rights. Is it fair to require some to give up their hard-earned property even if it will promote the general happiness? What about the policy of eminent domain, where the state can confiscate property for the sake of the common good? Is it fair to take people's homes or farms from them (against their will) to build public buildings that will benefit a larger segment of society?

These concerns lead many utilitarians to favor some form of rule utilitarianism that gives extra weight to special duties. They argue that once you sign a contract, maximum utility is promoted in the long run by a rule that says you are bound by the contract no matter what calculations you make in the future. But act utilitarians argue that contracts are only a means to utility. They can serve as rules of thumb (general guidelines), but they are not absolutes. They should not be allowed to stop the progress toward maximum happiness. But what about the contractee's right to have the contract enforced? Is it just to nullify a contract, even if it is for the social good? All of these considerations lead some critics to charge that utilitarianism is fundamentally flawed, since it cannot adequately account for common-sense notions of justice.

The Problem of Justice

> **For Study:**   What is the problem of justice? Why are utilitarians opposed to absolute rights? What is the difference between violating a right and overriding a right?

For our purpose we can say that a person has a ***moral right*** to something *when a person can make a legitimate claim to it.* (It is legitimate when justified at the proper level by an agreed-upon moral theory.) So, to have a right is to have the liberty to do or receive something because it is our "due." Just how extensive or inviolable are rights? Historically they arose as a way to protect individuals from others, including the government. Should rights also protect individuals from utilitarian calculations?

Utilitarians say all rights are extrinsic goods justified by their role in promoting utility, so there are no rights that are more fundamental than the principle of utility itself. Utilitarian critics, however, say that this is exactly the attitude that violates our sense of justice. They claim that utilitarians refuse to acknowledge that some rights are so important that they are indefeasible—such as rights to life, liberty, and equal opportunity. (***Indefeasible*** is a legal term meaning that *a right cannot be defeated or voided by other social considerations including the general welfare.*) These critics say that any theory is unjust if it would allow the indefeasible rights of individuals to be violated in order to promote general happiness.

Is utilitarianism an unjust theory? There is a whole series of strange "lifeboat" examples that are supposed to show that utilitarians will, at least in principle, sacrifice the rights of individuals in order to maximize social utility (e.g., if a boat will only hold ten people and there are twelve on board, should we throw the least useful people overboard to maximize the good of the whole even though that violates their right to life?). The most famous of these lifeboat scenarios is the claim that utility could be used to justify punishing an innocent person as a means for deterring crime by others (Anscombe, 1957, p. 16). This would clearly violate individual rights, since an individual should not be punished unless she is guilty of some crime. If utilitarianism would allow such practices it would seem to be a defective theory.

I am not going to discuss each of these esoteric criticisms here. I agree with Narveson (1967, chaps. 2–7) that all of the lifeboat examples are generally weak arguments. Utilitarians are advocating a world in which everyone is happy in the long run. Individual decisions are always made against that background. The lifeboat examples are taken out of context and treated as though they are cases existing in a social vacuum, which distorts the utilitarian agenda. For instance, with regard to punishing an innocent person, utilitarians respond that the example has to presuppose that people will be willing to favor an absurd policy of allowing governments to promote general happiness by using secret manipulations of innocent people at the discretion of the government. Why would any utilitarian favor such policies? If anything, the general fear of arbitrary punishment that such a policy would create would produce disutility rather than a sense of safety. In addition, lifeboat cases are so problematic that it will not be clear what should be done no matter what theory we are using. Any solution will wind up violating someone's intuition, so all theories will have problems with these tough cases.

The point at issue here does not, however, turn on the adequacy of the examples used to criticize the utilitarian agenda. We can forget about lifeboats and simply ask: Is it permissible at all to set aside an individual's fundamental rights if it will promote general happiness to do so? Most utilitarians will say yes, since there are times when conditions might call for this. Critics of utilitarianism say that this concession shows the theory conflicts with our sense of justice.

John Stuart Mill (1863, 1957, chap. 5) argues that utilitarians would never allow people or agencies to "violate" individual rights. Now and then, conditions may require us to *override* a claim that is normally legitimate, but only *when a higher moral claim takes precedence*. As mentioned in Chapter One, overriding is not the same as violating. Violating a right is done for some nonmoral reason (such as private gain), but overriding is done for moral reasons. When we override a claim that is normally legitimate, it is because the claim no longer has its usual moral status. Sometimes extraordinary circumstances occur and other moral values trump what is normally right. Mill also thinks critics of utilitarianism are confused about the status of rights. They seem to think that there are ***absolute*** rights when, in fact, there aren't any. An absolute is *universally binding in all contexts and has unconditional value*. But, according to utilitarianism, there are and can only be two absolute rights: (1) the right to have the principle of utility used to make decisions, and (2) the right to have your interests considered when utility is calculated. (This is required by logic, since utility cannot be accurately calculated unless all relevant interests are reviewed in the calculation.)

Mill argues that all rights are actually ***prima facie*** rather than absolute, which means there are important but not always conclusive reasons for them. Thus, they hold *on first appearance, other things being equal*. People have rights in the first place because they promote utility. So, *prima facie* rights put the burden of proof on anyone who wants to override them to prove there is a utilitarian reason to make an exception to the rule. If a new situation arises that destroys the utility of particular rights, however, then the rights are not being violated if we implement new policies for the sake of reestablishing conditions that will promote everyone's happiness. All extrinsic goods, including rights, have value only because they promote utility. When they stop contributing to happiness, they lose their utility, and have to be overridden. Some values are so important for promoting utility that it is hard to think of a time when they would lose value or need to be overridden. To recognize that these values are special, we give people a right to them (e.g., a right to freedom). But these rights are *prima facie* rather than absolute. We only have them other things being equal, that is, so long as they continue to function as a means to overall happiness. We should not become confused and start thinking of them as absolutes.

Nonconsequentialist Criticism

> **For Study:** Why do nonconsequentialists disagree with the consequentialist approach to ethics?

The consequentialist approach to morality is not the only approach that can be taken. For instance, many philosophers think that morality has its own special status; it is not only a means for promoting other nonmoral values. These philosophers argue that moral rights and duties logically precede, and are independent of, any particular theory of value. The ***nonconsequentialist*** approach argues that *the status of moral rights and duties does not depend on the consequences they lead to because there is some other more fundamental "right-making" characteristic that is independent of consequences*. In fact, nonconsequentialists argue that one function of moral theory is to place boundaries on the nonmoral values that can legitimately be considered under a theory of value. As far as nonconsequentialists are concerned, consequentialists are like moral mercenaries—they are loyal to morality only because it pays some dividend in terms of nonmoral values. But morality is supposed to obligate us because it is about what is right, not because it pays.

Nonconsequentialists argue that to know what the moral boundaries should be on strategic calculations of utility we need a *theory of obligation* that *prescribes moral rights and duties*. In other words, a theory of obligation logically precedes any theory of value since a particular theory of value cannot be completed until we figure out the moral boundaries. For instance, some pleasures and interests may look good to us at first glance, but once we see that they are temptations that might make us violate our duty, we appreciate that they are not really good after all. Apparent goods lose their value when they conflict with a theory of obligation. Thus, nonconsequentialists argue that a mature moral agent ought to reverse the historical order of things. That is, most of us begin our moral life as consequentialists pursuing some good so that what *is* right *seems* to be in the service of the good. However, as we mature, we begin to opt for a more abstract logical order where doing what is right or our duty comes before the choice of the good lifestyle. But we cannot know the proper way to reverse the priority between good and right until we first develop a theory of obligation. The four principles that remain all assume (in varying degrees) that some form of nonconsequentialism is the only legitimate approach to moral inquiry.

⌁ Natural Rights Theory

For Study: Why do the defining characteristics of human rights make them cross-cultural?

The foundational principle of the **natural rights** theory states that *everyone ought to act in accordance with inalienable, indefeasible natural rights*. It is a nonconsequentialist orientation, since natural rights have special status as boundary conditions that place constraints on any subsequent decisions about the value of other goods. Because natural rights are more than a means to some other end, they have their own intrinsic moral worth. Contemporary natural rights theory is usually discussed under the label "human rights." According to Winston (1989) for rights to have this special human status they must be

1. *universal* (since all humans have them);
2. *moral,* not civil (so they do not depend on the actions of any government);
3. *natural* (in the sense that we have them just because we are human—they are essential to our nature);
4. *equal* (in that we all have them to the same degree no matter what our cultural context);

5. *fundamental* (in the sense of being inalienable and indefeasible— *inalienable* means that *the rights are so important to our nature that we cannot be separated from them as we can be from extrinsic values* and *indefeasible* means these rights *cannot be defeated or voided by any other social conditions*);

6. *self-evident* (which means they do not have to be proven; that is, they are self-justifying, since to hear about them is to immediately recognize their validity); and

7. a *standard of legitimacy* that *gives individuals the power to make claims against governments and majority rule.*

There are two ways to determine if something is legitimate in traditional liberal philosophy, mainly *popular sovereignty* and *human* or *natural rights.* Popular sovereignty leads to the creation of democratic institutions and majority rule. But natural rights theory is based on the idea that individuals should have inherent control over their life and the freedom to pursue personal preferences without external interference (Habermas, 2001, pp. 115ff). Thus, the theory says human rights trump popular sovereignty. They ought not to be overridden, even by a majority.

Background: Values in Nature

> **For Study:** According to natural rights theory, how do we morally judge all institutions?

Although to many of us today natural rights or human rights seem like a fairly straightforward approach to morality, individual natural rights were not emphasized in ancient civilizations. There were, of course, historical trends that set the stage for this individualistic approach. Religious tradition contributed the idea that all of nature was created by God. Since we are all part of God's purpose, we are all individually equal in the eyes of God. The Roman Stoics then elaborated on the Greek idea that nature follows rational patterns or norms that can be known by any individual if he will use human reason to interpret events. Then Roman law was literally imposed on all the different cultures in the known Western world, which helped people accept the idea that some transcendent norms could in fact apply cross-culturally. As long as local customs were not inconsistent with the Roman law they were allowed to flourish in their own context, and this gave rise to the idea that local communities could have freedom to choose a way of life so long as it was compatible with the boundaries established by universal law. It is a fairly straightforward step from these historical trends to the modern conception that individuals themselves have universal human rights that ought to be protected in any society. In the eighteenth century, natural rights were the primary normative tool used by modern philosophers to fight against the conventional institutions that were based on hereditary hierarchies. The antiroyalists insisted that citizens were by nature free individuals who should be self-governed. In fact, natural rights theory has inspired liberation movements in many countries. For instance, it is instructive to think of the Declaration of Independence as the kind of account a group of morally autonomous revolutionaries would give to the rest of the world, if they were using a natural rights theory to justify their actions. Jefferson thought such an account would make sense to the reason (or moral sense) of all free people.

> When in the course of human events, it becomes necessary for one people to dissolve the political bands which have connected them with another, and to assume among the powers of the earth, the separate and equal station to which the laws of nature and of nature's God entitle them, a decent respect to the opinions of mankind requires that they should declare the causes which impel them to the separation.
>
> We hold these truths to be self-evident, that all men are created equal, that they are endowed by their Creator with certain inalienable rights, that among these are life, liberty, and the pursuit of happiness—That to secure these rights, governments are instituted among men, deriving their just powers from the consent of the governed, that whenever any form of government becomes destructive of these ends, it is the right of the people to alter or to abolish it, and to institute new government, laying its foundation on such principles, and organizing its powers in such form, as to them shall seem most likely to effect their safety and happiness.

Notice, that according to this abstract conception natural rights logically precede legal arrangements. Thus government is conceived of as a means for protecting rights, which gives natural rights priority over all contingent social arrangements. One of the Enlightenment's major contributions to Western moral theory is the argument that no one is obligated to obey any law that is not compatible with the dictates of universal human reason. It follows that governmental institutions lose their legitimacy when they cannot be trusted to protect the natural rights of individual citizens.

Ideal Theory: Self-governed Individuals

> **For Study:** How do we know about natural rights? Why do they seem to support a negative rights conception?

B. J. Diggs (1974, pp. 33ff) argues that John Locke should be given credit for making the logic behind the natural rights tradition perfectly clear. Locke (1689, 1968) explicitly states that the sovereign in a legitimate state can only be the universal rational will of the people. He believed mankind possessed a divine light of reason that enabled humans to know about inalienable natural rights to things like life, liberty, health, and property (pp. 4–11). Since these natural rights are sacred even for people who live outside the boundaries of a state, the natural condition of man is to be a free, equal, self-governing moral being. Thus, natural rights theory is inherently individualistic, since its purpose is to protect individuals from others and create a carefully defined political/ social space for individual autonomy within which individuals will be free to pursue personal preferences. Liberal individualism resolves the tension between the personal and the impersonal in favor of personal autonomy, and republican communitarianism resolves it in favor of the impersonal good of the whole community.

But if people in nature were ever free, rational, social beings with natural rights, why would they ever agree to give up this natural status and submit to a civil authority? Locke argued that the state was a necessary means for protecting individual rights. While all people have a natural right to seek justice and a duty to punish those who violate natural rights, because individuals and families tend to overreact to injustice, they cannot properly do the job. When they seek retribution against those who violate rights, their sense of moral outrage naturally leads them to overstep the boundaries of fair punishment. Friends of the punished individual will then seek retribution in return. They too will overreact creating new outrage, etc., and eventually natural social life will degenerate into a state of war (or tribal feuds like the Hatfields against the McCoys). To avoid this, Locke argued that rational people would agree to enter a social contract for the purpose of choosing a government that can be trusted to impartially protect their natural rights.

Locke's theory is developed against a background of individualism that leads to a negative rights conception of the state. In a manner similar to a night watchman whose job is to protect the store, government's main function is to stop institutions and people from infringing on the property rights of individuals, including their property interest in their own life. As we saw in Chapter Four, this kind of background assumption leads to the idea that all contributions to the general welfare are charity, that is, supererogatory acts that go above and beyond the call of duty. At one point in his career, Robert Nozick (1974) was a most impressive contemporary advocate of this approach. He argued that, while it is immoral to violate the natural rights of others, no one (including the state) has a positive duty to help others satisfy their rights (p. 30).

Implementation: Problems with the Natural Rights Theory

> **For Study:** What are some of the most common problems confronting a natural rights theory? Why should communitarians be cautious when objecting to the theory? Why is the word *natural* problematic in a postmetaphysical society?

One major problem with this theory is methodological. Natural rights are supposed to be self-evident, but different people see different lists of rights as self-evident. Whose list is right? Why should we trust a list of rights just because it feels self-evident to someone, when we know how introjection can influence feelings? What if the judgments that seem self-evident are only common local prejudices? Furthermore, how should we interpret the content of a particular right? For instance, the United Nations' Declaration of Human Rights has been accepted by almost every country, but what does it mean? The list of human rights gives everyone "a right to meaningful work." Is the proper interpretation of "meaningful" self-evident?

Even if we could agree to a formal list of rights, can we agree to a list of priorities about how to resolve conflicts between the rights on the list? Is the rich man's right to property violated if we tax him to feed young children who have a right to life, or a right to health care, or a right to education, or a right to—where does the list stop? All theories have to solve such *priority problems,* but the *natural rights theory has special difficulties since each right is inalienable and indefeasible.* Such vexing questions lead some theorists to argue that the moral world is by its nature complex. They argue that we have to accept the fact that pluralism in absolute rights is a fundamental fact. When conflicts arise, we will just have to settle them case by case with a direct appeal to intuition.

But this is not very helpful. Which intuitions are correct? Even if people claim they have stage-six intuitions, they still need to enunciate the principles behind their intuitive priorities. Did they empathize with all possible motives, or only those that were compatible with principles that follow from some previously well-thought-out moral theory? Pure intuitionist theories are just too silent about how we ought to analyze background conditions. Relying on intuition makes us especially vulnerable to the standard man problem, since our interpretation of the meaning of natural rights and how to implement them will be heavily influenced by our own personal background. This has led to deep suspicion on the part of postmodern Western intellectuals that natural rights theory has been used to further ideological agendas. In theory, human rights protect people regardless of race, creed, sex, age, religion, etc. But there is tension "between the universal meaning of human rights and the local conditions of their realization" (Habermas 2001, p. 118). Until natural rights get translated into positive law in the form of legal rights, the protection is moral only, not political. But because of the way politics plays out, the powerful control the institutions of positive law needed to implement human rights. Since the powerful implement rights in a paternalistic fashion using their own personal experience, their personal point of view affects the policies that supposedly implement human rights. We should not be surprised to find that human rights theory has been used to protect the special status of privileged groups of people by hiding the real status of oppressed minorities and the injustices already built into legal arrangements. Some critics argue we should drop the appeal to transcultural human rights since their ideological abuse is so pervasive that they can't really protect people from abuse.

But, the forces of modernity that created the human rights movement in Western societies in the first place have now reached many Third World countries. Indigenous populations and oppressed minorities are not so eager to "get beyond" human rights. In fact, they are now turning the theory back on the powers that oppress them, and demanding protection of their equal rights to freedom and self-governance. For instance, women in patriarchical cultures are now using human rights to insist that they have value as individual women. They are not only daughters, wives, and mothers, but also individual people who have "the right to be recognized as separate beings whose well-being is distinct from that of a husband's" (Nussbaum, 1999, p. 1144).

Communitarians criticize human rights for being too individualistic, abstract, and anticommunity. As we saw in Chapter Five, they claim an emphasis on individual rights leads to egoism and destroys the conditions for community that make life worth living. But in fact, the situation is not that clear. Human rights are also being used in the fight to protect the integrity of communities. For instance, to fight against the homogenizing effects of the forces of globalization, smaller cultural minorities are fighting for the right of their cultural survival through a politics of mutual recognition (Habermas, 2001, p. 74). Since individuals have identities that are inherently tied to the collective identity of their cultural group, their individual rights to lifestyle cannot be protected unless the integrity of their culture is protected as well. Thus, although the human rights record is mixed, the value of this moral appeal for oppressed minorities is beyond dispute. It raises them to a level of equal humanity, and gives them a voice that can prick the conscience of privileged classes.

A final minor criticism focuses on the way rights have been associated with the natural law tradition. In a postmetaphysical world it is not as clear what advantage can be gained by retaining the label "natural" rights. What makes natural rights so special? The mere fact that something is natural does not make it right. Many natural things do not appear to be right. It is natural to die of disease but we try to prevent it at every step. It is natural to feel emotions like jealousy, envy, revenge, and hatred, but are these emotions moral? Whatever the right-making criteria are for natural rights, it does not appear to be enough to merely point out that rights are natural.

Early versions of natural rights theory did not worry about such questions because natural rights were supported by *divine command theory*. This kind of moral theory is based on religious foundations that claim *the right-making characteristic in morality is God's commands*. It is moral to obey God, immoral to disobey. Since God created nature, if something was natural then of course it was right. We do not have space to discuss divine command theory here. In any case, it would not end the questions, since pluralism in religious traditions leads to the same confusing issues. I am not saying that religious ethics is unimportant, but rather that we can only do so much in a short text.

To make room for religious freedom, philosophers generally strive for a secular theory that can help those from different religions figure out how to live together in peace. Members of a particular religion, as responsible moral agents, will have to figure out how to make their religious convictions compatible with the dictates of secular morality. If a rational, secular morality gives them duties that are incompatible with their religious convictions, their religion and the secular society will have a social dilemma to solve. Such conflicts must be worked out on a case-by-case basis. In the next chapter we will turn to a non-consequentialist theory that tries to cover some of the same ground as natural rights theory, but without appealing to nature.

REFERENCES

ANSCOMBE, G. E. M. (1957). Modern moral philosophy. *Philosophy* 32, 16ff.

DIGGS, B. J. (1974). *The state, justice, and the common good.* Glenview, IL: Scott, Foresman.

ERICKSON, ERICK. (1963). *Childhood and society.* New York: W. W. Norton.

FIRTH, RODERICK. (1952). Ethical absolutism and the ideal observer. *Philosophy and phenomenological research* 12, 314–45.

HABERMAS, JURGEN. (2001). *The postnational constellation.* Max Pensky (Trans.). Cambridge, MA: The MIT Press.

HAMPTON, JEAN. (2002). Introduction to Thomas Hobbes. In Steven M. Cahn (Ed.), *Classics of political and moral philosophy* (pp. 383–85). Oxford: Oxford University Press.

HOBBES, THOMAS. (1839, 1962). *Leviathan.* Michael Oakeshott (Ed.). New York: Collier Books.

LOCKE, JOHN. (1689, 1968). An essay concerning the true original, extent and end of civil government. In Ernest Barker (Ed.), *Social contract* (pp. 1–144). London: Oxford University Press.

MILL, JOHN STUART. (1863, 1957). *Utilitarianism.* New York: Bobbs-Merrill.

NARVESON, JAN. (1967). *Morality and utility.* Baltimore, MD: The John Hopkins Press.

NOZICK, ROBERT. (1974). *Anarchy, state, and utopia.* New York: Basic Books.

NUSSBAUM, MARTHA C. (1999). *Sex and social justice.* Oxford: Oxford University Press. Cited in Steven M. Cahn (Ed.). (2002). *Classics of political and moral philosophy* (pp. 1136–61). Oxford: Oxford University Press.

RAND, AYN. (1999). Man's rights. In Aeon Skoble & Tibor Machan (Eds.), *Political philosophy* (pp. 425–32). Upper Saddle River, NJ: Prentice Hall.

WINSTON, MORTON E. (1989). *The philosophy of human rights.* Belmont, CA: Wadsworth.

Chapter   Nine

Nonconsequentialist Alternatives to Natural Rights Theory

Like the natural rights approach to morality, the following three theories are trying to explain our intuition that people have a special intersubjective *moral* status. Only after we have established social, political, and economic boundaries that honor mankind's special moral status can strategic reasoning be used to pursue personal agendas. Thus, each of these three theories insist that secondary strategic tasks cannot preempt the logical priority of moral reasoning. We can see these priorities clearly illustrated in social contract theory, since the type of constraints placed on contractual considerations convert this apparently strategic form of reasoning into a special form of moral reasoning that satisfies the impartiality required by the MPofV (moral point of view).

～ Social Contract Theory

> **For Study:**   What is the intuitive idea behind social contract theory? Why is the social contract purely hypothetical? Why are empirical criticisms of the method irrelevant?

According to contemporary *social contract* theory, we should be asking, "What rights and duties would all rational beings be willing to impose on themselves—whether rights are natural or not?" This is a very abstract question, since we have to conceive of people as being able to participate in a foundational justificatory discourse about the principles that ought to have regulated the institutions that socialized the people who are choosing. That is, fairness in a social contract requires that choosers start their deliberations prior to being bound by any other contracts that set up social relations of power and prestige. This means, theoretically speaking, that since no one can have an advantage at the start, we must conceive of people as beings who are by nature free, rational, and equal no matter what real social conditions are like. Thus, the foundational principle of *social contract theory* says that *moral principles are those that* **would be** *chosen* if *free and equal rational people were to enter a social contract to establish a moral community.*

The word "would" is emphasized in the principle to draw attention to the fact that there is nothing natural about a social contract. It is a purely hypothetical abstract device of reason designed to guide our moral intuitions by helping us think like hypothetically rational, autonomous agents who care about having a social existence. The intuitive idea behind the model is that humans should only be governed by rational laws to which they give their autonomous consent. We assume that if a principle would in theory receive universal consent by moral equals, then it is ideally suited for the task of guiding the reform of real institutions that distribute social, political, and economic goods.

Background: Hume's Empiricism versus Rousseau's Normative Prescriptions

Many critics of social contract theory fail to understand the point of this hypothetical, abstract perspective. For instance, the Enlightenment philosopher David Hume (1748, 1968) argued that because governments are founded on "utility" and "habitual" obedience to a prince who has come to power through "conquest or usurpation" (pp. 149, 154), those who say obedience to a system of government is or ought to be based on consent are simply mistaken.

> But would these reasoners look abroad into the world, they would meet with nothing that, in the least, corresponds to their ideas, or can warrant so refined and philosophical a system.

... It is strange that an act of the mind, which every individual is supposed to have formed, and after he came to the use of reason too, otherwise it could have no authority; that this act, I say, should be so much unknown to all of them.

... [One problem is that] this supposes the consent of the fathers to bind the children, even to the most remote generations, ... besides this, I say, it is not justified by history or experience in any age or country of the world. (pp. 150–51)

The proper response to this kind of empirical criticism is to say "So what?" The entire argument misses the point because it confuses the logic of a descriptive exercise in social science with the logic of a normative theory about what ought to be. It is true that most political structures are based on power and usurpation, but that tells us nothing about justice. Duties that stem from the strategic reasoning behind utilitarian necessity and habit amount to no more than the prudent adaptation to local power relations. They should never be conceived of as *moral* duties.

As mentioned in Chapter Seven, Rousseau rejects the empirical approach used by philosophers like Hobbes, Grotius, and Aristotle. He understands that social contract theory is not about how people in fact developed the habit of obedience. "To yield to the strong is an act of necessity, not of will. At most it is the result of a dictate of prudence. How, then, can it become a duty?" (Rousseau, 1762, 1968, p. 172). In order to make sense of the fact that we have moral as well as prudential reasons for obeying law, Rousseau says we must assume that the consent behind the social contract functions implicitly everywhere we find a legitimate form of government. It does not matter that consent was never explicitly given, it should have been (and will be as soon as people come to understand it). He says that even if the principles of such a contract "... may never have been formally enunciated, they must be every-where the same, and everywhere tacitly admitted and recognized" (p. 180). Thus, social contract theory invites people from any generation to speculate on how things ought to be. Future generations are no more bound by their fathers' real normative speculations than we are by our father's. That is, we are not talking about a concrete contract created in the context of current courts of law, but an abstract, ideal representation of the kind of contract that in princi-ple ought to be used to criticize courts of law.

Because we are always already embedded in ongoing social systems it is hard to imagine what it would be like to have a beginning position that is fair to everyone. For example, a letter to the columnist Ann Landers once com-plained that the Founding Fathers were wrong when they claimed "all men are created equal" because the world is full of people who suffer from all kinds of inequalities. Those who think about ethical foundations in such a concrete manner will not understand the logic behind a postconventional, theoretical discourse that tries to make sense of moral equality.

John Rawls's Explanation of the Logic of a Social Contract

> **For Study:**   Why is the veil of ignorance supposed to guarantee a kind of universal impartial empathy?

John Rawls (1971) tries to clarify what it would be like to think on the abstract level required by social contract theory. It would be like trying to imagine that principles of justice are chosen from behind a *veil of ignorance* (pp. 136–42). This hypothetical veil would *cloud our memory to allow each of us to forget particular details about who we are, thus insuring an impartial perspective.* We would know general things about humanity but would not know if we were rich or poor, male or female, black or white, old or young, and so forth. All personal knowledge about the self would be gone, yet we would still have to choose the principles that would regulate social arrangements.

It seems to me that, from a hypothetical developmental perspective, the question should be framed as, "What kind of ideal institutions would people choose to be born into if God gave fetuses general information and the capacity to reason before they were born as people?" To make this abstract decision procedure more concrete let's use the Zimbardo Prison Experiment to clarify how it would work. Zimbardo could have created some aspects of a veil of ignorance if he had said to the subjects in his experiment: "I am going to assign you roles in an experimental prison community. Before you learn which role you will have, however, I want you to sit down and draw up rules for the prison." What would a rational agent choose under these conditions, when facing the possibility that she might have to occupy any role, office, or station that is created? If Zimbardo also had the power to say, "And you won't know if your previous position in society was that of guard or prisoner, staff or visitor, rich or poor, old or young, male or female," then he would have imposed a complete veil of ignorance. In this way, all potential voices in the institution would have to be taken seriously, since you could wind up occupying any of the social, economic, political offices created by the contract.

The real inequalities that already exist must be treated as either accidents of nature or as the result of conventional historical choices that need to be justified. Other things being equal, we should justify inequalities by checking to see if they are compatible with the principles that would follow from the theory. Theoretically, all morally autonomous people would choose the same principles, if they had similar information and opportunity for public debate. For instance, from behind a veil of ignorance, if one free, equal, self-interested, rational being would reject slavery, so would all of them.

Of course, an abstract metaphor like the "veil of ignorance" is ambiguous by nature, thus it can carry contradictory meanings depending on how the metaphor is used. Some critics of the theory think the veil of ignorance implies that we must choose in the same way as isolated, socially unencumbered, fictional beings. Such a creature would have no interests, thus wouldn't be able to choose anything. Since this is ridiculous, it is probably a mistake to follow this concrete approach to the metaphor. Instead, the veil metaphor ought to give us insight into what it would mean to proceed in the opposite direction toward complete empathy for everyone. Because we could turn out to be anyone, we become so encumbered by human possibilities that we become completely empathic and thus truly impartial. As Habermas (1991) says, "the impartiality of judgment is expressed in a principle that *constrains all affected to adopt the perspectives of all others in the balancing of interests.* The **principle of universalization** is intended to compel the *universal exchange of roles* that G. H. Mead called 'ideal role taking' or 'universal discourse'" (p. 65) (emphasis added). If I don't know who I will become, the logic behind the veil requires me to evaluate every form of life with the same enthusiasm I would have if I were socially constructed to live in each of them. This is the point Kant was emphasizing in Chapter Six, when he said rational fellow workers must strive to think from the point of view of others. On a practical level, this means I should take steps to give voice to all perspectives, just as I would if I knew some perspective was my own. Thus, the logic of the veil points to an obligation to make a serious attempt to listen to all kinds of differences, not ignore them as we would if we were an unencumbered empty vessel.

The social contract approach, when properly used, clarifies some of our most basic ethical intuitions. For example, it clearly shows that institutions such as slavery are inherently wrong not because they violate some natural right or lead to bad consequences, but because they are inconsistent with humanity's moral nature. No rational, autonomous being would ever voluntarily establish an institution such as slavery (or ethnic cleansing) if she thought there was even the smallest chance she would have to be a slave (or suffer ethnic cleansing) herself. If we are not willing even in principle to choose slavery for ourselves, then how can we ever be justified in imposing it on someone else without violating their equal moral status as rational, self-governing persons? Slavery obviously is not an expression of the kind of general interest that Rousseau claims ought to lead to equality before the law. Because it is based on the interests of a few, allowing an institution like slavery turns the personal subjective inclinations of that few into a public privilege that oppresses others.

The Role of Qualitative Information

> **For Study:** Why is accurate, complete information of a qualitative nature crucial to the fairness of a social contract? Who is the best judge of qualitative information? Why do difficulties in interpreting qualitative information suggest that local people should be given the freedom to choose their own options?

The amount of information available to contractees is crucial. As new information becomes available to mankind, we will have to rethink what we believe would be chosen from behind a veil of ignorance. We can see the importance of adequate information to the fairness of a contract, if we consider the New Jersey court ruling in the Baby M. surrogate motherhood case (Wilentz, 1989).

For Instance:

Mrs. Whitehead signed a contract in which she agreed to give birth to a baby after being artificially inseminated with Mr. Stern's sperm. She agreed to financial compensation for giving up the baby to the Sterns, who would then raise the child as their own. Mrs. Whitehead changed her mind, however, and sued in court to keep the child. She eventually lost her case because of intervening variables that led the court to believe that it was in the best interest of the child to live with the Sterns. When the case was appealed, the appeals court agreed it was in the best interest of the child to stay with the Sterns; however, this court also ruled that the original surrogacy contract was invalid. They argued that this type of contract presupposed someone could contractually obligate themselves before they had access to the kind of qualitative information that is crucial for making a rational decision. Carrying a child to term creates new pressures and experiences that ought to figure into a rational, caring decision. In each pregnancy this information is not available until after the child is born. The court ruled that surrogacy contracts that do not allow a surrogate mother to change her mind in light of this new information are invalid.

"We do not know of, and cannot conceive of, any other case where a perfectly fit mother was expected to surrender her newly born infant, perhaps forever, and was then told she was a bad mother because she did not. We know of no authority suggesting that the moral quality of her act in those circumstances should be judged by referring to a contract made before she became pregnant . . . We have found that our present laws do not permit the surrogacy contract used in this case. Nowhere, however, do we find any legal prohibition against surrogacy when the surrogate mother volunteers, without any payment, to act as a surrogate and is given the right to change her mind and to assert her parental rights." (Wilentz, pp. 510–12)

The idea that valid contracts presuppose not just consent but consent informed by the right kind of information is crucial to social contract theory. It means the general information available behind the veil of ignorance would have to be qualitative as well as quantitative. It would have to contain case studies into types of lives as well as broad theory. Although they are trying to choose final principles, they must have the opportunity to change their mind when reflection on new experiences teaches them about better ways to interpret human experience. This is a serious complication, because the interpretation of qualitative information is influenced by one's previous experience.

For instance, the medical profession has tried to find universal empirical measures that can help professionals interpret the quality of a patient's life on the basis of certain inherent satisfactions that ought to be present in any life worth living. Even with clear empirical definitions of health-related conditions, however, studies show that "those who have not experienced a condition cannot accurately predict the impact that the condition will have upon their quality of life." In medicine at least, "the healthy appear to be ill equipped to make the necessary imaginative leap to evaluate a wide range of health states" (Edgar, 1998, p. 776) and this includes professionals who have not yet experienced the subjective feelings that accompany a specific illness. This implies that the opinion of those who have experienced a disease should have more weight than the opinion of others, including professionals who lack the experience. This is similar to J. S. Mill's (1863, 1957, p. 15) assertion that the person most competent to judge between two qualitative states is a person who has experienced both. Obviously, social contractees have a monumental task before them, if they think they can decide all the issues that will confront all ways of life ahead of time. For this reason, it makes sense to think that rational social contractees would choose principles that turn the power to make policy over to the real people that will be affected by policy choices. Paternalism would be permitted only as a last resort.

Ideal Theory: Rawls's Two Principles Are Really Three

> **For Study:**   Why must the theory of the good life be a thin theory at this level of morality? What priorities are emphasized in Rawls' three principles?

Generally, social contract theory lies halfway between consequentialist and nonconsequentialist traditions. On the one hand the social contractees are trying to make strategic choices that will maximize their conception of the good, and this makes it look like a consequentialist approach to ethics. But on the other hand, it is nonconsequentialist in that there are strict moral restrictions placed on choice that reflect our nature as moral equals. This means a conception of what is right logically precedes the choice of a good life. Rawls develops this point by emphasizing the fact that at the start of deliberations in the initial contractual situation, contractees can only have a "thin" theory of the good. They only know that no matter who they turn out to be, they will want to maximize their share of the ***primary social goods*** that are a prerequisite for having any kind of life at all. These are goods *distributed by all societies and include things like wealth, power, prestige, rights and duties, equal opportunities, freedoms (such as the freedom to form their own conception of the good), and even self-respect—insofar as it is affected by social relations.* Their conception of the good is thin because they cannot know the full details of their personal values until after they choose principles of justice that regulate the choice of any full theory of the good. This restriction makes social contract theory a nonconsequentialist approach to ethics.

Rawls (1971, pp. 60ff) believes contractees would choose a system that emphasizes the three central virtues of the eighteenth-century Enlightenment: liberty, equality, and fraternity. Fraternity is often ignored by Rawls's critics, but as we shall see, this relational term plays a central role in his theory. He argues contractees would consent to two major background principles (pp. 60ff). I have expressed them as three principles in order to isolate the three key constraints on the distribution of social goods that emerge from Rawls's argument.

1.   **A Liberty Principle:**   *Everyone ought to have an equal right to the most extensive basic liberty compatible with a similar liberty for others.* This principle would have top priority. Other calculations about how to distribute goods cannot even be considered until after a system of liberties has established maximum freedom for everyone (liberties such as voting rights, freedom of the person, citizenship rights, due process rights, the right to voluntary consent, and so forth).

2.   **An Equal Opportunity Principle:**   *Inequalities are unjust unless they are attached to offices open to all under conditions of fair equal opportunity.* This principle makes equal opportunity the second most important boundary condition for judging institutional arrangements. An unequal distribution of other social goods might be permissible, but only if everyone has a fair equal opportunity to compete for any social advantages that are allowed to enter the system. "Fair" emphasizes that equal opportunity should be substantive or real, not just a formal principle.

3.   **A Difference Principle:**   *Inequalities in the distribution of primary social goods are unjust unless they are to the advantage of everyone in the society (i.e., the bottom class must also benefit from the inequalities).* This principle is based on the assumption that self-interested, free, and equal rational agents would want to keep the equal status they have in the original contractual position, unless allowing inequalities to exist would benefit them. From behind the veil of ignorance, the only way we can be certain to benefit is if inequalities benefit everyone. For instance, differences in salary might be allowed, but only if they lead to an increase in productivity that would lead to more for all of us in the long run. This principle looks like the kind of consideration that would be chosen by people in a family or a relational net where all of them are concerned about the well-being of the others. This is why Rawls thinks that his method is compatible with the virtue of fraternity.

Implementation: Problems with Rawls's Social Contract Theory

For Study: What are the two major kinds of criticisms that are used against Rawls's social contract theory? Why is it useful to add the word "needy" to the characterization of social contractees? Why would social contractees want to protect the right of people to be different? Why does Sandel claim that the veil of ignorance biases Rawls' theory in favor of individualism? Is Sandel correct?

Most of the criticisms of Rawls's theory can be divided into two types. The first type accepts the methodology but disagrees with the conclusions about what would be chosen. For instance, some of these critics argue that contractees would not choose egalitarian principles. Instead they would risk greater inequalities for the chance to get greater rewards. Thus, they might choose a principle to maximize the average utility of society even though that means some people would lag behind. How much aversion to risk is rational is influenced by personal experience. Different experiences give people different intuitions about how to judge the quality of the risks in life. Thus, there is no way to respond to this kind of criticism about how much weight to give risk taking other than to continue discussions and see if we can mutually educate each other. Rawls believes that his principles of justice are rational. They would receive unanimous agreement because they protect our moral nature and leave individuals free to make their own local decisions about lifestyles.

Feminist critics who are sympathetic to the method, argue that portraying contractees as self-interested, autonomous, rational beings gives us a distorted view of how real people would think from behind a veil of ignorance. They claim we would get better insights from this theoretical device if we abandoned the idea that contractees had the qualities of abstract independent males and instead portrayed them in relational terms as rational, interdependent, dependent beings, that is, as beings who know they will have normal human frailties (see O'Neill, 1989, pp. 230ff). Without this assumption of vulnerability contractees will not be properly concerned about the quality of relationships that ought to evolve. Practical wisdom requires us to acknowledge humanity's social, political, and economic vulnerabilities.

If properly used, the veil of ignorance should take care of this concern, at least on the theoretical level. Since contractees could turn out to be anyone, they will have to sympathetically evaluate all types of vulnerabilities as well as the different kinds of human relationships. It is true that Rawls says contractees would be self-interested and want the best for themselves, but the veil of ignorance converts this self-interest into universal concern; that is, by stepping behind a veil, we move in one step from the personal motive of the wholly self-interested person to the impersonal decentered motive of someone who cares about every social position. If a self-interested person could wind up occupying any role, then his own self-interest would lead him to give every role a fair hearing. However, real people who use the social contract device are vulnerable to committing standard person errors, which may lead them to discount the fact that others can have legitimate needs that are greater than their own. Thus, to help real people stay focused on this point, it might be useful to add "needy" or "vulnerable" to the list of traits used to characterize the social contractees.

Since everyone seems so different in terms of lifestyle preferences, it seems as though the only interest that can be shared by everyone is the general interest in having others treat us with respect. Rawls (1993) confronted the problem caused by individual and group differences by accepting the fact that a heterogeneous population with a plurality of points of view is a permanent and desirable condition of democracy. Indeed, truly democratic institutions that protect liberty will promote a plurality of points of view by protecting freedom of religion. He argues, however, that rational people who recognize this fact should be able to reach an *overlapping consensus* on a political conception of justice that would protect their shared interest in liberty and equal opportunity. We will not pursue this new development in Rawls's theory here. In the next chapter we will pick up on the problem of difference and the need for a postconventional solution to it.

The second group of Rawlsian critics attacks the method itself. They argue that it is far too abstract and unrealistic (How can we get guidance by thinking about how people might think when they don't know who they are?) and is basically circular (since by carefully structuring an original contractual position ahead of time you can generate any kind of principle that you want). A serious version of this criticism accuses Rawls of so structuring the original contractual position that it is actually biased against the commitment to community. Sandel (1982, pp. 27ff) argues that the veil of ignorance is not really neutral toward lifestyle choices (conceptions of the good) since the desire to maximize one's share of the primary social goods favors choosing principles that would support atomistic individualism rather than dedication to community.

In response to this line of inquiry, Rawls (1985, pp. 228ff) argues that he is conceptualizing the logic of just political choice, not advocating an individualistic metaphysics. There is nothing anticommunitarian about wanting a larger share of primary goods in the original contractual situation. Without personal information, the inclination is neutral with regard to lifestyle choice and is consistent with someone's choosing to dedicate themselves to a community. If one has a larger share of goods than is needed, one can always turn one's share over to her community if that is the conception of the good one chooses. In addition, with his emphasis on moral development and the importance of fraternity, I believe that Rawls's theory of justice has a communitarian voice for anyone who cares to read it with that in mind. The approach shows just how inherently social moral nature has to be, especially when we are being impartial in the sense of feeling empathy for all representative positions. As we saw in Chapter Seven, this same concern for community is captured by the fully developed concept of moral autonomy. Those who are impressed with Rawls's approach are busy constructing rebuttals to these kinds of criticisms, so the literature on Rawls's theory is still unfolding. We will not pursue these matters here, because they would lead us into further metaethical concerns and away from applied ethics.

∽ Duty Ethics

For Study: What is Kant's major objection to the consequentialist approach to ethics? How does a good will distinguish humans from animals? Why is reverence different from other inclinations? Why is it autonomous rather than heteronomous?

Kant (1797, 1964) argued that all consequentialist theories of ethics are mis-conceived, because they distract us from those variables that are truly essential to morality. Kant claims the *form* of an action is more important for judging its moral worth than the *content* of the consequences that follow from it. Acting to make yourself happy is not immoral, but it is also not morally praiseworthy. We do not give moral praise to someone who says they did their duty because it was a clever strategic way to promote good consequences for themselves. Moral actions are special and can be used to clarify the difference between moral agents and other animals. Animals can only act on self-interest and in-stinctual social drives, but humans can also act out of duty.

This means moral agents can be dedicated to something beyond their own preferences. For example, in certain circumstances soldiers can intention-ally choose to die in support of a cause. They do not die because they expect to gain personally from dying. They do it because, under the circumstances, it is their duty to die. Kant claims that anytime we act for duty's sake, rather than to advance a personal goal, we are acting morally (remember Socrates' devo-tion to duty even in the face of death?). The willingness to do what is right even when it hurts is a sign that a person has a **good will**, which means *the capacity to intentionally do duty for duty's sake.*

Kant is careful to avoid confusing *moral law* with **positive law.** The lat-ter refers to all *those laws that are legislated into existence by a governmental body.* Thus, positive commands of a legal authority may or may not be con-sistent with the **moral law,** which is Kant's term for his *foundational moral principle, also called the categorical imperative.* It is only the moral law that can give us duties that we must follow for duty's sake.

The caring side of the moral point of view is developed in Kant's theory through the notion of *reverence* for moral law as such. Reverence is not an or-dinary inclination, since it is not like a desire that might cause us to adopt moral beliefs for strategic reasons. Reverence is caused by rational under-standing of humanity's moral nature. Kant (1797, 1964) says,

> Now an action done from duty has to set aside altogether the influence of incli-nation, and along with inclination every object of the will; so there is nothing left able to determine the will except objectively the *law* and subjectively *pure rever-ence* for this practical law, and therefore the maxim of obeying this law even to the detriment of all my inclinations. (pp. 68–69)

Kant clarifies what he means by reverence for the law in a footnote:

> Although reverence is a feeling, it is not a feeling received through outside influence, but one self-produced by a rational concept, and therefore specifically distinct from feelings of the first kind, all of which can be reduced to inclination or fear. What I recognize immediately as law for me, I recognize with reverence, which means merely consciousness of the subordination of my will to a law without the mediation of external influences on my senses. Immediate determination of the will by the law and consciousness of this determination is called "reverence," so that reverence is regarded as the effect of the law on the subject and not as the cause of the law. Reverence is properly awareness of a value which demolishes my self-love. Hence there is something which is regarded neither as an object of inclination nor as an object of fear, though it has at the same time some analogy with both. The object of reverence is the law alone—that law which we impose on ourselves but yet as necessary in itself. . . . All moral interest, so-called, consists in reverence for the law. (p. 69)

Why does Kant insist that reverence must be "self-produced" rather than influenced by something outside of the person's moral will (such as threats of punishments and rewards)? Actions and feelings that are truly moral have to be autonomous. If our moral will is going to be independent of desire, then the principles and feelings associated with it have to originate from within it alone, free from control by "inclination." Since our body and introjected values are external to our moral will, a morality developed to satisfy them is not an autonomous morality. Kant characterized this difference by saying that *actions controlled by forces from without the moral will* are **heteronomous,** those *controlled by the moral will alone* are **autonomous.** Reverence is the feeling that explains the subjective side of our respect for our moral nature as autonomous beings who can obey our moral will regardless of inclination. So, reverence is caused by reason's own contemplation of moral concepts; it is not a prior feeling that causes contemplation of moral concepts.

Developmentally speaking, I wonder if a person can be capable of reverence if the person has not had the prior opportunity to transcend egocentricism and become a social being. For instance, could a sociopath learn reverence purely through rational contemplation or would he first have to be taught how to care about something other than himself? *Learning to care* requires the development of capacities that are taught by outside interventions from caring people. As Temple Grandin said, we need some gentle squeezing before we can know what it means to be gentle. The need for developmental interventions is still compatible with Kant's notion of reverence. The feeling of reverence would not be possible if normal emotional structures had not previously developed. The point, however, is that although reverence builds on prior structures, it only emerges when we contemplate something that takes us beyond our animal heritage.

Background: Autonomy and Pure Reason

> **For Study:**   Why must the categorical imperative or moral law be based on pure reason? What is the difference between a categorical and a conditional principle? In what two ways can one fail the universalizability test when testing to see if an action is done for duty's sake?

Kant argued that the only way to make sense of morality, which is a practical necessity since we need it to have a social life, is to assume people are autonomous beings who can be held responsible. It is, therefore, a practical necessity to believe that moral agents have the mental capacities that are a necessary prerequisite for autonomy. Kant uses the term *pure reason* to refer to the *autonomous capacity to exercise the intellect without letting it be controlled by the body's heteronomous inclinations.* When reason is purified of inclination then it is autonomous because we have stripped away all inclination until nothing is left to control reason but reason itself. We cannot prove we are actually autonomous in a metaphysical sense, we can only assume it. Thus, autonomy is a regulative concept used to guide how we must think about creatures who can take up the MPofV. In Chapter Seven, I tried to make a case for the fact that a significant kind of moral autonomy may be possible, but Kant's discussion of these issues is much more cautious.

Since the only source of the moral law and thus moral duty is pure reason, to show respect for our autonomous nature we must always treat people according to ethical principles that could be derived from their own exercise of pure reason. Thus, moral duty is defined as acting on *maxims (principles or intentions)* that are consistent with pure reason's contemplation of moral law. Since pure reason is free of subjective inclinations, its maxims are universal because they are the same as the maxims of all other beings who are acting only on pure reason. If we will all act only on pure reason when we intervene in the lives of others, we will always be in a position to give them a moral account of our intervention that will make sense to their own autonomous will.

How can we know when our actions are motivated by duty for duty's sake rather than inclination? The difference is found in the form of the principle we are acting on, not in the consequences of our act. Actions based on autonomous moral law have the form of a *categorical principle* of autonomy, rather than a *conditional principle* of heteronomy. Conditional principles say: "IF (*some inclination*) THEN (*some "ought" command*)"; for example, if *you want to be successful,* then *you ought to be honest.* This kind of prudent command uses strategic rationality to make the moral virtue of honesty a means for satisfying a previous personal want. This is the kind of moral imperative that emerges first at the preconventional level of understanding.

A *categorical principle,* on the other hand, *applies universally no matter what the local inclinations;* for example, *you ought to be honest, no matter what you are inclined to do*. Kant believes that all truly moral acts are based on foundational moral maxims that have this structure. There is, however, only one principle that always has this form, the *categorical imperative* (or *moral law*). Although he gave four different versions of it, Kant believes they are all based on the same universalizability criteria. Everyone ought to *act only on that maxim through which you can at the same time will that it should become universal law* (p. 88). How are we supposed to interpret Kant's appeal to this abstract criteria of *universalizability*? The key is to focus on the social function of moral maxims. A maxim must not only be internally consistent, it must also function as a prescriptive social norm that can be voluntarily, consistently followed by everyone. So, there are two ways in which a maxim can fail the universalizability test for being a moral maxim.

First, moral maxims are *"conceptually incoherent"* if they contradict themselves. For example, Kant says if you make a promise with the intention of breaking it, the maxim on which your action rests cannot be turned into a universal law applicable to all people. The maxim of a false promise is: "Everyone should break their promises whenever it is convenient for them to do so." If this were the categorical principle behind the institution of promising, the institution itself would collapse because no one would accept any promise made. The maxim behind a false promise is conceptually contradictory, because it destroys the social conditions needed for making the promise itself.

Second, because there are many immoral maxims that do not seem to lead to this kind of straightforward internal logical contradiction, we have to ask about intentions that are clearly immoral but do not appear to be internally self-contradictory. Kant thinks they will lead to *"contradictions in the will"* rather than to "conceptual contradictions." For example, the normal principle of beneficence says, "We ought to help others." This maxim is easy to universalize without inconsistency. But what if we try to universalize its opposite? To universalize the maxim "We ought to never help others," we would have to say, "No one should ever help anyone else." This does not entail a conceptual contradiction, but according to Kant, this maxim is "volitionally incoherent." There will always be times when an agent is going to need help to achieve his goals (humans are interdependent, needy beings). It would be irrational to refuse available means to achieving your goals, so it is inconsistent with your ends to refuse the help you need when you need it. As O'Neill (1989) says:

> to will some end without willing whatever means are indispensable for that end, insofar as they are available, is, even when the end itself involves no conceptual inconsistency, to involve oneself in a volitional inconsistency. It is to embrace at least one specific intention that, far from being guided by the underlying intention or principle, is inconsistent with that intention or principle. (pp. 90–91)

The emphasis on universalizability seems very abstract and confusing. Without practice in philosophy, it is difficult to use such an abstract imperative on a day-to-day basis. Thus, Kant (1797, 1964) clarified the practical implications of the categorical imperative in a version that was supposed to be easier to implement. The practical version says, "Act in such a way that you always treat humanity, whether in your own person or in the person of any other, never simply as a means, but always at the same time as an end" (p. 96).

Ideal Theory: Rational Nature as an End in Itself and the Kingdom of Ends

> **For Study:**   How do rational people think of themselves? Why does this way of thinking give us positive duties to humanity? In what sense does Kant's theory give both positive and negative duties? Why would a kingdom of ends be a caring community with positive respect for diversity, rather than a community with only negative duties?

In Chapter One, we simplified this principle to read, "Always treat people as ends unto themselves, never use them as a means only." This version of the principle follows from Kant's belief that "Rational nature exists as an end in itself. This is the way in which a man necessarily conceives his own existence . . . it is also the way in which every other rational being conceives his own existence . . ." (Kant, 1797, 1964, p. 96). *Ends in themselves* are *autonomous beings, that is, beings that ought to control their own lives with their own principles, so they never think of themselves as objects to be used by others.* We don't treat people as "ends unto themselves" because it benefits us under our conception of the good to do this; *we treat them that way because as rational human beings we know we are obligated to do this no matter what local goods we value personally.* We do this as a matter of duty whether or not it promotes our favored lifestyle. Kant says that *a society composed of autonomous people all of whom use the categorical imperative as their foundational moral maxim* would be a **kingdom of ends** (pp. 100ff). What shape would such a society take? Would it be a place with negative rights only, or would there also be universal positive rights? The injunction to never use another person as a means gives us negative duties to do no harm (e.g., as seen in the Ten Commandments in the Bible). These are **perfect duties** (O'Neill, 1980, p. 288) in that they *do not allow for individual discretion about how or when to carry them out.* But, this is only half the categorical imperative. Positive duties are conceptually linked with the other half of moral law that tells us to treat humanity (ourself and all others) always as an end. Treating people always as an end requires us to act benevolently, which is "to seek others' happiness. This means we have to intend to achieve some of the things that those others aim at with their maxims"

(p. 288). However, these are *imperfect duties,* because *the exact context of the behavior and to whom it is required cannot be set out ahead of time.* People want too many things, and we only have so much time, so "it follows that we have to be selective" (p. 288). At bottom then, there is a deep background minimalist instruction not to rule out any way of life that can fit within the universal boundaries entailed by mutual respect between moral equals. But there is also the positive instruction that institutional arrangements ought to help further the ends of all these acceptable ways of life. As Kant (1797, 1964) says

> As regards meritorious duties to others, the natural end which all men seek is their own happiness. Now humanity could no doubt subsist if everybody contributed nothing to the happiness of others but at the same time refrained from deliberately impairing their happiness. This is, however, merely to agree negatively and not positively with *humanity as an end in itself* unless every one endeavors also, so far as in him lies, to further the ends of others. For the ends of a subject who is an end in himself must, if this conception is to have its *full* effect in me, be also, as far as possible, *my* ends. (p. 98)

Because the capacities for moral autonomy are a necessary means for realizing humanity's end "as an end in itself," and because we cannot intend the end without intending the means, the means to humanity's end should also become my end if the categorical imperative is to have its full effect in me. A kingdom of ends will naturally be a pluralistic society with regard to choices of the good life. People have been shaped by social construction under conditions of freedom, so it naturally follows that there will be genetic and cultural differences between both individuals and groups. People embedded in a way of life want those differences essential to their way of life respected by institutional arrangements. Because differences represent the particularized, substantive expression of our shared universal status as ends unto ourselves, mere toleration of difference is not enough. Forms of diversity ought to also be respected and supported as particular expressions of our shared humanity as long as they don't violate the moral law.

In this light, it seems odd that Kantian concepts are often criticized as being so abstract as to do a disservice to our actual embeddedness in different ways of life. This kind of criticism fails to understand that the purpose of these moral concepts is to help us focus on our obligation to treat the differences between fellow workers with respect. Iris Young (1990, p. 94) may be right that in the past the consequence of focusing on universal citizenship has been to force us to ignore relevant differences, but she is wrong in assuming that the logic of universal moral concepts entails that we must ignore those differences. However, since nonconsequentialist concepts are often misused at the level of implementation, maybe it is true that Kant's theory is too abstract to be useful.

Implementation: Too Abstract? Too Monological? The Family Example

> **For Study:** Why do critics think Kant's theory is so abstract that it is practically useless? How would a modern Kantian respond? Why would a monological emphasis contribute to misuse of the theory? How should people who are not yet morally autonomous be treated in a kingdom of ends?

So many people think nonconsequentialism is excessively abstract that there must be something to the accusation. It is well and good to tell us to do our duty, but what exactly is our duty? What should we do if two duties conflict? What if telling the truth conflicts with being kind? Should we always tell old ladies that we think their hats are ugly, or is there room for a white lie? When considered outside of any particular context, Kant seems to imply that we must always tell the truth no matter what. This seems rigid to his critics. Why can't we universalize the maxim: "When a small lie will spare someone's feelings we should lie." Would this nullify itself, since no one will believe us when their feelings are at stake? What about something more serious, like lying to save a life? Kant is rather strict in what he thinks the categorical imperative will allow. He says you should not even lie to a potential murderer who asks you where his victim is hiding. You can refuse to cooperate, of course, but if you choose to speak, you must tell the truth. Critics argue that this absolutism is counterintuitive.

A proper solution to this dilemma may require us to focus on establishing reasonable priorities between rules and principles. The categorical imperative is an absolute that should always be followed, but secondary principles and rules are *prima facie* norms that need to be coordinated with each other when we apply the moral law to specific circumstances. Moral agents will need to develop practical wisdom about how the moral law regulates the use of *prima facie* secondary principles. For instance, other things being equal, don't lie. On the other hand, if you think you can justify a lie, the burden of proof is on you to show how your exception is consistent with the moral law.

Kant has good reasons for not giving much guidance about how to settle these issues. Autonomous agents are supposed to reason their own way through such conflicts. Practical problems are tied to a context, and Kant is only providing a background against which we can judge the deepest formal elements of all contexts. All the theories eventually reach this point, since no theory can tell us exactly what to do in situations that have not yet arisen. O'Neill (1989) summarizes the problem quite well when she says,

> [Kant] . . . offers an ethic of principles, rather than one specifically of virtues, and principles can be variously embodied—both as virtues of individual characters or of institutions and also in practices and even in decision procedures. (p. 162)

. . . and he does not see human reason as merely calculative. His modernity lies in his rejection of a conception of human nature and its telos that is sufficiently determinate to yield an entire ethic. . . . Kant offers us a form of rationalism in ethics that . . . does not generate a unique moral code, but still both provides fundamental guidelines and suggests the types of reasoning by which we might see how to introduce these guidelines into the lives we actually lead. (p. 161)

Habermas (1993) argues that it would help if Kant were more concerned with context. There is a utopian element in Kant that seems to overlook how difficult it will be for real people to adopt a truly universal perspective. In the absence of guidance from Kant, people are likely to treat their local standards as though they are universal norms. Habermas (1993) addresses this point by arguing that a good deal of the abuse of principle can be overcome if we critique what he calls the *"monological"* emphasis in Kant. Too often, ideal theories encourage civil servants *to retreat inside their own "impartial spectator" (or Kantian "pure reason") to judge between right and wrong in isolation from the active participation of those affected.* In a multicultural setting a "monological" approach impedes "access to the intuitive knowledge of the [various] life-world[s]" (p. 13) that frame the perspectives of the affected people. Thus, although Kantian ethics is essentially right, it is difficult to implement because it fails to caution banal users about how difficult it will be to factor local information into principled decisions. Why didn't Kant worry about this application problem? Habermas (1998) speculates that Kant

tacitly assumes that in making moral judgments each individual can project himself sufficiently into the situation of everyone else *through his own imagination.* But when the participants can no longer rely on a transcendental preunderstanding grounded in more or less homogeneous conditions of life and interests, the moral point of view can only be realized under conditions of communication that ensure that *everyone* tests the acceptability of a norm, implemented in a general practice, also from the perspective of his own understanding of himself and of the world. (pp. 34–35)

Even if Kant's use of pure reason is too monological, it does not mean that his theory is devoid of practical implications. For instance, consider how the theory can be used to give insight into the structure of the family. Kantians would argue that all family members are to be thought of as "ends unto themselves," but we should not confuse being an "end" with having the actual capacity to live like an *autonomous moral agent (a being governed by a will that makes law for itself).* Too many people who follow abstract guidelines ignore what an extreme individualist like John Stuart Mill (1859, 1971) remembered. In concrete cases, liberty principles only make sense when they are applied to people of "ripe" years with "the ordinary amount of understanding" (p. 11).

Since no one is born ripe, even "ordinary" moral understanding is impossible unless people have experienced at least some form of supportive family (or tribal) heritage. Thus, insofar as all moral agents have an obligation to promote humanity's end, they have an obligation to support the development of the necessary means to that end. If we believe a kingdom of ends is an acceptable ideal, then we are being *volitionally inconsistent if we do not create social policies that provide the means to this end,* that is, *policies that help people develop the virtues needed for moral autonomy.* To be properly nurtured, we must each get the proper life experiences in the proper sequence. Families can be conceived of, then, as the first vital link in a supportive network designed to create the conditions for a kingdom of ends. But the family can fulfill this moral role only if it can support those "ends in themselves" who are not as yet morally autonomous. Some "ends" need more nurturing and protection than others, and some families need more outside social support than others. Since all autonomous agents have an imperfect duty to promote the means to humanities ends, helping families achieve their ends is a positive duty rather than only a supererogatory act of charity.

∾ Habermas and Discourse Ethics

> **For Study:** Why does Habermas believe communicative discourse is a practice that contains universal norms? Why do these norms indicate that it is part of our nature to be social beings? What does it mean to recast moral theory so that it is about argumentative discourse?

Habermas has set out to reconstruct Kantian ethics to make it more responsive to the concerns of postmodern philosophers and more useful to nonphilosophers who have to make practical decisions. Since universality is the standard for moral maxims in Kantian philosophy, Habermas begins by looking for a medium of social interaction that is found in all forms of life and contains universal moral norms. These norms should be able to provide a common background upon which to build cross-cultural moral solidarity and consensus about standards of justice. This kind of morality will have to be anchored at the level at which moral dilemmas initially emerge, mainly within the horizon of the various life-worlds (Habermas, 1991, p. 58).

Background: The Nature of Communicative Discourse

All individuals use *communicative discourse* to function as members of a life-world, thus the ability to be a member of any life-world presupposes the presence of a universal human capacity to communicate with the aim of reaching mutual understanding. *The intersubjective norms that make communication possible exist everywhere and are known on a procedural level by every individual who is a competent language user.* As discussed in Chapter Six, to consciously explore these procedural norms we will have to study *pragmatics*, which focuses on the kind of values people have to be committed to in order to engage in argumentative discourse at all.

No one can become a functional member of a language community unless they first learn the background procedural norms of honest discourse. We can take it as a given, then, that every competent language user already shares a tacit, procedural understanding of certain intersubjective norms that make possible symbolic communication with others in his language community. Because communication aims at reaching a consensus about how we should understand a topic, both the speaker and the hearer have to rely on the same normative expectations of what is legitimate in speech, and this is true in all communities. Thus, every competent speaker has internalized a social capacity that is vital to his or her individual development as a social being. The logic of this social capacity is the same everywhere, thus it is suitably universal.

By focusing in this way on the logic of the linguistic act, Habermas recasts moral theory so that it is about the type of argumentation that is used in justifying moral claims to other members of a community rather than about metaphysical phenomenon that supposedly exist independent of social practice. In a *communicative practice* people *coordinate their plans on a consensual basis and evaluate their agreements in terms of an "intersubjective recognition"* (p. 60) *of what can count as valid reasons for making claims.* Before a system of morality can work, then, all affected must agree on what it means to make a moral claim and what factors can serve as good reasons to justify the claim. This intersubjective dimension behind the individual's use of language provides morality with its abstract universal logic and its ability to get in touch with local cognitive content. So, to understand morality, we must first explore the logic of communicative practice.

Communicative Rationality

> **For Study:** How is each type of communicative claim justified? Why is communicative rationality required for moral justification and strategic rationality inadequate for this task? Why does the logic of honest communication suggest Kant was right about our moral nature? Why does a lie create moral indignation rather than only strategic anger?

As discussed in Chapter Six, in all intersubjective communicative practices, people assert the same three types of validity claims (pp. 58–60). They make truth claims about the objective world, for example: "The moon is a sphere." They make claims of rightness or appropriateness about the norms that regulate their shared social world, for example: "No one should lie for personal gain." And, they make claims about private or subjective experiences that depend on their truthfulness, for example: "I'm hungry now."

As argued in Chapter Six, truth claims and moral claims both require the support of good reasons that make sense in the public sphere. The type of reasoning appropriate for evaluating these communicative actions is different from the type of strategic reasoning that is appropriate for pursuing personal agendas. The act of making a truth claim or moral claim is not the same kind of linguistic activity as the act of making a strategic claim about what one wants. Strategic claims about a personal preference involve only a private agenda. When getting what I want is all that matters, it may even be strategically rational to use threats and bribes to get my way. But all competent members of language communities know that threats and bribes are inconsistent with what counts as good reasons in science and morality.

The aim in communicative discourse in these two areas is to honestly express your beliefs to another, so concerns for truth and rightness are essential to these intersubjective activities. It would be irrational to subvert true communication by telling lies. Thus, the rationality behind science and morality can only be explained by associating it with the type of *communicative rationality* that is *controlled by publicly agreed upon norms designed to regulate the logic of both "truth claims" and "claims about right and wrong."* Competent moral agents realize that real discourse is based on a bond between speaker and hearer that evolves out of their shared social expectation that each will honor the norms that make honest communication possible.

Habermas believes that the norms behind honest communication prove that Kant was essentially right about our moral nature. People not only do not want to be treated as a means only, but their moral talk shows that they develop a suprapersonal sense of what it means to be an end when they come to understand honest communication. Everyone expects to be treated with the kind of respect that ends unto themselves take for granted during honest communication. They feel discounted and abused when people speak to them without following communicative norms that are supposed to regulate speech between people who are honestly trying to communicate. We will feel properly indignant when people use language to confuse or distort communication, because respect for our audience requires us to play fair and give good reasons for our claims. To disrupt true communication is almost as evil as telling a lie. As Habermas (1991) says, the lie fills us with moral indignation, because it is a "violation of an underlying *normative expectation* that is valid not only for ego [who is lied to] and alter [who is the lier] but also for all members of a social group or even, in the case of moral norms in the strict sense, for all competent actors" (p. 48).

The basic idea is that we cannot be neutral with regard to communicative norms because they are essential to our existence as social moral beings. Our normative world exists only when we communicate using the norms of our life-world. If we start abusing the norms behind communicative speech in order to deceive people, then the trust on which the social bond is based is broken, and the normative world begins to unravel. We cannot be both a part of communicative practice and outside of it. It is all or nothing (p. 61). So, to imitate communicative discourse but not really mean it in a performative way is to be a liar. As Erickson says, trust is the first human need that has to be satisfied, because without it we cannot become social beings. If everyone can lie whenever they like, a trusting community becomes impossible. Thus, we feel indignation in the presence of those who lie and manipulate because they attack the core of our ability to have a committed social identity. Even when people tamper with this important intersubjective medium for fun, we might feel ill at ease. It is one thing for the entertainment industry to create comedies and melodramas which couch conversations in ironic terms, or for "fun" say the exact opposite of what they really mean, but what if everyone began to ignore the underlying norms needed for community by fabricating farcical stories whenever they felt like it? Would the bond of social trust needed for communicative discourse be destroyed?

For Instance:

I attended a conference on the teaching of philosophy about twenty years ago, before I had begun to study Habermas. During a break, a man from California said, "Isn't it odd how gullible people are. I flew to South Carolina to see my sister. Then I rented a car and drove up here to New York for the conference. When I stopped for gas the attendant started asking me about South Carolina. So I played along and made up a bunch of stories about my ancestors in South Carolina. We had quite a conversation. It is really amazing to me how people just buy into anything you say. You'd think they would become more sophisticated." He then laughed. No one else at the table laughed, and in fact we quickly changed the subject. At the time, I was not sure why we were all so uncomfortable. Was it just because we were embarrassed that a colleague was still playing sophomoric jokes on a decent fellow who was trying to be neighborly, or was there something deeper that could explain our sense of unease. I now think we were intuitively reacting to the potential social consequences that would result, if people in general started using language to toy with each other, rather than communicate with each other. This was an educated man, and yet he was distorting an ordinary intersubjective communicative exchange for no particular reason. The fact that the gas station attendant took his words on good faith and showed him respect by engaging in conversation is not surprising, he was a member of the language community and assumed the respect would be returned. What is surprising is that the philosopher would think it is odd for a member of the community to willingly trust his words. Is this what getting a Ph.D. in philosophy leads us to? Of course we can use our verbal skills to fool people who are trusting members of a language community, but that only proves that we ourselves are not members who deserve the mutual trust we receive. I wish I had read about communicative rationality prior to that exchange. It would be interesting to see if others at the table would have shared my sense of irritation at the fundamental lack of respect shown in the exchange, and how this practice has the potential to undermine communicative rationality. Imagine our world if we all had to talk like shyster salesman and preface each thing we said with: "Listen, you can trust me now. This time I'm telling the truth." We will return to this issue below when we consider Lyotard's concept of agonistics.

Ideal Theory: The Practical Normative Implications of Communicative Discourse

> **For Study:** Why does a legitimate moral norm entail that something besides force justifies it? Why does morality's nature indicate that a monological interpretation of moral norms is inconsistent with social impartiality? On a practical level, how should we interpret moral principles so as to avoid the standard person problem? What two assumptions underlie the whole of discourse ethics?

What does it take for a norm to gain general social acceptance? First, there is the matter of conviction. Communication can exist because speaker and hearer are both committed to the norms that make the communication possible. Second, there is the matter of sanctions or punishment. The community must show it supports a norm with sanctions that enforce its proper use (the general silence that greeted the philosophy teacher's attempt to amuse us was a kind of punishment). Sanctions alone are not sufficient to secure a norm's lasting social acceptance, there also has to be something about the norm that makes developing a social conviction about it seem like the reasonable thing to do. Thus, social acceptance depends ultimately on whether there are good reasons for a norm that made the sanctions legitimate in the first place. In the long run, then, there is no sustainable mass loyalty to norms without some conviction that they are supported by good reasons and are thus legitimate.

Legitimate sanctions must also be impartially imposed. The impartiality entails that the norm deserves social acceptance by all, not just some. Universal consensus about a norm would be impossible if people thought it was not going to be impartially applied. This is the insight behind Kant's claim that moral maxims must be capable of being universal laws of nature.

Moral impartiality means a norm must be acceptable to every perspective, and this is possible *only if universal principles can embody an interest that is held in common by all affected.* Only then can we come to believe that everyone will in fact be able to give his or her uncoerced consent to the norm (Habermas, 1991, p. 65). The skeptic claims that there is no evidence for the existence of a general interest that can support morally impartial universal norms. Can Habermas satisfy the skeptic?

Habermas (1991) argues that there is a ***universal principle of argumentation*** that specifies the conditions any norm must meet before we can assume that everyone will choose it. He believes this principle overcomes the skeptics' complaint that no one can come up with a principle that can represent a general interest shared by everyone. Habermas says the universal principle of argumentation entails a norm is universally valid only if

> *all* affected can *freely* accept the consequences and the side effects that the *general* observance of a controversial norm can be anticipated to have for the satisfaction of the interests of *each individual*. (p. 93)

> (and these consequences are preferred to those of known alternative possibilities for regulation). (p. 65)

As a rule of argumentation this principle gives us some reason to believe that we can get unanimous agreement, at least to the principle itself. This principle captures the general interest everyone has in not being bound by rules that are not acceptable to them. As a formal rule this "universal principle of argumentation" protects everyone from oppression but does not prejudge the substance of any particular way of life. So, there is no reason for reasonable people to reject it. It does not require anyone to stop being who they were socially constructed to be (unless of course, their construction has lead them into ways of life that are inconsistent with the principle, i.e., the right of all people to live according to their own social construction and ethical choices). It entails that any positive legal norms that are inconsistent with everyone's practical participation in social choice are illegitimate. Thus, on the practical level the moral "ought" which emerges from this universal rule of argumentation protects the right of all affected parties to be actual participants in the substantive decisions that create rules.

Habermas (1991) believes that if the norms in this universal principle of argumentation are explicitly emphasized in the foundational moral principle of a moral theory, then the foundational principle won't be so abstract that banal moral agents can easily misuse it at the level of application. Thus, the foundational "moral" principle of *discourse ethics,* which follows from the "universalization principle of argumentation" takes a form that emphasizes the need for social consensus at the application level, and not only at the abstract level of justification discourse, other things equal. His moral principle states that

> Only those norms can claim to be valid that meet (or could meet) with the approval of all affected in their capacity *as participants in a practical discourse.* (Habermas, 1991, p. 66)

A shorter version was stated in the first chapter of this text as one of the six principles of Western ethics, that is: "Just those action norms are valid to which all possibly affected persons could agree as participants in rational discourses" (Habermas, 1996, p. 107).

Habermas sees his theory of discourse ethics as shifting the emphasis of Kant's categorical imperative away from "What I can will to be a universal law" and toward "What all can will while in agreement to be a universal law" (p. 68). This shift draws attention to the two major assumptions that underlie the whole of discourse ethics. First, moral claims to validity have cognitive public meaning that all can evaluate. Moral claims are similar to claims to truth in that valid ones can be redeemed by the intersubjective good reasons that justify them. Second, justification of norms requires that a real discourse must take place between all those really affected. There is a qualitative change in life when we reach a point where we see the other, not as a means and not as someone to be controlled, but as a moral equal who has a right to participate with us in making the decisions that affect both of us. By emphasizing the virtues behind communicative rationality in our institutional arrangements (as in procedural democracy), we can help people learn that treating those who are culturally different with respect means giving them equal access to the dialogues that affect their lives. The intuitive idea is that each of us ought to be treated according to the same intersubjective consensual norms that make members of a language community trust each other. Under the discourse conception of justice, solidarity with the other should naturally develop, even between those who have different lifestyles. In Habermas's (1998) words, discourse ethics

> reminds us that moral consciousness depends on a particular self-understanding of moral persons who recognize that they *belong* to the moral community. . . . As members of this community, individuals expect to be treated equally, while it is assumed at the same time that each person regards every other person as "one of us." From this perspective solidarity is simply the reverse side of justice. (p. 29)

Solidarity amidst diversity is what communicative rationality leads to. Is there evidence that this kind of cosmopolitan moral perspective will continue to develop during the twenty-first century? To the chagrin of those who favor ethnocentric homogeneity, communitarian isolationist agendas, or policies based only on national self-interest, institutional structures are increasingly supporting those liberal policies that encourage open critical dialogue, mutual support, and acceptance of diversity. I think the research in constructivist developmental psychology indicates that this direction in the evolution of human consciousness will continue, barring nationalistic wars, or a shift in the direction of the global war on terror so that it begins to stampede people back into tribal enclaves.

Implementation: The Justification of Discourse Ethics

> **For Study:** Give examples of the normative transcendent pragmatic rules of argumentation.

The justification of discourse ethics is based on a transcendental pragmatic understanding of argumentative discourse. A *transcendental pragmatic* argument focuses on *isolating the background pragmatic (i.e., practical causal) conditions that are necessary prerequisites for an activity to exist at all.* A set of causal conditions or rules for argumentative practice will be "pragmatic" when they explain why the form of communication works. They will be "transcendent" with regard to the argumentative practice, when the practice itself cannot be conceived of as being possible if the set of causal conditions or rules are absent, since they are necessary prerequisites for the practice. Habermas argues that the following are the types of transcendent, pragmatic background norms that make communicative discourse possible (1991, pp. 87–94). In the first place, argumentation requires some minimal logical norms such as

1.1   No speaker may contradict himself.
1.2   Every speaker who applies predicate (f) to object (a) must be prepared to apply (f) to all other objects resembling (a) in all relevant aspects.
1.3   Different speakers may not use the same expression with different meanings, [and so forth]. (p. 87)

Since these are only logical rules that keep argumentation coherent by themselves they do not have moral content. To take the argument to another normative level, we have to isolate the procedural aspect of argumentation that leads to obligations. What pragmatic presuppositions focus on are (1) accountability and truthfulness between all involved and (2) the rules that tell us what can count as a contribution to an argument. The presuppositions at this level will have moral significance because they show that mutual recognition between participants is logically necessary for the social activity to exist. They force us to abandon merely personal strategies and adopt a position that has intersubjective respect. This is the point at which the conman has to begin to hide his true intentions when he is not really trying to communicate.

2.1   Every speaker may assert only what he really believes.
2.2   A person who disputes a proposition or norm not under discussion must provide a reason for wanting to do so. (p. 88) [People trying to communicate do not throw arbitrary wrenches into the mix, and they take the other seriously as someone who deserves an account.]

Finally, as a process of communication, argumentative speech must satisfy certain improbable but idealizing conditions. We need something like an "unrestricted communication community" (p. 88) that forbids coercion or force. The idealizing conditions presupposed by communicative argumentation (as opposed to strategic argumentation) "neutralize all motives other than that of the cooperative search for truth [and rightness]" (p. 89). This level relies on presuppositions such as:

3.1   Every subject with competence to speak and act must be allowed to take part in a discourse. [This really refers to "all moral agents," since the "amoral" are not yet participants. We will need to be guided by future oriented consent when choosing for the amoral. The goal would be to protect their equal opportunity to be part of future moral dialogues.]

3.2   a) Everyone is allowed to question any assertion whatever.
b) Everyone is allowed to introduce any assertion whatever into the discourse.
c) Everyone is allowed to express his attitudes, desires, and needs. [Obviously, when powerful groups do not allow others to participate in policy discussions, they violate this rule at the start. Thus, to capture the "we are all created as moral equals" notion underlying democracy we need another condition, such as 3.3.]

3.3   No speaker may be prevented, by internal or external coercion, from exercising his rights as laid down in (3.1) and (3.2).

Problems: How Does Language Really Function?

> **For Study:**   Why does the transcendental pragmatic argument indicate that a moral skeptic is involved in a performative contradiction? How can a developmental account of language acquisition help Habermas respond to Lyotard's theory of language? Why do moral theories need principles of appropriateness?

Are these norms just cultural conventions of Western styles of argument or are they truly transcendent universal norms that emerge in all forms of argumentative discourse? To be transcendental they have to be necessary conditions for the possibility of argumentative discourse, so that without them, this type of communicative practice could not exist. Habermas argues that these are not norms found in all communication, but they are found in that widely used form of communication called "argumentative discourse aiming at reaching a consensus." They are transcendental inescapable presuppositions for this type of communication because even the skeptic who claims he does not believe in universal norms has to use them. The skeptic is caught in a "performative contradiction" if he argues against them, because he will have to presuppose the validity of the norms of argumentation in order to argue against the norms of argumentation.

Some of Habermas's postmodern critics claim that his theory of communicative speech is simply contrary to empirical fact. Lyotard (1984; cited in Holub, 1991) argues that language is not a simple tool designed to reach consensus through communication, but is in fact a heterogeneous series of language games that function according to different rules that cannot be laid out in advance. What rules are appropriate evolve during the unfolding of the language game. Thus there are no universal norms that can serve as the foundation for all of speech. He argues that speech is "by its very nature *agonistic*, [which means it is] a *struggle for advantage over an adversary*" (cited in Holub, p. 141) (emphasis added). The true end of dialogue, then, is motivated by dissension, not a desire for consensus. This explains why speech is made up of "paradoxes, discontinuities, and undecidabilties of utterances. . . . [In short,] . . . linguistic contests rely on force and not consensus" (Holub, 142).

Lyotard fails to understand Habermas's point because they are talking about using speech for different purposes. Habermas is not talking about *all* speech, only all communicative speech aiming at mutual understanding. So, Habermas can easily agree on an empirical level that disputes often are resolved on the basis of power or coercion. But, a true attempt to reach agreement through communication is the most basic kind of speech, and it cannot be based on these forces. Habermas is interested in the prerequisite conditions needed to have any meaningful dialogue at all. The prescriptive norms behind attempts to communicate and reach understanding are anthropologically based universals inherent in language itself. No matter what kind of validity claim you are asserting, it must be governed by the norms of communication or else we will fail to understand one another.

Critics like Lyotard fail to take into account the constructivist developmental sequence of language acquisition. Before language can be used in an agonistic manner to engage in combat, one first has to learn speech as a neophyte in a language community. All parents who care about the intersubjective mental health of their children avoid using language in manipulative combative ways with their babies. When a child says, "What's that?" parents tell the truth. Good parents nurture children by basing communication on truth, appropriateness, and sincerity. After the lessons are learned, then we are well positioned for playing different types of language games, but by then we also know the difference between communication and combat. Habermas (1994) says,

> I never say that people want to act communicatively but that they have to. When parents bring up their children, when the living appropriate the transmitted wisdom of preceding generations, when individuals and groups cooperate, that is, when they work to get along with one another without the costly recourse to violence, they all have to act communicatively. There are elementary social functions that can only be satisfied by means of communicative action.

Our intersubjectively shared, overlapping life-worlds lay down a broad background consensus, without which our everyday praxis simply couldn't take place. (p. 111)

Habermas knows that language in general is a heterogeneous enterprise. He is aware that some philosophers will play games with some gas station attendants rather than speak to them in ways that are governed by the norms of communication. But we should not become confused by such games into thinking this kind of manipulative play or combat should have equal billing with the norms of communication. Argumentative communication is based on norms that precede playing games. There is an "intuitive preunderstanding that every subject competent in speech and action brings to a process of argumentation" (Habermas, 1991, pp. 89ff) that proves his point about the moral priority of the norms of communication. What does he mean by *intuitive preunderstanding*? He is referring to *the procedural understanding that competent members of language communities develop everywhere in the world when they become capable of using arguments to assert and defend validity claims.* For instance, when someone says she is going to convince you through communicative discourse, she has committed herself to the norms of communicative discourse, so it would be a performative contradiction for her to then use lies in an attempt to convince you. This same insight applies to excluding people from communicative discourse by silencing their input. On a procedural level we know it is nonsense to say we convinced people if they were forced into silence by threats or by being excluded from political participation (p. 91).

People everywhere take these universal expectations for granted within their own cultural group. The implementation problem to be overcome in application discourse is to find a way to make these universal norms come alive in communication across group lines between strangers and enemies. Because it is never easy to implement conceptions of legitimate commonality in diverse local circumstances, Habermas (1993) argues that any complete universal theory must be supplemented with *principles of appropriateness* (p. 37) designed to *help moral agents figure out how to apply fundamental, universal background norms in concrete particular situations.* He recommends that postmodern critics would do well to read Klaus Gunther's (1993) study of application discourses in law and morality to learn how to combine their concern for sensitivity to particular contexts with the requirements of universal background respect found in moral discourse.

At the level of application, to avoid standard person errors, a major principle of appropriateness can be stated as "Other things being equal, affected parties must actually participate in real discourses whenever issues of justice are involved." Because all lower level policies and substantive legal and moral principles are formulated at the application level, we need to ensure that the actual choice of such substantive content will "depend on real discourses (or advocatory discourses conducted as substitutes for them)" (Habermas, 1991, p. 94).

The most fundamental practical need is to find a way to make shared power and real interactive dialogue between different people a practical reality. Since universal, impartially based theories of morality all presuppose informed consent, perhaps a *prima facie* right to actual participation should be added to the universal background ideals of all theories as the first of many principles of appropriateness to guide application discourse during subsequent discussions at more substantive levels. As Habermas (1993) says, "In discourses of application, the principle of appropriateness takes on the role played by the principle of universalization in justificatory discourses. Only the two principles taken together exhaust the idea of impartiality" (p. 37).

Summary

It is not my purpose in this text to try to solve the philosophical disagreements between the six competing theories discussed so far. That would take me far beyond the scope of the text. It might be wise for a concerned moral agent to use insights from all of these theories when confronting moral dilemmas. But because they are inconsistent with each other, ultimately a choice will be required. Basically, every moral agent is responsible for choosing her own theory. I hope the kinds of considerations that we have been discussing will be considered relevant in helping us choose the best theory. We can always make the world a better place if we and other free people are willing to try. Applying theory to lived life increases both the quality of moral decisions and the excitement of living. To see this, we need to return to the practical side of normative ethics. How can we use the theories we have studied to attack ethical dilemmas in a pluralistic world? To answer this question, the next chapter considers *theory* of *implementation*.

REFERENCES

EDGAR, ANDREW. (1998). Quality of life indicators. In *Encyclopedia of applied ethics*, Vol. 3. (pp. 759–76). Academic Press.

GUNTHER, KLAUS. (1993). *The sense of appropriateness: Application discourses in morality and law*. John Farrell (Trans.). Albany: State University of New York Press.

HABERMAS, JURGEN. (1996). *Between facts and norms: Contributions to a discourse theory of law and democracy*. William Rehg (Trans.). Cambridge, MA: The MIT Press.

———. (1998). *The inclusion of the other*. Ciaran Cronin & Pablo De Greiff (Eds.). Cambridge, MA: The MIT Press.

———. (1993). *Justification and application: Remarks on discourse ethics*. Ciaran P. Cronin (Trans.). Cambridge, MA: The MIT Press.

————. (1991). *Moral consciousness and communicative action*. Christian Lenhardt & Shierry Weber Nicholson (Trans.). Cambridge, MA: The MIT Press.

————. (1994). *The past as future*. Max Pensky (Trans. & Ed.). Lincoln: University of Nebraska Press.

HOLUB, ROBERT C. (1991). *Jurgen Habermas: Critic in the public sphere*. New York: Routledge.

HUME, DAVID. (1748, 1968). *Of the original contract*. In Ernest Barker (Ed.), *Social contract* (pp. 145–66). London: Oxford University Press.

KANT, IMMANUEL. (1797, 1964). *Groundwork of the metaphysics of morals*. H. J. Paton (Trans.). New York: Harper Torchbooks.

LYOTARD, JEAN-FRANCOIS. (1984). *The postmodern condition: A report on knowledge*. Geoff Bennington and Brian Massumi (Trans.). Minneapolis: University of Minnesota Press.

MILL, JOHN STUART. (1863, 1957). *Utilitarianism*. New York: Bobbs-Merrill.

————. (1859, 1971). *On liberty*. In R. A. Wasserstrom (Ed.), *Morality and the law* (pp. 10–23). Belmont, CA: Wadsworth.

NOZICK, ROBERT. (1974). *Anarchy, state, and utopia*. New York: Basic Books.

O'NEILL, ONORA. (1989). *Constructions of reason: Explorations of Kant's practical philosophy*. Cambridge: Cambridge University Press.

————. (1980). Perplexities of famine and world hunger. In Tom Regan (Ed.), *Matters of life and death* (pp. 322ff). New York: Random House.

ROUSSEAU, JEAN-JACQUES. (1762, 1968). The social contract. In Ernest Barker (Ed.), *Social contract* (pp. 167–307). London: Oxford University Press.

RAWLS, JOHN. (1971). *A theory of justice*. Cambridge, MA: Harvard University Press.

————. (1985). Justice as fairness: Political not metaphysical. *Philosophy and public affairs* 14, 224ff.

————. (1993). *Political liberalism*. New York: Columbia University Press.

SANDEL, MICHAEL. (1982). *Liberalism and the limits of justice*. Cambridge: Cambridge University Press.

WILENTZ, C. J. (1989). New Jersey Supreme Court: In the matter of baby M. In Tom Beauchamp & LeRoy Walters (Eds.), *Contemporary issues in bioethics* (pp. 502–13). Belmont, CA: Wadsworth.

WILLS, GARRY. (1979). *Inventing America*. New York: Vintage Books.

YOUNG, IRIS. (1990). Part two: The politics of difference. In *Throwing like a girl and other essays in feminist philosophy and social theory*. Bloomington: Indiana University Press.

Chapter   Ten

Theory of Implementation:
The Best Means

⌒ Background: The Relationship Between Ends and Means

> **For Study:** What is the proper relationship between choosing means and the reasoning used to justify ideal positions? Why is the process of reform as important as the goals being pursued?

In previous chapters, we studied how people could use justification discourse to address "why" questions as they climbed the ladder of abstraction to the background universal moral vision that ought to govern their intersubjective world. Once this "discourse of justification" convinces us of the rightness of an ideal vision, then we have to turn to applied ethics to seriously consider questions about how the moral vision ought to be applied to actual cases. The goal of application is to figure out what intermediate steps ought to be taken right now to settle specific ethical and moral conflicts "all things considered." Given the MPofV (moral point of view) as a general background, the practical goal of *applied ethics* is to *use moral ideals contained in foundational principles to generate lower level principles and rules that can help us solve the ethical and moral conflicts that arise in local settings.*

Since the world is imperfect, one overriding concern in applied ethics is to achieve ideals in ways that do not betray the high standards previously chosen during the discourse of justification. As we saw previously, when people pay too little attention to this issue by relying solely on instrumental rationality (which is too simplistic for the moral world), then we see a corresponding increase in the types of administrative maneuvers that fall into the category of the "banality of evil." To avoid these problems, the means chosen must be compatible with the same communicative reasoning that was used to justify the background guiding ideals. Thus, we will need a *theory of implementation* or *application to guide the choice of the means chosen for achieving moral ideals "all things considered."*

Basically, every moral agent is responsible for choosing and defending her own ideal theory as well as the theory of implementation that logically follows from it. If we choose an ideal that cannot be implemented without having to

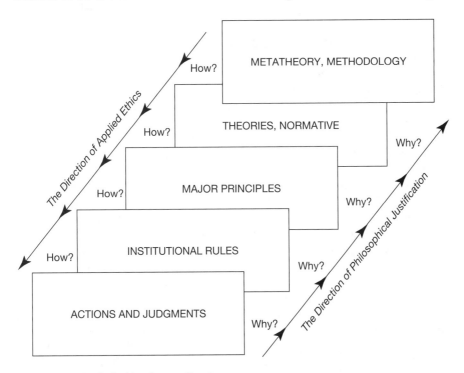

Figure 10.1   Applied ethics changes directions.

distort the ideal on the practical level, then we are to blame for choosing a poor background ideal theory. In applied ethics, we can say that any ideal moral philosophy that easily lends itself to immoral implementation strategies is a faulty moral theory. For instance, one criticism of Ayn Rand's (1999) brand of moral egoism is that ordinary people too easily abuse it at the implementation level. Since her approach confuses the virtue of individualism with selfishness, it gives aid and comfort to those who downplay the importance of intersubjective connection and commitment. When one's only obligation is to pursue personal preferences, concerns about accounting for intersubjective ethical and moral boundaries seem to disappear. The most obvious preliminary question, then, is "Which ideal moral theory should guide the development of our theory of implementation?" I hope that the kinds of considerations discussed in this text will help people sort through these issues, so that they will be more likely to make a wise moral choice on both the theoretical and the practical level.

The Way It Is

> **For Study:** How should the phrase "that is just the way it is" fit into moral theory and applied ethics?

An approach to applied ethics that can cause considerable confusion is expressed in the skeptical statement, "Well, that is just the way it is." What should we make of this phrase? It is sometimes used as a reform stopper, "Don't be idealistic because the way it is can't be changed." For instance, at our local prison, some inmates use the phrase to challenge the idea that being moral could ever be rational in the "real" world; that is, get out of the ivory tower of academia and look around at the way it is. As one student at the prison said to my colleague, "If you follow moral principles out here you will be eaten alive."

Now obviously there is an important point being made by the inmate. Principles point in a direction that we ought to follow, but occasionally we find ourselves in institutional settings that will punish people if they try to do the right thing. The prisoner is wise to notice that in his current setting, being honest, empathic, and open to dialogue makes him vulnerable to powerful scoundrels willing to take advantage of moral people. It is difficult to answer the inmate's complaint about ideals as long as he has to stay in a setting that punishes moral behavior. My colleague responded to the inmate's skeptical complaint in the most effective way possible. He asked the prisoners in the class if they all liked living in the prison, with its egoistic philosophy that put moral people at risk. To a man they hated their current environment, so he made his point. Their hatred is a powerful condemnation of "the way it is" in institutional settings that are unethical. Bad institutions do not prove that moral principles are wrong; they simply prove that there are evil environments.

Morality does not require us to be naively innocent about the way parts of the world work. On the contrary, if you will be "eaten alive" when you take the high road, then you ought to use appropriate strategic reasoning to cautiously apply ideals in ways that help you avoid inadvertently becoming someone's dinner. But, rolling over and accepting the inevitability of immoral approaches to life is not the way to proceed. The point of distinguishing between ideal theory and theory of implementation is to encourage people to develop the practical wisdom that is needed to apply moral principles in ways that do not defeat the spirit of the ideal. Since the so-called realistic approach of accepting the way it is can actually encourage the continuation of immorality, moral agents must occasionally reject the way it is or risk reinforcing immorality by cooperating with its demands.

Stop and think about the consequences for social life if the great moralists in human history always approached ethical issues by saying, "Well, that is just the way it is. We can't do anything different." What would have happened to the United States if the Founding Fathers of the country had followed this slogan? They were not a homogeneous group of abstract idealists. In fact, each colony had its own interests and agenda, so they did not trust each other (Wills, 1978). But even with all their diversity, they were able to *change* the way it is. The Constitutional Convention can be viewed as a nice example of pluralism in action that illustrates an important lesson about moral process. Although many of the participants in the Constitutional Convention were not abstract idealists to begin with, nonetheless, they seem to have been swept up by the *process of moral debate.* That is, the three-step process of (1) trying to *reform* a government, coupled with (2) constitutional debate between relatively *free and equal participants,* who were (3) motivated by the practical necessity to reach *unanimous agreement* on an idealistic document, took many of the Constitutional Convention members much further along the road toward an idealistic vision than they ever meant to travel.

∼ Ideal Theory: Combining the Empirical and the Prescriptive

> **For Study:** Why does the slogan "ought implies can" imply that ethical theory needs to be consistent with the results of empirical research? Why does the interdisciplinary nature of applied ethics make it a controversial discipline?

Rather than giving up because of "the way it has been," we would be better off pursuing the implications of the slogan *ought implies can,* which as discussed in Chapter Two, draws attention to the *logical connection between an agent's responsibility and her capacity to act in local situations*. If ethical theory is going to be useful at the implementation level, it must take into consideration the kind of empirical research that reveals what ordinary good people can and cannot do. As we have seen, by designing innovative empirical experiments (e.g., filling Zimbardo's pseudo prison with "good" people to see what they will do in a strange environment), social psychologists have shown us again and again that some of our common-sense intuitions about individual moral responsibility seem to be in conflict with research data that shows what people actually do when under institutional pressure. This kind of research is very useful at the implementation level, where we shift focus from "other things being equal, what ideals should govern morally autonomous agents?" to "all things considered, how do we apply our ideals to people in this institutional setting?" Application theory can only be practically useful if it is possible to cross back and forth between the borders of normative and descriptive disciplines. But, the structure of explanations in science is a bit different from the structure of normative justifications in philosophy. Both require good reasons, but the reasons have a different logical structure, for example, empirical versus rational normative agreement. Thus, how should the two disciplines be integrated? If we place a chart that diagrams the directionality of scientific explanations next to a chart illustrating normative justifications, then we get the differences illustrated in Figure 10.2.

Explanations in the social and natural sciences are causal accounts that describe "what" has happened and clarify "how" events occur. That is, scientists presuppose that they can get in touch with value-neutral facts in some

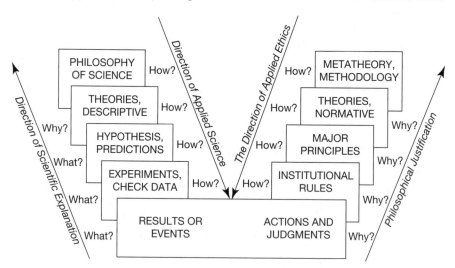

Figure 10.2   Science and philosophy ask different questions and are grounded in different ways.

significant sense, and they attempt to continually ground their descriptions with empirical investigations of these neutral facts. On the left side of Figure 10.2, applied science moves back and forth between observation and abstract scientific theory, always trying to keep theoretical hypothesis and applications in touch with something called "facts" or "the way it *is*." The applied scientists who work on the concrete level become skilled at applying empirically based theories to the choice of means for achieving normative goals. However, morality is more concerned with motives than with causes. On the right side of the chart, we see that a study of philosophical justifications for *why* people act as they do takes us to the level of ideal normative theories. Then, in applied ethics this normative process is reversed to study "how" people "ought to use" these reconstructed background norms to make judgments at the level of action—given the way it is right now.

The goal of traditional moral theory has always been to offer background justifications for principles; so it has never been particularly policy-oriented. Thus, the understanding one gains by analyzing abstract background theories does not automatically translate into insights about how the world works or about what to do in concrete situations. It is possible for a theoretician to have considerable background understanding of theory and principles but lack the experience that could give her practical wisdom about how to implement her theory. On the other hand, since policies for action are usually formulated at the concrete level of rules, which is below foundational principles, it is possible for people who create policy at the local or national level to lack vision into background ideals. It became clear centuries ago that theory and practice are not automatically integrated in people's decision-making skills, so the ancient Greeks found it useful to distinguish between theoretical wisdom (*theōria*) and practical wisdom (*phronēsis*). Policy decisions presuppose the existence of moral ideals, but they are often ignored when people become fixated on concrete values like efficiency and cost. As we have seen throughout the text, "concrete focus" on practical empirical issues and strategic reasoning can deflect attention away from background ideals. Yet moral wisdom requires that people learn how to integrate all these factors in their deliberations. Each generation will have to master this task in the face of increasingly complex challenges.

It should be clear that in applied ethics we must cross back and forth between descriptive and normative disciplines to integrate the information from both concrete studies and theoretical speculation. Once we reverse directions in ethics to start applying moral ideals to practice, then the concrete data from the empirically based social sciences become very important in ethics. The empirically based "how to do it" data helps us make decisions about proper means for achieving our goals, while the abstract insights from normative philosophy helps us become clear about which human values we ought to be pursuing in the first place.

Blending the Concrete with the Abstract

> **For Study:** Why is following rules without question an inappropriate way to implement moral theory? In what way do decision procedures help and in what ways are they limited? Why do we need to distinguish between questions about foundational justice and questions about the good life? Which should have priority when there is a conflict between them?

Theoretical moral concepts are based on abstract background universal norms, so justice cannot be reduced to a simple matter of obedience to concrete laws. Thus, a concrete approach that simply says, "Obey rules without question" will not work as a theory of implementation in morality. As Wilkins (1994) points out, even though there is a *prima facie* general obligation to obey the law, individuals are still not relieved of the burden of evaluating specific cases of legal compliance to insure that justified abstract norms of justice are being applied in the law. Because institutions may be just without being perfectly just, "there may not be an actual moral obligation to obey a specific law provided it can be shown that disobeying the law in question will not harm the state, or provided it can be shown that disobeying the law may succeed in making it a more just state, as, for example, in cases where civil disobedience may be justified" (p. 94). Given lack of perfection, moral agents are going to have to develop their capacity to use some discretionary moral judgment in adapting theories to the modern world. Moral issues have become so complex that even when people agree about general principles of justice, they can still find themselves unprepared for many of the moral contingencies that can arise at the level of application.

> The realization that we can never know all the relevant aspects of a situation because we would never have sufficient time to consider all the aspects—this insight confronts us with a structural indeterminacy of application situations; because of this indeterminacy there remains only the alternative of once again attempting a rationalization of the application problem from the perspective of morally acting persons, or of completely changing the perspective and of no longer tackling the problem within the conceptual framework of moral action. (Gunther 1993, p. 7)

Since Gunther's second choice of abandoning "the conceptual framework of moral action" will leave us ethically stranded, we need to choose the first option and create a new *discourse of application* that can *facilitate the development of the right kind of practical wisdom*. Because it is never easy to implement abstract universal norms, Habermas (1991) argues that all universal theories must confront the problems of application that are of concern to postmodern philosophers. He points out that since "moral norms do not contain their own rules of application," universal principles and good intentions are not enough. We also need "contextual sensitivity" and "hermeneutic prudence at the level of application" (pp. 179–82). Thus, as mentioned in the last chapter, abstract universal theories need to develop clearly worded **principles of appropriateness** to *help moral agents figure out how to apply universal norms in concrete particular situations.* This is one reason that codes of ethics are needed in the various professions. They can help guide professionals when they have to develop concrete implementation strategies to apply ideals to unique cases. As mentioned in Chapter Two, this is also one of the reasons ethicists often recommend that people use decision procedures to help them apply theory in ways that are sensitive to the various levels. In short, the recommendation that we focus on "background" first, and then "ideal theory" before considering "implementation strategies" is a way of developing some obvious principles of appropriateness for the application process itself.

However, because many people do not know how to calculate in the abstract manner required by these procedures, they may well make immoral decisions even when following principles of appropriateness. For instance, a person in Kohlberg's (1971) third stage of moral development might say he believes everyone should follow the principle of utility, but then he will use the rule of the peer group as his primary principle of appropriateness even though it conflicts with utilitarianism. His use of a decision procedure will turn out to be inappropriately ethnocentric since his peer-group orientation will make him vulnerable to the standard person problem—that is, he will treat everyone according to the rules of his own group. Decision procedures are tools; they are not substitutes for moral wisdom. It is not sufficient to simply hand people a decision procedure and a list of justified principles and rules if they have not been taught how to integrate rules, principles, and theories in the decision procedure.

Furthermore, if people adopt an approach to morality that treats a decision procedure as a concrete measuring stick that can be followed without theoretical reflection, then they are apt to treat universals as concrete rules needing no local interpretation. "A universalist ethics then appears as an abstract, obstinate rigorism blind to facts and of service to immoral intentions at any moment" (Gunther 1993, p. 6). This kind of concrete unreflective approach treats decision procedures as though they are systems of *pure procedural justice.* This means they would have to be procedures *that are so correct or fair that any outcome the procedure produces will likewise be correct or fair provided only that the procedure has been properly followed* (Rawls, 1971, p. 86). But only games like poker can distribute goods in this pure manner. That is, as long as no one cheats in a game of chance, then any distribution is just. In the real world, however, there are no pure procedures that can guarantee justice. As mentioned above, because universal principles are not concrete maxims for action, they need to be impartially interpreted in contextually sensitive ways with due regard to the ideals contained in the universal principles. So, agents will need both practical and theoretical wisdom when using any procedure to implement principles. On the whole, these procedures have remained too silent about their background presuppositions and the virtues that agents will need to use them. In general, they should warn users that people who suffer from bureaucratic thinking can be properly motivated by moral duty but still be deficient in the virtues needed to intelligently apply universal norms while using a decision procedure. As Gunther (1993) says,

> we know in most action situations which assertions of fact are true and which action norms . . . [are] valid, and yet often enough act "immorally" because we . . . overlook or incorrectly appraise certain aspects of the situation; or we underestimate the importance of particular precepts or prohibitions (worthy of recognition) in relation to the norms we then actually observe in the particular situation (p. 3).

Finding fault with **bureaucratic thinking** is not about claiming that people who use this style of thought intentionally distort decision procedures or lie. Instead, the moral drawbacks of this form of judgment have more to do with *"a lack of care in considering the relevant facts, to an absence of sensitivity to the particular circumstances, and to an insufficient aptitude for choosing the appropriate course of action in view of the particular situation"* (Gunther, p. 4) (emphasis added). Habermas (1991) believes that inability to understand these important conceptual distinctions results from harmful "deficiencies" in moral thinking that are responsible for some of the oppression in the name of universal values that worry the postmodern critics.

All of these complications give us good reasons to be skeptical of packaged concrete decision procedures that are supposed to lead everyone to the right decisions. It may be useful therefore to make a distinction between the complex nature of contemporary civilizations and the more homogeneous city-states of the ancient Greek world. We can no longer assume that the ethical choice of lifestyle (or the good life) and moral deliberations regarding matters of justice are simply two sides of the same coin. Habermas (1991) argues that the contingencies of lifestyle choice are so personal that they are not amenable to universalization. The choice of the good life involves issues of personal identity formation that are more a matter of aesthetic or clinical judgment within a local community than a matter of achieving justice between groups. Thus, he follows Kant's lead by restricting universal morality to deliberations about justice and human rights. This means at the level of implementation abstract and practical questions about justice must first be resolved to everyone's good-liking, before we can turn to the lower-level ethical and personal concerns about which lifestyle it is good to choose. Since justice concerns what is right it has priority over the choice of lifestyle or what is good. Once justice has been achieved then choice of lifestyle ought to be left to local deliberations between people who are tying to create a shared community. This strategy might help diminish the extent of the standard person problem in matters of justice, since concrete differences between ways of life will not be confused with the content of impartial justice between abstract moral equals.

∾ Implementation: Moral Agents and Institutional Settings

> **For Study:**   How does the development of moral understanding affect the strategy for implementing moral ideals? What is the first step in implementation that all moral theories should advocate? Why is it important to study our past before we try to implement ideals?

Because it is difficult to blend the normative with the descriptive and the concrete with the abstract when using decision procedures, implementation strategies must be realistic about what can be accomplished at the level of institutions. It is not enough to have a theory about where you would like to go; to have successful reforms you must also know how to build on the past. In his study of the failure of new settings (which were collective attempts to implement some ideal conception), Sarason (1972) found that the first step in any attempt at reform must be a historical study of the current setting. This requires us to consider conditions "before the beginning" of the "new" setting (p. xvii), but unfortunately, whether the goal is self-transformation, a marriage, or the creation of a new society, this first step in implementation is often overlooked. Sarason says, "consensus about values does not instruct one in how to create settings consistent with these values, and that is why the creation of settings is such an important problem" (p. 20). Time and time again, he found that people in agreement on values failed in their attempts at reforms because they were not aware of how much old forms structure the recommendations for reform itself. We must confront our history, build on it, and guard against it, if attempts at reform are not going to flounder. Sarason claims that

> Unless the compass that guides us has history built into it we will go in circles, feel lost, and conclude that the more things change the more they remain the same. . . . One can only sigh and say, "here we go again" when we see efforts to shape futures based on the rejection or ignorance of the past. . . . The creation of a modest setting proceeds (in the local sense) a-historically at its peril. (pp. 22–23)

The first long-range strategy in any general theory of implementation should be to figure out ways to distribute historical information, emotional adjustment, and thinking skills as widely as possible. For instance, integrity is less likely to develop in societies that fail to encourage the kind of relational bonding that leads to intersubjective commitment. Thus, in Norway they have recently passed legislation that gives state support for maternity leaves for both mothers and fathers. The policy is based on the idea that the emotional health of future generations of Norwegian citizens will be strengthened if policies support opportunities for emotional bonding with both parents during the first year of life. Policies designed to create opportunities for moral development, will allow us over the long run (1) to place responsibility where it belongs—on moral agents themselves, (2) to increase people's freedom of choice, and (3) to hold one another responsible for our intersubjective moral choices. If we have been introduced to the options and have the capacity to understand what we ought to choose, then ignorance or poor socialization will not be accepted as excuses for a failure to choose properly.

In general, developmental constructivist theory suggests that we are not stimulating moral development as well as we could. To avoid teaching hidden curriculums that interfere with moral learning, institutions should encourage all people to participate in discussions about the policies that affect them. People should also be encouraged to use sophisticated decision procedures that help people stay sensitive to the full range of moral variables. Decision procedures help to stimulate dialogue at the local level. But, to avoid misuse of decision procedures, people must be encouraged to use them under conditions of critical public debate between all people who are stakeholders.

At this point it becomes clear how developmental research makes an important contribution to normative philosophy. It demonstrates forcefully why advanced normative theories must all agree on at least one substantive moral right. All moral theories must advocate giving people the educational experiences that are a prerequisite for properly using a decision procedure that emphasizes the moral point of view behind the theories. Rawls (1971) recognizes this fact explicitly when he states that "the moral education is an education for autonomy" (p. 516), where autonomy is defined as the ability to live according to principles that would be chosen from behind the veil of ignorance. If moral autonomy is to become an increasingly practical guide in our daily life, then, other things being equal, as many of our institutions as possible ought to be designed to promote this ideal or at least not inhibit it—especially those institutions that affect human development or create and disseminate information (e.g., family structures, day-care centers, schools, universities, media agencies). To reform institutions so that they promote moral autonomy, we must begin with institutions that are already in place and then modify them in a judicious manner. To get an idea about how to implement background moral values in institutional contexts that are already established, it will be instructive to use a decision procedure to evaluate a couple of complex dilemmas, one involving legal theory and one involving a business contract.

∽ Applied Ethical Reasoning Using a Decision Procedure

The following two examples of ethical reasoning at the implementation level illustrate how one can use a simple decision procedure to guide deliberations about particular moral issues, even in well-established institutional contexts. Notice that even though I am using the same decision procedure in each example, the subcategories are not exactly the same. Each dilemma will have its own dynamic that dictates what needs to be considered. The point is to use the procedure as a guide; it should not be allowed to constrain reflective thought. Also, that a decision procedure is used to figure out how a case should be settled does not mean that the solution is obviously right. In ethics there is no guarantee that we won't err even when using a decision procedure. The questions addressed are complex, so it is possible for other reasonable professionals to disagree with reasonable conclusions. The possibility for error only means we are fallible. This should keep us humble and open to reasonable criticism. It also helps explain why it is important to include all people affected in the decision making; they can mutually encourage each other to consider all variables.

When using a decision procedure to analyze a case, much of the preliminary work will be done on scratch pads, going back and forth between the steps in the decision model. The goal is to sharpen our analysis as we increase our understanding of the relevant variables. In these examples, I am not going to show all of the preliminary work. Although I did spend some time thinking about each case on a scratch pad, at this point I'll go directly to the final stages of my analysis.

Example: The Jurisprudence of Difference

> **For Study:** What is the problem of difference in the law? Why are feminist critics and other minority groups suspicious of legal institutions? How does Rawls attempt to account for difference and what adjustments to Rawls's theory does Wilkin's recommend?

Background: The General Dilemma

The first move in the back-grounding step of the decision procedure mentioned in Chapter Two is to "state the specific dilemma, then place it at the proper level of ethical consideration by framing the dilemma as a general type." So the type of dilemma we will use as out first example of applied ethical reasoning deals with a common issue that confronts officers of the court in constitutional democracies. The following case was so complicated it led members of the U.S.

Supreme Court to conflicting conclusions. Specifics: In the state of Oregon, members of the Native American Church occasionally used peyote as part of their religious services. However, the drug laws in Oregon, which were passed to promote the general welfare of the society, have classified peyote as an illegal substance. Thus, it would appear that church members occasionally violate the law. Two members of the church were dismissed from their jobs in a drug rehabilitation program, because they ingested peyote during a church service. The State of Oregon then refused them unemployment benefits on the grounds that they were dismissed for violating a state law, a crime that makes them ineligible for benefits. The workers sued for their unemployment benefits because the Constitution guarantees individuals "the free exercise" of their particular religious beliefs. They claimed the local state laws unfairly discriminated against their religious practices. If the drug laws were unjust, then the dismissal from work would not be justified and should not be used as grounds for depriving them of unemployment benefits. In short, they want the court to take into account the special circumstances that make their use of peyote an exception to the rule.

What is the nature of this general dilemma, or at what level of abstraction does the conflict occur? When viewed as a conflict between levels of the legal system, the issue concerns the relationship that ought to exist between local laws that regulate the public sphere and the constitutional rights of citizens in general. The state's drug laws fall into the category of *laws of general applicability* because *"they apply to everyone equally."* Defenders of the Oregon drug laws say that such laws do not unjustly discriminate. The mere fact that these general laws "prohibit the exercise" of a particular religion's practices (which leads to harm to particular individuals in that religion), does not prove that the laws are unjust or that the plaintiffs have a legitimate claim to be treated as exceptions to the laws because they are different. The laws are secular regulations passed to promote the general welfare, and there was never any intention to discriminate against a particular religious practice.

An important background consideration that helps define who is a stakeholder in this issue, is the fact that the case arose in a constitutional democracy established to protect fundamental moral values. For instance, the preamble to the Constitution states that the purpose of the document is to "establish justice, insure domestic tranquillity, provide for a common defense, promote general welfare, and secure the blessings of liberty to ourselves and our posterity," etc. To implement these background ideals, federal and state governments are given the power to regulate individual behavior by passing laws of general applicability to set moral and practical boundaries on choice of lifestyle. The key stakeholders in this dilemma are, then, all people who want to be free to worship as they please, every citizen who wants the state to "establish justice, insure domestic tranquility, and promote the general welfare," and all the legislators and officers of the court who have the duty of station to see that justice is served.

To keep lower-level rules and laws compatible with constitutional ideals, amendments have been added to the Constitution that clarify which moral values should have the highest priority. For instance, Article I, the First Amendment to the Constitution, states, "Congress shall make no law respecting an establishment of religion, or prohibiting the exercise thereof . . ." It is clear that the moral ideal behind this amendment is to protect freedom of religion from state oppression. So, other things being equal, it looks like freedom of religion should have top priority and trump general regulatory laws. On the other hand, to ensure domestic tranquility, promote the general welfare, etc., legislators also need to confront the drug problem in the United States. So, how should judges and legislators balance these values when they collide in cases such as the one under discussion?

This kind of case is important because similar conflicts are bound to occur in the future. By their nature, when constitutionally constrained democratic societies protect the rights of minorities to religious freedom, they automatically promote a plurality of religious points of view. That is, since there are so many different ways to worship, freedom of religion guarantees that there will be different forms of social life within civil society. Protecting religious diversity guarantees that some people will be so different from the norm that mere formal equal treatment under a law of general applicability might create an injustice.

Rawls (1993) explicitly addresses the problem of difference in his moral theory. He acknowledges that a heterogeneous population with a plurality of points of view is a permanent and desirable condition of constitutional democracies. He argues that in liberal democracies extended real discourses between people who are living under various *reasonable, comprehensive doctrines* (such as a traditional religious belief) should lead people to an **overlapping consensus** about what secular political conception of justice is best for protecting everyone's rights, including their own right to be religiously different from each other. As we saw in Chapter Nine, Rawls believes the overlapping consensus about justice would include liberty, equal opportunity, and concern for equality in the distribution of primary social good. These are the types of "transcendent" principles that are supposed to guide us when we consider how the legal system should deal with value diversity.

Ideal Theory, Other Things Being Equal

Western democracies assume that formal moral equality is the background ideal against which we should judge the justice of legal institutions (i.e., "all men are created equal"). To avoid unjust discrimination we protect moral equality with substantive due process rights that ensure equal treatment under the law. In the United States, this emphasis in procedural law on impartial equal treatment has been enshrined in the Equal Protection Clause of the Fourteenth Amendment to the Constitution of the United States. (The discussion on the next three pages is an adaptation of Cooper and Cooper, 1999.)

On the other hand, ideal assumptions about formal equal treatment have to be made compatible with the background moral ideal that we should respect persons as individuals. The background principle of justice as fairness obligates us to take the individual's special circumstances into consideration; for example, children cannot be treated as equal to adults. It would simplify justice concerns if at the lower levels of implementation we could assume that everyone was in fact the same in all respects. Then we would be able to treat everyone exactly the same and ignore their unique differences and their special circumstances. But, in pluralistic societies, disputes between majorities and minorities and between governmental power and private preferences will in fact complicate the relationship between the formal assumptions in the law and the reality of the lives of individual citizens. So, given that there is a need for consistency required by equal treatment according to general laws, how can we also promote the kind of fairness needed to respect each person's unique historical circumstance? This is a conflict at the level of moral principles that will make all lower-level legal decisions quite complicated. How can the legal profession honor both the concept of **justice** as *consistent equal treatment in the law* and as *fairness to unique individuals in the law*?

Problems for Ideal Theory

The legal profession's attempts to balance concern for formal equal treatment with concern for protecting individual liberty and legitimate differences has led to an area of study called the *jurisprudence of difference,* where legislators try to *decide when a difference ought to make a difference in the law*. Historically, it has been dangerous to encourage people to pay attention to differences between groups of people, because differences were all too often used to justify the kind of unequal treatment that led to unjust discrimination. For instance, race was used as a reason to keep African Americans from participating as equals in the public sphere, and gender was used to deprive women of the vote and exclude them from public life by restricting their role to the private sphere of the family. However, over time people challenged these explicitly unjust policies by applying the concept of moral equality to actual institutional practices. Slowly, the law shifted from protecting the unjust privileges of the powerful minority to protecting the right of all people to be treated as equals in spite of their differences.

Currently the burden of proof is now placed on those who want to discriminate to prove that there is a difference that is so important that it can justify unequal treatment in the law. A typical example of how one can meet the burden of proof, and thus justify discrimination, can be found in the way the law discriminates against children. They are not allowed to vote or form enforceable contracts without the consent of a legal guardian. Since this kind of paternalistic discrimination in the law protects children's interests, the deviation from equal treatment to emphasize fairness to children is justifiable. If a similar kind of paternalistic protection were extended to adults, however, the resulting discrimination would be controversial. For instance, it is difficult to see how using differences in sex or race as criteria for treating people differently with regard to voting rights could be justified on the grounds of fairness to these groups. In order to decide when justice obligates us to discriminate to protect people, the law must have clearly developed standards, that is, principles of appropriateness that can help courts and citizens discriminate in ways that are fair.

Principles of Appropriateness: Because the standard person problem is endemic to the human situation, postmodern skeptics point out that existing legal structures "always already" presuppose a taken-for-granted background that reflects the sexual, racial, cultural, and other stereotypes of whatever privileged group controls the passage of legislation. Thus, the law will always be biased in some ways, even when the explicit intention is to build in protection for minorities who are different. Privileged groups are simply poorly situated for judging the discriminatory potential of their own legal structures. So, we should either avoid the looming bias by treating everyone the same, or we should just accept the fact that the law has to be unjust to someone and ignore minority complaints.

Rather than accept this defeatist attitude, the Supreme Court has tried to avoid abuse by establishing standards of appropriateness to guide attempts to apply the law with sensitivity to differences. Thus, *"rational basis review"* should be used to interpret cases under the equal protection clause of the Fourteenth Amendment. For instance, the Court held in Gulf, C. *& S. F. Ry. Co.* v. *Ellis,* 165 U.S. 150 (1897) that *any deviation from equal treatment must be based on some reasonable ground that can justify treating people differently.* For something to be a *reasonable ground* in the law it *must have a just and proper relationship to the purpose of the particular legislation.* The Supreme Court has also developed other standards such as intermediate scrutiny, strict scrutiny, etc. to help evaluate the relationship between the goals of a legal regulation and the means used to achieve those goals. Using these standards has led to a number of court rulings that have expanded the application of the equal protection clause beyond its initial aim of protecting African Americans from arbitrary discrimination. For instance, the equal protection clause has been used to evaluate the reasonableness of gender-based legislation to make sure legal distinctions between men and women are not based on arbitrary claims. The courts have also used the equal protection clause to evaluate discrimination based on other classifications, such as age, disabilities, class, previous discrimination, legitimacy in birth, sexual orientation, and so forth. In the face of increasing diversity, jurisprudence will need to continuously reevaluate historical applications of the background liberal theory of equal protection to extend the universal and elastic language of the Fourteenth Amendment to other classifications. So, although there is an "other things being equal" assumption of equal treatment in justice, there are also precedents for making fine-tuned adjustments when practical wisdom requires adjustments to account for differences "all things considered."

Implementation, All Things Considered

Obviously, as the laws dealing with children illustrate, unequal treatment can be justified when differences are so great that it is unreasonable to think that formal equal treatment will promote justice. But, can unequal treatment of "adults" ever be justified? We can gain valuable insight into this question if we consider some recent feminist criticisms of the legislative attempt to protect women by giving them formal, equal legal standing with men. Mackinnon (1989) argues that since privileged white males have historically defined the baseline from which all considerations start, background universal definitions that affect considerations of "gender" and "difference" are already biased in ways detrimental to the interests of most women. When this kind of unfair discrimination is already built into the definitions used to structure the legal system itself, *formal equal treatment* that *simply treats everyone the same regardless of differences* will merely perpetuate existing unfair advantages (pp. 216–34). Thus, feminist legal critics argue that because the legal status quo glorifies abstract, universalist thinking, it ignores real differences. Thus, the liberal attempt to extend equality to all amounts to no more than a formal adjustment that ignores the concrete reality of the inequality that already exists in the lives of women. If legislation based on formal equality merely eliminates gender as a basis for discrimination and yet leaves the system's historical discriminatory structure unchanged, then women as a class will be stripped of the few gender-based protections they have but receive nothing in the way of substantive equality that can compensate for the lost protection.

All things considered, formal equal treatment does not guarantee justice. By its nature it ignores relevant historical differences that call for legitimate adjustments in treatment. (The debate surrounding the issues of maternity leave for workers is a perfect example.) The logic behind this argument can be applied to many other contexts as well. We examined one such context in Chapter Five when it was mentioned that women of color claimed that the voice of mainstream feminism had been infected with the exclusive background agenda of privileged white women. The mainstream voice was ignoring relevant racial and cultural differences that have greater impact on some minority women's lives than does the mere fact of being women (Crenshaw, 1989). Others have argued against the biased baseline of heterosexuality in mainstream feminism, and others have examined the issue of race, and so forth.

General Normative Strategies: The major theories we have reviewed seem to agree on a general strategy for the impartial application of the ideal of moral equality. As moral equals, all stakeholders have the right to *equal substantive protection*. This means protection must be *more than formal; it must have a concrete local impact as a result of taking differences into consideration.* However, what has concrete impact can vary from locality to locality. Thus, rather than assume that the law only needs to protect one standardized substantive version of needs, difference jurisprudence must find a way to make the equal protection clause sensitive to situational differences. This is the primary concern behind Habermas's (1996) insistence on real participatory discourse in the law. Since the reality of difference entails that "standard persons" are not properly positioned to figure out by themselves how to give "different" people the equal protection they need, moral equality requires everyone to participate in finding solutions to legal problems. Furthermore, since principles protect at a variety of theoretical and conceptual levels, different groups must be represented in the deliberations at all the levels of abstraction.

Creating institutions that encourage real participation will not be easy, and as Habermas (1997) says, it may require the majority to give up its historical prerogative to always set the political agenda (p. 117) in order to protect the participation of minority communities. This sentiment is echoed by Wilkins (1994) when he says he hopes that majorities in democratic cultures will feel secure enough in their liberties that they will allow members of minority collectives "a certain amount of slack" (pp. 95–96) in terms of legal compliance with those laws the collectives find troubling to their conscience, for instance, in a situation where a religious group feels that it cannot in good conscience take a loyalty oath, but is "in other respects willing to obey the laws of the state" (p. 96). Diversity between reasonable comprehensive doctrines would be less of a problem if people would develop the transcendent postconventional forms of consciousness that help us accommodate diversity.

Specific Strategies for This Case: Keeping these background issues in mind, we can return to the clash between the religious practice of the Native American Church and the laws of general applicability to consider ways to resolve the problem without violating background ideals. When parties in a dispute can't agree, it is useful to ask them to consider the MPofV, to see if it will help. So, how does this case look from the point of view of a device like Rawls's veil of ignorance? (The following section is adapted from Cooper, 2001.) In an original position behind the veil of ignorance, social contractees would know about the application difficulties that have plagued human history. They would want to protect their specific heritage (whatever it might be) from people with power who will inevitably be inclined to impose standardized solutions on them. For instance, they would worry that a liberal society that emphasizes neutrality in the law might itself pose a threat to some reasonable comprehensive religious doctrines, because neutral laws only give formal equal protection that ignores substantive differences. They would ask, "How can we create opportunities for justified unequal treatment when it is required by equity or fairness concerns?" As Wilkins (1997) says,

> the problem for a theory of justice is . . . How to be neutral without being inhibiting? (p. 15). [Even] laws 'neutral' toward religion may burden the free exercise of religious beliefs as surely as laws intended to interfere with free exercise (p. 16).

To guard against the standard person problem, the impact of liberal neutrality, and the tendency for bureaucrats to distort the intent of universal values, social contractees would choose a principle specifically designed to protect those reasonable, cherished differences that make up each group's unique identity. In a move compatible with this insight, the U.S. Congress recognized that there was a need for this kind of adjustment when they passed the Religious Freedom Restoration Act of 1993 (Public Law 103-141). They were concerned about "the impact of so-called neutral laws of general applicability upon the exercise of religious freedom" (Wilkins, 1997, p. 17). They wanted legislation that made it clear that "the government should not substantially burden a person's exercise of religion even if the burden results from a *"rule of general applicability"* unless it can demonstrate that the application of the burden is in furtherance of a compelling state interest" (pp. 16–17).

The Religious Freedom Restoration Act appears to conflict with the spirit of Justice Scalia's opinion as expressed in *Oregon Employment Services Division* v. *Smith,* which involved the two dismissed Native American employees. In effect, Scalia ruled that if we use the "compelling state interest" criteria to protect religious freedom, then we will usher in "a parade of horribles." Scalia is worried that "anarchy would prevail if, for every state regulation that might have a negative impact upon some religion, the state be required to justify such regulation by appeal to some compelling state interest" (cited in Wilkins, 1997, p. 18). Justice O'Connor, who shows much more sensitivity to the need to protect diversity, believes the compelling state interest provision is necessary to ensure the free exercise of religious belief. Her interpretation of the Constitution sends the proper message to legislators, since it is in tune with a principled approach that claims "principle must prevail over policy even if this places a considerable burden upon the efficiency of government" (Wilkins, pp. 18–19). In short, if we are to protect religious diversity, then the burden of proof should be on those who favor policies that impact on religious communities to show that the impact does not harm religious ceremonies and the requirements of a group's faith (p. 20). At the level of application, then, we must treat the claim of a religious community that it is being harmed as "presumptively correct barring overwhelming evidence to the contrary" (p. 19).

Solution: All things considered, what kind of substantive legal procedures do we need at the application level to implement equal protection and protect religious freedom in this kind of case? Because this issue would be so important to contractees, they would want to start the protection at the level of justification discourse rather than place their fate in the hands of local authorities at the application level, who may or may not be banal. That is, protection must be seen to be more than a policy decision at the level of application, or else some future legislative body might think it is legitimate to weaken the protection of religious freedom as a trade-off for some other more popular local agenda. To emphasize the importance of this fundamental right, contractees would want a third principle at the level of justification that would serve as a background ideal to regulate all future moves legislative bodies might make at the level of application. Wilkins (1997) argues that protection at this level would look something like the following principle:

> A constitutional regime, acting in accordance with the protection of the basic rights and liberties and equality of opportunity, shall insofar as possible avoid adopting rules with harmful effects upon those comprehensive doctrines which satisfy the conditions of reasonable pluralism. Such rules would include those which (a) may be directed against specific comprehensive doctrines or (b) may be of general applicability but which may result in unintended but foreseeable harms against some comprehensive doctrine(s). Any "neutral" rule which substantially burdens comprehensive doctrine(s) can be justified only if it furthers a compelling state interest. (Wilkins, p. 23)

I think a principle of this kind is appropriate, since we can expect many people in power to share Justice Scalia's worries about diversity. When people can only see diversity as a problem, they are apt to be inclined to marginalize those who are different in order to protect *formal equality,* which, in the absence of sensitivity to difference, gets interpreted as *adherence to a version of a neutral status quo which feels most familiar to a governing body or majority.* Even though social order could also be achieved by protecting the right of minority people to be reasonably different, the first impulse of powerful people is often to protect social order by voting to impose constraints on those others who are different, even if the group being constrained may consider the constraints quite oppressive.

The most compelling issue in applied ethics for the foreseeable future may well be how to give adequate support to those reasonable groups who live in ways that appear deviant to the majority of conventional citizens in democratic states. Given that each new decade ushers in a new wave of ethnocentricism, a just society needs to provide constitutional protection against the possibility that those with a conventional mind-set might use political power to try and oppress others who live under the reasonable, comprehensive doctrines with which they disagree. This means that constitutional protection at the level of application must be reinforced by background principles that emerge at the level of justification.

Should members of the legal profession incorporate some of these considerations into their code of ethics? In the first place, as emphasized in Chapter One, a professional is not supposed to be a mere technocrat. Technocrats can ignore the concrete evil that sometimes follows from the blind use of technical skills, but professionals have an obligation to be more sophisticated than that. It is so banal as to be evil to engage in professional practice without paying attention to the actual consequences of that practice on all stakeholders. Professionals ought to understand that professions are institutions designed for the purpose of serving universal human values for all people in ways consistent with their legitimate differences. Thus, in a pluralistic world, it is important that we do more than strive to master the abstract logic behind the skills of our professional existence. We also must strive to insure that our professional way of life helps to implement ideal values in the world.

It should be clear from these remarks that I think a case can be made for allowing the practices of the Native American Church to be categorized as an exception to the rule. Allowing this kind of exception will, of course, create problems of the kind that worry Justice Scalia. However, future cases will have to be dealt with on a case-by-case basis, and courts will simply have to learn to seriously consider and communicate with minority churches.

The need for professional guidance seems to be increasing at all levels in the public domain. Somehow, the reliance on experts has to be balanced with respect for persons and fairness to individuals. Since professions have generally dealt with this problem in admirable ways, the normative standards behind professionalism should be able to give us some insight into the kinds of relationships that ought to exist between experts and the lay public. It will be useful to end the section on implementation theory with an example of applied ethical reasoning from a context where professionalism bleeds over into a domain that is not usually governed by the expectations found in professional practice. This will help us see how the normative implications of professionalism can be used to restructure economic relationships in a business setting where esoteric knowledge has become a crucial factor.

Example: Contractual Dispute, Business or Professional?

> **For Study:**   What is the usual background status quo for business transactions? What features of Ms. Jones's case indicate that her relationship with the dance studio is similar to a professional relationship? Should these features change the nature of the financial contract?

What follows is a short summary of a case discussed in Braybrooke's text, *Ethics in the World of Business* (1983). (All quotations are taken from Braybrooke's account.) The names of the people involved have been changed, but the facts are summarized as accurately as possible. The case went all the way up to the Florida Appeals Court, but I will not focus on the court's reasoning in this analysis. While it is instructive to compare legal analysis with ethical analysis, it is not necessarily the best way to approach an ethical dilemma. Legal judgments presuppose prior legal contexts that may or may not themselves be ethical, but of course, if a legal context makes up part of the background in an ethical case, it needs to be taken into consideration during the application process.

Background: The General Dilemma

Should business contracts signed by adults always be enforced, or can a party to a contract have the contract nullified in court over the objections of the other party to the contract? We have to accept that the following facts as presented by the parties in this dispute are accurate. It might be useful to have more details, but often in ethics, because we do not have access to all the information we would like, we have to make decisions in a partial state of ignorance. The facts indicate that Mrs. Jones, "a widow of 51 years and without family, had a yen to be 'an accomplished dancer' with the hopes of finding 'new interest in life'" (p. 68). On February 10, 1961, she attended a promotional party at a dancing school where she was confronted with the school's accomplished sales technique. "Her grace and poise were elaborated upon and her rosy future as an 'excellent dancer' was painted for her in vivid and glowing colors" (p. 68). Eventually, for $14.50 cash, the school sold her eight-half-hour dance lessons to be utilized within a month. This started her on a course of action that led to her buying fourteen "dance courses," which in less than sixteen months would add up to "2302 hours of dancing lessons for a total cash outlay of $31,090.45" (p. 68). All fourteen courses were agreed to in writing and paid for in advance, so there is apparently a series of legal contracts in this case. Each contract had the following addendum in heavy black print: "No one will be informed that you are taking dancing lessons. Your relations with us are held in strict confidence" (p. 68). (Notice: Strict confidentiality is usually one of the marks of a fiduciary relationship.) The dance school assured her that she had "grace and poise" and was making progress that would soon make her a skillful dancer. They implied additional lessons would do the trick; soon she would become a beautiful dancer,

> "capable of dancing with the most accomplished dancers"; that she was "rapidly progressing in the development of her dancing skill and gracefulness," etc. She was given dance aptitude tests for the ostensible purpose of "determining" the number of remaining hours of instructions needed by her from time to time . . . (pp. 68–69)

Her complaint to the court alleges that she has no dance aptitude and has trouble hearing the beat. She claims the dance instructors knew their statements were

> false and contrary to the plaintiff's true ability, [but] the truth was withheld from the plaintiff for the sole and specific intent to deceive and defraud the plaintiff and to induce her in the purchasing of additional hours of dance lessons. . . . In other words, while she first exulted that she was entering the "spring of her life," she finally was awakened to the fact there was "spring" neither in her life nor in her feet. (p. 69)

Mrs. Jones asked the court to do an accounting of how much she owed for actual time spent in dance lessons, deduct that amount from the $31,090.45 already paid, nullify the dance contracts not yet used, and then return the balance of the money not already used up by dance lessons. The dance school, on the other hand, argued that

> contracts can only be rescinded for fraud or misrepresentation as to a material fact, rather than an opinion, prediction or expectation, and that the statements and representations set forth at length in the complaint were in the category of "trade puffing," within its legal orbit. (p. 69)

The defense attorneys for the dance company are arguing that ideal business transactions are defined by the expectations of reasonable people. A dominant background business norm is that reasonable people need honest information regarding *material facts* in a transaction in order to make intelligent decisions. This means that all those *factors that will substantially affect a reasonable person's choices in a transaction* must be shared with other parties, for example, if your car has a cracked block, that is a material fact that ought to be shared with other parties who might buy your car. However, reasonable consumers also expect *puffery,* which refers to *harmless exaggerations allowed in the law to entertain consumers.* Reasonable people do not confuse harmless puffery with material facts. The dance school maintains that its behavior did not go beyond the legal limits placed on the use of puffery in the business world between reasonable people. In using a bit of puffery, the instructors were only giving their opinion; they were not engaging in fraud by selling a material good that was in fact misrepresented. Since Mrs. Jones was an adult consumer who voluntarily signed the agreements, the dance company is right to consider her to be a reasonable person. They want her to keep the contracts she made.

Business Norms and Trader's Morality: This dispute occurred in Florida, in a free enterprise economy, where sellers and consumers meet as individuals under conditions of fair competition. A major assumption of the *free market* philosophy is that *all transactions between autonomous adults are based on voluntary consent.* Under conditions of voluntary consent all contracts are just, since people do not consent to being harmed. In general, then, consent theory draws our attention to the fact that contracts are valid because autonomous agents are capable of looking out for their own interests (which is why children are not allowed to sign contracts). However, since law governs business transactions, traders cannot do anything they please. Practices such as fraud, coercion, theft, and misrepresentation of material facts are not considered to be fair. Because they compromise consent, they are immoral and illegal business practices. So long as there is no obvious coercion or fraud on the part of either party, however, we assume both parties have a legitimate claim to have a contract enforced as is. People of good faith will uphold their contracts.

Traders in the market place are assumed to be rational autonomous agents, who voluntarily enter into financial transactions at arms length. They do not worry about the other trader as they might if selling a product to a friend or relative. This means it is normal for them to have different conflicting interests, and they have no special duties to look out for the well-being of others. In a free market many people assume "trader's morality" ought to be used as the primary background principle of appropriateness. *Trader's morality* assumes *"the relationship between strangers in the marketplace is best ... conceived of as ruling out force and outright fraud (for example, not delivering the goods specified) but of licensing both sides of a transaction to take advantage of the other's mistakes"* (Braybrooke, 1983, pp. 70–71). This principle leads to *caveat emptor,* or *"buyer beware."* You can't assume a seller will tell you everything you might like to know, so two people engaged in a trading transaction are expected to be wary, bargain tough, and then sign the contract. Since the contract is based on autonomous consent, no matter what the outcome, the agreement can be considered to be just. It follows from this, that since traders only sign contracts when they believe they have something to gain, other things being equal, an analysis of any particular contract will reveal how both parties to the contract expected to benefit. This is the approach that the lower court apparently used in evaluating the contract between Mrs. Jones and the dance company. They treated her as a trader, and told her to pay up. She appealed to a higher court.

Trader's morality should not be confused with professionalism, since the governing norm in trader's morality is the pursuit of self-interest, not the pursuit of a professional value. In fact, businesses will generally reject professional standards in so far as they want to emphasize the doctrine of "buyer beware." According to trader's morality, the only reason to be honest or benevolent or kind in market relations is if it will contribute to your profit margin. Business people do not have ethical duties as business people to take care of the other. We need to consider whether Mrs. Jones's case ought to be decided using trader's morality or the morality behind professional practice.

Trader's morality assumes that because business transactions are private undertakings between rational autonomous agents, other things being equal, the content of contracts should not be matters of public concern. The general public is simply not a stakeholder in most contracts. Eliminating the public as a stakeholder, however, can have public consequences in itself. Teaching that people do or ought to pursue self-interest in all transactions has an impact on how students begin to interpret the world. It teaches egoism, which leads to the economization of human relationships. This by-product of trader's morality ought to be of concern to the public, because as a background context for the business world it fosters moral skepticism that leads to questions such as: "Isn't the idea of business ethics an oxymoron?" This skeptical point of view is captured in simple jokes such as: "Dad, what is business ethics anyway?" "Well, son, it's like this. What if a little old lady comes into the store and inadvertently overpays by 100 dollars?'" "Oh, I see, Dad. The ethical part has to do with the question: 'Should I tell her she made a mistake or should I keep the extra 100 dollars?'" "No, Son, that's not it. Business ethics is about whether or not to tell my partner about the sudden extra profit."

Professionalism in a Contractual Context: "Trader's morality" with its "buyer beware" principle of appropriateness represents one possible background from which to view the case between Mrs. Jones and the dance company, but it is not the only option. As discussed in Chapter Two, professions are institutions that serve social values under the principles of appropriateness contained in their codes of ethics. When a relationship is not between traders but between a professional and a client, different expectations hold. The relationship that exists between a professional and a client is typically characterized as a fiduciary relationship, which means a relationship of mutual trust. The professional is in a position of having superior knowledge, and she has an obligation to use that superior position to serve the client, society, the profession, and herself. Thus, the contract between a professional and a client is not the kind of contract we find between typical traders in a marketplace. In other words, profit is not considered the primary value in this context. But, what do we do with business institutions and practices that are not so clearly defined by a background professional code of ethics? For instance, what is the appropriate ethical background from which to view a dance studio's relationship with its "clients?" Should we use the professional model, or the model of trader's morality?

Ideal Theory

As stated earlier, I usually begin my own analysis of problems by asking Kantian questions. I see the business world as a subset of a larger world governed by the regulatory ideal of a kingdom of ends. Kant is clear that in an interdependent world we must use each other to get our needs met, but we should not use each other as a means only. The mere fact that there is a dispute does not mean that the parties are not respecting each other as ends unto themselves. It is possible that both sides feel they are treating the other with respect in enforcing a contract, because they assume the other entered into the contract in good faith. The burden of proof is on anyone who would want to nullify a signed contract. They will either have to reject Mrs. Jones's capacity to give voluntary consent, question the honesty of the communication between the parties involved, find some special duty that is being violated by the contract, or argue that society has an overriding interest in forbidding contracts of this particular type.

It is possible for principles such as benevolence and caring to enter into this kind of dispute, for example, what if the contract will lead to abject misery for one of the parties? However, we do not have enough information to appeal to either of these two principles. We do not know how wealthy Mrs. Jones might be; perhaps $31,000 means little to her and she is only disappointed because her dancing has not improved. We do not know how financially strapped the dance school might be; perhaps they will have to declare bankruptcy and lay off employees if they return the money. Without additional information, the best policy is to stay focused on the nature of the obligations that logically follow from the norms behind contracts.

Implementation, All Things Considered

Even when issues of private profit are concerned, moral theories are still used to set boundaries on how profit ought to be pursued. For instance, often societies decide that it is not ethical to allow certain practices in the business world, for example, child labor, fraud, coercion, theft, deception, or taking unfair advantage of necessitous circumstances (e.g., gouging people during earthquakes, hurricanes, droughts, war, or emotional crises). I assume, therefore, that business practices are and ought to be covered by moral norms. As a moral agent affected by what goes on in the business world, why should I accept the view that business is only about private profit? Why not characterize *business* as first, *an institution sanctioned by society to be the arena within which we meet the survival and economic needs of the people,* and, second, as *a place where people can engage in fair exchange of commodities for their mutual advantage?* When characterized in this public manner, placing ethical boundaries on business transactions does not seem so inappropriate; business ethics seems like less of an oxymoron.

From this perspective it is possible to see many business transactions as similar to (but not synonymous with) professional transactions. The system of business can be considered to be in the service of broad human values. It asks participants to be dedicated to something beyond self-interest, and to voluntarily submit to codes of fair and just business practices for the good of the whole. Profit is good, but it's not the only value. Thus, there are more stakeholders in this case than may appear at first glance. Obviously Mrs. Jones and the dance school are stakeholders since it is their contractual dispute. But other stakeholders include the members of the business world who have a vested interest in seeing contracts that are signed upheld (to them, the burden of proof is on Mrs. Jones to show cause why the court should overturn this contract), as well as the members of society who will be affected by general business practices. What tone do we want to establish for business practices in general?

Since this case has reached a state's appeals court, the state is an additional stakeholder that has an interest in having the case resolved in a way that will set the proper precedents for the future. Do we want policies that allow courts to enter into business transactions after the fact and reverse contracts that were signed by adults? What background standards do we want to establish for valid contracts between consumers and businesspersons, and between clients and those that provide a service? Let's return to the nature of this specific contract and offer a solution.

Solution: There are elements of a fiduciary relationship between Mrs. Jones and the dance school, so this is not a typical contract that we would expect to find between traders who are simply negotiating an exchange of commodities. It is a psychological fact that Mrs. Jones is not a business-woman engaged in a trading transaction. She is going through a period when she is emotionally vulnerable; she is alone, without family, and looking for a new beginning in life. So, this transaction involves a person's fundamental hopes and dreams. Why is this relevant? Traders do business "at arm's length," (p. 70) with a clear head, and no pretensions to intimacy or to duties to watch out for the well-being of the other party. The Florida Appeals Court argued that because the dance lessons were not conducted at arm's length, a special fiduciary duty was incurred that is similar to those in a professional relationship. Professional practice is not conducted "at arm's length," because professionals are serving vital human needs and the relationship with clients is not between people equal in power. People come to them precisely because they are led to believe the professional can help them with their needs. Clients are vulnerable parties who must place their trust in the professional's competence and his willingness to live up to the obligation to communicate honestly. These expectations give partners to a contract extra duties not to take advantage, which includes being cautious with puffery.

Overall, the practices of the dance school in this case seem unethical. If I assume she had been honestly dealt with as a participant in a Habermasian practical discourse, I cannot see how a reasonable trader could have expected a sufficient return on the investment to have voluntarily signed such an agreement. Thus, I conclude Mrs. Jones was either deceived by *puffery* that went beyond what is legally permissible, or she was in a legally relevant condition of instability at the time she signed the contract. Should the dance school have looked after her needs with more care? They presented themselves in a professional light to a fairly vulnerable needy person who is not a normal "at arm's length" trader. There was a fiduciary relationship involving confidentiality (they promised her they would keep her lessons a secret). They presented themselves as being experts with the skills and esoteric knowledge to make her a dancer who would be able to dance "with the most accomplished dancers." Given that Mrs. Jones was hoping to develop a way of life around these accomplishments, she was not simply buying a luxury item. To her, this was a matter vital to the rest of her life. So she hired experts to satisfy her fundamental needs; they portrayed themselves in a professional light, and she was more like a client than a trader in the market place. It follows that special obligations to care for the other were created by this contract. She was not in a good position to judge her own progress, and the "experts" should have used their esoteric knowledge to give her sound advice about how bad her investment really was. In short, I think the dance school portrayed themselves as trustworthy, and then used puffery to confuse the client, making it possible to take advantage of her necessitous circumstances. A reasonable trader, who had been honestly dealt with, would never sign so many contracts, and they should not be allowed to stand. The dance school has a right to that portion of the payment that went for honest lessons, but the rest should be returned to Mrs. Jones.

As a citizen, I want to encourage the institutions in my society to be honest, fair, and not take advantage of vulnerable parties. There is still plenty of room for fair competition and dynamic business activities without letting businesses take advantage of people going through transitional crises. In this particular case, the findings of the Florida Appeals Court paralleled portions of my analysis. For similar legal reasons, they also nullified the contract.

~ Summary on Application Discourse

> **For Study:**   What is the major limitation of trader's morality? What general steps need to be taken to begin the implementation of moral equality?

Habermas claims that the way we have institutionalized bureaucracy under the banner of instrumental reason is only one possible form of implementation among many. He argues that "the discontents of modernity are not rooted in rationalization as such, but in the failure to develop and institutionalize all the different dimensions of reason in a balanced way" (cited in McCarthy, 1984, p. xxxix). Trader's morality falls into this trap by taking a form of strategic reasoning that is appropriate for a limited set of financial transactions, and then trying to generalize it to account for all the relationships that involve money. This is at odds with what we would expect to see if we were consistently using universal metaphors that give each of us equal moral status as fellow workers. Thus, in so far as professional practices contribute to modern bureaucratic forms of economization that reduce our moral status from that of fellow workers to that of dependent clients, they need to be radically reformed so that they get back in line with the Enlightenment's agenda of mutual respect between moral equals who are not equals with regard to knowledge and power. And certainly they should never turn clients into equal traders, who have the responsibility to beware of the professional.

Given that we are individually embedded in particular ways of life, what steps should be taken to make universal values practically useful rather than red flags for possible oppression? An adequate theory of implementation will tie local contexts to the more abstract levels of ideal theory to help people stay focused on the abstract reality of "moral equality" and "moral autonomy." So we will need to do the following kinds of things:

First, we should critique institutional structures and our codes of ethics to make sure that they remain consistent with the logic of universal morality.

Institutions should not be overly paternalistic, so they ought to encourage people to become active moral agents who can accept responsibility.

Second, the lesson learned from contemporary developmental, constructivist, and clinical psychology indicates that a reconstructed liberalism should lobby for institutions that give everyone a "place" in which not only their standard basic needs can be satisfied but also their particular need to define their own unique approach to life.

Third, the theory should emphasize that institutional design cannot be determined ahead of time by "outsiders" to the way of life under consideration, even if they are sympathetic to that way of life. We have seen how easy it is for people to project their own special interests onto other people's contexts. Thus, in complex cases, it is banal to assume that well-meaning representatives who share only the standardized interests of a privileged group can decide for others who are fundamentally different in their outlook.

Fourth, all the people affected by institutional arrangements need to participate in decision making at all levels. Obviously, as the laws dealing with children illustrate, unequal treatment can be justified when differences are so great that it is unreasonable to think of people as free and equal adults. But, if legislators, judges, and lawyers (and all other professionals) all come from a homogeneous privileged group of planners, then their decisions are bound to remain myopic to a degree, even if, as good philosophical liberals, they strive mightily to be neutral, rational, and empathic. The same problem will arise if we stack professions with representatives from any homogeneous segment of society.

Fifth, we need to strive for broad representation in the professions. Thus, we need to reform the system that determines entry into professions so that they will be open to fellow workers from all walks of life.

Sixth, at the very least, we should feel some pressure to reform current professional structures so as to adjust for the bureaucratization and economization that have infected them. The goal should be to help those who are affected by professional practice to speak with their own voice and to be heard during consultation with members of a profession.

Seventh, because our differences represent the particularized, substantive expression of our shared universal status as ends unto ourselves, mere toleration of difference is not enough. Most forms of diversity should also be welcomed as particular expressions of our shared humanity. Moral metaphors ought to be designed to help us focus on our obligation to treat the differences between fellow workers with respect. Under this conception, reform would start with people where we find them; it would acknowledge their differences and encourage them to participate in rational, empathic dialogue to construct out of the materials of their different histories as good an account of mutual understanding as they can. This insight is the basis for Habermas's insistence on a participatory principle, and Rourke's (1992) insistence that professionals need to be trained so that they become experts in talking across differences.

Eighth: And so forth.

The Practical Impact of a Course in Ethics

> **For Study:**   How is an ethics course supposed to affect student attitudes?

Habermas (1976) is surely correct when he argues that the knowledge gained through ethical reflection changes not only the way we see ethical events but also the type of event we are capable of considering. He makes the intriguing observation that inquiry into ethical theory ought to be at the same time self-reflective inquiry into how our own norms ought to be normed (p. 86). In an important sense, then, reflection about ethical theory is also historical self-reflection at the formal operational level. There is a basic incompatibility between saying "I believe people are morally obligated to do X" and saying "I don't have to ever do X even if I do believe that people morally ought to." Moral and ethical "ought" statements are not matters of taste. Once you understand them, you cannot choose to reject them for personal reasons without feeling obligated to give some kind of account that should make sense to other moral agents. If you refuse to try and act on what you claim is morally right, it will be hard for us to believe that you really care about doing the right thing. People who act in such a contradictory manner are either terribly confused or they are telling lies. Thus, we assume that if you learn anything important about what people ought to do, this knowledge will change you on a practical level. In fact, I have research data that suggests a college ethics course has a practical effect on the attitudes of most students. Over a five-year period, I gave the University of Minnesota DIT (Defining Issues Test) test in all my ethics classes at the beginning and end of each semester. This test has been nationally normed, and it tests how much a person thinks she ought to take a principled approach to solving moral dilemmas. That is, the higher the score, the more likely a student is to approach moral dilemmas from a postconventional principled position. In general, college students will move up 10 points on the DIT test after four years of college (Rest, 1986). However, most of my students move up ten points after one semester of applied ethics. Thus, we are clearly intervening in student lives when we teach ethics, and this text is partly an attempt to justify this kind of intervention.

The fact that an ethics course can have this kind of practical impact explains why there is a certain danger to taking an ethics course. You may come to believe that some of the things you enjoy doing are not morally acceptable. If you do not know that a behavior is immoral, then doing it is not really immoral, it is amoral. You may be banally ignorant, but at least you are not evil. However, once you come to understand that an action is a violation of a norm you believe in, you can never again perform the behavior in an amoral fashion. With knowledge of right and wrong comes the burden of guilt (the proverbial apple in the Garden of Eden). After an ethics course you will be even more accountable, for you will have ethical knowledge that you did not have before.

On the other hand, you should also be in an improved position to give a theoretical justification for your moral behavior. The benefits of rational ethics far outweigh possible inconveniences, and improving one's ethical abilities is itself a moral duty.

REFERENCES

BRAYBROOKE, DAVID. (1983). *Ethics in the world of business.* Totowa, NJ: Rowman & Allanheld.

COOPER, DAVID. (2001). An introduction to applied ethics with contributions by Burleigh Wilkins. In Aleksander Jokic (Ed.), *Festschrift in honor of Burleigh Wilkins* (pp. 193–228). New York: Peter Lang.

COOPER, DAVID & COOPER, KATHERINE. (1999). The Jurisprudence of difference. In C. Gray (Ed.), *The philosophy of law: An encyclopedia* (pp. 205–7). New York: Garland.

CRENSHAW, KIMBERLÉ. (1989). Demarginalizing the intersection of race and sex: A black feminist critique of antidiscrimination doctrine, feminist theory, and antiracist politics. *University of Chicago Law Forum* 139, pp. 139–67.

GUNTHER, KLAUS. (1993). *The sense of appropriateness: Application discourses in morality and law.* John Farrell (Trans.). Albany: State University of New York Press.

HABERMAS, JURGEN. (1976). *Communication and the evolution of society.* Thomas McCarthy (Trans.). Boston: Beacon Press.

———. (1991). *Moral consciousness and communicative action.* Christian Lenhardt & Shierry Weber Nicholsen (Trans.). Cambridge, MA: The MIT Press.

———. (1996). *Between facts and norms: Contributions to a discourse theory of law and democracy.* William Rehg (Trans.). Cambridge, MA: The MIT Press.

———. (1997). The European nation-state—Its achievements and its limitations. On the past and future of sovereignty and citizenship. W. Krawietz, E. Pattaro, & A. Erh-Soon Tay (Eds.), *Rule of law: Political and legal systems in transition* (pp. 109–22). Berlin: Duncker & Humblot.

KOHLBERG, LAWRENCE. (1971). From is to ought: How to commit the naturalistic fallacy and get away with it in the study of moral development. In T. Mischel (Ed.), *Cognitive development and epistemology.* New York: Academic Press.

MACKINNON, CATHERINE A. (1989). *Toward a feminist theory of the state.* Cambridge, MA: Harvard University Press.

MCCARTHY, THOMAS. (1984). Translator's introduction. In Jurgen Habermas (1984), *The theory of communicative action, Vol 1.* Thomas McCarthy (Trans.). Boston: Beacon Press.

RAND, AYN. (1999). Man's rights. In Aeon Skoble & Tibor Machan (Eds.), *Political philosophy* (pp. 425–32). Upper Saddle River, NJ: Prentice Hall.

RAWLS, JOHN. (1971). *A theory of justice.* Cambridge, MA: Harvard University Press.

———. (1993). *Political liberalism.* New York: Columbia University Press.

REST, J. (Ed.), (1986). *Moral development: Advances in research and theory.* New York: Praeger.

ROURKE, NANCY. (1992). Talking across difference: An experiment in perspectivism. AMINTAPHIL Conference. October 1992. Also, see her work in progress: Toward a theory of lawyering in a world of difference: Implications for the adjective law.

SARASON, SEYMOUR B. (1972). *The creation of settings and the future societies.* Cambridge, MA: Brookline Books.

WILLS, GARRY. (1978). *Inventing America.* New York: Vintage Books.

WILKINS, BURLEIGH. (1994). The moral *prima facie,* obligation to obey the law. *Journal of social philosophy* 25 (2), Fall 1994. pp. 92–96.

———. (1997). The third principle of justice. *The journal of ethics* 1 (4), January 1997. pp. 355–74.

Glossary of Key Terms

Absolute: Cross-cultural universal values that are binding in all contexts and have unconditional value.

Accountability procedure: A set of institutional rules designed to encourage people to remain thoughtful about their actions, just as they would if they had to explain what they were doing to a third person.

Age of Enlightenment: The eighteenth century, when philosophy tried to transcend social and cultural idiosyncrasies by grounding moral judgments in universal absolute values.

Agonistic: Refers to use of language as a tool in a struggle for advantage over an adversary, as opposed to its communicative use.

Always already: A phrase to draw attention to the fact we are always situated in a social setting, which means we are biased by our past experiences and language, so there is no privileged position outside of history from which to make moral judgments.

Amoral: People who are not responsible because they lack either the knowledge and/or the capacity needed for moral choice (e.g., babies, the retarded, the insane, the comatose).

Applied ethics: Investigates how theoretically justified abstract ideals contained in foundational principles can be applied at lower and lower concrete levels to help resolve the kinds of value conflicts that arise in local contexts.

Application discourse: Discussions about what ought to be done to make a concrete situation conform to an abstract ideal.

Argumentation, Universal principle of: A principle that is universal, since everyone engaged in argumentation can agree that the principle should be used to judge norms before they can be imposed on them: *All* affected can *freely* accept the consequences and the side effects that the *general* observance of a controversial norm can be anticipated to have for the satisfaction of the interests of *each individual* (and these consequences are preferred to those of known alternative possibilities for regulation).

Autonomous moral agent: In Kant's duty ethics, a being governed by a will that makes law for itself, controlled only by one's own moral will. Autonomous people are influenced by, not controlled by, external factors. (See moral autonomy.)

Autonomy: Independent control of one's own life, or not being controlled from the outside. (See *personal autonomy* and *moral autonomy*.)

Banality of evil: Evil that results from motives that are not in themselves wrong in a proper context, but which seem excessively trite, thoughtless, or careless as moral motives in complex contexts that require a careful evaluation of right and wrong.

Bias paradox: That condition arising when, if all criticisms are equally biased, then "the critique of oppression" is just another bias even though the critic wants to be taken more seriously than the oppressors whom she criticizes.

Black/white fallacy: A form of dualistic thinking in which the possibility for compromise is denied: There is no middle ground on complex issues; positions are black or white, there are no shades of gray.

Burden of proof: Whoever wants to challenge or change the moral status quo has the burden of justifying the challenge or change.

Categorical Imperative: Kant's moral law. There are four versions; the easiest to apply is: Always treat humanity as an end unto itself never as a means only.

Categorical principle: A principle that applies in all situations; its application is not restricted by any local conditions. Kant says there is only one categorical principle: the categorical imperative, which is called the moral law.

Ceteris paribus: Latin equivalent for "other things being equal." Used to exclude extenuating circumstances for a time to allow a discussion to focus on the ideal case.

Claims about truth and morality: They are intersubjective claims that require us to take a position that can be judged according to agreed upon public standards versus the private preferences of one person or group.

Codes of ethics: The published rules and principles that regulate the behavior of officeholders within particular institutional settings.

Cognitive moral theories: Based on universal standards that are supported by good reasons that will make logical sense to any rational being.

Communicative discourse: For this type of communication to be possible intersubjective norms of communication must be known on a procedural level by each individual who is a competent language user.

Communicative rationality: Refers to the social and structural universal norms of discourse that make it possible for people to come together in communicative exchanges where they attempt to reach mutual understanding. It is rational to accept noncoercive, logical, normative, processes that facilitate reaching understanding, and since disruption makes discourse impossible, it is irrational to disrupt these normative processes when the goal is communication.

Communitarians: The perspective that says commitment to community has priority over individualism and/or concerns about autonomy in ethics.

Concrete operational thought: Ability to think logically in causal terms about standard solutions to common concrete problems.

Conditional principle: Applies only when certain local conditions are satisfied. It has the logical form of: If you want x, then you ought to do that which will lead to x, which makes the ought appropriate only if the condition of "wanting" is satisfied first.

Consequentialist: Right is determined by good consequences. Look at the various options to see how much nonmoral value or good can be promoted by each option.

Conventional level: A developmental step where one becomes loyal to the rules and norms of one's group. Related idea: an ethnocentric commitment to the status quo.

Critical self-reflective dialogue: To engage in critical dialogue with those who have opposing points of view so that our own background assumptions will be evaluated at the same time that they are being used to analyze and judge all the other background assumptions that are used to attribute meaning to human experience.

Cultural relativism: A metaethical position that claims ethical values can only be judged relative to the particular culture within which they arose. Rejects the possibility that there could be absolute or universal ethical values that transcend cultural boundaries.

Decentering: A process of moving from the egocentric child's capacity to understand and care about him or herself, through ethnocentric understanding and caring about the family or tribe, to a universal perspective where we understand and care about the abstract ideals of humanity.

Decision procedure: A device to help people achieve a clear focus on all the relevant factual and moral variables in dilemma situations.

Declarative knowledge: Is expressed consciously in symbolic form using words and signs, in contrast to procedural knowledge that is unconscious and not declared in words.

Deontological: Another term for nonconsequential ethics. Some property besides good consequences determines what is right and wrong.

Deontological reason: An impartial point of view is arrived at by abstracting from the concrete particularity of the person's situation.

Developmentalist, constructivist approach to ethics: Emphasizes the way that cognitive and ethical orientations are constructed out of background maturational stages and social experiences that evolve as we adjust to conflict situations.

Difference principle: Rawls's third principle of justice: All inequalities in the distribution of primary social goods are unjust unless they are to the advantage of everyone in the society (i.e., the bottom class must also benefit from the inequalities).

Difference, the problem of: How do we treat people as equals in morality or in the law and yet show respect for the diversity caused by their unique individual differences.

Discourse ethics: Uses the norms of honest practical communication as the foundation for a universal ethical theory. Principle: Everyone ought to always follow those norms that claim to be valid because they meet (or could meet) with the approval of all affected in their capacity as participants in a practical discourse.

Discourse of application: To critically reflect on how universal principles ought to apply to concrete cases.

Discourse of justification: To critically reflect on the background values that ought to govern other things being equal, and that ought to justify lower-level acts and rules.

Discretion in professions: When professionals have leeway to use their esoteric knowledge to figure out the best means for carrying out the goals of their profession in specific cases.

Divine command theory: Any ethical system based on religious foundations that says the right-making characteristic in morality is the commands of a deity.

Duties of station: All the special duties (and rights) that apply only to people who move into an institutional setting to take responsibility for the specific social roles defined in the code.

Dysfunctional from the moral point of view: When an institution produces agents with such extreme personality styles that they cannot function as morally autonomous adults on either the rational or the caring dimension.

Economization: When we convert relationships into ones based purely on financial incentives, in effect allowing market forces to determine the quality of the interactions between client and professional.

Egocentric: Only capable of understanding and caring about one's own point of view.

Emancipatory virtues: Enabling virtues that help people become Socratic in their ability to care about social norms, gain theoretical understanding about them, and yet critically evaluate and choose between the available concrete and theoretical options.

Emotivism: A metaethical position that claims all value statements are merely expressions of emotion, and therefore, that all moral claims could only have the logical status of emotional exclamations that lack the cognitive content that truth claims are supposed to have.

Ends in themselves: Autonomous beings, that is, beings that ought to control their own lives with their own principles, so they never think of themselves as objects to be used by others.

Enlightenment philosophy: A period primarily in the eighteenth century when philosophers tried to find universal ideals that would be seen as self-evidently true by all rational people.

Equality, formal: Treating everyone exactly the same according to a standard, regardless of local contingencies or differences.

Equals, moral: When people share the same moral status, for example, as seen in the phrase "all men are created equal."

Equal substantive protection: Is more than formal, it must have a concrete local impact that takes differences into consideration.

Esoteric knowledge: Information that is so theoretical and technical that the general public does not easily acquire it. To obtain it usually requires years of higher education in professional and graduate schools.

Ethical egoism: A moral theory based on the foundation that one's own good is the ultimate value. Thus, the foundational principle states: "Everyone ought to promote his or her own best interest."

Ethics, academic: A dialogical discipline that tries to understand in a rational, self-critical manner how we ought to resolve various kinds of value conflicts.

Ethnocentric: When one only has the ability to understand and care about the point of view of one's own group.

Extrinsic goods: Useful things. Those things we value because they are useful for getting other things of value.

Fellow workers: Kant's name for all of those who engage in dialogue together to search for truth while rationally evaluating justifications for moral claims.

Fiduciary relationship: When a client/professional relationship is built on mutual trust and a sense that obligations must respect the equal moral status of everyone in the relationship.

Form/content distinction: Form refers to the type or kind of reasoning used, and content refers to the specific example of the kind. For example, "I hate you" and "I love you" have radically different emotional content, but both have the same form since both are emotional expressions.

Formal operational: A capacity that makes it possible to think on a theoretical level. The capacity to use mental operations or skills to create a hypothesis, to conceive of new possibilities before they exist, to theorize, to think about thinking, and/or to evaluate the logic of our evaluations.

Foundational principles: The most basic principles in a system of morality; they obligate us to give certain values top priority in all our moral decisions.

Future-oriented consent: To try to make better decisions for vulnerable others by asking: "What would these people consent to in the future when they better understand their position."

Good versus Right: Considerations of the good are about what makes us happy; considerations of the right are about what ought to be done as a matter of duty.

Good reasons: Reasons that satisfy intersubjective standards that are acceptable to all members of a group.

Hermeneutics: The practice of interpreting stories or written texts or the study of methods of interpretation.

Heteronomy: A condition in which actions are controlled by forces outside the moral will, including being controlled by desire rather than reason.

Human rights: Rights that are universal and protect individuals from local "isms of exclusion" by giving them moral status that transcends national borders.

Ideal theory: Any theory that attempts to justify the prescriptive principles and rules that are constructed to tell us what we ought to do other things being equal.

Ideals: Are abstract values representing perfect states of affairs that people think should exist when things are what they ought to be, but which may exist only in our discussions until we learn how to implement them.

Impartial judgment: To avoid personal agendas when making judgments by using the moral point of view to give all people equal consideration.

Impartial spectator: Our internal ability to observe and judge our own behavior from an impartial perspective, as though we were outside of ourselves.

Imperfect duties: Obligations where the extent of a duty and to whom it is owed cannot be specifically established ahead of time. For example, the duty to be charitable is imperfect because it does not perfectly define how much charity is required or to whom the charity is owed.

Implementation: Similar to application discourse; the study of the best strategies to use to build ideals into the structure of concrete institutions all things considered.

Inalienable right: A right that is so important to human nature that we cannot be separated from it, as we can be from extrinsic values.

Incommensurables: Values that are so radically different that there is no common standard that can be used to measure the properties of one set against the properties of the other.

Indefeasible: A term meaning that a right cannot be defeated or voided by other social considerations.

Integrity: When a person has emotional commitment to legitimate ends or rules of conduct.

Intersubjective: When the logic, value, or meaning of a social setting is determined by the shared expectations of everyone in the setting.

Institution: Any rule-governed relationship.

Instrumental or strategic rationality: The use of rational processes to choose the means to a predetermined goal that may or may not itself be rational.

Intrinsic good: Something that is valued for its own sake. It is always a goal or an end.

Introjection: To unconsciously internalize values that originated externally.

"Isms" of exclusion: Ideological systems of belief that allow people to marginalize, exclude, oppress, or ignore those with whom they disagree.

Justice: Concerns the area of morality that deals with justifying and protecting rights or giving people their due.

Jurisprudence of difference: The study of how the law ought to deal with the fact we are not only moral equals but are also different. This jurisprudence tries to decide when a difference should also make a difference in the law.

Justification, levels of: Policies and actions need to be justified, and the justification must be logically appropriate for the level of abstraction, i.e., act, rule, principle, theory.

Justification discourse: Dialogue where the goal is to justify actions, rules, principles, and universal norms by basing them on a theoretically justified moral theory.

Kingdom of ends: A society composed of autonomous people all of whom use the categorical imperative as their foundational moral maxim.

Laissez-faire capitalism: Implies unimpeded, absolute individual discretion on the part of property owners to use, trade, or sell their property without government regulation, even in emergencies, wars, and catastrophes.

Legitimation crisis: When many members of a community begin to challenge the legitimacy of basic institutions.

Life-world: In Habermas, it is the historically learned value heritage of a language community that makes the world seem "always already" familiar when people begin to reflect.

Liminality: A condition that exists temporarily when a tribal member enters a rite of passage that allows him or her to take on a new tribal role and thus critically compare the new role with previous roles.

Logical positivism: A metaphilosophy that asserted propositions could not be true or false unless they could be empirically verified by some observation or experience. This emphasis on empirical validation led to the metaethical position called emotivism in ethics.

Matters of taste: Subjective values that are so private they do not significantly affect other people; they only need to be judged from the point of view of the person who has them.

Maxims: Intentions or principles that explain or justify actions.

Metaethics: Attempts to answer questions about the nature of an ethical point of view, the nature of ethical theories, the meaning of ethical terms, and the types of reasons that can serve as justifications in morality.

Metaphorical extensions: A capacity of the human imagination that allows us to carry meaning from one level or domain of experience to another.

Metaphors: Language constructions that can be used to carry meaning from one context to another in order to clarify the second context.

Metaphysical society: A society that relies on a common system of beliefs about the ultimate nature of reality and the place of citizens in that reality.

Monological: The idea that an ideal observer can retreat inside his or her own pure reason and judge between right and wrong in isolation from the active participation of those affected. Or, when one person, choosing by himself under the constraint of pure reason, or behind a veil of ignorance, can figure out all by himself what is right and wrong.

Moral accountability: In principle, moral agents must be prepared to give those they affect an explanation that will show how their actions respect the moral autonomy of those affected.

Moral authority: The authority you appeal to when you justify the rightness of actions or rules. A statement condemning an action has moral authority when all competent agents in the language community reach an intersubjective agreement that the violation in question should not happen to anyone.

Moral autonomy: To be governed by social principles that are self-imposed, because as a caring moral agent, you believe these are the kind of principles that would at least in principle be acceptable to all other agents who also rationally impose moral principles on themselves.

Moral claims: Are intersubjective statements about what is right or appropriate. They must be redeemed (validated) with good reasons that make sense to others in a life-world.

Moral dilemma: A situation in which mutually exclusive moral actions or choices are equally binding. A social moral dilemma occurs in a society when rational people can be found on both sides of a dispute.

Moral drift: When people make a series of small decisions, without paying attention to the overall goal toward which the series of small decisions is gradually carrying them.

Moral emotions: Appropriate visceral responses to situations governed by duties and obligations. These include feelings such as empathy, sympathy, commitment, loyalty, guilt, shame, resentment, outrage, etc. They are emotional responses that only make sense in an intersubjective context of mutual obligation and shared expectations about how people ought to behave.

Moral equality: We are all equal members of the moral family, with equal moral status, even while we live with the reality of unequal status in the political and economic world.

Moral law: Kant's term for his foundational moral principle. Also called the categorical imperative.

Moral point of view: The standpoint from which moral questions can be judged impartially. It must (1) meet publicly acknowledged rational standards, (2) satisfy conditions of universality, (3) be self-critical rather than ideological, (4) promote generalized empathy and respect among all people, and (5) be compatible with cross-cultural dialogue aimed at mutual agreement.

Moral principles: Are reasons for acting that can justify our actions to other members of our moral community. They prescribe intersubjective reasons for acting.

Moral rationality: A level of reasoning that impartially asks the intersubjective question: "What are the good reasons that can support constraints of justice that must be observed in all life-worlds?"

Moral sense: Scottish communitarian belief in a kind of sixth sense or faculty of perception that allows us to naturally see and approve of benevolent relations and disapprove of selfish ones.

Moral theory: Used to justify the claim that there are moral values that can have universal validity.

Morality: A system of intersubjective norms that give all people mutually understood expectations of how they ought to treat one another.

MPofV: See moral point of view.

Natural rights theory: A theory based on the foundational belief that individuals naturally have special moral standing as holders of rights. Principle: Everyone ought to act in accordance with everyone's inalienable, indefeasible natural rights.

Naturalism: The assumption that values are objective properties existing naturally in the world.

Negative duties: These duties command us to avoid doing something that is harmful, i.e., they tell us what we ought to avoid.

Noncognitivist: A belief that ethical judgments lack the kind of cognitive content that can be considered true or false.

Nonconsequentialism: The status of moral rights and duties does not depend on the consequences they lead to because there is some other more fundamental "right-making" characteristic (such as natural rights or God's commands) that is independent of consequences.

Normative discipline: A discipline that tells us what "ought to be" is normative. To judge or evaluate the validity of belief systems, norms, standards, values, etc. Prescribing norms in contrast to merely describing norms.

Objective: The third-person perspective that avoids subjective bias.

Ought implies can: A famous motto in ethics that draws attention to the logical connection between an agent's responsibility and his or her capacity to act. It is absurd or illogical to give ought commands to people who lack the ability to carry out the command.

Override a claim or right: To set aside a claim that is normally legitimate because a higher moral claim takes precedence. Overriding is not the same as violation.

Paternalism: To make decisions for others for their own good, even if they do not agree with our intervention on their behalf.

Particularist: Explicitly rejects universal assumptions, acknowledges the possible relativity of all interpretations of reality, and asserts that different cultural groups will always be embedded in incommensurable ways of life so to even try to be universal is apt to lead to oppression.

Perfect duties: Duties that are clearly defined in the sense that they do not allow for individual discretion about how or when to carry them out, for example, a duty not to kill, lie, steal, etc.

Performative contradiction: To argue that x is not possible or true even though to make your case you must make use of x.

Personal autonomy: To be controlled by an independent will with a stable, fairly consistent set of beliefs, in contrast to being controlled by (1) biological or introjected social desires that we consciously reject, or (2) social and external forces that we consciously reject.

Philosophical ethics: The disciplined critical study of the validity of moral theories.

Pluralism: When numerous worldviews occupy the public sphere. When there is a number of irreducible ways of living, none of which can have absolute priority over the others, and they occupy the same political space.

Positive duty: Obligation to do something to help people.

Postconventional, autonomous, principled level: The third level of development in Kohlberg's theory of moral development that transcends the ethnocentric conventional level. At this level, one's moral authority becomes abstract universal theory or principled conscience.

Postmetaphysical age: The contemporary human situation where consensus on background moral principles has to be reached without relying on the assumption that everyone in a society conceives of the ultimate nature of the world in the same way.

Postmodernism: A metaethical position encompassing a variety of post-Enlightenment theories, all of which reject the concept of universal foundations for human knowledge and ethics, and which emphasize contextual interpretation, the deconstruction of universal ideas, and the challenging of Enlightenment ideas about universal norms.

Practical reason: The mental capacity to act on the basis of good reasons.

Practical wisdom: The capacity to judge wisely in a variety of practical situations. Aristotle: The capacity to determine what is right whatever the situation. Sometimes called "case wisdom" in the professions.

Pragmatic or strategic reason: Rationality is used in a strategic way to determine the best means for attaining given goals during social interactions, for instance, as in bargaining contexts.

Pragmatics: A linguistic field that studies the performative aspects of *speech acts* rather than the grammatical and syntactical structure of *language*. Focuses on the implications of the underlying universal norms required if discourse is going to allow competent members of speech communities to reach mutual understanding and consensus.

Preconventional Level: The first level of moral development, where people are egocentric and define "ought" statements by reference to personal desires for rewards and attempts to avoid punishments.

Prescriptive versus descriptive: Statements that prescribe how events ought to be as opposed to describing how they are.

Prima facie: Background foundations or ideals on which we ought to base our ethical decisions, other things being equal. *Prima facie* obligations are those for which there is a strong but not always conclusive reason for doing whatever the obligations require.

Principle of appropriateness: Principles designed to help moral agents figure out how to apply universal norms in concrete particular situations.

Principles: moral ones: Statements that justify or give reasons for acting.

Procedural knowledge: A type of knowledge that is based on bodily procedures that allow us to do things automatically without reflection or conscious awareness. Modes of knowing that are so basic that they precede language use or our ability to talk about them. Habit, automatic behavior without thought.

Profession: Any state-supported organization staffed by licensed experts with esoteric knowledge, and to whom the government has given the privilege of autonomous, monopolistic control over the delivery of services that are essential for promoting certain vital social values.

Pure reason: The autonomous capacity to exercise the intellect without letting it be controlled by the body's heteronomous inclinations.

Qualitative data: Involves subjective states of experience that include feelings, values, and the meanings we give to the world.

Quantitative data: Relating to "objective" aspects of experience that can be measured and recorded by third-party observers.

Rational person standard: Emphasizes that moral decisions must be based on reasons that are universal because they can in principle be accepted by everyone affected after critical public debate.

Rationality: An intersubjective stance requiring one to take a position that can be judged according to agreed upon public standards versus the private preferences of one person or group.

>   **Ethical level of:**   Intersubjective goals are not fixed only by preexisting *personal* preferences. Preferences themselves must be reevaluated in light of concerns about self-realization as a social being in a community.

Instrumental level of: Focusing on the best means to achieve ends that are already given and may or may not be rational.

Moral level of: The highest order of decentered intersubjectivity, because people confront interpersonal conflicts resulting from opposed cross-cultural interests. Good reasons are tied to intersubjective, cross-cultural consensus on norms of justice for all life-worlds.

Strategic or pragmatic level of: What a person rationally ought to do is relative to the person's subjective wants or ends which may or may not be rational.

Reasonable man (person) standard: The morality of the average man in the street or the feelings of standard members of a society that are historically passed on as part of cultural heritage.

Reductionist: One who attempts to take sophisticated complex material and reduce it to a type that can be described in simpler terms, often distorting the original conception one hoped to describe.

Relativism: A metatheory about morality that claims there are no universal values, so that the meaning of all values is constrained by the context that gave rise to them.

Right before the good: When duty or justice concerns have priority over concerns for happiness or the good life.

Situational control: When features of the environment seem to shape and control individual behavior to such an extent that an individual does not appear to be acting in the voluntary or free manner we would expect from good moral agents.

Social contract theory: An ethical theory based on the foundations of hypothetical ideal conditions for moral consent. Principle: Everyone ought to act in accordance with principles of justice that would be chosen by free and equal rational people who come together to form a social contract to establish a model community.

Social impartiality: Is possible only if universal principles can embody an interest that is held in common by all.

Social moral dilemma: A value conflict that is so complex that reasonable members of a community can disagree with each other about the proper solution.

Solidarity: A feeling of commitment between members of a social group.

Stakeholder: A person (or institution) whose interests will be affected by a decision that is going to be made.

Standard person problem: When some group assumes without reflection that its beliefs can accurately serve as a standard for judging everyone else's experience, just because historically the group's particular beliefs have always worked well for its own group.

Subjectivists: Assert that all value statements are merely expressions of the internal feelings of some individual. Since internal feelings are private, that makes all the value statements expressing them publicly arbitrary.

Supererogatory act: Any action that goes above and beyond the call of duty.

Suprapersonal: To transcend or go beyond merely personal concerns to a higher level of intersubjective understanding.

Taste versus morality: The private realm of values as opposed to the intersubjective obligatory realm of ethics and morality.

Technical rationality: A way of thinking and living that emphasizes the scientific-analytic mind-set and the belief in technological progress.

Theory of implementation: A theory that guides the application of ideal values to local contexts, all things considered.

Theory of obligation: An ethical theory that puts boundaries on other value choices by prescribing moral rights and duties.

Theory of value: A theory that prescribes what nonmoral values ought to be pursued in life.

Transcendence from within: To develop emancipatory virtues that help a person go above and beyond his or her previous position. Ethnocentric transcends egocentric since it leads to intersubjective understanding. The universal orientation transcends the ethnocentric since it allows for cross-cultural understanding.

Transcendental norms of argumentative discourse: Necessary normative prerequisites for the possibility of any argumentative communication at all. The same transcendental norms support argumentative discourse in all societies.

Transcendental pragmatic: An argument that focuses on isolating the background pragmatic (i.e., practical, causal) conditions that are necessary prerequisites for an activity to exist at all.

Universal morality: Transcends both first level codes of ethics and second level community morality by providing a background context for judging the adequacy of the first two levels. It prescribes rights and duties for everyone, no matter what their station or what community they inhabit.

Universal norms: Values that apply or ought to apply to everyone.

Utilitarianism: An ethical theory based on the idea we are obligated to maximize nonmoral good in the world. Principle: Always choose the option that promotes the greatest amount of happiness for everyone.

Validity claims: Assertions that should be accepted if they can be supported or redeemed with good reasons.

Veil of ignorance: A device of reason in social contract theory, to help us adopt the moral point of view. Hypothetically speaking, one thinks of the veil as clouding our memory to allow each of us to forget particular details about who we are, thus insuring an impartial perspective.

Virtue: Refers to any human strength that makes one excellent at performing some task or function or helps us live like we ought to.

Virtue ethics: Tells us to develop those traits of character (virtues) that help moral agents function well in situations calling for moral judgment.

Voice: A reference to the life experiences that are shared by groups in various life-worlds that lead them to share a perspective on moral matters.

Subject Index

Name Index